T0329981

Innovation in the Pharmaceutical Industry

To Akemi, Sotaro, Koshiro and Nozomi

Innovation in the Pharmaceutical Industry

The Process of Drug Discovery and Development

Takuji Hara

Graduate School of Business Administration, Kobe University

Edward Elgar

Cheltenham, UK • Northampton, MA, USA

Published by
Edward Elgar Publishing Limited
The Lypiatts
15 Lansdown Road
Cheltenham
Glos GL50 2JA
UK

Edward Elgar Publishing, Inc.
William Pratt House
9 Dewey Court
Northampton
Massachusetts 01060
USA

A catalogue record for this book
is available from the British Library

Library of Congress Cataloguing in Publication Data
Hara, Takuji, 1962–
     Innovation in the pharmaceutical industry : the process of drug discovery and development / Takuji Hara.
          p. cm.
     Includes bibliographical references and index.
          1. Drug development—Japan. 2. Drug development—Great Britain. I. Title.

RM301.25 .H37 2003
615' .19'0941—dc21

2002034703

ISBN 978 1 84376 050 4

Contents

Figures

Tables

Acknowledgements

This book explores the process of drug discovery and development conducted in Japan and the United Kingdom. Although the main disciplinary perspectives of this study are historical and sociological, economical and organizational perspectives are also incorporated into the analysis. The interdisciplinary examination demonstrates how the process of drug discovery and development is heterogeneous, interactive, and contingent. It also provides implications for technology management in the pharmaceutical industry and industrial policy in the biomedical area. This book is in substantial part based on my PhD dissertation submitted to and admitted at the University of Edinburgh.

Without the help of many people, I would not have completed this work. First of all, I wish to thank Donald MacKenzie and Graham Spinardi for their supervision, valuable suggestions and critical comments. It is their excellent academic guidance and warm-hearted inspiration that enabled me to achieve this undertaking.

Empirical material is also indispensable to the achievement. I should like to thank the interviewees who talked to me about their stories of drug discovery and development. They are: Sir James Black, Akira Endo, Sir David Jack, Barry Furr at AstraZeneca; John Wood and Angela Palmer at GlaxoWellcome (now GlaxoSmithKlein); Mike Nakayama at GlaxoWellcome (Japan); Kazuyuki Nakagawa, Hideyuki Miwa and Shinya Tashiro at Otsuka Pharmaceutical; Masao Kuroda at Sankyo; Masahiko Fujino, Katsura Morita, Mitsuo Numata, Yasuaki Ogawa, Tai Matsuzawa, Kenji Okonogi, Nobuyoshi Hiramatsu and Kouji Sonoi at Takeda Chemical Industries; and Toichi Takenaka and Isao Yanagisawa at Yamanouchi. I should also like to thank Andrew Bliski for providing me with information about the discovery and development of atenolol. I also wish to thank two anonymous interviewees who talked to me about their laboratory life. My thanks are also due to Christopher Henderson at AstraZeneca, Anita Kidgell at GlaxoWellcome, Masamichi Nishi at GlaxoWellcome (Japan), Shinji Masaki at Otsuka Pharmaceutical, Sakae Katayama at Sankyo, and Toshihiko Murate and Kyoko Iida at Takeda Chemical Industries for their help with the arrangement of interviews. I am also indebted to Gail Turner at the Association of the British Pharmaceutical Industry and Takeshi Shinba at Japan Pharmaceutical Manufacturers Association for providing me with information about the British and Japanese pharmaceutical industry, and to Nobuo Aoyama, Soichi Arakawa, Satoshi Kagawa, Sadao Kamidono and Takeshi Tsujino at Kobe University School of Medicine for providing me with information about the treatment of the diseases for which the drugs discussed in this study are used.

I am also indebted to many people for their help in writing and improving the study. I should like to thank Graham Spinardi and Donald MacKenzie again for helping me correct English errors in my writing. Special thanks are due to Gerri Kirkwood for helping me transcribe interview tapes and correct the English errors in part of my writing. I wish to thank Wendy Faulkner and Andrew Webster, who were the examiners of my dissertation, for their constructive criticisms. I also wish to thank two anonymous referees of this book who gave me helpful comments on rewriting my work. My thanks are also due to Sang-Hyun Kim for providing me with valuable resources from his knowledge of science and technology studies. I should like to thank the many members of Edward Elgar Publishing who diligently supported me in the publishing process of this book.

Without the comfortable life in Edinburgh, I could not have conducted the research. I wish to thank Kobe University for supporting my life in Edinburgh financially. I also wish to thank the faculty members of the Graduate School of Business Administration, Kobe University, for allowing me to study abroad for such a long time. I should like to thank specially Masayuki Munakata for his intellectual and social support since my student years. Many thanks are due to Gerri and Colin Kirkwood, Tom Schuller and Unni Hagen for helping my family live happily in Edinburgh. I should also like to thank my wife's and my parents, Yasuko and Sakuichi Morino and Keiko and Yoshine Hara, for supporting my family on various occasions while we were in the UK. Lastly, I owe a special debt of thanks to my wife Akemi for supporting and encouraging me constantly. Thank you, Sotaro, Koshiro and Nozomi, for tolerating my always being 'busy father'.

The Publishers wish to thank the following who have kindly given permission for the use of copyright material:
GlaxoSmithKline plc for the data on the 1994 market share of cimetidine, ranitidine and famotidine in the US, Europe and Japan.

1. Introduction

1.1 UNDERSTANDING THE PROCESS OF DRUG DISCOVERY AND DEVELOPMENT

This study is an attempt to explore the process of technological change, particularly in pharmaceuticals. Pharmaceuticals are important products for our lives. They are indispensable for patients. They are often lifesaving. Some of them are not lifesaving but improve the quality of life. The longer the lives of people become, the more beneficial this type of drug will be. However, at the same time, they are potentially dangerous. Their wrong administration may cause death or serious damage. Mainly because of this, modern governments strictly regulate every aspect of the industry: research, development, manufacturing, marketing and delivery. Enormous sums of public money are spent on the distribution and regulation of pharmaceuticals. In addition, the pharmaceutical industry becomes more and more important for the competitive advantage of industrialized countries. The production of pharmaceuticals requires high-quality skills, sophisticated equipment, and a highly controlled environment. Moreover, research and development (R&D) for new pharmaceuticals is on the cutting edge of biomedical sciences. The pharmaceutical industry is one of the most research-intensive industries. R&D costs in the industry are more than 10 per cent of sales (Association of the British Pharmaceutical Industry 1997, p. 29; Japan Pharmaceutical Manufacturers Association 1997, p. I-35). They are also the main outlet of biomedical and other researches conducted in academic institutions, and contribute to the justification of investment in those researches. The pharmaceutical industry also supports various industrial and professional activities because it takes about a decade involving a complex procedure and costs a huge amount of money to develop a drug. Thus, pharmaceuticals can be regarded as one of the most crucial technologies, in particular for industrialized countries.

Despite the importance of pharmaceuticals, outsiders including social scientists only partly understand the process by which drugs are shaped. As will be seen in Chapter 2, a large body of literature in economics and management and organization studies has explored the aggregated, abstract and/or cross-sectional pictures of drug R&D. Sociological literature in this field has described in detail parts of the process of drug R&D. However, there are few empirical studies that examine the social process of drug discovery[1] and development fully and closely. This is possibly because most social scientists hesitate to open the black box of pharmaceuticals, which seems to be formidable stuff. Another possible reason is the high confidentiality of pharmaceutical companies, in which the greater part of the innovation process is included.

Without sufficient empirical investigation, the process of drug discovery and development is sometimes regarded as following the linear model. The linear model of technological change suggests that technological change starts from scientific research, goes through technological development and production, and ends with consumption. An alternative version of the linear model implies that technological change starts from social needs, followed by research and development, production and marketing, and ends with the satisfaction of the initial needs. Nowadays, these linear views of technological change are in general regarded as too simple to represent the actual process of technological change. However, the pharmaceutical industry is sometimes seen as an exception. Indeed, the innovation process in the industry 'looks' as if it were linear, because the government regulates the procedure of drug discovery and development one by one based on a linear scheme. But the appearances and the realities of social phenomena are often different. Without sufficiently detailed empirical studies, how can we say that the innovation process of pharmaceuticals is linear?

The main objective of this study is to fill the gap with a close examination of the process of drug discovery and development. My approach to this target is basically a sociological one, namely the social shaping of technology, which emphasizes the intertwining relationship of society and technology, the myriad ways society shapes technology, the attention to both local and wider societal relationships, the intractability of the material world, and the empirical investigation of the contents of technology and the process of technological change. Although the fundamental discipline of this approach is sociology, a number of concepts and ideas of other disciplines including institutional economics and management studies are also incorporated into the analysis (MacKenzie and Wajcman 1999, pp. xiv–xvii, 3–27; Williams and Edge 1996). This study can be regarded as an attempt to explore the social shaping of pharmaceuticals. It aims to reveal how drugs are shaped in society and what kinds of relationships exist among relevant agents and elements. Not only the sociological aspect of the process but also its economic, organizational and pharmacological aspects are examined.

Based on the view of the social shaping of technology, this book demonstrates the heterogeneity, interactivity, uncertainty and contingency of the process of drug discovery and development. The shaping of pharmaceuticals is an interesting issue from a sociological point of view, because various social groups seem to be involved in the process. As a result, pharmaceuticals have several different meanings: for researchers, they are chemicals; for patients and doctors, they are therapies; for companies, they are products for sale; for regulators, they are objects of regulation; for some industrial workers, they may be the means of intra-organizational politics. If we divide relevant people into smaller social groups, there are probably even more meanings. For example, chemists and biologists probably attribute different meanings to the same chemical. Patients and doctors probably regard the same medicine as having different therapeutic values. The production and marketing divisions of the same pharmaceutical company probably evaluate the same product from different points of view. Thus, different social groups give different meanings to the same drug. A drug is shaped through interactions among these actors. How do they interact with each other?

Various non-human entities also seem to be involved in the process of drug shaping. It is obvious that without things such as drugs, tissues, animals, experimental instruments, production facilities, computers and means of communication, no drug can be shaped. As will be seen in the next chapter, there is a body of literature discussing the relationship between people and artefacts in the sociology of science and technology. Although this philosophical controversy is beyond the scope of this study, it is certainly interesting for us to look at the roles various non-human entities play in the innovation process of pharmaceuticals. What kinds of non-human entities are involved in the process of drug shaping and how do they interact with human actors?

In addition, institutional and structural factors cannot be ignored in the study of the process of drug shaping. There exist the social relationships that are beyond the interactions between the 'relevant' human actors and non-human entities. No one lacks his/her historical, structural and cultural position and no one can be free from the influences of these positions, though he/she is often unaware of being influenced. Non-humans are also given positions and meanings by institutional and structural factors. For instance, who their possessors are is defined not only by the interactions among directly related social groups but also by institutional and structural factors such as laws, patents and the economic structure. Thus, institutional and structural factors, which are also affected by local history and culture, influence the process of drug shaping. What kinds of institutional and structural factors affect the process and how do they do so?

The influence of historical and structural context on the process of drug shaping is also interesting from the viewpoint of industrial policy. This seems to help us to understand why the pharmaceutical industry in some states is more successful than in others. In particular, it is often argued that the Japanese pharmaceutical industry is not internationally stronger than its British counterpart though in many other industries Japan is globally stronger than the UK. Why is the Japanese pharmaceutical industry internationally uncompetitive?

In sum, this study aims at answering a set of questions: In what way are drugs discovered and developed? What kinds of human actors are related to the process? What kinds of non-human entities are critical in the process? What kinds of institutional and structural factors affect the process? How do human actors, non-human entities, and institutional and structural factors interact with each other? Can the process of drug shaping be described by the linear model of technological change? If not, what kind of model plausibly describes the process of drug discovery and development? Are there any distinct patterns in the process of drug shaping? How different are the processes in different countries? Why is the Japanese pharmaceutical industry weak? What are the theoretical and practical implications of the findings?

In order to answer these research questions, I conduct multiple case studies consisting of 16 cases of drug discovery and development in different therapeutic areas in Japan and the United Kingdom. To analyse the cases I divide the process of drug shaping into four different aspects, namely the shaping of the compound, the shaping of the application, the shaping of organizational authorization, and the shaping of the market. Relevant human actors, non-human entities, and institutional and structural factors are identified and their interactions are examined. The relationships between different aspects of drug shaping are also investigated. Then, the different cases in different settings are compared, and similarities and differences are explored. Based on these analyses, I discuss the distinct pattern of drug discovery and development, the influences of national settings on the process of drug innovation, and theoretical and practical implications.

1.2 DISTINCTIVE FEATURES OF THIS STUDY

This study possesses two uncommon features compared with most other innovation studies. First, I venture into the contents of relevant academic literature in medicine, physiology and pharmacology. This is because academic literature has a lot of historical evidence and information to help us understand the process of drug shaping. To minimize misunderstanding, I conducted interviews with key researchers and corporate staff who were involved in the discovery and development of the drugs. I also consult other sorts of literature such as review articles, textbooks, biography and corporate history. I emphasize again that I used the contents of academic literature only as evidence for a sociological and historical study of drug innovation, and that I have no intention of discussing the contents themselves.

The second unique feature of this study is that I also explore the organizational processes *inside* pharmaceutical companies. This was achieved by interviewing relevant people and consulting some internal documents which were obtained by courtesy of these people or their companies. As mentioned above, pharmaceutical companies are especially sensitive about confidentiality. However, probably because of their awareness of the importance of public relations and because most of the cases I examined were no longer at the cutting edge of research, they were generally cooperative. All the researchers I met seemed proud of their achievements in drug discovery and development, and were happy to talk about them to me. There is again a potential risk as regards the accuracy of their stories. To reduce this risk, I also consulted academic papers, patents and other sources of information. This study demonstrates that a company is not a monolithic unit but that there are a lot of conflicts and politics within it.

1.3   THE STRUCTURE OF THIS BOOK

This book consists of nine chapters. Chapter 2 reviews various perspectives on technological change, in particular, the linear model and its criticism consisting of several non-linear perspectives on technological change. The chapter also describes some basic features of R&D activities in the pharmaceutical industry. Then, literature on drug R&D from different disciplinary viewpoints is reviewed. Based on the literature review, I propose a new framework of analysis for this study, which includes the different aspects of drug shaping: the compound, the application, organizational authorization, and the market. At the end of the chapter, the methodological matters of this study are set out.

In each chapter from Chapter 3 to Chapter 6, several cases of drug discovery and development in the same therapeutic area are described. Each chapter includes at least one British and one Japanese case. Chapter 3 deals with cardiovascular drugs, especially the ones that are used for the treatment of hypertension. The innovation processes of two β-blockers, namely propranolol and atenolol, and of one Ca-antagonist, nicardipine, are examined. Chapter 4 addresses the cases of anti-asthma drugs including β-stimulants such as salbutamol, salmeterol and procaterol, and inhaled steroids such as beclomethasone dipropionate and fluticasone propionate. Chapter 5 describes the cases of drugs called histamine H_2-antagonists, used for the treatment of peptic ulcer. They include cimetidine, ranitidine and famotidine. Chapter 6 depicts the R&D process of two LHRH analogues, leuprorelin and goserelin, which are used in the treatment of prostate and breast cancer and several gynaecological diseases. These case studies revealed the complex interaction between various human actors, non-human entities, and institutional and structural factors in the process of drug discovery and development. In addition, a few different patterns of drug shaping are also found, which are confirmed in Chapter 7.

Chapter 7 explores three more cases of drug discovery and development which took place in Japan. These cases include an HMG-CoA reductase inhibitor, mevastatin, which reduces the level of cholesterol in the blood, an α_{1c}-receptor antagonist, tamsulosin, which is used for the treatment of urinary disorder accompanying benign prostatic hypertrophy, and an cephalosporin antibiotic, cefotiam. Although they belong to different therapeutic areas, they are intentionally brought together in order to confirm the findings of previous chapters about the different patterns of drug discovery and development, which I name types of drug innovation. The drugs dealt with in this chapter are clearly different in novelty in terms of chemical structure and medical application. Mevastatin is the exemplary compound of other HMG-CoA reductase inhibitors such as lovastatin, simvastatin and pravastatin. It is paradigmatic as a compound and as a therapy. Therefore, I name this type paradigmatic innovation. Tamsulosin is not very novel as a compound; however, its application is innovative. It is used for the treatment of urinary disorder whereas existing α-receptor antagonists are used for the treatment of hypertension. I name this type application innovation. Although cefotiam has some unique structure in its molecule, it is not a paradigmatic drug. It has exemplary compounds and its application is the same as the exemplars. I name this type modification-based innovation. These case studies clarify distinct properties of each type of drug innovation by going into the details of the process of drug discovery and development.

Chapter 8 integrates the findings of empirical studies in previous chapters with the theoretical framework. First, general features of the process of shaping drugs are described. Four different aspects of drug shaping are discussed respectively. Different human actors, non-human entities, and institutional and structural factors involved in each aspect are identified. The interactions between them are also described. In addition, it is argued that the different aspects also interact and are interdependent with each other. Based on these, I suggest an interactive model of drug shaping. Second, based on a comparative analysis of different cases, three different types of innovation in the pharmaceutical industry, namely paradigmatic innovation, application innovation and modification-based innovation, are explained. The chapter explores several distinguishable characteristics of each type, with regard to interactions between human actors, non-human entities, and institutional and structural factors. Third, based on the comparison between British and Japanses cases, the distinctive features of Japanese pharmaceutical innovation are discussed. Several institutional and structural factors affecting the innovation process are considered. Finally, in Chapter 9 this study ends by summarizing findings and discussing theoretical and practical implications.

NOTE

1. A drug discovery is defined here as a discovery of the 'fact' that a natural or synthesized chemical has a profile of biological activity which can be applied to the treatment of diseases. However, from the viewpoint of the social shaping of science and technology, I do not intend to suggest that the 'fact' is an objective matter, which exists independently of social processes. I use the words 'drug discovery' only for convenience because the usage is common among people.

2. Technological change and the pharmaceutical industry

2.1 PERSPECTIVES ON TECHNOLOGICAL CHANGE

2.1.1 Linear Model of Technological Change and its Criticism

Among various perspectives on technological change, there is a simple dichotomy between two extreme positions. One of these is 'hard' technological determinism, which regards scientific progress and its natural consequence, technological change, as autonomous phenomena and as the ultimate factors that decide the style of society (Marx and Smith 1994, pp. ix–xii). Another simple perspective is the exact opposite of 'hard' technological determinism – what I shall call 'hard' social determinism. 'Hard' social determinism views society as the absolute planner of scientific and technological change (Williams and Edge 1996, p. 866). We can find several sub-versions of this perspective, including 'demand-pull' theory of innovation (Coombs *et al.* 1987, pp. 94–7), 'mode of production' determinism and organizational choice perspective (Thomas 1994, pp. 1–9). Either the 'hard' version of technological determinism or that of social determinism can be put as a linear model (Figure 2.1).

'Hard' technological determinist linear model

Scientific research →	Technological development →	Product development →	Production →	Marketing and sales →	Social impacts

'Hard' social determinist linear model

Social needs →	Scientific research →	Technological development →	Product development →	Production →	Marketing and sales

Figure 2.1: 'Hard' technological determinism and social determinism

However, few researchers in social sciences nowadays seem to believe in either version of the linear model. Most believe that there are both aspects in the process of technological change. These include, for example, economists of technological change (Nelson and Winter 1974, 1977, 1982; Dosi 1982; Coombs *et al.* 1987, pp. 102–3; Rothwell 1994; Steinmueller 1994; Nelson 1996; McKelvey 1996; Freeman and Soete 1997), historians of technological change (Rosenberg 1976, 1982, 1994; Hughes 1983; David 1985) and researchers on technology management (Abernathy 1978; Kline 1985; Tushman and Anderson 1986; Henderson and Clark 1990; Tushman and Rosenkopf 1992; Utterback 1994; Thomas 1994; Christensen 1997).

Among these strands of criticism of the linear model, a group of economists called evolutionary economists provide a particularly useful theoretical framework for the understanding of the non-linearity of technological change. Although there seem to be several traditions of evolutionary economics with long histories (Hodgson 1999, pp. 127–8), the one that is discussed here is established by Richard Nelson and Sidney Winter. They criticize the profit-maximization firm theory based on neo-classical economics, and advocate an alternative theory of the behaviour of firms. According to them, the behaviour of firms follows the principle of satisfactory choice from a set of recognized options, rather than the principle of optimum choice from all possible options. Each firm operates largely based on its unique routines, the decision rules that are heuristically and cumulatively obtained and altered. This results in the emergence of diversity of behaviour among different firms. Then, the different behaviours face the selection environment consisting of the market and other institutions, in which some behaviours are successful but others fail. It should be noted that the selection environment is also affected by the aggregated behaviour of firms. When a firm recognizes that the performance of its behaviour in the selective environment is unsatisfactory, it will start searching for a better set of routines. Based on this evolutionary model of firm behaviour, R&D activities are also regarded as interacting, heuristic search processes. Thus, various R&D strategies arise. Technologies, which are the conditional probabilistic outcome of the strategies, are also different from each other and go through the selection in the institutional environment. As a result of these processes, specific paths of technological change often emerge, which are named 'natural trajectories' (Nelson and Winter 1974, 1977, 1982).[1]

This evolutionary model of technological change suggests that technological change is not driven by any one kind of force, because it is a compound result of the search activities of the subjects, mainly firms, and the selection mechanisms of its institutional environment. Various factors including cognitive, material, and practical capabilities of the organizations, market conditions, the conditions of other institutions, and the interactions between these are involved in the process of technological change. Because each organization has a partly different set of routines and capabilities, the resultant directions of technological change are also different from each other though it may be possible to identify common technological trajectories (McKelvey 1996, pp. 40–5). Thus, the process of technological change is neither driven by one force nor orientated towards one direction. The linear model of technological change, therefore, is regarded as inappropriate by evolutionary economics.

Although the theoretical framework provided by evolutionary economists is helpful in understanding the interactive process of technological change at the firm, industrial and national levels, it does not seem to be sufficient to understand the social processes within a corporate organization or between different kinds of social groups and institutions, or the interactions between the social and the material. The perspectives of the sociology of science and technology[2] in particular seem to be complementary here. Sociologists in this strand also criticize the linear model of technological change based on detailed empirical studies and deep theoretical insights, and provide us with various concepts and theories to understand the complex process of technological change involving heterogeneous actors. In the next three sub-sections, we examine several variations of this strand, which help us deepen our understanding of how the linear model is distant from the reality of technological change.

2.1.2 Interpretative Flexibility and Closure: the Social Construction of Technology

The first variation of sociological criticism against the linear model of technological change is done by the social construction of technology (SCOT) approach. SCOT, like most of the other strands of the sociology of technology, stems from the sociology of scientific knowledge, especially the empirical programme of relativism (EPOR) developed by Harry Collins (Pinch and Bijker 1987; Collins 1981). Pinch and Bijker, the leading proponents of SCOT, regard the process of technological change as an evolutionary process, as do evolutionary economists. As a result, they also advocate a 'multidirectional' model of technological change and deny the linear model (Pinch and Bijker 1987, p. 28).

The essential concepts of SCOT are 'relevant social groups', 'interpretative flexibility' and 'closure mechanisms'. A relevant social group is that in which all members share a meaning of a certain artefact. Different relevant social groups often give different meanings to the same artefact. For example, in the history of bicycle development, the high-wheeler had the meaning of the 'macho machine' for young men of means and nerve, but for older people and women it had the meaning of the 'unsafe machine'. This divergence of meanings is named interpretative flexibility. A relevant social group gives a specific meaning to an artefact and perceives a set of specific problems with respect to the artefact. Around each problem, several different solutions can be developed. As a result, a number of variants of the artefact are developed. This is the explanation of variation of an artefact by SCOT (Pinch and Bijker 1987, pp. 30–44; Pinch 1996, pp. 24–5).

However, variation based on interpretative flexibility does not continue forever. Some artefacts appear to have fewer problems than others and become increasingly dominant forms of the technology. This closure and stabilization of technology occurs through closure mechanisms. It is not necessary for all relevant social groups to be convinced of a certain interpretation of the artefact: what is required is that each major group can see its own problem as being solved. There are different closure mechanisms of technological change including the manipulation with rhetoric and the redefinition of problems. The closure and stabilization of technology, however, may not mean the disappearance of all rivals, and a few different technologies may coexist. In addition, it does not mean that the technology reaches its final form. New problems can emerge and lead the technology to another session of interpretative flexibility (Pinch and Bijker 1987, pp. 44–6; Bijker 1995, pp. 84–8; Pinch 1996, p. 25).

The SCOT perspective indicates that social diversity prohibits technological change from being developed in such a way as the technological determinist linear model assumes. At the same time, it indicates that various social processes, called closure mechanisms, lead technological change in a specific direction, or create a technological trajectory in terms of evolutionary economics, though the driving forces of closure mechanism are not necessarily clear.

2.1.3 Non-human Actors: Actor-Network Theory

Although SCOT is a very strong opponent of the technological determinist linear model, it does not seem to be a strong opponent of the social determinist linear model to the same degree. However, it is obvious that technological change is by no means free from the laws of nature. Although most scholars probably recognize this, it is actor-network theory (ANT) that most strongly emphasizes the role of non-human elements of nature in the process of technological change. According to ANT, technology should be seen as a product shaped by an actor-network in which not only human actors but also non-human 'actors' such as electrons, catalysts, electrolytes and lead accumulators are playing their roles (Callon 1986, pp. 22, 28–33; Latour 1987, pp. 121–44; Law 1987). An actor-network is also a dynamic network, which can connect up further heterogeneous elements, redefine itself, and transform itself constantly (Callon 1986, pp. 28–33; 1987, p. 93). The activity that builds a relatively stable system (or network) within an indifferent and unstable environment (or field) from various human and non-human actors is named 'heterogeneous engineering' (Law 1987, pp. 113–16) or 'translation' (Callon 1986, pp. 24–8). In heterogeneous engineering, or in actor networking, society is not given a higher position than nature (Law 1987, p. 130; Latour [1992] 1999). There has been controversy over this symmetrical position on human and non-human actors (Collins and Yearley 1992; Callon and Latour 1992; Latour [1992] 1999; Bloor 1999; Latour 1999a). In addition, recent discussion amongst ANT proponents is developing beyond these issues (Law 1999; Latour 1999b). However, what is important here is that the view of ANT is incompatible with the social determinist linear model. Rather, their perspective on technological change is more reciprocal and simultaneous: society, technological artefacts and knowledge of nature are coevolving (Callon 1986, p. 20).

Thus, ANT provides us with another alternative perspective on technological change: it rejects not only the technological determinist linear model but also the social determinist linear model. Not only human actors but also non-human entities matter to technological change. This view also reminds us of the active side of technological change through the notions of heterogeneous engineering and translation.

2.1.4 Structural and Historical Context: the Social Shaping of Technology

Both SCOT and ANT help us understand the complexity of technological change, but some social scientists have criticized them for their tendency to disregard the structural and historical context. For example, Russell and Williams (1988, pp. 7–10, 26) point out that actors must be shaped not only by a tangible relationship to other actors, but also by an intangible historical and structural context. They argue that the historical and structural context is important in technology studies because there are several differences between science and technology. First, technological practitioners are more heterogeneous than scientists because they often work beyond the boundaries of the disciplinary community. Second, technological knowledge is more directly concerned with economic and political purposes than science. Third, technology consists of not only knowledge but also material: in technology studies, it is necessary to investigate the implementation and the use of technology.[3] These differences force technology studies to embrace various institutional, structural and historical matters more than science studies (ibid., pp. 4–6).[4]

This (re-)attention to structural and historical context as well as to interacting actors in technological change is the key characteristic of an approach called the social shaping of technology (SST) (MacKenzie and Wajcman 1985, p. 23; MacKenzie 1988; Williams and Edge 1996; MacKenzie and Wajcman 1999, p. 22). Structural and historical context concretely includes, as we know from the literature of SST, classes, modes of production, markets, gender, democracy, and so on. By taking these into consideration, SST can enjoy various intellectual fruits from existing social studies on technological change including Marxist technology studies (see, for example; Braverman 1974; Noble 1984), the economics of technological change (see sub-section 2.1.1), studies of innovation management (see sub-section 2.1.1), feminist technology studies (see Wajcman 1995) and critical studies of technology policy (see Williams and Edge 1996, pp. 870–1).

It is important to note that SST is not the 'hard' social determinism of technology. The proponents of SST explicitly recognize the following two factors: first, social actors cannot construct technology at will because nature also limits technology (MacKenzie and Wajcman 1999, pp. 16–18); second, technology, as an element of the structural and historical context, restricts the behaviour of social actors (Williams and Edge 1996, pp. 866–7; MacKenzie and Wajcman 1999, pp. 22–3). They are not arguing that society determines technology, but that it is important for us to understand the myriad ways in which society shapes technology (MacKenzie and Wajcman 1985, p. 24). They stress the room for technological and social choices, the negotiability of technology, the temporary stability of technology and the reversibility of earlier choices (Williams and Edge 1996, pp. 866–7). This flexible view of SST is mostly compatible with both the perspective of SCOT and that of ANT. In contrast, it is completely at odds with both the technological determinist linear model and the social determinist linear model. What is unique to SST is that it enriches the potential causes of the variation and convergence of technology beyond visible social groups and actors, by taking structural and historical context into consideration.

Thus, the SST perspective seems to be the broadest and most balanced theoretical approach. However, this may reduce the sharpness of the perspective, that is to say, because the SST perspective takes more factors into consideration, it is more difficult to decide what is the most important based on the perspective. Despite this dilemma, in order to understand technological change, I think it necessary to tolerate this ambiguity, because what is the most important factor in technological change does not seem to be a question that can be given a single general answer. On the contrary, this position may go further: the social shaping of technology is still limited by the word social. As Latour and Woolgar did in the second edition of their book (Latour and Woolgar 1986), I think that it is acceptable to remove 'social' from SST: the shaping of technology. This is obviously very broad, maybe too broad, and we perhaps need a reminder of our sociological point of view. However, at least as a starting point of empirical investigation into technological change, it seems better to be free from the priority of the social.

2.1.5 The Linear Model Still Exists!

As we can see in the sections above, the linear model has been criticized by various disciplinary groups of social scientists. Rothwell (1994) suggests five generations of innovation model: technology-push model as the first generation (1950s–mid-1960s); market-pull model as the second generation (late 1960s–early 1970s); 'coupling' model as the third generation (mid-1970s–early 1980s); integrated model as the fourth generation (mid-1980s–1990s); and system integration and network model as the fifth generation (1990s onwards). Among them, the first two can be seen as the technological determinist linear model and the social determinist linear model. This clearly suggests that the linear model of technological change is regarded as obsolete.

However, the linear model, especially its technological determinist version, still persists as a policy driver and as a standard model in several specific industries. Tait and Williams (1999, p. 2) suggest four reasons why the linear model has been resilient in the minds of policy makers: first, some policy makers are still unaware of its reputed problems; second, it is attractive as a metaphor for policy makers who want a simple understanding of technological change; third, existing policy repertories based on the model are well-entrenched in the minds and relationships of policy makers; fourth, the model matches the interests of academic research scientists and some research councils because it justifies the expenditure of large amounts of public money on basic research (see, for example, 'Government focuses on science base', *The Financial Times*, 26 July 2000). Tait and Williams (1999, pp. 2–3) indicate that a revised version of the linear model, named the 'linear plus' model, has emerged. The 'linear plus' model stresses the relationship between academia and industry and the cooperation between various disciplinary groups, though it still assumes linearity from research to market.

The linear model is often regarded as reality in several exceptional industries such as the chemical industry (Cadogan 1997, p. 938) and the pharmaceutical industry. Fleck (1996, p. 14) writes: 'In practical terms [the linear model] is applicable to situations characterised by a mature market structure and the presence of a scientific research intensive infrastructure, as is found in biotechnology and pharmaceuticals'. Faulkner and Senker (1995, p. 211) also state: 'pharmaceutical innovation conforms more to the linear model'. This view is also reflected in the word 'pipeline', which is often used in the pharmaceutical industry, as below:

> SmithKline Beecham will today announce it is buying rights to a cancer drug as part of continuing efforts to improve its *product pipeline*. ('SB and Glaxo take stock of drugs' cabinet', *The Financial Times*, 25 July 2000)

> Yamanouchi's formidable *R&D pipeline* is its engine of future growth. (Yamanouchi, *Annual Report 1999*, p. 4)

> BMS is confident it has enough in the *pipeline* to more than offset any shortfall. ('Bristol-Myers remedies scepticism', *The Financial Times*, 29 November 1999)

The linear-model-like appearance of the pharmaceutical industry is created by regulation in the industry to a considerable degree (Tait and Williams 1999, p. 8). Each step of the research and development (R&D) process of pharmaceuticals in modern society is strongly regulated by the government. Without satisfying the requirements of the current stage, the pharmaceutical company cannot advance its drug to the next stage. In sum, the linear model of technological change has been criticized by various disciplines of social science. But, in the practical world, it is still believed and used. In particular, even social scientists who in general criticize the linear model seem to believe that it is still applicable to a few industries, in particular the pharmaceutical industry.

The claims that technological change in the pharmaceutical industry is like the linear model, however, do not seem to be based on detailed study of the innovation process. Therefore, it is still questionable whether the process of drug discovery and development is truly the one that is described by the linear model. This question gives us an opportunity for re-evaluating the linear model as one perspective on technological change. This question is also practically important because the pharmaceutical industry is one of the key industries for such countries as the UK, the US and Japan. It may have further significance when we consider that the industry may represent a group of 'research-intensive' industries which are expected to sustain the economy and culture in 'advanced' countries. Therefore, answering the question 'Is it the case that the linear model of technological change can at least be applied to pharmaceuticals?' is an excellent challenge in attempts to understand technological change in modern society. And this is the objective of this research. I try to find an answer to the question by examining some cases of the R&D process in the pharmaceutical industry in detail. However, before we move to case studies, let us glance at the general characteristics of the pharmaceutical industry and the literature on it. Let's begin with a visit to a modern research institution in the pharmaceutical industry.

2.2   RESEARCH AND DEVELOPMENT IN THE PHARMACEUTICAL INDUSTRY

2.2.1 Visiting Laboratories[5]

The first room   This room is well lit and partitioned into booths by frosted acrylic boards. Science equipment is crammed and piled into quite a large booth. Perhaps these machines are used for measuring or analysing chemicals. Most of them seem to be computerized. Machinery analyses chemicals and the display conveys the results to people. There are, however, few people apart from us. Maybe it is because strangers are looking at the laboratories. Maybe it is because it is not the time to check the results. Anyway, the laboratory is not an automation system, because each machine looks separate, unconnected to others. Each machine, however, looks very expensive. In fact, they are expensive, according to the director who shows us the laboratory. I have been hearing continuous sounds of motors and compressors. In the next booth, I can smell chemicals. I see several ordinary refrigerators. There are also a number of bottles of chemicals on racks, cupboards and laboratory benches. They are neither very tidy nor in a mess. Then, there are several smaller booths, which look like personal offices. Women are not in the minority. The next booth is again full of science equipment and personal computers; there are various logos of makers on the machines, but most of them are unfamiliar. Then, we go out of the room. There are a lot of doors before we get to the next room.

The second room   This room is dark. A female researcher sitting in front of a sophisticated microscope and a display beside the microscope demonstrates to us how to use the apparatus. On the display, we can see part of a cell. According to the researcher, they can analyse a microscopic image on the computer screen by dyeing different proteins within cells with different colours. When she chooses a particular colour, we can see the distribution of a particular protein in the cell. It is said that the microscope can secure images every 30 seconds. If you become interested in the movement of proteins inside the cell, you can reconstruct images. You can also analyse the movement because it is digitally coded. You can download the data onto a disk, take it with you and observe the movement anywhere you can open your laptop computer. Because it is digital, you can erase visual noise so you can get a clearer image than with an ordinary microscope. The researcher explains everything cheerfully and proudly. The software of the apparatus looks very specialized and customized, and the operator seems to be well accustomed to it. It is said that they bought in the software but they also modified and improved it.

The third room   This room is again well lit. In the centre of the room there is a large table with a large, transparent plastic box on it, occupying quite a large part of the room. The box is roughly 30 feet in length, 10 feet in width and 6 feet in depth. In the box, a robot is working. The robot does not look very flexible; its thee-dimensional motions are rectilinear. The robot first picks up a sample case from the piles of them at the end of the box. Then it takes it to a bar-code checker. Then it takes the case to the point where some sort of reagent is added to the samples. Finally, the robot takes the case to an analyser. And then it goes back and repeats these motions. This equipment is connected to a computer and the results of analysis can be seen on the display. By the side of the plastic box there is a set of red, amber and green indicator lights, such as those often seen in a modern factory. But there is neither the loud noise nor the alarming music you may hear in a factory. On a bench by the wall there are a lot of things: pipettes, sample cases, something looking like an electronic thermometer, a roll of sellotape, a pair of scissors, papers, a calculator and so on.

2.2.2 The Formal Process of Research and Development of Pharmaceuticals

In this study, I deal with the R&D process of prescribed drugs. Prescribed, or ethical, drugs are normally given to patients either by pharmacists based on the prescription issued by doctors or directly by medical practitioners in hospitals and clinics. Large pharmaceutical companies earn most income from their prescribed drugs (Davis 1997, p. 8; Association of the British Pharmaceutical Industry 1997, p. 13; Japan Pharmaceutical Manufacturers Association 1997, p. I-5). Almost all major product innovations in the pharmaceutical industry are for prescribed drugs. To secure profits from novel prescribed drugs, pharmaceutical companies file patents for new compounds, often together with their analogues and derivatives, immediately after they discover the compounds and their potential clinical applications. Therefore, newly discovered prescribed drugs are sometimes called patented drugs. These drugs are normally given brand names on the market: this is why they are also called brand-name drugs, in contrast with generic drugs, which are marketed by other manufacturers after the relevant patents have expired.

Most prescribed drugs that are currently used work through their interactions with receptors within our bodies. The human body, as well as other animals' bodies, is regulated by various chemicals, such as hormones and neurotransmitters. These chemicals are used for communication between different cells and different organs in the body. On the membrane around cells, there are a lot of special proteins called 'receptors'. There are also some types of receptors inside cells. Each receptor catches a specific kind of hormone or neurotransmitter as if they were a lock and a key, and then sends a specific signal inside the cell, which causes the cell to respond in a specific way (Stone and Darlington 2000, pp. 1–10). Drugs combine with these receptors and promote or inhibit the reaction of cells. A drug which has the same actions as a natural hormone or transmitter is called an agonist or stimulant. Normally, a clinically used agonist possesses stronger potency and/or longer duration of action than a natural hormone or transmitter. In contrast, a drug which inhibits the actions of a hormone or transmitter is called an antagonist or blocker. Although agonists and antagonists of the same receptor have opposite functions, their molecular structures are often very similar, because they have to combine with the same receptor (Patrick 1995, pp. 61–3). All the drugs I examine in the case studies in this research belong to this type, except mevastatin and cefotiam which inhibit specific enzymes in the body or bacteria cell walls, and nicardipine which blocks specific channels (also made by proteins) in the cell walls. There are also other types of drug, which target transport enzymes, nucleic acids and specific types of cells such as cancer cells. In the near future, drugs which target specific genes are likely to appear (Stone and Darlington 2000, pp. 12–13). All drugs have potentially harmful side effects, partly because chemicals within the body normally play more than one role, partly because they have to be metabolized, that is to say, be transformed into other chemicals, which may have toxic effects within the body, and partly because the body sometimes rejects strange chemicals (allergic reaction). Prescribed drugs are normally more potent than non-prescribed, so-called over-the-counter, drugs but, at the same time, are potentially more dangerous because their side effects are often stronger. This is one of the main reasons medical and regulatory authorities in advanced countries strictly control the manufacture and distribution of prescribed drugs, although it is not the only reason (Abraham 1995, pp. 36–86; Davis 1997, p. 120).

R&D in the pharmaceutical industry is conventionally split into two stages: research and development. According to the conventional view, research activities in pharmaceutical companies are aimed at the 'discovery' of drugs, whereas development activities mainly refer to clinical trials (Chiesa 1996). A drug discovery is defined as a discovery of the 'fact' that a natural or synthesized chemical has a profile of biological activity that can be applied for the treatment of diseases. The 'fact' does not necessarily include a clear explanation about the action mechanisms. Until recent times, drugs could be approved for use without a clear explanation about the mechanisms. Nowadays, this is more difficult, but as we shall see in the case studies, there still exists uncertainty about the mechanisms. Strictly speaking, therefore, the 'fact' is nothing more than a system of beliefs (Barnes *et al.* 1996, pp. 69–73; MacKenzie 1996b, p. 248). Sometimes, a drug discovery is regarded as a discovery of a chemical which has a profile of biological activity, but this view may be misleading, because the chemical is often not naturally occurring, but intentionally synthesized. Invention is a more appropriate word here and should be distinguished from discovery. In this research, however, I use the word discovery, referring to the first learning of the causal relationship between the chemical and the biological activities, not to the chemical itself. My using the word discovery implies no ontological commitment to the correspondence between that learning and reality.

Both chemists and biologists play a core role in the research process and the interaction between the two disciplines is the key to the achievement of drug discovery. However, it should not be ignored that other disciplines such as physics, mathematics, statistics, computer sciences, electronics, mechanical engineering and material engineering also support the process of drug discovery, as we can see in the laboratories described in sub-section 2.2.1.

After a drug discovery, the compound is examined in detail by testing it on various animals. The toxicological, pharmacological and pharmacokinetic properties of the compound are investigated. This process is often called pre-clinical tests or pre-clinical development. At this stage, initial studies on the production process of the compound start, because it is necessary to supply a larger amount of the compound for clinical trials and the development of preparations (Pisano 1997, p. 122). Development of preparations is more important today than previously because now the notion of drug delivery systems is taken seriously into consideration (see Chapter 6). If the data from the pre-clinical tests are favourable, the compound goes into clinical trials. Before that, however, a managerial decision is made because clinical trials require an enormous amount of money. Also, approval by the regulatory body is needed, because clinical trials use humans (McIntyre 1999, p. 73; Ministry of Health and Welfare 1996, pp. 85–105).

Clinical trials before marketing, which are conventionally a synonym for drug development, are normally divided into three phases. In phase I, a drug candidate is given to healthy volunteers to investigate its toxicological and pharmacological profiles. In phase II, the drug is given to a small number of patients at various dosage levels and with different dosage forms in order to examine its efficacy and safety, and to determine the appropriate dosage profiles. In phase III, the drug is given to a much larger number of patients at multiple sites for quite a long time in order to confirm its efficacy and safety. The trials in phases II and III are normally controlled and the drug is compared with a placebo and/or an existing major therapy (Chiesa 1996, pp. 639–40; Pisano 1997, pp. 119, 123–4). The governmental authority strictly regulates these phases of clinical trials. Phases can overlap with the permission of the authority but cannot be waived. This regulatory system of clinical trials has been constructed in particular since the disaster caused by thalidomide in the early 1960s. The relevant institutional changes happened first in 1962 in the US, and around 1967 in the UK and Japan (Temin 1980, p. 125; Abraham 1995, pp. 66–74; Nihon Yakushi Gakkai 1995, p. 132; Kaufer 1990, p. 154; Timmermans and Leiter 2000, pp. 45–6). Most of the drugs I examine in case studies in this research experienced these phases of clinical trials. It is also important to notice that clinical trials are conducted by a number of doctors and patients who are outside the control of the pharmaceutical company. Factors such as protocols, organizing doctors, schedule management and informed consent are necessary (Smith 1985, pp. 80–8). Statisticians also play a significant role in clinical trials because results of controlled studies are statistically analysed and interpreted (Marks 1997, pp. 129–248).

As a matter of course, a drug must be produced on a much larger scale than the laboratory level before the large-scale clinical trials and commercialization. Therefore, process development must be done between the discovery of a drug and the large-scale clinical trials. A specialized process R&D group in the pharmaceutical company normally conducts this function in parallel with product development. Process development is not a once-for-all sort of activity but a continuing effort. Each stage of pre-clinical and clinical studies requires a certain amount of the drug. At each moment, the production of the required amount of the drug must be achieved, even if the process is far from the optimum one for large-scale production. Regarding the values in process development, cost reduction is in general important. However, reduction of development time is also particularly important in the pharmaceutical industry because it may constitute a bottleneck in the whole process of drug R&D, which is crucial in terms of competition in the market. Flexibility is also required because changes of product profile often arise in the process of drug development (Pisano 1997, pp. 81, 95–102). Process development includes identification of several alternative routes of synthesis and the selection of the best route among them in terms of quality, safety, simplicity and costs. It also includes high uncertainty because scaling-up means the entry of further heterogeneous factors, both the material and the social (Pisano 1997, pp. 125–34; Smith 1985, pp. 111–16). Human actors such as chemists, chemical engineers, system engineers, electricians, mechanics, operators and managers play a role in a plant. Non-human entities such as tanks, pipes, censors, thermometers, pressure gauges, cables, computers, software, terminals and clocks also play a role.

When clinical trials and process development of a drug are successfully completed, the manufacturer applies to the regulatory body for approval of its manufacture and marketing. The application requires the detailed results of pre-clinical tests and all clinical trials, detailed description of the clinical protocols, statistical analysis of the results, expert opinions on the data, detailed description of the manufacturing process and other prescribed data and analysis (Pisano 1997, pp. 124–5; Reich 1986; Ministry of Health and Welfare 1996, pp. 127–206). When the regulatory body approves the application, the company can 'basically' launch the drug. The word basically is used because a further procedure may be needed in some countries. In Japan, for example, without obtaining an official price determined by the Ministry of Health and Welfare, it is virtually impossible to sell the drug in the country (Reich 1986, p. 23; Campbell and Ikegami 1998, p. 154). It is reported in the early 1990s that the whole process of R&D of a drug, except the research before the discovery, took more than 10 years and cost more than $350 million (Weisbach and Moos 1995, p. 244).

Thus, the formal R&D process of a drug consists of a number of stages: very roughly, research, pre-clinical tests, clinical trials (phases I, II, III), process development in parallel with product tests, and filing. The process is strictly regulated by the governmental authority stage by stage. Given the regulation and huge investment required in the later stages of development, the management of pharmaceutical companies also strictly controls the progress of the R&D process by the milestone approach. This explains why the R&D process in the pharmaceutical industry is regarded as similar to the linear model. It can be schematized as in Figure 2.2.

Research and drug discovery	Pre-clinical tests →	Clinical trials →	Application for approval	Marketing and sales	Use
→	Process development etc. →		→	→	

Figure 2.2: Formal drug R&D process schematized by the linear model

However, even though the formal R&D process can be schematized in a linear process, there is a significant question of whether this is the case in the *actual* process of drug discovery and development. To what extent do existing works explore the process of R&D in the pharmaceutical industry?

2.2.3 Literature on Technological Change in the Pharmaceutical Industry

Because innovation is a crucial problem for the pharmaceutical industry, many researchers in economics and organization studies write on innovation in the pharmaceutical industry. In contrast, literature on this topic by sociologists seems to be limited.

From the economic viewpoint
According to Comanor (1986), there are three strands in economic studies of R&D in the pharmaceutical industry, namely: the determinants of research expenditure; scale economies in R&D; and the costs and returns from R&D. On the determinants of research expenditure, factors including firm size, research productivity, product diversification, the level of internally generated funds, the level of research and the direction of research have been suggested as determinants of research spending (ibid., pp. 1190–1).

On the scale economies in R&D, there is disagreement among researchers about whether larger pharmaceutical companies have an advantage in innovation over the smaller ones. Comanor provides two alternative views about this: the disagreement may be due to the difference in the periods of data collection; or it may be due to the definition of innovation, that is to say, 'larger firms are relatively more important when all new drugs are included but not so in regard to the most important innovations' (ibid., pp. 1192–3). However, more recent studies tend to support the importance of firm size for R&D productivity (Jensen 1987; Thomas 1990; Alexander 1996; Henderson and Cockburn 1995). Jensen (1987) and Alexander (1996) argue that increase in firm size does not affect or possibly negatively affects the marginal productivity of R&D while it positively affects the average R&D productivity. Henderson and Cockburn (1995) argue that economies of scope are as important as the economies of scale *per se*. Two different but related economies are included in their economies of scope. One is from the 'free-riding' effect among different research projects based on the public goods aspect of knowledge; the other is from internal spillovers of knowledge between projects that benefit each other.

On the problem of whether the returns generated by R&D are sufficient to cover their cost, a body of literature from the mid-1980s indicates that the average returns for new drugs have declined and may be less than average development costs in recent years (Comanor 1986, p. 1195). Diminishing average returns in the pharmaceutical industry is also indicated in more recent works (for example, Alexander *et al.* 1995). Comanor, on the other hand, points out that the returns from a small number of very successful products are now especially critical to success in this industry (Comanor 1986, p. 1195). This also seems to be consistent with the results of more recent studies (Grabowski and Vernon 1990, 1994, pp. 398–400).

There seem to be two more strands of research on the economics of R&D in the pharmaceutical industry. One strand is concerned with the effects of regulation on innovation, in particular on R&D productivity defined as the number of new chemical entities discovered and introduced in the market per R&D expenditure. While Grabowski *et al.* (1978), Wiggins (1981) and Jensen (1987) suggest the negative effect of regulation on innovation, Thomas (1990) later argues that the larger US pharmaceutical firms benefited from Federal Drug Association (FDA) regulation due to reduced competition but smaller firms suffered reductions in research productivity because of regulation. Another strand of research is on the general trend of decline in research productivity. Henderson and Cockburn (1995) and Graves and Langowitz (1993) can be categorized in this strand.

These works on the economics of R&D in the pharmaceutical industry indicate that there seem to be economies of scale, economies of scope, the declining trend of return, the declining trend of research productivity and the effect of regulation in pharmaceutical R&D. Although quantitative relationships between various empirical data related to technological change in the industry are shown by these studies, the process of technological change remains untouched.

McKelvey (1996) is, however, an exception. Although it might be inappropriate to classify her work with economic literature because she declares that her approach is multidisciplinary (p. 298), I place it here because it is more closely related to 'evolutionary economics' established by economists of technological change including Nelson, Winter and Dosi, than to organization studies of technology and innovation or sociology of technological change. She argues that a fundamental assumption of evolutionary economists that technological change is evolutionary has been little examined in detail by empirical studies (p. 257). She, therefore, shifts the focus of research from innovations as objects to those as processes (p. 2) and examines a case history of R&D process in genetic engineering, in particular that of human growth hormone made with recombinant DNA techniques (rDNA hGH) as her empirical base. She identifies in the process various agents, including academic scientists, biotech firms, established pharmaceutical companies, governments, doctors and the general public. She describes the shifts of knowledge-seeking activities of these agents from scientific to scientific-economic and techno-economic environments, with the advance of the process towards practical uses. She concludes that the innovation process of rDNA hGH is more accurately described as evolutionary, that is to say, includes the dimensions of diversity, retention and selection through the complex interactions among these agents and among agents and environmental conditions, rather than as linear, which appears to be the case on a hasty reading (pp. 26–36, 258). She also emphasizes the cross-stimulating relationship between science and technology. This relationship became more obvious when the knowledge-seeking activities of agents entered scientific-environment and techno-economic environments. In particular, she emphasizes the importance of production, where interaction between science and technology is very crucial, in the process of biotechnological innovation (pp. 291–4). Thus, McKelvey's work is especially close to my interest, and partly answers my question about the linearity of the drug R&D process. However, her answer is still insufficient on several points. First, her work does not include sufficient examination of the social process of drug R&D inside organizations. Second, the economic aspect of social processes is particularly emphasized, whereas sociological and political aspects are only briefly inspected in her study. Third, her work is based on only one area of pharmaceuticals, which is a relatively new area in the pharmaceutical industry and it may therefore be problematic to regard it as representative. Although her conclusions seem quite convincing, it is necessary to examine them through further detailed case studies with a more balanced viewpoint. Literature from organizational and sociological viewpoints (see below) seems to be helpful in this regard.

From the managerial and organizational viewpoint
Most of the recent works on the management and organization of the pharmaceutical industry highlight R&D and innovation, because they are regarded as the critical factors of competitive advantage. I roughly categorize the discussions here into three: discussions on technology strategy; on networking for innovation; and on the management of research organization.

Discussions on technology strategies in the pharmaceutical industry tend to identify trends of technology as a crucial environmental factor and then discuss the strategy. Bogner and Thomas (1996) identify several technology trajectories and other trends of technology in the history of the US pharmaceutical industry. They identify, for example, the organic chemistry trajectory (p. 54), the anti-infectant research trajectory (p. 59), trajectories of non-antibiotic drugs (p. 82) and the trajectory related to biotechnology (p. 117). Then they examine strategies of pharmaceutical companies and identify several strategic groups characterized as 'traditionally antibiotic', 'broad organic-chemistry focus', and so on in the 1970s; and 'narrow focus research firms', 'broad focus research firms', 'genetic firms', and so on in recent years (pp. 142–4). Achilladelis (1993) focuses on the sector of antibacterial medicines, and from historical analysis identifies four technological trajectories in the sector, namely, sulphonamides, natural product antibiotics, semi-synthetic antibiotics and synthetics. He also found corporate technology traditions in several companies. The concept of a corporate technology tradition, defined as the 'concentration of a company's R&D resources on a particular technology for a very long period of time leading to the introduction of many innovations embodying this technology' (p. 281), implies that there may be further diversity of company strategies in a single therapeutic area.[6] Hara (1997) identifies similar trajectories and corporation technology traditions in the development of antibacterial drugs in Japan. Galambos and Sewell (1995) identify four scientific and technological cycles in vaccine development, the latest of which is related to biotechnology. Many other authors also notice the impact of biotechnology on the pharmaceutical industry (for example, Sharp 1991, 1995; della Valle and Gambardella 1993; Whittaker and Bower 1994; Gambardella 1995; Otero 1995; Zucker and Darby 1997) and discuss the strategic linking of organizations. Sapienza (1997) looks at the opposite direction: from strategy to technological trajectories. She regards technological trajectories as the results of overall R&D as well as of programme- and project-specific decisions. She argues that technology strategy is the blueprint for the technological trajectory (pp. 5–7).

The research on the external linking and networking of pharmaceutical R&D for innovation is probably the most flourishing area in the organization studies of the industry. Most works in this area discuss it with reference to biotechnology. Whittaker and Bower (1994) show that the R&D alliance between pharmaceutical and biotechnology companies increased dramatically in the 1980s. They argue that this is not temporary but long-standing because their relations shift toward functional specialization. Gambardella (1995) also points to radical change in the pharmaceutical R&D associated with the development of biotechnology and molecular biology, and its implication for the division of labour between the large pharmaceutical companies and small to medium-sized biotech companies, universities and other research institutions. He argues that because scientific capability embedded in individuals is often the critical resource for drug discovery, on the one hand, and because the commercialization of drugs needs solid financial and managerial capabilities, on the other, the division of labour between small organizations with the former capabilities and large organizations with the latter is very hopeful (pp. 163–4). Faulkner and Senker (1995) identify changes in the relationship between the pharmaceutical industry and public sector research (PSR) from the early era of biotechnology (1983–4) to more recent times (1990–1). They identify that the role of PSR in the linkage shifts from being somewhat informal and random towards being more formal and specialized under the growth and penetration of biotechnology in the industry. Powell *et al.* (1996) indicate that when the knowledge base of an industry is both complex and expanding and the sources of expertise are widely dispersed, as is seen in biotechnology, innovation will stem from organizational learning in networks, not individual companies. These studies argue that network-form organizations are appropriate and sustainable in the era of biotechnology-based pharmaceutical innovation. Zucker and Darby (1997) provide a case study of the transformation of a large incumbent pharmaceutical company by 'the biotechnological revolution'. By detailed observation through a case study, they reveal that formal networking is insufficient to absorb the impact of biotechnology. Galambos and Sewell (1995) examine the history of vaccine development in the US pharmaceutical industry. The most remarkable feature of this work is that they regard drug developments as consistently being accomplished through networks. They identify four cycles in the history of vaccine development: namely, the bacteriology cycle; the virology cycle; the cycle associated with the new bacteriology of polysaccharide capsules; and the cycle grounded in biotechnology and molecular biology. According to them, new cycles were accompanied with new science and medical networks and the vaccine companies sought to accommodate them. Their historical investigation reveals that external networking did not begin in the biotechnology era, but had existed previously and that the era of biotechnology has brought a new arena for networking.

The third interest of research on the management of pharmaceutical innovation is management of the R&D organization. The effective and efficient assimilation of external knowledge seems to be one of the most important issues here. Specialized scientific competence within the organization is emphasized for evaluation and absorption of external knowledge. Gambardella (1995, p. 165) argues that companies with better in-house knowledge assets in biotechnology use more intensively external linkages. Faulkner and Senker (1995, p. 97) and Sapienza (1997, p. 188) also emphasize the in-house assessment capability of external knowledge. Bierly and Chakrabarti (1996) argue that technology cycle time, from initial development to product launch, is shorter in internal knowledge exploitation than in external knowledge utilization. They argue that this is because the relationship between organizational learning and new product development is moderated by strategic flexibility, controlled by flexibility in manufacturing, finance and marketing, and the range of knowledge base. Fitzgerald (1992) indicates that the assessment process of external technology involves many functions, namely, pharmacologists, toxicologists, pharmacists, physicians, marketing, legal experts and representatives from the major international markets. This heterogeneity might make prompt organizational learning and accurate assessment much harder. Another issue in the management of pharmaceutical R&D is the difference between research function and development function. Chiesa (1996) identifies several differences between research and development. According to him, research in the pharmaceutical industry is characterized by unpredictable timing, informality, modest expenditure and unpredictable results, while development is characterized by predictable timing, formality, huge expenditure and planned results. He indicates that these differences result in difference between research management and development management. For example, research management has characteristics such as direct communication and pressure from a sense of urgency, while the management of development has characteristics such as formal communication and pressure on deadlines.

The literature on pharmaceutical innovation from the managerial and organizational viewpoint highlights the relationship between technological change and corporate strategy, the inter-organizational network as the key organization form, the in-house scientific capability as the key factor for success in the pharmaceutical business and the differences between research function and development function in the industry. The studies show us some aspects of the process of technological change in the industry. However, the detailed interaction between various social and material factors in the process is not sufficiently described in these studies. In particular, social and political interaction within an organization, which has been described in several case studies in other industries (Whipp and Clark 1986; Thomas 1994), has not yet been explored in this industry.

From the sociological viewpoint
Despite the potential opportunities for sociological analysis, there does not seem to be much literature on technological change in the pharmaceutical industry from the sociological point of view. On the one hand, according to Bartley (1990), the sociology of medicine has traditionally been outside the construction of medical knowledge. Rather, it has been concerned with the ways in which medical knowledge is applied. In particular, how medical technologies are developed and introduced into practice has often been viewed in a technological deterministic way (Elston 1997, p. 4). Recently, however, the advent of the sociology of scientific knowledge (SSK) and other strands of the sociology of science has extended the opportunity for sociology to investigate the construction of medical science and technology. This can typically be seen in the sociology of medical science and

technology, which has recently emerged (Elston 1997). Nevertheless, pharmaceuticals do not seem to be the dominant topic even in this area. They are at most a one-of-them topic there. In this section, we review several sociological studies related to the process of drug discovery and development.

Bodewitz *et al.* (1987) analyse the drug regulatory process in which the efficacy and safety of the drug are adjudicated. They identify four social groups, each occupying a specific position in the social system of medical care and expressing a specific perspective on drug regulation practices: the general public, the pharmaceutical industry, the representatives of drug regulation agencies, and medical scientists and practitioners. They argue that science provides the yardstick for assessing their rationality for all groups. However, according to them, the asymmetry between standards of efficacy (double-blind methodology) and standards of safety (no commonly accepted standards) gives room for the diversity of assessments and leads to a complex mixture of factual and value-laden judgements. They indicate that standards of safety evolved along different lines between the US and European countries. They conclude that scientific procedures and certified knowledge are outcomes of the social process of acceptance.

Richards (1988) deals with the debate over the efficacy of vitamin C in the treatment of cancer. She compares it with cases of two other drugs, namely, 5FU and interferon. According to her, whereas vitamin C was rejected by the medical society because of the lack of 'sufficient' evidence of its efficacy for the treatment of cancer, the other two drugs were recognized as cancer treatment without the same level of evidence as was required in the former case. Moreover, the methods of the 'crucial' clinical trials that showed the inefficacy of vitamin C were conventionally 'rigorous' but fundamentally inconsistent with the theory and ideology of the proponents. Richards suggests that vitamin C was incompatible with the then established treatment of cancer, the interest of the medical authority, the interest of funding organizations and the interest of most of the pharmaceutical companies, whereas the other two drugs were more compatible with them. She concludes that the evaluation of medical therapies is inherently social and political and that this social character of medical knowledge cannot be eliminated by methodological reform: the randomized, controlled clinical trial, no matter how rigorously organized and operated, can neither guarantee objectivity nor definitively resolve controversy over competing therapies or technologies (ibid., pp. 686–7).

Abraham (1995) also highlights drug testing. His interest is whether, and how, corporate bias may influence the scientific processes of evaluating the safety and effectiveness of a new drug (p. vii). As a student of a realist sociology of science, he presumes interests of profit maximization for the pharmaceutical industry and of good health for patients. He also presumes that 'rational' companies and consumers will pursue those respective interests. Based on several case studies, he indicates that bias exists among many industrial scientists; that the bias coincides with the commercial interests of the pharmaceutical company; that such corporate bias becomes entangled with some reward systems of science; and that the British regulators are more biased than their American counterparts because of the close institutional relationship in the UK. Based on these findings, he insists on reform to reduce corporate bias.

Clarke and Montini (1993) examine how various actors were related to the construction of an oral abortion-inducing drug, RU486, by using 'arena analysis'. Arena analysis emphasizes multiple views of various actors: it attempts to view the constructed world metaphorically over the shoulders of all the actors, rather than only of scientists and engineers. Thus, they identify various actors and their different views of RU486. For example, for reproductive scientists it is 'the second generation pill'. For family planning, population control and abortion provider organizations, it is a means of mobilizing women to fight for new birth control. For pharmaceutical companies, it was a headache. For the clinicians who conducted its clinical trials, it was a means of 'doing science'. For medical groups, it is a means for greater safety in the practice of medicine and a means of fighting for medical autonomy. For antiabortion groups, it is another means of killing the child in the womb and a means of intentionally inducing a miscarriage. For feminist pro-choice groups, it is a means of mobilizing feminists. For women's health movement groups, it is a means of safe abortion for some women who so choose. For some politicians in California, it was a strategy to become the governor. They conclude that a fuller and more historicized arena of the construction of technology can be obtained by following all these actors.

Prout (1996) describes the mutual constitution of the metered dose inhaler (MDI) and various human actors by applying actor-network theory. Although the MDI is not a drug, its actor-network seems similar to a drug's because it is used together with a drug. Prout identifies both human actors including patients, doctors, technicians and scientists, and non-human actors including aerosol gases, the Bernoulli principle, metering valves and the lung in the actor-network. He describes the interactions between these actors and transformation of the actor-network: configuring the users, anti-programmatic actions of users and modifications of the MDI. He argues that 'ANT can help in understanding the intricate and mutually constitutive character of the human and the technological in the processes and relationships of sickness and healing' (p. 214).

Epstein (1996) describes the social history of the production of biomedical knowledge, specifically, knowledge about the causation of and the treatment of AIDS. His approach is a synthesis of conceptions coming from the sociology of scientific knowledge, the social history of science and theories on social movement. In the analysis, he especially focuses on the role of lay people, in particular that of AIDS activists, in the formation of the biomedical knowledge. According to him, the role of the activists in the treatment controversy was greater than that in the causation controversy. He states that the activists have challenged the calculation of risks and benefits by the traditional experts such as researchers, doctors and statisticians, and have helped to change the rules governing the kinds of evidence required to determine the efficacy of AIDS drugs by becoming 'lay experts'. He argues that 'analysts of science and medicine should attend to the strategies pursued by lay actors in their attempts to speak credibly about science and medicine' (p. 332), because lay actors, as well as experts, can and do transform research.

Timmermans and Leiter (2000) examine how thalidomide, the notorious drug which caused horrific disaster in the early 1960s, has reappeared as a life-saving drug for the treatment of leprosy, erythema nodosum leprosum, and AIDS wasting syndrome in the US since the mid-1990s. A standardized drug distribution system, which was newly devised by a pharmaceutical company called Celgene and the Food and Drug Administration (FDA), played a key role in the transformation of the drug. By the 1990s, the advantage of thalidomide for the treatment of those diseases was known to patients, and its underground trade arose. The FDA called for the cooperation of the pharmaceutical companies and Celgene took it up. The distribution system that the company proposed and the FDA approved consisted of several elements: education of physicians, pharmacists and patients; contraceptive counselling; regimen of pregnancy testing; informed consent; managed distribution and mandatory outcomes registry survey (ibid., p. 48). This system was constructed by not only the company but also other players, including physicians, pharmacists, patients, thalidomide victims, the FDA and the drug itself. The jurisdictions and identities of the players were in turn redefined by the system. The risk of the drug has not disappeared but become more controllable and acceptable by the system of the standardization of drug distribution.

These sociological studies of technological change in pharmaceuticals, together with sociological investigations of related issues such as biomedical laboratory life (Latour and Woolgar 1986), the genetics of cancer (Fujimura 1996), and the aetiology of peptic ulcer (Thagard 1999), provide us with detailed pictures of various aspects of biomedical research and development. They are obviously incompatible with the linear model of technological change. They suggest that various human actors, non-human entities, and institutional and structural factors together shape the biomedical science and technology. However, these works do not necessarily show us the full process of drug discovery and development. The processes of clinical trials and regulatory examination have been well investigated (Bodewitz *et al.* 1987; Richards 1988; Abraham 1995; Epstein 1996). Marks (1997), as a historian of science, also explores a detailed history of clinical trials in the US and the controversy over the randomized, controlled clinical trials. The processes of marketing and distribution of drugs and related instruments have also been examined but to a lesser extent (Clarke and Montini 1993; Prout 1996; Timmermans and Leiter 2000). The process of biomedical research is described and studied in most detail (for example, Latour and Woolgar 1986; Fujimura 1996; Thagard 1999). However, the whole process of drug discovery and development has been little explored. This lack of a full picture is a grave problem when we try to understand technological change in the pharmaceutical industry. In addition, most of these works tend to regard a pharmaceutical company as monolithic. Even worse, some regard the pharmaceutical industry as one unit of interest. However, as organization studies indicate, private companies consist of heterogeneous entities (Whipp and Clark 1986; Thomas 1994). A number of companies in the industry compete with each other. Without admitting the heterogeneity of the pharmaceutical industry and pharmaceutical companies, we cannot fully understand the process of drug discovery and development.

2.2.4 New Framework for Analysing Drug Discovery and Development

In the literature review above, we find that what we need in order to understand technological change in the pharmaceutical industry is to examine the entire process of drug discovery and development including the social process both inside and outside drug companies. The reviewed works in different disciplines have provided only partial pictures of this process. This book aims at filling this gap in the knowledge. However, it seems necessary for us to have an appropriate framework to analyse the process of drug discovery and development. With the great aid of reviewed studies, I set up a new framework for analysis of the process. Let me explain it.

I regard the process of drug discovery and development as a mix of social, organizational, political, economic, and material processes. The fact that different disciplines including economics, management and organization studies, sociology and pharmacology have actually studied the process so far supports my view. In other words, the process seems to be a process of heterogeneous engineering in a historical and structural context. If so, the process is most likely to be explored from the perspective of the social shaping of technology (SST). As was discussed in sub-section 2.1.4, the SST regards technology as being shaped not only by relevant social groups and related non-human entities but also by historical and structural factors including markets, regulation, and professional societies. Based on this view, the SST approach possesses the flexibility to absorb the fruits of different disciplines including evolutionary economics, management and organization studies, the social construction of technology, actor-network theory, and even medicine and pharmacology. This property makes the SST approach probably the most appropriate to grasp the richest picture of the process of drug discovery and development. I, therefore, adopt this approach for the analysis of the process of drug discovery and development. Putting it differently, I regard this study as an examination of the shaping of drugs. I dare to drop the word 'social' here because the process is also an economic and a material one.

According to the SST approach, not only the heterogeneity of elements but also the interactions between them are important to understand the process of technological change. In other words, dynamic relationships between elements involved in the process of technological change should also be investigated. However, these views of the approach are still schematic and do not prescribe particular analytical frameworks. They must be developed in relation to specific settings and concerns, which is the shaping of pharmaceuticals here.

As was seen above, in the process of drug discovery and development, the discovery of compounds, the choice of the application, the managerial decision to start the clinical development, and the creation of the market through clinical trials and regulatory approval are key events. Therefore, I divide the process of drug shaping into four aspects: the shaping of the compound; the shaping of the application; the shaping of organizational authorization; and the shaping of the market. The shaping of the compound refers to the creation of the material aspect of a drug. The shaping of the application refers to the defining of the therapeutic meaning of the compound. The shaping of organizational authorization refers to the acquisition of approval of corporate management in regard to the development of the drug. Finally, the shaping of the market refers to the establishment of the social legitimacy and the economic rationality of the drug outside the company. I shall examine each of these aspects and the relationships between them to analyse the complex process of drug shaping.

Each aspect of the shaping of drugs seems to involve heterogeneous elements. Reviewed literature in different disciplines is extremely useful here. Economic studies suggest that economic factors affect the process of drug discovery and development. They also address the effect of regulation on drug innovation. Among them, McKelvey (1996), based on the evolutionary model of innovation, argues that various agents including scientists, start-ups, large drug companies, governments, doctors and the general public are involved in the process of drug R&D. She also argues that the process includes interactions among these agents. Several sociological studies, including Bodewitz *et al.* (1987), Clarke and Montini (1993), Epstein (1996) and Timmermans and Leiter (2000), are consistent with her argument in terms of the heterogeneity of relevant social groups and their interactions in the process of drug shaping. They also add other actors such as patients, activists, politicians and statisticians to the list of participants. From organizational studies, Fitzgerald (1992) provides more detailed classification such as pharmacologists, toxicologists and pharmacists. The arguments of Bierly and Chakrabarti (1996) and Chiesa (1996) suggest that there exists a diversity of interests and cultures inside a pharmaceutical company due to the division of labour, for example, research, development, manufacturing, finance and marketing. Organization studies also indicate that institutional factors, including technology strategy, external organizational linkage, human networks, organizational capabilities, and financial and material resources, contribute to the shaping of drugs. Both economic and organizational studies emphasize the high uncertainty of the process of drug innovation. Sociological studies, such as Bodewitz *et al.* (1987), Richards (1988) and Abraham (1995), go further and reveal that there exists interpretative flexibility even about the properties of a drug, including efficacy and safety. The existence of diversity in the process of drug R&D is also indicated by McKelvey (1996). Sociological works, such as Richards (1996), Epstein (1996) and Timmermans and Leiter (2000), highlight the constructive feature of drugs. The mobilization and linking of heterogeneous elements are emphasized. Furthermore, Prout (1996), inspired by actor-network theory, adds non-human entities to the participant list. Timmermans and Leiter (2000) also pay attention to the drug itself.

Thus, the process of drug discovery and development can be regarded as involving heterogeneous elements including:

1. human actors such as chemists, pharmacologists, toxicologists, different functions in the company, corporate managements, academics, doctors, patients, government officers, politicians, activists and the general public;
2. non-human entities such as drugs, materials, instruments and facilities; and
3. institutional and structural factors such as strategies, organisational linkages, human networks, organisational capabilities, funds, markets, regulations, sciences and clinical trials.

Interactions, mobilizations and combinations of these elements in each aspect of drug shaping should be examined to understand the process fully.

In sum, my analytical framework consists of seven components. First, the process of drug shaping is divided into four different aspects, namely the shaping of the compound, of the application, of organizational authorization and of the market. Second, various human actors, non-human entities and institutional and structural factors involved in each aspect of drug shaping are identified. Third, interactive relationships among these heterogeneous elements and between different aspects are investigated. Fourth, the characteristics of different drug shaping processes in different settings are compared to reveal similarities and differences between them. Fifth, the reasons for the differences are searched. Sixth, the results of analysis are integrated to establish a model of the shaping of drugs. Seventh and finally, theoretical and practical implications are extracted from the model.

2.3   METHODOLOGICAL NOTES

To explore the process of drug R&D, I use case studies. One of the strengths of the case study as a research strategy is its thickness, that is to say, its richness in both the quantity and variety of information it includes. This thickness enables a case study to provide us with a means of retaining 'the holistic and meaningful characteristics of real-life events'. It also makes a case study appropriate for 'how' and 'why' research questions because answering these questions deals with operational links that need to be traced over time (Yin 1994, pp. 3–6). These characteristics are appropriate for this study to explore the detailed process of drug discovery and development.

Partly to achieve 'analytic generalization' (ibid., pp. 30–2) and partly to clarify invisible factors affecting the process of shaping drugs, I conduct multiple case studies. I compare different drug R&D processes in the same therapeutic area. I also compare drug R&D processes in different therapeutic areas. In addition, I compare drug R&D processes in two different countries, to understand in particular the influences of historical and structural context. In these comparisons, I investigate what kinds of differences there are and how and why these differences arose.

As the sites of case studies, I chose β-blockers and Ca antagonists (drugs for hypertension and other cardiovascular diseases), H_2 antagonists (anti-ulcer drugs), β-stimulants and inhaled steroids (anti-asthma drugs), LHRH analogues (anti-prostate cancer drugs), HMG-CoA reductase inhibitors (anti-cholesterol drugs), a cephalosporin antibiotic and an α_{1c}-blocker (a drug for urinary disorder) as areas for case studies. They were chosen because they were successful on the market and properly 'mature'. The successfulness and maturity of these drugs enabled me to access the information necessary for this research to cover the full process of R&D, partly because the relevant literature on such drugs is rich both in amount and in range, and partly because the relevant people and companies feel easy talking about their R&D process. If the cases were newer, it would be much more difficult to gain access to the relevant information because of the confidentiality surrounding pharmaceutical R&D.

I chose cases in Japan and the United Kingdom for the international comparison. There are two reasons for this. First, most of the literature on technological change in the pharmaceutical industry reviewed in the previous section deals with American cases. In contrast, both British and Japanese cases are investigated much less. This makes research on the British and Japanese pharmaceutical industry interesting and useful. Second, and perhaps more interestingly, although Japanese products such as automobiles and electronics have often enjoyed competitive advantage in overseas markets, this does not seem to be the case with pharmaceuticals (Howells and Neary 1995, p. 1). The overseas sales of 81 large and medium-sized Japanese pharmaceutical companies contributed only 2.5 per cent of their total sales in 1996; even those of 20 leading Japanese companies accounted for only 7.2 per cent of their total sales (Japan Pharmaceutical Manufacturers Association 1997, I-21). Nevertheless, Japanese companies dominate the domestic market, which is the second largest single market for pharmaceuticals. They accounted for about three-quarters of Japanese pharmaceutical sales in 1996.[7] In contrast, the UK is one of the leading exporters of pharmaceuticals in the world (Owen 1999, p. 360), with exports amounting to 41 per cent of gross output (Association of the British Pharmaceutical Industry 1997, p. 13). Thus, the British pharmaceutical industry's performance in the world market is outstanding, though its machinery and electronics counterparts are only modestly successful (Howells and Neary 1995, p. 1). Because of these contrasts, the comparison between Japan and the UK is very interesting.

In regard to data collection, I used a variety of published material related to the cases, including academic articles, patents, textbooks, biographies, corporate histories, business journal articles, newspaper articles, statistics, publications of companies and those of industrial associations. I also conducted interviews with key researchers and staff related to the discovery and development of the drugs we examine here (in total 22 interviewees). I obtained causal and situational information related to meaningful interactions between actors from interviews. Unfortunately, most internal documents related to the cases were not available for reasons of confidentiality. The quantity and quality of data used in each case study are not the same, mainly because of differences in the degree of publicity and confidentiality.   Interviews to Japanese researchers were conducted in Japanese. The transcriptions cited in the case studies were translated into English by the author.

For understanding of the process of drug R&D, I reconstructed the cases by organizing collected information historically and qualitatively. In order to reconstruct the process of drug R&D, written information and verbally obtained information were both used. The written stories of drug R&D were checked against the contents of interviews. The unwritten stories of drug R&D process, in particular the social aspect of the process, which is rarely conveyed in the scientific literature analysed, were obtained through interviews. On the other hand, the contents of interviews were also checked against and supplemented by the contents of relevant literature. I also tried to use writings by authors other than interviewees when they were available in order to obtain a more balanced picture of the drug shaping processes. In this way, I tried to minimize the danger of misunderstanding due to my limited scientific expertise, the tendency towards the conventional realist explanation of drug R&D, the risk of lapses in interviewees' memories and the biases of interviewees' opinions.

There are a few methodological limitations. First, the use of scientific papers in this study as one of the main sources of information might be taken as hampering a symmetrical, 'relativist' treatment of scientific and technological knowledge because such papers usually incorporate a view of science as objective, cumulative and progressive,[8] though some of those papers explicitly suggest the existence of uncertainty and controversy in their research areas, which I tried to uncover. The uncertain and controversial aspects of drug R&D were also confirmed by and elaborated through the interviews. Second, this research might be criticized for being a 'great men' account, because it appears to be too dependent on interviews of key researchers. Interviews with other researchers must have countered this risk. However, it would have been extremely difficult to achieve this without the help of relevant pharmaceutical companies, and they are very sensitive about confidentiality. Some companies were more cooperative than others in this respect, but even in such cases I was unable to obtain many informants for a single case study. To minimize the potential biases and the lapses of memory of interviewees, therefore, I checked the contents of interviews with relevant literature as much as possible. I believe that any remaining potential bias is not significant enough to undermine the major findings of this study.

NOTES

1. For further discussions about the trajectories of technology, see Dosi (1982, 1988), MacKenzie (1996a, pp. 54–9) and McKelvey (1996, pp. 29–32).
2. For an overview of the sociology of (science and) technology, see, for example, Bijker *et al.* (1987); Webster (1991); Williams and Edge (1996); and MacKenzie and Wajcman (1999).
3. It should be noted that science is also based on not only knowledge but also material. See, for example, Collins (1992); Latour and Woolgar (1986); and Pickering (1992). I think that this difference is a matter of degree.
4. See also Faulkner and Senker (1995, pp. 31–4); Hamlin (1992); Pavitt (1987); Constant (1980); Vincenti (1990); and McKelvey (1996) on the differences between science and technology.
5. This visit to a laboratory, which was located in England, was conducted on 15 February 2000.
6. See also Achilladelis and Antonakis (2001), in which they expand the scope of investigation and identify technological trajectories and corporate technology traditions in a wider area of pharmaceuticals.
7. The author's estimate based on Japanese Pharmaceutical Manufacturers Association (1997, I-5) and *Yakuji HandoBukku* (2000, p. 97).
8. On the relativist, symmetrical treatment of scientific and technological knowledge, see Bloor (1991); Collins and Yearley (1992); and MacKenzie (1996a, pp. 9–18).

3. Cardiovascular drugs

3.1 INTRODUCTION

In this chapter, we shall see three cases of drug discovery and development in the cardiovascular area. Two of them, propranolol and atenolol discovered by ICI in Britain, are what are called β-adrenergic receptor antagonists, commonly known as β-blockers. The third one, nicardipine discovered by Yamanouchi Co. Ltd in Japan, is a drug classified as a calcium antagonist. Propranolol (Inderal®) was discovered in 1962, it eventually became the first practically used β-blocker and is still widely used. Atenolol (Tenormin®), which was discovered in the early 1970s, is the successor of propranolol and the best selling β-blocker in the world. Nicardipine (Perdipine®) was discovered in 1971 and is one of the most frequently prescribed calcium antagonists in Japan. Of the four categories of anti-hypertension drugs, namely, diuretics, β-blockers, ACE (angiotensin-converting enzyme) inhibitors and calcium antagonists, β-blockers are the most frequently used group of drugs in Britain, whereas calcium antagonists are most often used in Japan (*Scrip Yearbook* 1991, p. 63).

3.2 PROPRANOLOL

3.2.1 Introduction

The first β-blocker that was investigated clinically was pronethalol (see Table 3.1). Pronethalol was discovered by Sir James Black and John Stephenson of ICI in 1960. Although it showed efficacy for the treatment of angina pectoris in clinical trials, it was replaced by propranolol partly because of its toxicity. Propranolol was discovered by Black's team in 1962. It showed about ten times higher potency than pronethalol and no serious side effects. Its clinical trials started in 1964 and it was marketed in 1965 under the trade name Inderal. It was developed for the treatment of angina and arrhythmias at first, but later it was found to be also useful as an anti-hypertension drug. It was highly successful in the market, and many pharmaceutical companies including ICI itself rushed into syntheses of its analogues.

Table 3.1:   Major events related to the discovery and development of propranolol

Year	Events
1958	Research project on β-blocker started at ICI
1960	Synthesis of pronethalol
1962	Clinical trials of pronethalol
	Synthesis of propranolol
1963	Launch of pronethalol under restriction
	Clinical trials of propranolol
1965	Launch of propranolol

3.2.2 Discovery of β-blockers

At a symposium on the history and the future of β-blockade in Amsterdam in September 1975, James Black stated that his discovery of β-blockers was based on the adrenergic receptor theory of R.P. Ahlquist and the discovery of DCI (dichloroisoproterenol) by researchers from Eli Lilly, an American pharmaceutical company (Black 1976). Ahlquist examined the responses of various organs to several sympathomimetic amines, which mimic the actions of noradrenalin (which is released from the sympathetic system and causes stimulatory or inhibitory responses of various organs). He found that there were two different orders of activity of the amines on various organs and suggested that there were two distinct types of adrenergic receptors, namely, the alpha- and beta-receptors (Ahlquist 1948). This theory however had been almost ignored until the discovery of DCI (Black 1976). Ahlquist himself later, in 1973, described the adverse circumstances when he published his paper:

> The original paper was rejected by the *Journal of Pharmacology and Experimental Therapeutics*, was a loser in the Abel Award competition, and finally was published in the *American Journal of Physiology* due to my personal friendship with a great physiologist, W.F. Hamilton.
>
> Bursting into print in 1948, it was ignored for more than 5 years except when someone referred to the methods used or the result obtained, but never to the concept. The reasons for this are obvious today: the concept did not fit with ideas developed since the 1890s on the actions of epinephrine. (Ahlquist 1973, p. 121)

Black offered a more detailed explanation. According to him, Ahlquist's concept 'can be seen to have been hidden in the long shadows cast by two giants – H.H. Dale, in England and W.B. Cannon, in the USA' (Black 1976, p. 11). Dale, who closely investigated the activities of sympathomimetic amines on the body in the early 1900s, came close to Ahlquist's receptor idea. He wrote with G. Barger in 1910: '[t]here must evidently be something in those cells, or connected with them and them only, which has a strong affinity for these amines' (Barger and Dale 1910, p. 55). However, in the same paper, they also commented that the theory of receptive side-chains was very difficult to apply to their results because of the lack of common chemical characteristics among examined amines that plausibly explained the different affinity to the specific site of tissue where specific receptive side-chains were assumed to exist (ibid., pp. 56–7).[1] According to Black, Dale never referred to receptors again in his writing and never gave receptor theory the benefit of his huge scientific support. Because Dale was one of the most influential figures of his time, his neglect of receptor theory functioned as a strong negative signal from scientific 'authority'.

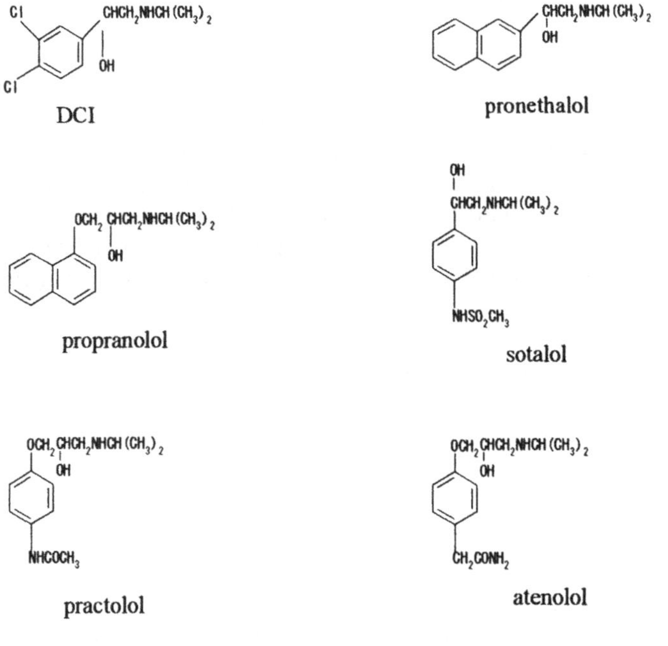

Figure 3.1: Various β-blockers discussed in Chapter 3

Another and equally strong negative sign against receptor theory was an alternative explanation offered by Cannon. In 1933, he and A. Rosenblueth suggested new hypothetical substances: sympathin E and sympathin I. Black explained their idea plainly: a transmitter substance A was released at sympathetic nerve endings, and A then combined with either excitatory E or inhibitory I substances in the tissues to form complexes AE or AI (sympathin E and sympathin I) (Black 1976, p. 12). They explained elaborately the excitatory and inhibitory actions of sympathomimetic amines without using the concept of different receptors. It worked like the phlogiston theory (Kuhn 1970). Thus, Black wrote: 'the contemporary combined forces of a theory of multiple transmitters and a low regard for receptor theory as a basis for classifying drug actions were too much for the new hypothesis to overcome on the first round' (Black 1976, p. 12).

Then came the discovery of DCI. When a group of researchers at the Lilly Research Laboratories of Eli Lilly, in Indianapolis in the US, discovered the compound, they were not looking for an adrenergic receptor antagonist but for a long-acting bronchodilator compound (Maxwell and Eckhardt 1990, pp. 6–7; Sneader 1985, pp. 111–12; Shanks 1984). They synthesized a series of analogues of isoprenaline, a bronchodilator, and assayed them. They found that one of the compounds, DCI, blocked selectively some of the effects of adrenaline and isoprenaline. They suggested that DCI was combining with certain 'adrenergic inhibitory receptor sites' without itself causing much physiological effect, and yet was competing for these sites with physiologically active amines (Powell and Slater 1958, p. 488), such as adrenaline and isoprenaline. They reported their discovery at a scientific meeting in 1957. Neil Moran at Emory University in Atlanta, Georgia, became interested in the report and asked Eli Lilly for a sample of DCI (Sneader 1985, p. 112; Shanks 1984). He and M.E. Perkins tested it immediately and confirmed that DCI antagonized the changes in heart rate and muscle tension produced by adrenaline in 1957. They also found that DCI blocked the cardiac responses to adrenergic stimuli after the initial increase in heart rate, which indicated its partial adrenergic agonist activity. What was very important was that they linked this phenomenon with Ahlquist's receptor theory. These results were published in 1958 (Moran and Perkins 1958). However, at that stage, they had not yet labelled DCI a 'beta-adrenergic blocking agent', as they did later in 1961; neither did Eli Lilly seem to notice fully the value of their discovery of DCI at that time. According to Black, this was also related to the dominant idea at the time, mainly developed by Walter Cannon. He developed the idea of homeostasis. He thought that the function of the sympathetic nervous system was the mediation of the 'fight, fright and flight' reaction, that is to say, the sympathetic nervous system was working for survival (Black interview; Black 1976).[2] For the people who believed the idea, it was not very wise to think about blocking the action of the sympathetic nervous system.

It was Black who clearly saw the values of the Ahlquist's theory, the discovery of DCI and the initial combination of these two events by Moran and Perkins. He had been a senior lecturer of physiology at the Veterinary School of the University of Glasgow since 1950 until he joined the ICI Pharmaceutical's laboratory at Alderley Park in Cheshire in July 1958 (Kennedy 1993, p. 130). During this period he had been interested in the treatment of angina pectoris. At the time, angina was treated by the strategy of increasing the supply of oxygen (Black interview; Shanks 1984). Though there were surgical ways of doing this, pharmacologists started with nitro-glycerine, which was and has been widely used to treat angina. Nitro-glycerine dilates blood vessels; this was believed at that time to help increase the supply of oxygen to the heart (Sneader 1985, p. 142). Many attempts were made to find a new vasodilator drug that was specific for the coronary artery, but they were not fruitful.

Black came to examine another approach. When he worked with George Smith, a vascular surgeon in Glasgow, he saw Smith's experiment with dogs to increase the small amount of oxygen in the plasma to stop ventricular fibrillation. Black raised a question: if a small increase of oxygen works, would a small decrease in the need of the heart for oxygen do the same thing? He then directed his attention to the heart rate and sympathetic nervous system. His knowledge of clinical medicine helped there. On the one hand, he knew that not only exercise but also stress caused pain to patients with angina. On the other hand, he also knew from observations of surgical operations that stopping the heart beating faster would relieve angina. Thus, he wondered if it was possible to decrease the need of the heart for oxygen by slowing down the heart rate, which was known to be controlled by the sympathetic nervous system. As he put it: could one make the heart go a bit more slowly by stopping the activity in the sympathetic nervous system? Thus, he began to look at adrenaline and in a textbook of pharmacology came across Ahlquist's theory of the two types of adrenergic receptors.[3] Although neither endocrinologists nor physiologists made much use of the concept of receptors at that time because of the reasons stated above, pharmacologists used the concept because it could explain beautifully the relationship between the concentration of a drug and its effectiveness in the body. He came to realize that what he wanted was a β-adrenergic receptor antagonist (Black interview).

In 1958, Black moved to ICI Pharmaceutical's laboratories at Alderley. ICI had established all its pharmaceutical business in a separate division at the new site in 1957 to strengthen the business, especially, in the cardiovascular drug area. Garnet Davey, then Head of Biological Research of the new Pharmaceutical Division of ICI, had learned of Black's interests and offered him a job (Kennedy 1993, p. 130). Before long Black came upon the discovery of DCI and Moran's report on it (Black interview; Black personal communication, January 2000; Kennedy 1993, pp. 130–1). In January 1959, he proposed a new project, saying: 'The search for compounds which will block cardiac sympathetic responses constitutes a clear-cut pharmacological problem' (Shanks 1984). He and his colleagues made their own sample of DCI and tested it on the heart. They saw that the compound stimulated the heart rate, which meant that it would not work for the treatment of angina. However, it otherwise worked as a β-adrenergic receptor antagonist. He decided to search for β-adrenergic receptor antagonists devoid of the heart-rate-stimulating effect.

In February 1960, John Stephenson, a chemist at Alderley Park, synthesized a new compound by replacing the two chlorine atoms in DCI with another phenyl ring (Sneader 1985, p. 112; Shanks 1984, p. 131; British Patent No. 909357). Black found that 'the compound blocks the cardiac rate of tension changes produced by catecholamines, but differs from DCI in being free from intrinsic sympathomimetic [agonist] activity' (Black and Stephenson 1962, p. 314); in other words, the compound was an effective antagonist of β-adrenergic receptors. The compound was named pronethalol (or nethalide, Alderlin®). It was subsequently tested on humans by A.C. Dornhorst and B.F. Robinson at St George's Hospital, London. In 1962, they confirmed that the drug blocked the cardiac action of catecholamines effectively in man and that exercise tolerance was increased by the drug in patients with angina pectoris (Dornhorst and Robinson 1962). Furthermore, the full-scale clinical trials of pronethalol showed that the drug was effective for angina (Alleyne *et al.* 1963), arrhythmias (Stock and Dale 1963), and hypertension (Prichard 1964). However, frequent occurrences of minor side effects of the drug were reported (Alleyne *et al.* 1963). Moreover, long-term toxicity tests revealed that the drug could cause cancer of the thymus gland in mice (Paget 1963; Shanks 1984; Sneader 1985, p. 112).[4] The British government and British people in general had become very sensitive about the safety of drugs after the revelation of the thalidomide disaster in 1962. The toxicological problem of pronethalol, therefore, was a major setback for the marketing of the drug. Eventually, it was marketed in the UK in November 1963, but under a restricted licence (Shanks 1984).

Meanwhile, Black did not stop searching for a better β-blocker, because he was not convinced that he had obtained the ideal drug in pronethalol. He put it thus:

> The first one was what is called a prototype. And a prototype is just good enough. So, out of the principle, these studies in man showed in principle this thing would work. But it had many problems with it. One was that quite a number of patients got their bad dreams and also it was then found to be a carcinogen in mice. But, we didn't wait. We were trying to get something, which should be

more potent and more selective and less toxic. We kept going. (Interview)

Elsewhere, Black stated: 'I don't think there were any pressures to market pronethalol as a drug, rather than use it as a stepping-stone or probe, but if there were, Garnet [Davey, the research director] kept them away from me' (Kennedy 1993, p. 132).

After a large number of compounds were made (Black *et al.* 1964), Leslie Smith and Albert Crowther, chemists at Alderley Park, at last synthesized an analogue of pronethalol in 1962 (British Patent No. 994918; Shanks 1984), which was later shown to be about ten times as potent as pronethalol, with fewer side effects, and not a carcinogen, by Black and his colleagues (Black *et al.* 1964). The compound was named propranolol (Inderal®). Shortly after the synthesis of propranolol, pronethalol's carcinogenic effect in mice was first reported in December 1962 (Shanks 1984), and the weight of R&D efforts rapidly shifted from pronethalol to propranolol. The first pharmacological and toxicological report of propranolol by Black and his colleagues was published in May 1964 (Black *et al.* 1964), and the clinical trials of the drug commenced in the summer of the same year. These soon indicated that propranolol was a safe and effective drug for the treatment of angina pectoris, hypertension and cardiac arrhythmias with a low incidence of side effects (Srivastava *et al.* 1964; Gillam and Prichard 1965; Rowlands *et al.* 1965; Sloman *et al.* 1965; various papers in the *American Journal of Cardiology*, 18(3), September 1966; Shanks 1984). The drug became the first β-adrenergic receptor antagonist on the market when launched in July 1965. It took only two years and eight months from the first experiment of propranolol in an animal to its market launch (Shanks 1984). It is obvious that the experience with pronethalol shortened the time for propranolol to achieve the required criteria for the approval. Pronethalol was withdrawn from the UK market in October of the same year (Shanks 1984). Then, on 10 and 11 November 1965, a major symposium entitled 'Symposium on Beta Adrenergic Receptor Blockade' was held in Buxton, England, with sponsorship from ICI (Braunwald 1966). The success of propranolol roused rival companies to the search for a better analogue of the drug (Sneader 1985, p. 113).[5] ICI also continued their research on β-blockers without interruption (Howe *et al.* 1968, 1969; Crowther and Smith 1968; Howe and Rao 1968; Crowther *et al.* 1969; Howe 1969; Dunlop and Shanks 1968). Black left ICI in the middle of 1964. He put it thus:

When a company has made a discovery of a new compound, what they want the scientists to do is to help them to promote the drug. So [ICI] wanted me to go to meetings and give papers ... And they did not want me to stop working on beta-blockers. I wasn't interested in marketing. And I got interested in [histamine receptor antagonist], so I said I wanted to do this, and they didn't want me to do. So, I said, 'All right. I'll go.' (Interview)

Later, it was learned that propranolol had previously been synthesized by H. Koppe of C.H. Boehringer and Co., Ingelheim, shortly before pronethalol had been discovered. However, the company did not recognize the clinical potential of the compound, and no patent was claimed at that time (Sneader 1985, p. 113; Shanks 1984). Black recognized the value of the compound, and ICI took out the patents related to it. Shanks wrote: 'Black had made the crucial contribution to the discovery of β-adrenoceptor blocking drugs by realizing that they might be of value in the treatment of cardiac diseases and instituted a research programme to develop acceptable drugs' (Shanks 1984). Other authors also wrote: 'The major contribution of Black was to appreciate the possible value of developing compounds to inhibit the sympathetic to the heart, and to then persuade, and then lead a team of scientists at ICI to translate the idea into reality' (Cruickshank and Prichard 1987, pp. 2–3).

Propranolol was very successful in the market. The biggest share of its sale was due to its efficacy in the treatment of hypertension, though the original researchers did not expect this use. The anti-hypertension activity of β-blockers was discovered by Brian Prichard when he was testing pronethalol in hypertensive patients at University College Hospital Medical School, London, in 1963 (Prichard 1964). He and P.M.S. Gillam found that propranolol also had an anti-hypertensive action in man in 1964 (Prichard and Gillam 1964). However, the anti-hypertensive activity of propranolol was not accepted immediately. There were some negative results, which Gillam and Prichard attributed to inadequate doses of the drug. They suggested that confusion arose from a misconception following an observation that showed that a relatively low dose of a β-adrenergic blocking drug would completely work in another application (Gillam and Prichard 1976, pp. 71–2). The use of propranolol for the treatment of hypertension was well established by the early 1970s (Morrelli 1973; Simpson 1974, p. 90; Fitzgerald 1982, p. 104; Beevers and MacGregor 1999, pp. 159–60), though the mode of the anti-hypertensive action of β-blockers has not yet been completely understood (Lewis 1976; Kaplan 1998, p. 206). β-blockers were the second most popular anti-hypertensive drugs after diuretics until 1991 (Kaplan 1998, pp. 189, 205), and propranolol was the leading β-blocker until it was superseded by a new generation of β-blockers such as atenolol. Garnet Davey, the then Research Director, stated that the discovery of the application for anti-hypertension was 'absolute luck' (Kennedy 1993, p. 133). Hypertension became the largest single use for propranolol and has enormously increased its market (ibid.). Black modestly commented that 'commercial success has nothing to do with the quality of the science. It's the fact that so many people suffer from high blood pressure that has led to the attention. If high blood pressure had been as uncommon as multiple sclerosis, there wouldn't have been the same amount of notice taken of it' (ibid., p. 134). However, the discovery of propranolol supported the theory of receptors, promoted further research into it, and changed the treatment of hypertension, angina pectoris and arrhythmias. This is shown in current textbooks in various disciplines: pharmacology (for example, Rang *et al.* 1995, pp. 24, 148–70, 286–91, 295, 317–19, 433); medicinal chemistry (for example, Patrick 1995, pp. 94–5, 102–3); physiology (for example, Berne and Levy 1996, p. 165); and hypertension treatment (for example, Kaplan 1998, pp. 205–12, 231, 277).

3.3. ATENOLOL

3.3.1 Introduction

Atenolol is a cardio-selective β-blocker discovered and developed by ICI. It possesses the advantages both of propranolol and of practolol. Practolol was the first cardio-selective β-blocker, also discovered and developed by ICI in the mid-1960s, but ICI withdrew it in 1975 after it was found to be toxic. Practolol was also less potent than propranolol. Atenolol is as potent as propranolol, as cardio-selective as practolol, without the side effects that were frequently observed in the use of propranolol and without the serious side effects seen in the use of practolol. Atenolol was launched in the market under the trade name Tenormin in 1976, and became the best selling β-blocker in the world in the 1980s and 1990s.

Table 3.2: Major events related to the discovery and development of atenolol

Year	Events
1964	Synthesis of practolol
1965	Launch of propranolol
1966	Discovery of cardio-selectivity of practolol
	Clinical trials of practolol
1968	Synthesis of atenolol
1970	Launch of practolol
	Pre-clinical studies of atenolol
1975	Withdrawal of practolol
1976	Launch of atenolol

3.3.2 In Search of a Better β-blocker: from Propranolol to Atenolol

As mentioned in sub-section 3.2.2, ICI continued research on β-blockers without interruption after the discovery of propranolol. They synthesized and tested a number of analogues of propranolol and pronethalol (see, for example, Howe *et al*. 1968, 1969; Crowther and Smith 1968; Howe and Rao 1968; Crowther *et al*. 1969; Howe 1969). They also studied β-blockers synthesized by other companies (Dunlop and Shanks 1968). Of these intensive and extensive studies on β-blockers at ICI, two sets of studies focused on a particular problem related to the local anaesthetic property of propranolol.

In 1965, Vaughan Williams reported that both propranolol and pronethalol are local anaesthetics (Vaughan Williams 1966). This raised a question whether the beneficial effect of the drug in angina resulted from the β-receptor blocking effect or a local anaesthetic effect (Shanks 1984). Researchers at ICI resolved propranolol into two optical isomers and found that the (–)-isomer was shown to be 60–100 times more potent than the (+)-isomer in blocking β-receptors, whereas both propranolol and its (+)-isomer were equally potent local anaesthetics but the (–)-isomer was less potent in local anaesthetic activity (Howe and Shanks 1966; Shanks 1984). The researchers decided to begin studies with the D- (that is, the (+)-)isomer of propranolol to determine the contribution of local anaesthetic activity to the therapeutic effect (Shanks 1984).

Another approach taken by ICI to this problem was to develop a β-blocker that was not a local anaesthetic (Shanks 1984). Besides propranolol, another β-blocker that was synthesized outside the company helped the researchers' thinking. This β-blocker was synthesized by A.A. Larcen at the Mead Johnson Pharmaceutical Company in October 1960, though the company was not searching for a β-blocker at that time (Sneader 1985, p. 113; Shanks 1984). The compound was named sotalol, and was later found to be a β-blocker. What was important was that sotalol was devoid of local anaesthetic activity (Lish *et al*. 1965; Shanks 1984). The compound was also devoid of side effects on the central nervous system due to its hydrophilic nature. Propranolol had this effect and could cause vivid dreams after taking it: this was one of the major side effects of the drug (Sneader 1985, p. 113; Simpson 1974). The ICI researchers synthesized sotalol and its derivatives, including its phenoxy derivative (ICI-50232) and the acetamido derivative of ICI-50232 (ICI-50172) in the summer of 1964. ICI-50172 was found to be a β-blocker without local anaesthetic activity like sotalol, though less potent in β-blocking than propranolol. ICI-50172 was named practolol, and ICI decided to develop it for clinical studies in which a comparison would be made between practolol and the D-isomer of propranolol to determine the role of blockade of β-adrenergic receptors and of local anaesthetic activity in the effectiveness of propranolol in angina and arrhythmias (Shanks 1984).

The comparative studies between practolol and the D-isomer of propranolol did not come to fruition because unique and more interesting pharmacological properties of practolol were unexpectedly discovered and research efforts were concentrated on understanding these properties. During 1965 and 1966 detailed pharmacological studies were made in animals with practolol. In April 1966, Robin Shanks and his colleagues at ICI almost by accident discovered that practolol blocked β-adrenergic receptors in the heart but not those in bronchial or vascular smooth muscle (Dunlop and Shanks 1968). Practolol was described as a cardio-selective β-adrenergic blocking drug (Shanks 1976). This property was especially important because the biggest problem of propranolol was a lack of selectivity in its affinity for β-adrenergic receptors. The β-receptors are widely distributed in the body, and are related not only to the heart but also to the bronchi and some other organs. The most serious problem is that β-adrenergic receptor antagonists without selectivity cause constriction of the bronchi, which can be life-threatening in patients with asthma. This side effect was obvious in the use of propranolol, because it affected equally both the β-receptors on the heart and those on the bronchi (Rang *et al.* 1995, pp. 150, 166–7). Practolol blocked the β-receptors on the heart selectively, and was almost devoid of this side effect.[6]

This phenomenon was explained by the hypothesis of Lands and his colleagues at Sterling-Winthrop Research Institute that there were two types of β-adrenergic receptors: β_1 receptors mediating responses in the heart and β_2 receptors mediating responses in bronchial and vascular smooth muscle (Lands *et al.* 1967). Practolol blocked those receptors that Lands had classified as β_1 and had little effect on β_2 receptors. In subsequent studies, practolol was shown to be cardio-selective in man (Brick *et al.* 1968), and was taken forward to clinical trials. The clinical trials confirmed that practolol did not block the bronchodilator action of isoprenaline and did not produce wheezing in asthmatic patients (Powles *et al.* 1969). An international conference on practolol was held on 5 and 6 June 1970 in London (Lewis 1971). Practolol (Eraldin®) was launched on the market in 1970 (Sneader 1985, p. 114).

Practolol, however, was withdrawn from general use in 1975 because it caused serious side effects (in the worst case, loss of eyesight) in a small number of patients who had taken it orally for a long time (Shanks 1984; Sneader 1985, p. 114; *British Medical Journal*, 14 June 1975, editorial; Cruickshank and Prichard 1987, pp. 835–9). The use of the drug was restricted to specialized hospital units after that. The drug which eventually took over the market for practolol in 1976 was ICI-66082 (atenolol), which had been synthesized by David Le Count in 1968, a year before the market launch of practolol (Fitzgerald 1977; British Patent No. 1285038). This compound, therefore, was not searched for because of the withdrawal of practolol, but had already been discovered in the continuous research on β-blockers at ICI, where the researchers had looked for a drug with the advantages of both propranolol and practolol.

Practolol had two obvious drawbacks, apart from the side effect mentioned above: it was less potent than propranolol on the heart and it also had a partial agonist activity (Barrett 1971, 1977; Fitzgerald 1977; Le Count 1982, p. 124). These two drawbacks were the main targets of the research after the discovery of practolol because its long-term toxicity had not been known when the research was conducted (Wiseman 1971). Therefore, the profiles demanded of the next drug to practolol were to be as potent as propranolol on the heart and to be devoid of partial agonist activity, and it was also necessary for it to have less effect on the bronchial and vascular smooth muscle (that is, cardio-selective) and to be free of local anaesthetic activity, like practolol (Barrett 1977; Fitzgerald 1977; Le Count 1982, p. 119). In addition, it was required that the drug be highly water soluble (hydrophilic) so that it did not penetrate the central nervous system and cause side effects such as vivid dreams (Barrett 1977). To find a drug that satisfied these profiles was important not only for improving the therapies for angina and hypertension but also for understanding the mode of action of β-blockers. All β-blockers available at that time had mixed activities: general β-blocking activity, cardio-selective β-blocking activity, local anaesthetic activity and partial agonist activity (Table 3.3).

Table 3.3: Some pharmacological properties of β-blockers

Drug	β-blocking potency	Cardio-selectivity	Local anaesthetic activity	Partial agonist activity
Available:				
Propranolol	++	—	+	—
Sotalol	+	—	—	—
Oxprenolol	++	—	+	+
Practolol	+	+	—	+
Required:				
Atenolol	++	+	—	—

Sources: Fitzgerald (1977) and Heel *et al.* (1979), partially edited by the author

Knowledge about the effects of each activity on the body was poor. Scientists in the industry wanted to know the contribution of each activity to the safety and efficacy of β-blockers. They particularly wanted a drug that had β-blocking activity only so that they could compare its effects with those of other β-blockers (Fitzgerald 1977).

The ICI research team at that time was led by Arthur M. Barrett, a pharmacologist, and included both pharmacologists and chemists (Fitzgerald 1977). Both sorts of expert were required to change their approaches. The pharmacologists needed to modify biological screening procedures so that they could identify each activity of the examined compound (Barrett 1977): a screening sequence with five stages was devised (Le Count 1982, pp. 120–6). For the chemists, it was relatively easy to achieve potency as strong as propranolol, but it was not easy to achieve the other demanded profiles; this was because the structural features responsible for the presence or absence of the other properties were not obvious. First of all, in order to achieve cardio-selectivity, the unique structure of practolol was carefully studied. One of the chemists, Roy Hull, considered that the acidic nature of the proton in the unique structure of practolol, $-NHCOCH_3$, contributed to the cardio-selectivity. He suggested an alternative side-chain to his colleague, Le Count (Fitzgerald 1977; Barrett 1977). Because the original suggestion was difficult to synthesize (Fitzgerald 1977), Le Count tried another side-chain, $-CH_2CONHR$,[7] in place of $-NHCOCH_3$ in practolol, based on Hull's hypothesis and his own thought that the NH chain could also play a crucial role (Le Count 1982, p. 126). The parent compound, atenolol, was the one with H at the R position of the side-chain, $-CH_2CONHR$ (that is, $-CH_2CONH_2$), which was synthesized through a unique, but very convenient, method (ibid., pp. 126–7). Within two months of its synthesis in December 1968, the compound was found to be a cardio-selective β-blocker, as expected. To the researchers' surprise, however, it was found to be devoid of partial agonist activity and also devoid of local anaesthetic activity (ibid., p. 126; Barrett *et al.* 1973; Fitzgerald 1977). Thus, the compound unexpectedly achieved all the targets at the same time.

A number of analogues of the compounds were also synthesized (Le Count 1982, pp. 127–31). Many of them were cardio-selective β-blockers.[8] However, none was closer than atenolol to the initial target. Any additional modification led to the loss of one or more demanded profiles. For example, a modification that enhanced the potency reduced the hydrophilic property (ibid.). Several compounds based on other approaches were also compared with atenolol, but none satisfied all the initial requirements (Fitzgerald 1977).[9] Although atenolol was not an 'ideal' β-blocker with cardio-specificity (that is, active on the heart only), it was at least the closest to the 'ideal' (Barrett 1977). In addition, it is said that atenolol was chosen particularly because it was believed to be the most potent one in anti-hypertension activity (Fitzgerald 1982, pp. 113–14; Bilski personal communication). As mentioned in the previous section, hypertension was the largest market for β-blockers; thus, atenolol was chosen to be developed as a drug.

Clinical trials confirmed the efficacy of the drug for the treatment of hypertension and angina pectoris, its cardio-selectivity, and its lack of serious side effects, including the one that was reported in the long-term use of practolol (Hoffbrand 1977; Heel *et al.* 1979). Many of the clinical trials included the comparison with propranolol (for example, Åström and Vallin 1974; Roy *et al.* 1975; Singh *et al.* 1975). Atenolol was not more potent than propranolol but its cardio-selectivity, its absence of local anaesthetic activity and its lack of partial agonist activity were regarded as advantages. An unexpected, additional advantage of the drug was that it was longer acting so that it could allow once a day dosage for the treatment of the hypertension (Fitzgerald 1977; Heel *et al.* 1979). It is notable that the number of papers on clinical trials of atenolol was much larger than those of propranolol. Atenolol was launched in 1976 under the trade name Tenormin (Zeneca 1993 *Annual Report and Accounts*, p. 16). An international symposium on atenolol was held 4–6 October 1976 in Nice, France (Hoffbrand 1977). Atenolol became one of the world's best-selling cardiovascular drugs in the 1980s. Even in 1991, 15 years after its launch, it was amongst the top five selling drugs in the world with sales amounting to $1180 million. (*Scrip Yearbook* 1993, p. 47). In 1993 the drug accounted for 25 per cent of the sales of pharmaceutical products at Zeneca, which has been separated from ICI since 1993 (Zeneca 1993 *Annual Report and Accounts*, p. 15).

3.4 NICARDIPINE

3.4.1 Introduction

Nicardipine is one of the drugs called calcium antagonists. It was discovered and developed by Yamanouchi Co. Ltd in Japan in the 1970s. When it was discovered, the researchers at Yamanouchi did not know its mechanism of action; however, because it showed remarkable potency in coronary and cerebral vasodilation, it was chosen for development. During its clinical trials, the concept of calcium antagonism arose and provided an explanation for the action of the drug. Nicardipine was launched in the Japanese market under the trade name Perdipine in 1981, and became one of the best selling cardiovascular drugs in Japan in the 1980s.

Table 3.4:   Major events related to the discovery and development of nicardipine

Year	Events
1966	Synthesis of nifedipine (patented in 1967)
1969	Clinical trials of nifedipine in Japan (in Germany in 1970)
	Finding of the calcium antagonist activity of nifedipine (published in 1972)
	Start of research on the analogues of nifedipine at Yamanouchi
1972	Discovery of nicardipine
1974	Clinical trials of nicardipine as a cerebral vasodilator (in Japan)
1976	Launch of nifedipine for anti-angina (in Japan)
1977	Clinical trials of nicardipine for anti-hypertension (in Japan)
1981	Launch of nicardipine as a cerebral vasodilator (in Japan)
1982	Extension of application of nicardipine for anti-hypertension (in Japan)
1985	Extension of application of nifedipine for anti-hypertension (in Japan)
	Suspension release tablet of nifedipine (in Japan)
1988	Suspension release tablet of nicardipine (in Japan)

3.4.2 Discovery and Development of a Calcium Antagonist in Japan

When Toichi Takenaka joined Yamanouchi Pharmaceutical after graduating from university in 1964, he was interested in the activities of vasodilators. However, vasodilators at that time were not highly rated as drugs for angina pectoris and hypertension, partly because existing vasodilators such as hydralazine, dipyridamole and cyclandelate were not very effective, and partly because the advent of β-blockers in the mid-1960s attracted most researchers' and physicians' attention to the new type of drugs. Yamanouchi also went with the tide, and eventually discovered a β-blocker, indenolol, in 1968. Takenaka had to stop his research on vasodilators because he was involved in the research of the β-blocker. However, not long after he finished the work on the β-blocker, he came across a new series of compounds, 1,4-dihydropyridine derivatives (Takenaka interview).[10]

The compounds did not originate with Yamanouchi. Since the mid-1960s, an American company and a German company had been studying them. In the United States, Bernard Loev and his colleagues at SmithKline and French Laboratories were interested in 1,4-dihydropyridine derivatives, a simple synthesizing procedure which had been discovered by A. Hantzsch in 1882, because the pharmacological properties of this category of compounds were not well-known even though dihydropyridines were involved in various biochemical processes (Loev *et al.* 1972; Loev and Snader 1965). They studied the derivatives and found that a compound had a long-lasting hypotensive activity in dogs when administered by injection. However, it did not work when given orally. They synthesized a large number of compounds to find an orally active compound. Eventually, they found one potent hypotensive compound (SKF-24260) that was active even by the oral route, and published in 1972 (Loev *et al.* 1972; Sneader 1985, pp. 143–4). They tried to develop the compound as a drug, but gave it up later because of its toxicity (Takenaka interview).

In Germany, F. Bossert, a chemist at Bayer AG, had been studying coronary dilating agents since 1948. He and W. Vater, a pharmacologist, found that 1,4-dihydropyridines possessed a strong coronary dilating activity. They synthesized and tested more than 2000 of its derivatives, and finally discovered a highly potent coronary vasodilator (BAY a 1040) in 1966 (Bayer (Japan) 1994; Bossert and Vater 1971). The compound was orally effective. They patented this and similar compounds in 1967 before the SKF team protected their work by patents (Sneader 1985, p. 144). The clinical trials of the drug started, first in Japan in 1969, then in Germany in 1970, for the treatment of angina pectoris. This was because some Japanese medical experts had been interested in coronary dilating agents for the treatment of angina. The drug, named nifedipine (Adalat®), was approved in Japan as an anti-angina drug in 1975, and launched in the market in 1976; in Germany, it was launched in 1975 (Bayer (Japan) 1994; *Gekkan Mikusu*, 24(14), 1996, p. 62). Meanwhile, Albrecht Fleckenstein at the University of Freiburg had been studying the mechanism of the vasodilating activity of nifedipine since 1969. He found that the drug was a strong calcium-ion channel blocking agent (in short, a Ca antagonist) and published his results in 1972 (Fleckenstein *et al.* 1972; Fleckenstein 1977, 1988). Vascular muscle cells contract when the intracellular calcium concentration rises. The entry of Ca^{++} into cells is regulated by calcium-ion channels on the cell membrane. Therefore, by blocking the entry of Ca^{++} into vascular muscle cells, vasoconstriction can be stopped. Fleckenstein had elaborated the concept of Ca antagonists from 1963, and nifedipine contributed to establishing the concept. He wrote in 1988:

> No doubt, the discovery of the top Ca^{++} antagonist nifedipine marked the definite breakthrough of the concept of Ca^{++} antagonism and induced enormous efforts by the pharmaceutical industry to expand the new Ca^{++} antagonistic drug family by further syntheses. (Fleckenstein 1988, p. 6)

In the late 1960s, Yamanouchi licensed three vasodilators from an overseas company, though they were not 1,4-dihydropyridine derivatives. In order to test the properties of these compounds, they had to learn the methods of biological tests on vasodilators, because the company, which had started its own research for new drugs in 1963, did not have sufficient skills. They learned the related techniques of experiments by sending their researchers to domestic universities. Using the compounds and the techniques, they obtained methods of assay for vasodilators. Although none of the compounds turned out to be a promising drug, the technology obtained through this experience contributed to their later work (Takenaka interview).

Masaru Iwanami and his fellow chemists at Yamanouchi started pharmacological studies on 1,4-dihydropiridine derivatives in order to discover a vasodilator in 1969 (Yamanouchi 1994b). They learned about the substances from information found by a team of literature and patent investigators in the company. The original sources in this case were the patents of Bayer and SmithKline. They synthesized a number of the analogues. Takenaka, who had at that time been conducting the biological screening of hundreds of compounds to find a potent vasodilator, tested these 1,4-dihydropiridine derivatives as well and found that one of them showed a remarkable potency he had rarely seen before. He put it: 'I didn't know the concept of calcium antagonists at that time. But I observed the reactions of animals given the compound, and strongly felt that this was very much different from the existing vasodilators.' Takenaka, Iwanami and their colleagues decided to continue examining the compound and its analogues (Takenaka interview).

Although the compound was highly potent, it was less soluble in water than Bayer's 1040 or SKF-24260. This meant the compound would not work when given orally. Therefore, the efforts of the Yamanouchi team of chemists were directed to finding more water-soluble analogues. Many approaches to getting high water solubility reduced the potency of the compound. The productivity of reactions was also important. After enormous effort, they had a few candidates to develop as a drug. There was a trade-off between water solubility and potency. They selected one of the most active compounds in their study though it had a relatively low water solubility; nevertheless, even the selected compound (YC-93) had very high water solubility compared to existing alternatives: it was more than 100 times higher than that of Bayer's 1040 or SKF-24260 (Iwanami *et al.* 1979). The selection was made in view of the potency, bioavailability (that is, water-solubility), duration and uniqueness of the compound (Iwanami *et al.* 1979; Takenaka interview). YC-93 was discovered in 1972 (Takenaka interview) and patented in 1974 (Iwanami *et al.* 1979; Japanese Patent No. 109384; Belgian Patent No. 811324).

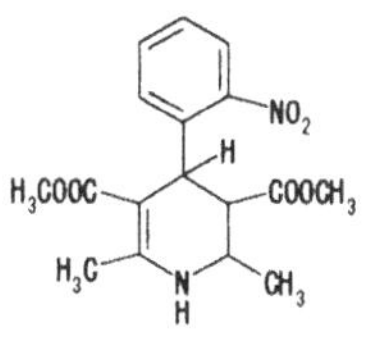

nifedipine 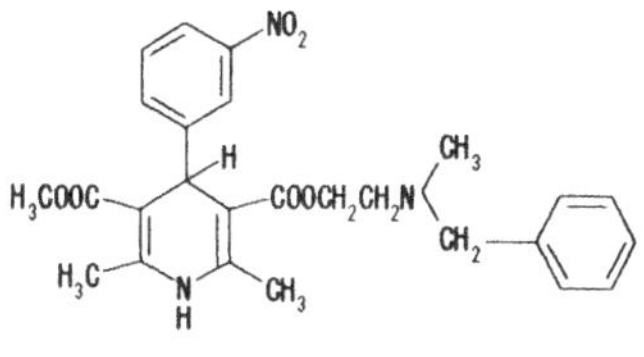   nicardipine (YC-93)

Figure 3.2: Nifedipine and nicardipine (calcium antagonists)

In pre-clinical tests with animals, YC-93 was found to be a potent cerebral and coronary vasodilator with low toxicity. Takenaka and his colleagues also confirmed that it was well absorbed by the oral route (Takenaka 1974; Takenaka *et al.* 1976). It seemed, however, that they had not yet noticed that the drug had a calcium antagonistic activity. In the paper published in 1976, they only mentioned: 'The coronary vasodilator mechanism of YC-93 seemed to be different from that of dipyridamole.' Later, they learned the concept of calcium antagonism from the literature and used it effectively to persuade medical doctors to conduct clinical trials of the drug (Takenaka interview).

Takenaka and his colleagues decided to propose the development of the compound. Since the company had only recently started its own research for new drugs, it did not have a systematic procedure to evaluate a drug development project when YC-93 was discussed.[11] Masuo Murakami, who was then director of the central laboratory of the company and had been a professor at the Research Institute of Industrial Sciences, Osaka University before joining the company, had absolute discretion on research policy and management. Researchers at Yamanouchi used to propose their projects directly to him, and he decided whether to take up or to drop their proposals. Takenaka put it thus:

> At the time, we used to ask the director to let us do this research, and he used to say, 'OK, go ahead.' We were in such atmosphere. Research management wasn't strict. We did what we wanted to do, and when we got good results on it, we would propose its development. We enjoyed an extremely high freedom about research. Later, when [famotidine] was developed, the atmosphere was less free and there was a formal procedure of project proposal. But, in [YC-93, nicardipine] case, we didn't have such procedure. I briefly explained the results to the director in a research meeting and asked, 'I've got such a good compound. Let me do this.' (Interview)

Murakami immediately gave Takenaka an OK. Although Takenaka

succeeded in obtaining organizational authorization in this way, he heard some anxieties expressed by the marketing side. They were anxious about the resistance of medical doctors whom they asked to conduct clinical trials of the drug. Only a few years previously, in 1967, a modern approval system for new drugs was introduced in Japan, and this drug was the first one Yamanouchi sought to develop under this new regulatory system. In fact, some doctors doubted the clinical value of vasodilators. Yamanouchi's representatives and researchers faced a lot of difficulty in obtaining the cooperation of these doctors. They were trying to persuade doctors by using data from animal experiments, but it was not easy.

Just in time, they learned of the concept of calcium antagonists from the literature on nifedipine (Takenaka interview), which I mentioned above. Because of the similarity between the structure of nifedipine and that of YC-93, it was obvious that the mechanism of action of YC-93 could also be explained by calcium antagonism. At that time, nifedipine was also in its clinical trials in Japan. Furthermore, another drug with a different chemical structure from 1,4-dihydropyridines, diltiazem, which had been serendipitously discovered by researchers at Tanabe Pharmaceutical in the mid-1960s and was also undergoing clinical trials at the time, was found to be a calcium antagonist as well (Nakajima *et al.* 1975; Tanabe 1994; Fleckenstein 1977; Fleckenstein 1988). That is to say, three potent vasodilators were clinically tested in Japan at almost the same time, in the 1970s, and during their clinical trials it became clear that all of them were calcium antagonists, a group of drugs whose mode of action was newly explained. This new concept attracted doctors, especially leading doctors at universities (Takenaka interview). Yamanouchi, the latecomer of the three, was able to enjoy the benefit of the popularity of the concept of calcium antagonism among academic physicians. As Takenaka put it: 'Voices from outside are very important in Japan. What opinion leaders say is crucial. ... In Japan, especially at that time, people didn't trust any Japanese work until someone else announced it's OK' (interview). Probably, for leading academic physicians in Japan, Fleckenstein was 'someone else', whereas, for other physicians, the leading academic doctors were the 'someone else'. However, it might be worthwhile noting that people at that time did not know whether calcium antagonists would work practically even though they had obtained the concept. People were beginning to recognize calcium antagonism as a new approach to the treatment of hypertension, but the clinical value of calcium antagonists was far from established. Although many aspects of calcium antagonism were still uncertain, the concept helped Yamanouchi's representatives persuade doctors and the company was able to start clinical trials of YC-93 in 1974.

These trials of YC-93 started first on its application as a cerebral vasodilator. There were two reasons Yamanouchi chose this application rather than as a coronary vasodilator. On the one hand, specialists in coronary medicines at that time were doubtful about the effectiveness of coronary vasodilators for the treatment of angina, because it was known that the then existing vasodilators such as dipyridamole dilated only the healthy coronary artery and that this might worsen the shortage of blood supply to the diseased coronary artery (the 'coronary steal' phenomenon). Calcium antagonists increase blood supply to both healthy and diseased coronary arteries, but at that time it was not possible to measure separately each blood flow to show this. As to cerebrovascular disorders, however, it was known that the total blood supply was related to the patient's condition. On the other hand, the number of patients with cerebrovascular disorders in Japan was higher than that of patients with angina at that time. It would have taken more time and cost more to have conducted clinical trials of the drug for the treatment of angina (Takenaka personal communication, December 1999).

In 1975, the drug progressed into Phase II, in which it was given to patients with blood-flow disorder in the brain. Then, it experienced Phase III: double-blind tests with an existing drug. Yamanouchi cleared clinical trials and applied for the approval of manufacturing of the drug in 1979. The drug, named nicardipine, was approved in 1981. It was launched in the market under the trade name Perdipine in the same year (Yamanouchi 1994b; Takenaka interview).

Meanwhile, the clinical trials of YC-93 as an anti-hypertensive drug also started in 1977. This was partly because its anti-hypertensive activity was confirmed in the course of its clinical trials as a cerebral vasodilator (Yamanouchi 1994b).[12] However, there was another reason why the clinical trials as an anti-hypertensive drug came late: the anticipated official price of YC-93 as a cerebral vasodilator was higher than as an anti-hypertensive drug (Takenaka interview). That is to say, this choice of application was made not only from a medical but also from an economic point of view. Of course, Yamanouchi did not give up the huge and growing anti-hypertension market. After clearing another set of clinical trials of nicardipine for the treatment of hypertension and after the drug was approved as a cerebral vasodilator, Yamanouchi applied for approval of the extension of nicardipine's application. This extension of application was approved in 1982, and nicardipine became the first calcium antagonist approved for the treatment of anti-hypertension (Yamanouchi 1994b). Although nifedipine had been approved as an anti-angina drug in 1975, it was not until 1985 that the drug became available in Japan for the treatment of hypertension (Bayer (Japan) 1994).

The dose of nicardipine tablets was originally three times daily. Later, the suspended release tablet (twice daily) of the drug was developed especially for the treatment of hypertension. This was approved in 1988. The injection formula for its use during a surgical operation was also developed and approved in 1988; its water-solubility made injection possible. Nicardipine was also launched in other countries, including the United States, France, Italy and the United Kingdom in collaboration with American and European companies (Yamanouchi 1994b). However, in these countries the applications of this drug are anti-angina and anti-hypertension, like nifedipine, rather than cerebral vasodilatation (*British National Formulary*, 35, March 1998, p. 99; Bowles *et al.* 1981; Gelman *et al.* 1983; Iliopoulou *et al.* 1983; Lambert *et al.* 1985; Ryman *et al.* 1986).

Nicardipine was very successful in the Japanese pharmaceutical market. Annual sales in the 1980s and early 1990s were about 40 billion yen (about £200 million at an exchange rate of £1 equals 200 yen). It was among the top five selling drugs in Japan from 1986 to 1990. Three years after nifedipine was approved for anti-hypertensive use and its suspended release tablets were launched in 1985, sales of nicardipine in Japan were surpassed by those of nifedipine (*Gekkan Mikusu*, 24(14), 1996, p. 41). In 1996, the estimated sales of nicardipine and nifedipine were 24 billion yen and 38 billion yen respectively, whereas that of atenolol, the top selling β-blocker even in Japan, was 11 billion yen (*Yakuji Handobukku* 1997, p. 268). The official prices of nifedipine, nicardipine, propranolol and atenolol per day in 1994 were 666–1220, 626–1200, 619–1436, 1290 yen respectively (*Yakka Yakkou Hayamihyou* 1994). Therefore, β-blockers are not always cheaper than calcium antagonists in Japan. Yamanouchi discovered and developed another calcium antagonist later. However, their third calcium antagonist project (YM-430) was stopped for economic reasons. Takenaka put it thus:

> We quit [YM-430] because of its cost rather than its technical concerns. That's because the prices of anti-hypertensive drugs have been severely getting lower. There are already a lot of good anti-hypertensive drugs on the market, and their patents have expired one after another. So, they are getting cheaper. We would have to accept a low price in this situation. Because we knew the drug would have needed massive production, we gave up from the point of view of costs. (Interview)

3.5   A BRIEF ANALYSIS

In the shaping of propranolol, the role of Black was very important. It was he who connected the discovery of DCI with the Ahlquist's theory, and he who played a central role in mobilizing resources to materialize the idea of a β-blocker for the treatment of angina. His role in the shaping of the compound, its application and its organizational authorization is, therefore, key in the shaping of propranolol, a new kind of drug. In the shaping of propranolol as a compound, the chemists who synthesized a series of compounds, the managers who championed the project, and the market needs that justified the project also played essential roles, as well as relevant materials including DCI and pronethalol and relevant scientific works such as those of Ahlquist (1948) and Moran and Perkins (1958). In shaping the applications of propranolol, external academics such as Prichard and Gillam (1964), who demonstrated the anti-hypertension activity of β-blockers were particularly important, because this aspect obtained the largest share of the drugs' sales. In the shaping of market, the efforts of ICI in promotion, academic journals and conferences that promoted the drug and gave it credibility, and the regulator who restricted the use of pronethalol played a significant role in the creation of the market of propranolol.

In the shaping of atenolol as a compound, more systematic and intensive approach seemed to be adopted by ICI because uncertainty about the technology and the market for β-blockers was much reduced. The roles of chemists and biologists, marketed and potential β-blockers made by ICI and other companies – particularly practolol which serendipitously showed cardio-selectivity, and Lands' theories on the two subtypes of β-adrenergic receptors were all significant in the shaping of atenolol, but it should be noted that effort was strongly orientated towards the improvement of pharmacological properties, including cardio-selectivity and the elimination of local anaesthetic activity and of partial agonist activity, which appealed to the market.

In the case of nicardipine, the research strategy of the Japanese company, the interest of the leading researcher in vasodilators, nifedipine as an exemplar drug, and the relevant techniques of experiments that were transferred from domestic universities contributed to the shaping of the compound, though the theory of calcium-ion channel antagonism had nothing to do with it. The applications and markets for the drug were orientated towards anti-hypertension and anti-angina before the compound was discovered, but the application as a cerebral vasodilator was intentionally given priority over anti-hypertension for strategic and demographic reasons. In the shaping of the market, the theory of calcium antagonism played a crucial role in persuading doctors of the efficacy of the new drug. The rival calcium antagonists such as nifedipine and diltiazem, which were developed at that time in Japan, also helped the diffusion of the concept of calcium antagonism among medical practitioners and the regulator. It is worth noting that the slow-release tablets were developed after the initial launch of the drug for reasons of competition against nifedipine. This implies that the shaping of the compound does not necessarily precede the shaping of the market.

Thus, different human actors within and outside pharmaceutical companies, non-human entities including chemical substances and experimental animals, and institutional and structural factors such as academic journals, conferences, scientific societies and patient population are involved in the process. The four aspects of the process of drug discovery and development, namely the shaping of compounds, of applications, of organizational authorization, and of markets are not sequential but rather reciprocal. For instance, the shaping of the application for hypertension came after the shaping of organizational authorization in the case of propranolol; the shaping of atenolol as a compound came after the shaping of application; and the shaping of the slow-release tablets of nicardipine came after the initial launch of the drug. In addition, these aspects interact with each other. Without recognition of the profitable application for anti-hypertension and its sizable market, ICI might not have made such a large effort to discover better β-blockers, while without the shaping of propranolol as a paradigmatic compound, the large market for β-blockers might not have emerged. This also demonstrated difference in the pattern of drug discovery and development between the case of propranolol and that of atenolol. The different patterns of drug discovery and development will be confirmed in the following chapters.

NOTES

1. Receptors are not simple side-chains, as Dale thought, but protein molecules and are flexible enough to bind many different substances. Therefore, agonists and antagonists exist. See, for example, Patrick (1995, pp. 45–67).
2. This interview with Sir James Black was conducted on 3 March 1999.
3. Ahlquist wrote the chapter on adrenergic drugs in *Drill's Pharmacology in Medicine* (McGraw-Hill; 1954), which Black read.
4. According to Sir James Black, no one has ever repeated this observation (personal communication, January 2000).
5. Consequently, by 1975 the market for beta-blockers became what was described as an 'overcrowded field' (see *Lancet*, 26 April 1975, pp. 961–2). Another factor that promoted the rush of research into the area was the relative simplicity of synthesizing an agent with a good chance of being a β-blocker (see Le Count 1982, p. 120).
6. Practolol was not absolutely devoid of this side effect (see *Lancet*, 26 April 1975, pp. 961–2).
7. R in molecular structures represents a generalized group of atoms, which are replaceable and to be examined with each other in order to obtain the best one. Typically, this includes hydrogen, methyl, ethyl and other alkyl groups.
8. Ironically, a subsequent analysis with those related compounds showed that the Hull's hypothesis was not necessarily correct. See Barrett (1977).
9. According to Dr Andrew Bilski, an expert in β-blockers at AstraZeneca (formerly ICI), there were three other candidates apart from atenolol, namely ICI-72222, ICI-78748 and ICI-89406. They had different advantages and disadvantages. For example, ICI-89406 was more cardioselective than atenolol. However, all but atenolol had partial agonist activity, which was

thought to result in less anti-hypertension activity than atenolol. ICI-78748 had an activity to induce histamine release, which was another reason why it was not chosen (personal communication, May 2000).

10. This interview with Dr Toichi Takenaka was conducted on 22 January 1999.

11. Costs, rather than estimated sales, was the only economic factor that was taken into consideration about R&D in the company at that time (Takenaka interview).

12. The efficacy of calcium antagonists for the treatment of hypertension was established in the 1980s. See Kaplan (1998, p. 216).

4. Anti-asthmatic drugs

4.1 INTRODUCTION

In this chapter, we examine cases of the discovery and development of several anti-asthmatic drugs. Asthma can be roughly defined as a syndrome in which there is recurrent reversible obstruction of the airways in response to stimuli which are not in themselves harmful and which do not affect non-asthmatic people. Three of the anti-asthmatic drugs examined here, salbutamol, salmeterol and procaterol, are drugs called β_2-stimulants, which stimulate β_2-adrenergic receptors on the airway smooth muscle and dilate the muscle. The other two, beclomethasone dipropionate inhaler (BDP inhaler) and fluticasone propionate, are drugs called inhaled glucocorticoids (commonly called inhaled steroids), which ease the mucosal inflammation inside the airways. Salbutamol, salmeterol, BDP inhaler and fluticasone propionate were discovered by researchers at Glaxo in England, led by Sir David Jack and Roy Brittain. Salbutamol and salmeterol were discovered in 1966 and 1984 respectively. BDP inhaler and fluticasone propionate were originally discovered as topical glucocorticoids in 1964 and 1981. They were 'rediscovered' as anti-asthma drugs in the late 1960s and in the mid-1980s. Procaterol was discovered in 1974 by a research team at Otsuka Pharmaceutical in Japan, led by Kazuyuki Nakagawa and Shiro Yoshizaki. Salbutamol (Ventolin®), salmeterol (Serevent®), BDP inhaler (Becotide®) and fluticasone propionate (Flixotide®) were first marketed in 1969, 1990, 1972 and 1993 respectively, and became the world best-selling drug in each area. The worldwide sales of salbutamol and BDP inhaler in 1995 were £526 million and £397 million respectively (GlaxoWellcome, *Annual Report and Accounts*, 1996). The sales of salmeterol in the world in 1997 were £406 million and surpassed those of salbutamol in the same year, which were £391 million. The world sales of fluticasone propionate in 1997 were £315 million and close to those of BDP inhaler in the same year, which were £331 million (GlaxoWellcome, *Annual Report and Accounts*, 1998). Procaterol (Meptin®) was marketed in Japan in 1980 and became the best selling bronchodilator there in 1982. Its sales in 1996 were about 15 billion yen (*Yakuji Handobukku*, 1997).

Table 4.1: Major events discussed in Chapter 4

| Year | Glaxo | | Otsuka |
	β-stimulants	Inhaled steroids	β-stimulants
1963	Research starts		
1966	Salbutamol discovery	Research starts	
1969	Salbutamol launch		
1972		BDP inhaler launch	Research starts
1974			Procaterol discovery
1980			Procaterol launch
1981	Research restarts	Research restarts	
1984	Salmeterol discovery		
1992	Salmeterol launch		
1994		Fluticasone launch	

4.2   SALBUTAMOL

During World War II, H. Konzett at C.H. Boehringer in Ingelheim, Germany, found that a new analogue of adrenaline had a strong bronchodilating action with fewer side effects than adrenaline itself (Konzett 1940a, b). Knowledge of this discovery became generally available after the war when the US State Department was investigating the wartime work carried out by German chemical manufacturers. The compound, isoprenaline (isoproterenol in the US), was introduced clinically in 1951. It was considered the drug of choice for the relief of acute asthmatic attacks for the next 20 years (Sneader 1985, pp. 102–3). However, the introduction of its aerosol form during the 1960s led to a large number of deaths because of the effects of overdose on the heart due to the lack of selectivity of isoprenaline (Greenberg and Pines 1967; Inman and Adelstein 1969). Another disadvantage of isoprenaline was that it was too short acting (Sneader 1985, p. 103; Brittain *et al.* 1970, p. 200). Several pharmaceutical companies tried to overcome these disadvantages. In 1961, C.H. Boehringer developed a new drug called orciprenaline, which was different from isoprenaline only in the position of a hydroxyl group in the molecule. Like isoprenaline it was about equally active on bronchial muscle and the heart but it was more stable in the body. Therefore it was longer acting than isoprenaline, though it was less potent. In 1964, Mead Johnson Company in the US discovered another adrenaline analogue, soterenol. Although soterenol was an effective and long-acting bronchodilator, it was found to be toxic in animals and was not marketed (Sneader 1985, pp. 103–4; Brittain *et al.* 1970, pp. 206–13; Jack personal communication, July 2000).

It was Glaxo that had the greatest success in solving the problem. David Jack and his fellow researchers at Allen & Hanbury in England, which had been a subsidiary of Glaxo since 1958 (Davenport-Hines and Slinn 1992, pp. 170–2, 198), started their research on β-stimulants in 1963. Their early objective was a long-acting β-stimulant to replace isoprenaline. Jack, who joined the company as the research director in 1961, explained his situation[1] at that time:

> I started with 122 R&D staff after being assured by the managing director of Allen & Hanbury's and the chairman of Glaxo that the staff would be increased to 200 because this was the minimum needed to find and develop a significant new medicine. A second assurance was that we in Allen & Hanbury's would be given at least 5 years to show if we would do something useful. (Interview)

Jack chose the area of anti-asthmatic drugs as one of the targets at his laboratories because asthma was a very common illness but its treatment was underdeveloped at the time. As Jack put it:

> [T]he secret of success in the pharmaceutical business is to find better medicines for common illnesses. ... It's so obvious, but people forget it. I considered asthma in 1963 because it was a badly treated common serious illness. Isoprenaline, the most effective bronchodilator, was too short-acting and was a powerful cardiac stimulant. Theophyline, the best available orally active bronchodilator, also had use-limiting side effects. There was clearly need for a better bronchodilator.
>
> The other drugs which were available by 1962 were anti-inflammatory steroids, analogues of cortisol. And by then, prednisone, prednisolone were available and so too, I think, would be dexamethasone and betamethasone. These drugs were of great value in asthma because they control the inflammation within the lungs. Unfortunately, although they were effective, they had major systemic side effects. (Ibid.)

The search for a better β-stimulant was, thus, the first work carried out by Allen & Hanbury's researchers in the anti-asthmatic area. At an early stage in the research, Larry Lunts, a chemist in the research team, reached the conclusion that inhaled isoprenaline was short acting because it was rapidly metabolized by catechol-specific mechanisms. Catechol is a chemical group included in isoprenaline molecules (see Figure 4.1). Therefore, he considered that non-catechol analogues of isoprenaline would be expected to be longer acting. He replaced one of the two hydroxyl groups of the ring by a CH_2OH group. The resulting compounds are called saligenin analogues of isoprenaline. Lunts made several saligenin analogues, side chains of which were different from each other in structure (Lunts 1985; Jack 1996, p. 6). In 1966, five years after Jack's agreement with his boss, the research team found that one of the analogues had not only the expected longer duration of action (3–4 hours against 1–1.5 hour in isoprenaline), but also unexpected high selectivity for the bronchi: the latter property meant that the compound had a much less pronounced side effect on the heart, which constituted the other major disadvantage of isoprenaline. The compound was named salbutamol (Hartley *et al.* 1968; Brittain *et al.* 1968; Cullum *et al.* 1969; Jack 1998, p. 141). A number of clinical studies in humans confirmed the longer duration of action and the selectivity of salbutamol in comparison with isoprenaline (for example, Choo-Kang *et al.* 1969; Chatterjee and Perry 1971; Tara *et al.* 1971; Conolly *et al.* 1971b; Schmann and Herxheimer 1971). Although salbutamol was effective by mouth, the duration of action was found to be less than when it was given by inhalation (Simpson 1971; Minette 1971).

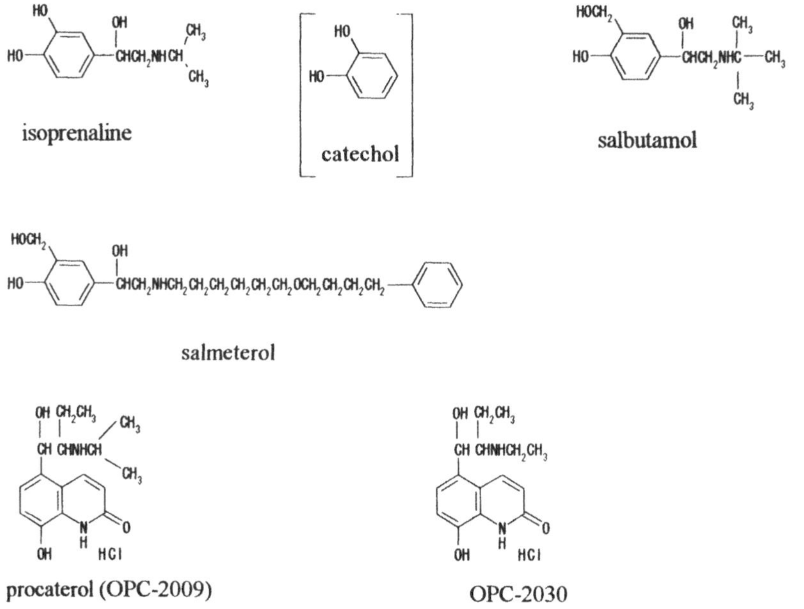

isoprenaline

catechol

salbutamol

salmeterol

procaterol (OPC-2009)

OPC-2030

Note: Catechol is not a β-stimulant but the ring of an isoprenaline molecule, which was replaced with the saligenin ring in making salbutamol.

Figure 4.1: Various β-stimulants discussed in Chapter 4

The selectivity of salbutamol was strong evidence for the theory formulated by Lands and his colleagues at Sterling Winthrop in the US that β-adrenergic receptors could be subdivided into β_1 and β_2 subtypes. There are many more β_1 than β_2 subtypes in the heart, whereas there are many more β_2 than β_1 in the airway (Lands *et al.* 1967; Cullum *et al.* 1969, p. 150). Salbutamol was found to be a β_2-selective stimulant. Jack wrote later: 'We were naturally disappointed that our discovery of selectivity within β-adrenergic effects had been anticipated but were comforted by the fact that salbutamol was clearly a better drug than any of the catecholamines' (Jack 1989, p. 173). Because salbutamol was β_2 selective, its short-term adverse effects were limited (Chatterjee and Perry 1971; Minette 1971; Conolly *et al.* 1971b). Salbutamol was marketed in 1969 and became the most commonly used bronchodilator in the world (Sneader 1985, p. 104; Jack 1998, p. 143), though controversy over the safety of the long-term, regular use of salbutamol and other β_2-selective bronchodilators arose later. This is discussed in sub-section 4.4.2.

4.3   BECLOMETHASONE DIPROPIONATE INHALER (BDP INHALER)

The next project for Allen & Hanbury's researchers after the discovery of salbutamol was the search for an anti-inflammatory agent to ease the inflammation inside the airways of asthma patients, which is another main cause of asthma. They focused on glucocorticoids, a group of anti-inflammatory steroid hormones, which are often called just 'steroids' (Jack 1996, p. 7).

The clinical value of the glucocorticoids as anti-inflammatory agents was generally known after a report that Philip Hench at the Mayo Clinic in the US had successfully used cortisone, one of glucocorticoids, for the treatment of rheumatoid arthritis in 1948 to 1949 (Hench *et al.* 1949; Sneader 1985, p. 222). The application of cortisone for the treatment of asthma was reported as early as 1950 (Carey *et al.* 1950). However, the problem of how to reduce systemic side effects prevented the application of cortisone and its analogues for the long-term treatment of asthma except in severe cases (Wilcox and Avery 1973, pp. 85, 88). Inhalation of corticoids had been tried since 1951 but these trials did not bring good results even when dexamethasone, a strong glucocorticoid, was used. Systemic side effects were observed at effective dosage levels of the drug (Morrow Brown *et al.* 1972, p. 585; Lal *et al.* 1972, p. 315; *Lancet* 1977, 2, p. 695, editorial). In the 1960s, the topical application of corticoid derivatives, such as triamcinolone acetonide (Sneddon 1976, p. 193) and betamethasone valerate (Williams *et al.* 1964), to skin diseases was successfully introduced. Based on these successes, around 1966 the application of such topical anti-inflammatory steroids inside the airways by inhalation was proposed within the Glaxo group by Wilfred Simpson at Allen & Hanbury and by Gordon Philips and Eric Snell at Glaxo Laboratories, independently (Jack 1996, p. 7).

Glaxo had many years experience in manufacturing cortisone and its analogues (Davenport-Hines and Slinn 1992, pp. 186–90, 196; Elks and Phillipps 1985, pp. 176–9; Sneader 1985, p. 223). Research on gluco-corticoid had also been conducted in the Glaxo group. Betamethasone valerate, one of the successful topical glucocorticoids, was synthesized there. Following this, Glaxo researchers synthesized a new glucocorticoid called beclomethasone dipropionate in 1964 (Caldwell *et al.* 1968; Fukai 1988, pp. 549–50). These experiences and the consequent knowledge, skills, facilities and other material resources possessed, individually and collectively, by the organization, probably played a significant role in connecting the needs of anti-inflammatory agents in asthma treatment with the idea of using topical glucocorticoids by inhalation.

The proposal to use topical glucocorticoids by inhalation, however, posed several questions: Would the bronchial mucosa resemble the skin in being sensitive to their anti-inflammatory action? Would the treatment favour the spread of infection in the lung? Would it cause all the kinds of side effects associated with glucocorticoids? (Jack 1990, p. 9; Jack, interview). Anti-inflammatory activity of glucocorticoids was (and is still) not fully understood (Jack 1998, p. 159; Le Fanu 1999, p. 28). Tests in animals and in humans played a key role in the selection of glucocorticoids for use in asthma. In the case of the use of glucocorticoids on the skin, there was an established test called the McKenzie skin-blanching test (McKenzie and Stoughton 1962), which was found to give sufficiently accurate forecasts of clinical potency because it used humans themselves without hurting them (Elks and Phillipps 1985, p. 176; Jack 1998, p. 159). However, it was questionable whether this was relevant to their use inside the airways by inhalation. Despite these uncertainties, Jack and his colleagues went ahead. They chose beclomethasone dipropionate (BDP) as an inhaled steroid, because it was more potent than betamethasone valerate and relatively limited in systemic activities. The topical anti-inflammatory activities were measured with the McKenzie and Stoughton skin-blanching test, and the researchers believed that the test also represented the activity inside the airways. The systemic activities were measured through suppression of early-morning plasma cortisol levels in volunteers. The weakness of systemic activities of BDP was later explained by its inactivation due to oxidation in the liver during first pass metabolism (Caldwell *et al.* 1968, pp. 111–12; Jack 1998, pp. 159–61). Then, they tested the drug in dogs. Six months of administration of BDP by mouth and by inhalation made the dogs develop a condition similar to Cushing disease, in which there is too much secretion of hydrocortisone. However, at the end of the experiment, the lungs of the dogs were found to be normal and infection had not been a problem. They were encouraged by the results to proceed to human trials (Jack 1990, p. 9). Clinical trials in humans produced favourable results (Morrow Brown *et al.* 1972; Clark 1972; Lal *et al.* 1972). Beclomethasone dipropionate inhaler was marketed in 1972 and became one of the major treatments of chronic asthma during the 1980s and 1990s (Jack 1990, p. 9; Jack 1998, pp. 159–60).

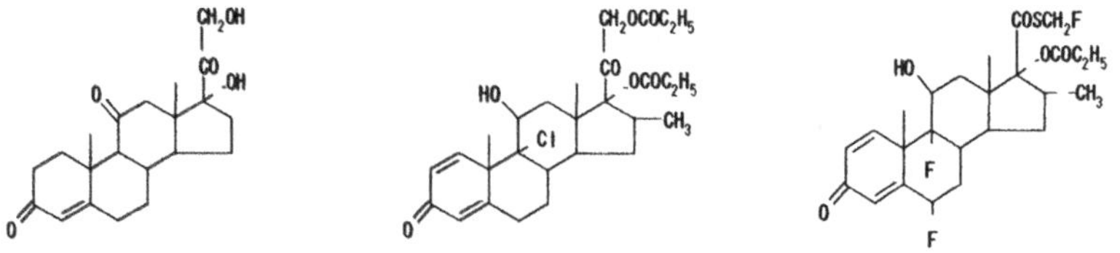

cortisone   BDP   fluticasone propionate

Figure 4.2: Various glucocorticoids discussed in Chapter 4

4.4 SALMETEROL

4.4.1 Discovery and Development of Salmeterol

With the launch of salbutamol in 1969 and of BDP inhaler in 1972, Glaxo obtained a combination of drugs against the two major causes of asthma: constriction of the airways and mucosal inflammation inside them. However, once the two drugs solved the initial problems – the treatment for the two causes on a basic level – a new set of problems on a higher level appeared.

Salbutamol had several problems. First, its duration of action, 3–4 hours, is too short to prevent worsening of asthma during the night. The level of adrenaline in the blood drops during the night, and asthma patients often suffer severe attacks when this happens (Jack 1998, p. 144; Jack interview). Second, a number of β-stimulants such as terbutaline, fenoterol and pirbuterol were marketed after salbutamol and competition in the area became more severe. Terbutaline, discovered and developed by Astra in Sweden, was the most powerful rival (Sneader 1985, pp. 104–5; Jack interview). Third, a 12-year delay in its launch in the US lessened salbutamol's competitive advantage in the important new market (Jack

1991, p. 504). In addition, the patents of salbutamol were getting close to expiry (Jack interview).

Jack and his colleagues tried to discover a better orally active β-stimulant during the 1970s. They also tried to find a better bronchodilator based on other physiological mechanisms, however, they failed in both (Jack 1998, p. 144; 1991, p. 504; interview). Furthermore, Jack and some of his colleagues were at the time involved in two other big projects: H_2 antagonists and 5-hydroxy-tryptamine (5HT, serotonin) related agents (see sub-section 5.3: ranitidine; Jack 1989, p. 182; Jack interview). Therefore, it was in 1981, the year in which a conference was held in Boston to promote salbutamol in the US, that Jack had to think about the future of brochodilators, and he 'concluded that the desired drug would have to be given by inhalation if side effects were to be avoided and would have to be much longer acting than salbutamol and similar $β_2$-agonists to prevent nocturnal attacks of asthma' (Jack 1998, p. 144; 1991, pp. 504–5).

Jack then considered how the prolongation of action might be achieved with an inhaled β-stimulant. The target duration of action was at least 8 hours to prevent nocturnal asthma worsening (Jack 1998, p. 145). He considered two ways: one was to make a drug which would be more slowly absorbed from the bronchi; the other was to make a drug which sticks firmly at its site of action in the receptor protein and remains efficacious for a long time. He chose the latter approach because it 'was simpler and seemed more likely to work' (Jack 1991, p. 505). The hypothesis for achieving this was to keep the ring structure of a β-stimulant molecule with high affinity for the adrenaline binding site in the receptor protein, and to make a large flexible non-polar side chain to ensure selectivity of action and to anchor the drug with the receptor protein (Jack 1996, p. 10; 1998, p. 145).

Jack believed that there were two types of agonism: in type 1 agonism the affected cells were capable of responding continuously to continuing stimulation, whereas in type 2 agonism the cells, having responded to an effective stimulus, must recover before they can respond to another (Jack 1991, p. 504). He also believed that adrenergic agonism must belong to type 1 agonism because adrenaline remains efficacious despite being continuously present in the extra-cellular fluid (Jack 1998, p. 145). Although his classification of agonism seems not to have been generally used in academic literature, it did lead him to the search for a better β-stimulant (Jack 1991, p. 504).

Based on this thinking, Jack commenced the research project in 1981. However, some of his colleagues were doubtful about the approach, because there was a large amount of literature (for example, Conolly *et al.* 1971a; Jenne 1977; Greenacre *et al.* 1978; Plummer 1978; Harden 1983, p. 25) on desensitization of β-receptors exposed to β-stimulants for a long time and reports of tolerance to β-stimulants in patients (Jack 1991, p. 505; 1998, p. 145). On the other hand, there were some studies (Larsson *et al.* 1977; Peel and Gibson 1980; Shepherd *et al.* 1981) that did not find the tolerance to β-stimulants by regular use of them. Persuading the doubtful researchers was not practical because scientific controversy over the issue obviously existed: 'The only way to settle the matter was to find and test the desired drug' (Jack 1991, p. 505). Jack, as the research director, showed his leadership by insisting that they test his hypothesis. He put it:

> [Some colleagues] said, 'You're wasting your time, David.' ... How did I persuade them? I told them to do it. [laugh] But then when they found that what I was saying was not mad, it then became theirs. But at the beginning I had to tell them to do it. (Interview)

Larry Lunts, who was the originator of salbutamol and responsible for chemistry in the new project, decided to seek the required drug in analogues of salbutamol with increasingly large non-polar side chain, based on Jack's hypothesis. The rates of onset and offset of action of these analogues were measured using guinea pig tracheal muscle. Interest in the team rose sharply when it was found that this preparation was not easily desensitized by continuous superfusion with isoprenaline or other β-stimulants, and that the rates of onset and offset of action of the analogues varied considerably. These findings supported Jack's hypothesis. The researchers who had at first doubted the idea became convinced that it would work. By painstaking optimization, they succeeded in finding salmeterol, a selective, very long acting (more than 12 hours) β-stimulant with a long non-polar side chain, in 1984 (Jack 1998, p. 146; Jack interview; Bradshaw *et al.* 1987; Ball *et al.* 1987, 1991; Brittain *et al.* 1988). The potency, the duration of action and the safety of salmeterol were confirmed in clinical trials (Britton *et al.* 1992; Brogden and Faulds 1991; Jack 1998, pp. 163–6). It was also suggested that the unusual effectiveness of salmeterol might be due in part to its anti-inflammatory activity in the airways (Twentyman *et al.* 1990; Butchers *et al.* 1991; Whelan and Johnson 1992). Salmeterol was marketed in 1992 (Jack 1996, p. 12).

4.4.2 Salmeterol and the β-stimulant Controversy

When salmeterol was marketed, there was a widespread doubt about regular use of β-stimulants (Jack 1996, p. 12; Jack 1998, pp. 162–3). There had been a long-lasting controversy over their regular, long-term use (*Lancet* 1990; Löfdahl and Svedmyr 1991; Chung 1993; Sears and Taylor 1994; Boulet 1994; Crane *et al.* 1995a; Ernst 1998). After the high incidence of death during the use of isoprenaline aerosol, doubt arose over tolerance to β-stimulants during long-term, regular use. Some researchers concluded that mortality was due to the side effects on the heart by overdose of isoprenaline, a non-selective β-stimulant (Greenberg and Pines 1967). However, other researchers thought that it might be due to the resistance to β-stimulants which was built up by their regular use (Conolly *et al.* 1971a; Jenne *et al.* 1977; Greenacre *et al.* 1978; Plummer 1978; Harden 1983, p. 25). There were also studies which supported regular use of β-stimulants (Larsson *et al.* 1977; Peel and Gibson 1980; Shepherd *et al.* 1981; Harvey and Tattersfield 1982). They could not reach a consensus because differences in test situations, such as *in vivo* versus *in vitro* (Shepherd *et al.* 1981 vs. Greenacre *et al.* 1978) and normal subjects versus asthma patients (Holgate *et al.* 1977 vs. Harvey and Tattersfield 1982), made the controversy more complicated. However, this controversy might have faded out had it not been for the incidence of a sharp increase of asthma mortality in New Zealand from the mid-1970s (Taylor and Sears 1994, pp. 261–2).

The 'epidemic' of asthma mortality from 1977 was internationally reported in the early 1980s (Jackson *et al.* 1982; Grant 1983). The medication was suspected as its cause early on: at first, combined treatment with oral theophylline and β-stimulants, and then β-stimulants themselves (Grant 1983). In 1989, the first case-control study on the relationship between the regular use of β-stimulants and asthma mortality by researchers at Wellington School of Medicine (New Zealand) was published (Crane *et al.* 1989). The authors claimed that use of fenoterol, a powerful β-stimulant developed by Böhringer Ingelheim, by inhaler increased the risk of death in asthma. This study was criticized by several groups in terms of both methodology and interpretation (O'Donnell *et al.* 1989; Buist *et al.* 1989; Sackett *et al.* 1990; Poole *et al.* 1990). The two important points of criticism were whether the regular use of fenoterol was the main cause of asthma mortality or just the marker of fatal asthma, and whether the relationship with asthma mortality was limited to fenoterol or was a general problem for β-stimulants as a class. The Wellington group conducted further case-control studies because of this criticism, but the results supported their original arguments: it was regular use of fenoterol that caused the epidemic in New Zealand (Pearce *et al.* 1990; Grainger *et al.* 1991). Other researchers also supported this and suggested that it might be due to the very large dose and the lesser β_2 selectivity of fenoterol (Wong *et al.* 1990; *Lancet* 1990; Löfdahl and Svedmyr 1991).

One major group opposing the Wellington study was researchers at Böhringer Ingelheim, the manufacturer of fenoterol (Staudinger and Haas 1992a, 1992b; Schuijt and Staundinger 1995) and advisory researchers of the company (Buist *et al.* 1989; Spitzer and Buist 1990; Spitzer *et al.* 1992; Suissa *et al.* 1994). The advisory researchers conducted their own large-scale case-control studies in Canada (Spitzer *et al.* 1992; Suissa *et al.* 1994). Although they admitted that there was strong correlation between the regular use of fenoterol and asthma mortality, they claimed that fenoterol might be a marker of severe asthma because it tended to be prescribed for that due to its high potency, and that there were no significant differences in selectivity between fenoterol and other β-stimulants, particularly salbutamol, but overdose of β-stimulants might cause the serious side effects. According to them, fenoterol was prone to be overdosed because its originally recommended dose was larger than that of salbutamol despite its relative potency in β-stimulation. They insisted that β-stimulants were safe when they were used properly, and that β-stimulants should be used with glucocorticoids to control inflammation inside the airways because this could not be done by β-stimulants. Some other researchers shared their view (Blauw and Westendorp 1995; Wanner 1995).

Another major opposing group of the Wellington study was Malcolm Sears and his colleagues at University of Otago Medical School, who claimed that although the relationship between regular use of β-stimulants and asthma mortality was causal, this was not limited to fenoterol alone but was potentially applicable to any other β-stimulant, including salbutamol and salmeterol. They insisted that asthma mortality was due not to cardiac side effects of less-selective β-stimulants but to worsening asthma caused by regular use of β-stimulants (Sears *et al.* 1990, 1992; Sears and Taylor 1992, 1994; Taylor *et al.* 1993; Taylor and Sears 1994; Sears 1995).

The argument by Sears and his colleagues caused further debate because it claimed that no β-stimulants should be used regularly and that emerging longer-acting β-stimulants such as salmeterol might have the same risk as regular use of short-acting β-stimulants. Several researchers supported their view (Crompton 1991; van Schayck *et al.* 1991). On the other hand, there were also several critics, including the Wellington group and researchers at Glaxo, of the generalization of the results from fenoterol to β-stimulants as a class (Palmer and Jenkins 1991; Dahl 1991; Crane *et al.* 1991; Clark 1991; Chapman *et al.* 1994). In particular, researchers at Glaxo, based on their post-marketing clinical studies of salmeterol, strongly opposed the claim of the Otago group that salmeterol might exacerbate asthma (Jenkins *et al.* 1991; Shepherd *et al.* 1991; Castle *et al.* 1993). Sears's group, William Inman at the Drug Safety Research Unit, which was conducting a post-marketing surveillance study of salmeterol, and two other specialists argued that Glaxo's study underestimated mortality of asthma related to salmeterol (Inman 1993; Bunney 1993; Crompton 1993; Sears and Taylor 1993). The Glaxo researchers defended themselves (Fuller *et al.* 1993). However, the guidelines on the management of asthma issued by the British Thoracic Society in 1993 showed a cautious attitude towards the regular use of bronchodilators, especially salmeterol. It advised that regular use of bronchodilators should come after high-dose inhaled steroids and that long-acting bronchodilators such as salmeterol should be used for more serious cases only, because of the uncertainty about regular use of bronchodilators (British Thoracic Society 1993, pp. S4–5, S10–11, S18).

There was another strand of the β-stimulant controversy: Jeff Garnett and his colleagues at Green Lane Hospital in Auckland, New Zealand, insisted that increasing financial barriers to primary health care against a background of social and economic decline were likely to have contributed to asthma morbidity and mortality in New Zealand. They also argued that the reduction in asthma mortality in the 1980s was mainly due to an improvement in utilization of hospital services, and that the further reduction in asthma mortality since 1989 would best be explained by an increase in the use of inhaled steroids and by an improvement in the management of asthma, that is, more careful treatment for asthma (Garnett *et al.* 1995). Both the Wellington group and the Otago group opposed this view and argued that the socio-economic factor was not the main cause, but regular use of fenoterol (or β-stimulants) was (Crane *et al.* 1995b; Taylor and Wong 1995). On the contrary, there were also studies which strongly doubted the relationship between use of β-stimulants and death from asthma (Mullen *et al.* 1993).

The β-stimulant controversy seemed to be fading in the late 1990s. This decline may be partly because the 'epidemic' in New Zealand ended, partly because simultaneous use of β-stimulants and inhaled steroids provided every party involved in the debate with a satisfactory answer in practice, and partly because long-term clinical trials of long-acting β-stimulants, especially salmeterol and formoterol, did not find exacerbation of asthma when they were used with inhaled steroids. The end of the New Zealand 'epidemic' of asthma death, in fact, led to another debate. The Wellington group sought the cause of reduction of mortality from the withdrawal of fenoterol (Pearce *et al.* 1995). Researchers at Böhringer Ingelheim and the advisory researchers of the company argued that the cause was advances in patient education and adequate anti-inflammatory treatment (Schuijt and Staudinger 1995; Ernst and Suissa 1995). As mentioned above, Garnett and his colleagues emphasized the socio-economic factor as one of the major cause of the reduction (Garnett *et al.* 1995); however, this debate was less heated. It is probable that the end of the epidemic was less interesting for researchers than its outbreak.

The second factor which probably contributed to the quasi-closure of the debate was that there was a consensus over the practical problem of how to manage asthma: simultaneous use of β-stimulants and inhaled steroids. Almost all researchers recognized and often argued that inhaled steroids should be used to treat airway inflammation, which causes asthma symptoms. Therefore, they would not oppose concurrent use of β-stimulants and inhaled steroid. In fact, most of them did promote the treatment (Crane *et al.* 1995a; *Lancet* 1990; Staudinger and Haas 1992a; Ernst and Suissa 1995; Sears *et al.* 1992; van Schayck and van Herwaarden 1993; Rees 1991; Chung 1993; Heino 1994; Boulet 1994; Greening *et al.* 1994; Woolcock *et al.* 1996; van der Molen *et al.* 1996; Wilding *et al.* 1997; Jack 1998). The British Guidelines on Asthma Management and its Japanese counterpart also adopt this treatment (British Thoracic Society *et al.* 1997; Makino *et al.* 1998, p. 69).

The third plausible factor in the decline of the controversy was the accumulated results of the use of long acting β-stimulants. In 1994, another long-term study of salmeterol, supported by Glaxo, showed that there was no evidence that regular use of salmeterol contributed to asthma exacerbation when using it with BDP (Greening *et al.* 1994). The Drug Safety Research Unit, which had initially opposed Glaxo's results, also stated that there was no evidence that salmeterol contributed to deaths from asthma after completing the study. It explained that its early overestimation of asthma mortality in patients using salmeterol was due to the assumption that deaths would be evenly distributed throughout the study; this was not the case because 39 of the 73 deaths occurred in the first seven months of a 25 month long study (Mann 1994). Based on these studies, the British Guidelines on Asthma Management, revised in 1995 and issued in 1997, showed a somewhat more favourable attitude to salmeterol. It was recommended that low dose inhaled steroids plus salmeterol be regarded as an alternative in step 3 treatments, while the former guidelines placed the drug after step 4 treatments, which is for more severe asthma (British Thoracic Society *et al.* 1997, pp. S2, S11). Several studies supported the safety of salmeterol (Woolcock *et al.* 1996; Wilding *et al.* 1997). A study on formoterol, another long-acting β-stimulant developed by Ciba-Geigy, also claimed that its use with inhaled steroids improved patients' condition (van der Molen *et al.* 1996). There were also studies warning that use of salmeterol might cause subsensibility to salbutamol (Grove and Lipworth 1995), and that use of salmeterol could delay recognition of increasing airway inflammation (McIvor *et al.* 1998). However, the attitude to salmeterol seems to have become less hostile recently. In 1997, sales of salmeterol for the first time were greater than those of salbutamol. Despite this, it is important here to notice that the β-stimulant controversy obviously limited the sales of salmeterol (Ernst 1998).

4.5 FLUTICASONE PROPIONATE

Although inhaled BDP was found to be an effective and generally safe treatment for asthma, it had significant systemic side effects when used in high dosage. Because of this and because the patents for inhaled BDP, like those of salbutamol, would expire in less than 10 years, Jack was forced in the early 1980s to consider how it might be replaced by a superior drug. What was required was an inhaled glucocorticoid with more intense anti-inflammatory activity than inhaled BDP in the airways but devoid of systemic side effects at therapeutic dosage. He consulted the Glaxo list of potential topical glucocorticoids and chose fluticasone propionate as a candidate (Jack interview and personal communication). In the early 1980s, G.H. Phillipps at the company discovered this during an unsuccessful search for a topical steroid which did not cause skin thinning (Dutch patent application 81 00707, 1981; US patent 4335121, 1982; Jack personal communication). Fluticasone propionate had been shown to be about twice as active as BDP in the McKenzie and Stoughton skin-blanching test in humans but almost inactive after oral administration in rats and mice (Phillipps 1990; Jack 1998, p. 160; Jack personal communication).[2] The compound was later found to be similarly inactive orally in humans and this was attributed to the first pass hydrolysis in the liver into two inactive fragments. This lack of oral activity was favourable for the treatment of asthma, because part of the inhaled drug absorbed from the gut would not cause unwanted systemic side effects (Jack 1998, pp. 160–2; Jack personal communication).

Fluticasone propionate was thus chosen for clinical trials and shown to be twice as active, on a weight basis, as BDP and at least as safe as BDP in asthmatic patients (Lundback *et al.* 1993; Barns *et al.* 1993; Holliday *et al.* 1994). It was also reported that treatment with fluticasone propionate was less associated with reduction in leg growth velocity in children than with BDP, which implied less systemic effects of fluticasone propionate (Wolthers and Pedersen 1993). The high potency of fluticasone propionate was explained by its persistent binding to the glucocorticoid receptor protein (Högger and Rohdewald 1994). Fluticasone propionate was marketed in 1994 and became a very successful inhaled steroid (Jack 1998, p. 162).

Thus, the combination of salmeterol and fluticasone propionate became a successor to that of salbutamol and BDP. By analogy with the game of poker, Jack compared each combination to a 'full house' consisting of a selective β_2-stimulant (equivalent to two of a kind) and a topical glucocorticoid steroid (equivalent to three of a kind). Both are a 'full house' but the former is a better one. However, this idea was not intended from the beginning but emerged and evolved in the research and development process. Jack put it:

> **Jack**: And don't forget that a full house is a good hand, but is not the best hand in poker. Similarly these combinations are unlikely to be the best hand for asthma. Better treatments are likely to be discovered.
> **Hara**: Did you aim at a full house?
> **Jack**: Not at the beginning. All of this happened with increasing understanding of the problem. One profound thing that not everybody knows is that we think with what we know. As years go by and one 'lives' with asthma, knowledge and, with it, understanding become more and more, increases and increases, and the way you think is correspondingly changed. OK? (Interview)

4.6   PROCATEROL: A β-STIMULANT MADE IN JAPAN

Otsuka Pharmaceutical in Japan began its research on adrenergic drugs in 1971. Until then, the company had mainly been a manufacturer of nutritional preparations for clinical uses and over-the-counter (OTC) products (Otsuka 1999, p. 32). Shortly before the establishment of its own laboratories, the company planned to manufacture an existing β-blocker, which was at that time a new type of drug. However, the supply of a key material was stopped by the parent company of the supplier and the plan failed. When Otsuka decided to start its own research, therefore, it chose a β-blocker as its first target (Miwa interview).[3]

A research team at Otsuka Tokushima Laboratories led by Kazuyuki Nakagawa started research on β-blockers in January 1972 and, one month later, succeeded in the discovery of a β-blocker, cartelol (Nakagawa *et al.* 1974; Nakagawa interview). This was the first product of their research and was marketed in 1980. In the synthesis, they chose pindolol, which was synthesized by a Swiss company, Sandoz, in 1964 (Saameli 1967; Hill and Turner 1969; Fukai 1988, p. 232), as the lead compound. This was because there had already been a lot of analogues of propranolol whereas pindolol analogues seemed less exploited (Nakagawa interview). They tried to replace an indole group in the pindolol structure and chose a dihydrocarbostyril group, partly because it has a proton which an indole group also has, and partly because it has a shape as if the side chain of acetaminophen were cycled, which seemed to be as active as acetaminophen but less toxic than it. This approach was found to be successful, and Nakagawa and his colleagues were able to find compounds which blocked β-receptors (Nakagawa interview). At least 45 derivatives were synthesized and cartelol was chosen as a drug (Nakagawa *et al.* 1974).

Beta-blockers, which attach to β-adrenergic receptors but do nothing to them, and β-stimulants, which also attach to the receptors and stimulate them as if they were adrenaline, are clinically opposites but chemically very similar. This means that if cartelol is effective as a β-blocker, there may be an effective β-stimulant among its analogues. Additionally, cartelol was found to be well distributed to the trachea. This property was advantageous as a bronchodilator. Based on these ideas, they started the research on β-stimulants in April 1973. Although the research was temporally suspended because the researchers had to support the development of cartelol, it did not take long for them to find a β-stimulant. The search for a β-stimulant was relatively easy, according to Nakagawa. This was because they already had the basic structure, a dihydrocarbostyril group, the same as cartelol, and it was the side chain that had to be devised (Nakagawa interview). There were several effective β-stimulants at that time; Shiro Yoshizaki, the project leader, and his colleagues at Otsuka examined these, for example isoprenaline, salbutamol, terbutaline and isoetharine, and synthesized a series of compounds with carbostyril and dihydrocarbostyril groups (Yoshizaki *et al.* 1976; Nakagawa interview). Despite the interruption, they found a highly potent compound as early as February 1974: it was the ninth compound in the research. This compound, with a carbostyril group and an isoetharine-type side chain, was at first named OPC-2009. After the synthesis of OPC-2009, the researchers continued to make various derivatives partly because there might be a better one, and partly because it was needed to ensure sufficient patent coverage so that rival companies could not make similar compounds to compete against Otsuka's. By April 1974, they had synthesized about 50 compounds. About 30 of them had strong β-receptor stimulating activity, and two of them were considered as final candidates for development: OPC-2009 and OPC-2030 (Nakagawa interview; Takayanagi *et al.* 1977).

OPC-2009 was more active than OPC-2030, but its activity on the heart was also stronger than that of OPC-2030. As a result of discussion among researchers and staff in charge of development, OPC-2009 was eventually chosen. It was said that the opinion of Akihiko Otsuka, who was then Tokushima plant manager and who also headed the laboratories, had a strong influence on the decision. Otsuka was a member of the owner family of the company and later became its president. The reason for the choice was that it was probably better that the efficacy was outstanding for clinical trials and for marketing. However, this was a subtle problem. Nakagawa put it:

It was a very hard question. If we had chosen OPC-2030 and had failed, nobody would have known how different the results would have been if we had chosen OPC-2009. This is because there was just one chance. ... Japanese people then had, perhaps still have, a tendency to prefer mild drugs with fewer side effects to very potent drugs with some side effects. Therefore, OPC-2030 might have been successful. (Nakagawa interview)

According to Nakagawa, there were few organizational obstacles to the development of OPC-2009, now renamed procaterol, because there was only one other project. The main obstacles were more technological ones. These occurred in the development of the tablets and the inhaler of the drug. Procaterol was easily soluble in water and this property was convenient to make a variety of preparations. However, because the drug was so active, it was necessary to ensure that each tablet or puff of inhaler equally contained a specific, very small amount of drug. There were two major technological problems there: one was to achieve this equality, and the other was to measure the equality. They made a considerable effort to solve these problems and were able to cope with them. In particular, the establishment of liquid chromatography in the 1970s helped solve the latter problem. Another problem was the interaction between the drug and a very small amount of water or impurities contained in diluents, packaging materials and components of inhalers: collaboration with the suppliers of various materials was important (Nakagawa interview).

The next problem in the development of procaterol was how to proceed to clinical trials because the company had little experience of these. They asked Yuichi Yamamura, a professor at Osaka University and an authority on immunology and allergology in Japan, to be the chairman of the clinical trial committee of procaterol. Yamamura accepted it and organized the committee (Miwa interview). Otsuka's staff described this process:

> **Miwa**: It was very important to ask Professor Yamamura to organize the clinical trials.
> **Tashiro**: Yes. When we asked doctors for clinical trials for the first time, they often declined because they did not believe in the drug made by Otsuka, a maker of nutritional preparations. But when they found the organizer of the clinical trials was Professor Yamamura, they changed their attitude and accepted us. ... Professor Yamamura also directly asked some doctors for cooperation, saying: 'Ten [patients] for you.' Without this strong lead by Professor Yamamura, it would have taken much longer to complete the clinical trials. (Interview)

Pharmacological tests of procaterol with animals started in April 1974, and showed that procaterol was more potent, more selective and longer acting than salbutamol (Yabuuchi *et al.* 1977; Himori and Tira 1977). Clinical trials began in January 1976. Phase I, tests in healthy people, finished in June 1977. Phase II, trials in patients, started in August 1976 and finished in November 1978. Meanwhile, Phase III, which included double blind tests, was conducted from January 1977 to July 1978. Here, again, salbutamol was used to compare and procaterol was shown to be more potent and longer acting (Yagura *et al.* 1979; Shida *et al.* 1979). This considerable overlapping of the different phases of clinical trials was common in Japan at that time. They applied for approval to manufacture the drug in December 1978 and this was approved in October 1980 (Nakagawa interview). Procaterol was marketed in Japan in the same year. This drug was also tested clinically in the US and some other countries, which supported the efficacy and safety of the drug (Zenetti *et al.* 1982; Crowe *et al.* 1985; Siegel *et al.* 1985). A comparative study of procaterol and salbutamol did not identify any difference in potency and safety between the two (Crowe *et al.* 1985), whereas another study supported the finding that procaterol was longer acting (8 hours) (Siegel *et al.* 1985).

After its launch the marketing staff of Otsuka had the problem of differentiating procaterol from existing β-stimulants. Shinya Tashiro explained the strategies for its promotion:

In the early marketing, making the characteristics of the drug clear was essential. We regarded salbutamol as a main rival, because it was at the time the best selling β-stimulant in Japan. First, we emphasized the higher selectivity of procaterol. We said that the drug was more β$_2$ selective and had fewer effects on the heart than existing others. Second, it was longer acting. Because asthma fits often occur on rising in the morning, they will be avoided if the duration of action is long enough. Another point was that the drug was said to have an anti-allergy activity. I heard that this was the first β-stimulant which had such activity. Then, Professor Kazuhiko Ito at Nagoya University suggested that this was the first one of the third generation β-stimulants, whereas isoprenaline belonged to the first generation and salbutamol belonged to the second generation. This was the strongest help in the marketing. (Tashiro interview)

Kazuhiko Ito at Nagoya University classified β-stimulants into three generations. The first-generation drugs, including isoprenaline, were short acting and not β$_2$ selective. The second-generation drugs such as salbutamol were more β$_2$ selective and longer acting. The third-generation drugs, in which procaterol was included, had the strongest β$_2$ selectivity and the longest duration of action of the three generations (8 hours or longer) (Kawai *et al.* 1987). This classification made salbutamol in the second generation sound obsolete in comparison with procaterol in the third generation.

Another aspect of the post-marketing promotion of procaterol was the development of a variety of administration forms. They marketed smaller tablets, granules and syrup of the drug mainly for younger patients in October 1982 (Shiota *et al.* 1981; Baba *et al.* 1981). They also added aerosol, aerosol for children and inhalation solution of procaterol in June 1987 (Hamada *et al.* 1986; Mikawa *et al.* 1986). As a result, procaterol had the largest variety of preparations of all β-stimulants available in Japan.

This was important because the variety of asthma patients is also high: from babies to old people. Variety of preparation gives doctors flexibility of treatment; therefore, Japanese practitioners welcomed the rich variety of procaterol, according to Tashiro (Tashiro interview). This development of additional preparations of procaterol also helped to maintain the sales of the drug (Miwa interview). In Japan, the government has regularly revised the prices of drugs and in general they have been gradually decreasing (Campbell and Ikegami 1998, p. 158). The price of procaterol also has decreased by almost half of the original price 19 years ago. The drug had sales of more than 13 billion yen in 1998; they consisted of 3.9 billion yen sales of its tablets, 1.7 billion yen of its mini tablets, 2.7 billion yen of syrup, 4.4 billion yen of its aerosol, and so on (Tashiro interview).

In fact, procaterol was such a success in the Japanese market that it outsold salbutamol, the best-selling β-stimulant in the world. The sales of salbutamol in Japan were about 40 per cent of those of procaterol (GlaxoWellcome (Japan), internal documents). Two reasons for this have already been mentioned: first, procaterol was more potent and longer acting that salbutamol; second, procaterol had a variety of forms. It should be noted that both doctors and patients traditionally prefer oral medicines to inhaled medicines in Japan. Both were accustomed to the former. In addition, the latter needed a doctor's instruction to patients about how to use inhalers. Doctors were unwilling to do this under the notoriously busy situation described as the 'three minute consultation', according to Mike Nakayama, the product manager at GlaxoWellcome (Japan).[4] Third, in European countries and the United States, doctors preferred salbutamol because its efficacy and safety were recognized through its long-term use and because it was cheaper. On the contrary, under the traditional health care system in Japan, doctors tended to prefer new drugs because doctors and hospitals benefited from a bigger gap between the reimbursement price and the real price they paid and because the new drugs were usually better than the older ones. Finally, Glaxo in Japan, strategically, did not put stress on the marketing of salbutamol, because its market size was relatively modest compared with other products of the company. Even in the respiratory drug area, the company put more stress on inhaled steroids (Nakayama interview). Salmeterol has not so far been sold in Japan.

4.7   A BRIEF ANALYSIS

As with the case of atenolol in the previous chapter, every case in this chapter had a rather specific target: in the case of sulbutamol, it was to obtain a longer-acting β-stimulant than isoprenaline; in the case of BDP, to reduce the systemic side effects of existing glucocorticoids when inhaled; in the cases of salmeterol and procaterol, to extend the duration of activity longer than salbutamol; and in the case of fluticasone propionate, to gain a less harmful inhaled steroid. This series of improvement in the area of anti-asthmatic drugs can be described by the concept of the reverse salient, which was proposed by Thomas Hughes. A reverse salient in technological change is a component in the technological system that has fallen behind (Hughes 1987, pp. 73–5; 1983, p. 79). The lack of selectivity in inhaled steroids, which causes side effects, and a short duration of activity in β-stimulants can be regarded as reverse salients. The researchers at Glaxo and Otsuka regarded them as critical problems and made a great effort to dissolve them, resulting in the shaping of sulbutamol, salmeterol, BDP inhaler, fluticasone propionate and procaterol. The main driving force of their effort was economic. However, other factors such as corporate strategies, researchers' interests, company-specific research traditions, existing exemplary drugs, theories, experimental skills and other relevant resources the companies owned also affected the recognition and the resolution of the critical problems. The series of improvement can be also described as a technology trajectory in β-stimulants and another in inhaled steroids, borrowing the terminology of evolutionary economists (Nelson and Winter 1977; Dosi 1982).

Various elements are involved in each aspect of the process of drug discovery and development in the area of anti-asthmatic drugs. For example, human actors such as project leaders, chemists and corporate managers, non-human entities such as existing exemplary drugs, experimental animals and inhalers, and institutional and structural factors such as corporate strategies, organizational assets, competitive situations and patents are related to the shaping of the compounds. In contrast, the shaping of their markets included human actors such as corporate employees, medical doctors and regulators, non-human entities such as compounds, academic articles and different drug forms, and institutional and structural factors such as clinical trials, academic journals, medical societies, guidelines for the treatment of asthma and price-setting systems.

The shaping of the market for salmeterol is particularly interesting because it demonstrates how much scientific controversy affects the construction of the market. Different academic research groups and different pharmaceutical companies participated in the controversy over the relationship between the 'epidemic' of asthma mortality in New Zealand and the regular use of β-stimulants. We can see interpretative flexibility on the cause of the epidemic and its end. We can also identify several closure mechanisms of the controversy, which contributed to the shaping of the market of salmeterol. The contribution of scientific issues to the shaping of the market is also shown in the case of procaterol. Ito's classification, in which procaterol was classified as a third-generation β-stimulant, played a significant role in the shaping of its market. In addition, it can be seen that several structural and cultural factors in Japan affect the process of market formation: the hierarchical structure of medical society made the relationship to the authoritative figure essential; a low familiarity with inhaled drugs among Japanese made other drug forms popular; and a unique price-setting system in Japan made new drugs preferable to old ones. These contributed to the shaping of the market of procaterol, which was larger than that of salbutamol in Japan. Procaterol was also promoted by direct comparison with salbutamol, in which the higher selectivity and the longer activity of the former were emphasized. Such emphasis on the differences when compared with existing drugs was also seen in the other cases in this chapter. This seems to indicate a characteristic of the process of drug discovery and development when there is/are (an) exemplary drug(s). In such a case, because the target of the project is well formulated, the search for an application seems less problematic. Organizational resistance also seems less serious. However, in the case of salmeterol, it occurred because of the controversy over the regular use of β-stimulants. Jack's authoritative power was used to overcome the resistance. His theory on the two types of agonism also played a role in justifying the project.

Thus, various interactions were seen in the discovery and development of anti-asthmatic drugs. It should be noted that the prospect of profits affected the shaping of the compounds and relevant scientific knowledge while science controversies and concepts affected the shaping of the markets. This shows that scientific knowledge, compounds and markets shape each other through social (including economic) processes. With regard to the pattern of the drug discovery and development process, salbutamol was rather paradigmatic: it was the first selective β-stimulant. BDP inhaler was paradigmatic not as a compound but as an application: it was the first inhaled topical steroid for the treatment of asthma. However, the rest seem to be the likes of atenolol in the previous chapter: having an exemplary drug, the discovery and development process was more focused; the compounds were similar to each other; and the application was the same. The process of discovery and development of these drugs was organized towards the creation of a few advantageous characteristics compared with the exemplar and other drugs of the kind. The different patterns of the drug discovery and development process will be discussed further in the next chapter.

NOTES

1. This interview with Sir David Jack was conducted on 26 April 1999.
2. The intense skin-blanching activity was significant because it indicates tight binding of the steroid to its receptor protein and, therefore, high topical anti-inflammatory activity. Oral inactivity in mice was unusual because that species is extremely sensitive to glucocorticoid steroids (Jack personal communication).
3. This interview with Dr Kazuyuki Nakagawa, the former head of chemical research, Mr Hideyuki Miwa, the director of research and development, and Mr Shinya Tashiro, the respiratory group leader in the development department was conducted on 9 November 1999.
4. This interview with Mr Mike Nakayama was conducted on 24 March 2000.

5. Histamine H$_2$ antagonists

5.1 INTRODUCTION

Histamine H$_2$ antagonists are a group of drugs which are used for the treatment of peptic (both duodenal and gastric) ulcer. One of the main causes of peptic ulcer is believed to be an excessive secretion of acid in the stomach, due to various factors such as stress and doses of aspirin. (Another main cause is now believed to be *Helicobacter pylori*, a kind of bacterium discovered in 1983, which destroys the mucous membrane of the stomach.) Unlike previous drugs which just neutralized the gastric acid, histamine H$_2$ antagonists reduce dramatically the amount of acid secreted in the stomach: they inhibit histamine, one of the important chemical transmitters in the body, from fitting into the receptors, called histamine H$_2$ receptors, which play an essential role in acid secretion in the stomach. Histamine H$_2$ antagonists were discovered by Sir James Black and his colleagues at the British subsidiary of SmithKline and French (now GlaxoSmithKline) in the early 1970s. Though the first marketed histamine H$_2$ antagonist was cimetidine (Tagamet®) made by SmithKline and French, it had two precursors called burimamide and metiamide, both of which were also discovered in the same company by Black and colleagues. The second histamine H$_2$ antagonist to be marketed was ranitidine (Zantac®) discovered by Sir David Jack and his colleagues at Glaxo (now also GlaxoSmithKline). And the third was famotidine (Gaster®, Pepcid®) discovered by Isao Yanagisawa and his colleagues at Yamanouchi in Japan. These histamine H$_2$ antagonists brought a major breakthrough to the area. First, therapeutically, they have eliminated the need for surgery for the treatment of peptic ulcer: the disease has been increasingly treated by physicians rather than by surgeons since the advent of these drugs. Second, they were extremely successful in the market: cimetidine and ranitidine were two of the top-selling drugs in the world, and famotidine was one of the top-selling drugs in Japan and was also considerably successful in other countries. Each of them has provided each company with enormous profit and contributed to the company's further investment in R&D and other operations. In this chapter, we look at these histamine H$_2$ antagonists.

Table 5.1:   *Major events discussed in Chapter 5*

Company / Year	SmithKline & French	Glaxo	Yamanouchi
1964	Research starts		
1968		Antigastrin research starts	
1970	Burimamide discovery		
1971	Metiamide discovery		
1972	Burimamide report Cimetidine discovery	H₂ antagonists research starts	
1976	Cimetidine launch	Ranitidine discovery	Research starts
1980			Famotidine discovery
1981		Ranitidine launch	
1985			Famotidine launch

5.2   BURIMAMIDE TO CIMETIDINE

5.2.1 Introduction

James Black applied the same approach to the discovery of histamine H_2 antagonists as to his discovery of β-blockers, that is, he started from a naturally occurring molecule, and then modified its structure to enhance the selectivity and stability to a particular type of receptors. The natural molecule this time was histamine, whilst for β-blockers it was adrenaline. Although the idea was quite simple, its realization was not at all easy. It took Black and his colleagues six years to discover the first H_2 antagonist, burimamide, in 1970. However, burimamide had a decisive flaw which prevented its practical use as a drug. They modified it and discovered metiamide in 1971. Though metiamide was free from the problem which burimamide had, it had undesirable side effects. They modified it further and eventually succeeded in the synthesis of cimetidine in 1972. Cimetidine finished clinical trials successfully and was marketed in the UK in 1976 and in the US in 1977 (Duncan and Parsons 1980). In the early 1980s, it became the top-selling drug in the world (Ganellin 1985, p. 115).

5.2.2 Discovery of the Histamine H_2 Antagonist

For a long time, the relationships between histamine, gastrin and gastric secretion were poorly understood. Gastrin as the gastric secretion stimulant was first reported by J.S. Edkins in 1906, when he derived it from an extract of the stomach (Edkins 1906). Histamine was discovered by H. Dale and P.P. Laidlaw in 1910 (Dale and Laidlaw 1910; Sneader 1985, pp. 165–6). Gastric secretion stimulants were found in many kinds of extracts of other tissues later (Koch *et al.* 1920; Ivy 1930). Because at that time it was known that histamine stimulates acid secretion (Koch *et al.* 1920; Popielski 1920) and it exists in many tissues (Abel and Kubota 1919), some researchers concluded that histamine and gastrin were identical (Rothlin and Gundlach 1921; Sacks *et al.* 1932; Gavin *et al.* 1933). However, in the mid-1930s, researchers at McGill University, Canada, claimed that gastrin and histamine were different substances (Babkin 1934; Komarov 1938; McIntosh 1938). S.A. Komarov repeated Edkins's experiment more systematically and showed that even histamine-free extract of the stomach could cause the secretion of gastric acid whereas histamine-free extracts of other tissues could not (Komarov 1938). Moreover, F.C. McIntosh compared the increase of histamine caused by injection of histamine with that caused by stimulation of the vagus nerve, a widely distributed nerve, and suggested that histamine functioned as a 'local hormone' working indirectly for acid secretion rather than as a 'true hormone' (that should have been 'gastrin') working directly (McIntosh 1938). Thus, they showed that gastrin was different from histamine and suggested that gastrin might work more directly in gastric secretion and be more important than histamine. After that, many efforts were made to unveil the new hormone, gastrin (for example, Uvnäs 1943; Harper 1946; Jorpes *et al.* 1952). However, the controversy continued until gastrin was identified chemically. For example, C.F. Code discussed gastrin as follows:

> 'Gastrin' then, may be simply another histamine releaser. Study of whether this action is confined to the release of histamine in the gastric mucosa or whether it is shared by other tissues is hampered by the lack of a ready source of purified 'gastrin' and, apparently, by the difficulty of preparing it so that it will be free of histamine. (Code 1956)

At last, in 1964 gastrin was isolated (Gregory and Tracy 1964) and its chemical structure, a polypeptide hormone, was identified subsequently

(Gregory *et al.* 1964). Then, '[m]any researchers turned their attention to seeking specific inhibitors of gastrin-induced acid secretion' (Ganellin 1982, p. 4).[1] This is exemplified by the statement below about gastric secretion in a physiology textbook published in 1968:

> Histamine and gastrin deserve some special consideration, histamine because it has for such a long time been involved in theories of gastric secretion as well as other activities, and gastrin because it is now firmly established as playing a major role in gastric activity and also is the first gastrointestinal hormone whose chemical nature has been determined. ...
>
> The role of histamine as a physiological agent in gastric secretion can still not be regarded as either proved or disproved. (Davson and Eggleton 1968, p. 619)

Similarly, L.R. Johnson in his paper, 'Control of Gastric Secretion: No Room for Histamine?', argued that 'histamine may have nothing to do with the direct stimulation of acid secretion' (Johnson 1971).

This view was reinforced by the fact that existing antihistamine drugs at the time could not stop acid secretion (Ganellin 1982, pp. 2–3; Patrick 1995, p. 283; Sneader 1985, p. 170),[2] though they could stop other body responses caused by histamine, particularly allergic symptoms such as urticaria and hay fever (Sneader 1985, pp. 167–8; Ganellin 1982, p. 2). In addition, in the 1950s M.I. Glossman and his colleagues at the University of Illinois College of Medicine, supported by Eli Lilly, examined the gastric acid secretion-inhibitory activity of various histamine analogues, but no effective inhibitor was discovered (Glossman *et al.* 1952; Ganellin 1985, pp. 99–100). Therefore, the idea of using histamine antagonists as the way of inhibiting acid secretion was generally regarded as 'played out' (Ganellin 1982, p. 4). For example, when Glaxo started its research programme for anti-acid drugs in 1968, they first did it by searching for an anti-gastrin compound.[3]

James Black described the atmosphere at the time:

> Suddenly [in 1938], we had the discovery of gastrin. Everybody went alive. And they were able to show its structure and they synthesized it. ... we now have up until 1938 everybody saying histamine, after 1938 everybody saying gastrin. So when the anti-histamine drug didn't stop acid secretion, it was said that that was because acid was stimulated by gastrin. Now that is why no one was looking for a histamine antagonist because they didn't think histamine was involved. (Interview)[4]

Why then did Black follow a different way? Two reasons have been put forward. One is his experience of adrenaline receptors: Black had succeeded in finding beta-adrenergic receptor antagonists before joining SmithKline & French (see Chapter 3). His familiarity with two types of adrenaline receptors led him to the analogy of the histamine receptors (Duncan and

Parsons 1980, p. 620; Black interview). The other is previous research on histamine by other scientists. Conventional antihistamines failed not only to inhibit acid secretion in the stomach but also to block dilation of blood vessels and some other actions caused by histamine. Therefore, in 1948, B. Folkow, K. Heager and G. Kahlson speculated that there might be two types of receptors sensitive to histamine (Folkow *et al.* 1948).[5] These two reasons led Black, the newly appointed Head of Biological Research at the British laboratories of SmithKline & French (UK), to propose a research programme on the unidentified second histamine receptor in 1964 (Duncan and Parsons 1980, p. 620).

The research programme began in September 1964 with the expectation that it would be over by Christmas. It consisted of Black and M.E. Parsons as pharmacologists, W.A.M. Duncan as a biochemist and G.J. Durant as a chemist. As they found the programme unexpectedly difficult, J.C. Emmett and C.R. Ganellin joined in the team in 1965 and 1966 respectively (Duncan and Parsons 1980), in order to reinforce the chemistry part.

Because there was only an hypothesis, they started to modify histamine itself. Many different approaches were tried, including a straightforward analogy with β-blockers, to fuse together a benzene ring and an imidazole ring. But none of these early trials worked (Ganellin 1982, pp. 5–6). Numerous failures raised doubts about the hypothesis; only the results that showed the different stimulating effects on the different receptor sites between 2-methylhistamine and 4-methylhistamine, implicating the two types of receptors, encouraged them to continue. However, this did not lead to the discovery of selective antagonists (Ganellin 1982, p. 7). In the first four years, about 200 compounds were synthesized and tested, with no success. Meanwhile, Parsons found that the assay they had been using was not able to detect partial agonists (partial agonists are compounds that have characteristics as both agonists and antagonists). He suggested a new assay able to find even partial agonists (Duncan and Parsons 1980). They re-examined some of the compounds synthesized earlier which had some potential from the theoretical point of view (Ganellin 1982, p. 7). By this screening, they found one compound that showed a weak blocking activity. This had been synthesized by Durant in 1964, the very first year of the research programme (Duncan and Parsons 1980).[6] It had not been detected in the first screening because it was a partial agonist. The compound, SK&F-71448 (N^{α}-guanylhistamine) became the lead compound for the next stage (Ganellin 1982; Duncan and Parsons 1980).

Before they discovered SK&F-71448, they had also found a compound[7] which inhibited acid secretion. However, its activity was not by antagonism at the histamine H_2 receptors but by another mechanism. There was strong pressure both within the research team and from the company to develop it, and eventually some temporary effort was diverted along this track. However, Black succeeded in reminding the team members that they were not interested in an antisecretory compound *per se*, but in a competitive non-H$_1$ receptor antagonist (Duncan and Parsons 1980; see also note 5 of this chapter). As Black said:

> I was looking for a histamine antagonist. I was not looking for something which would inhibit acid secretion. ... This particular compound inhibited acid secretion. And then I was put under great pressure to develop this as an anti-acid secretory compound. And I was able to show that it was the salt of dichlorobenzene sulphonate which was doing the inhibition, and there is nothing to do with histamine at all. And so, 'Go away! Don't follow this.' (Interview)

Black's reputation was important for the survival of the project. He himself observed: '[The company] would have to have really good reasons, if you understand, for cutting me off. But they had a problem. Because I had by this time, what you might call, a track record' (ibid.).

After the discovery of SK&F-71448, the research team made many of its analogues. One of them, SK&F-91486, which was synthesized in 1968, had a longer side chain and showed a stronger antagonist action though it was still a partial agonist. This made the research team more confident (Duncan and Parsons 1980).

The organizational pressure, however, increased more and more. The 1967 annual report of SmithKline & French announced that they ' began to concentrate [their] efforts on a smaller number of research areas and to give these areas more intensive study' (SmithKline & French, *Annual Report* 1967, p. 7). Several research programmes in progress were mentioned there but Black's project was not. Duncan and Parsons described the situation very well:

> The parent company in the United States had had a major reorganization of its research activities, and questions were being raised about the relevance of the research program in the British laboratories. This probing led to the resolve by the British workers that the survival of the UK Research Institute within the SK&F organization required that it make a major discovery and that it should do it soon. Duncan was now Research Director and it was decided that of the various research programs being worked on in Welwyn, the histamine-receptor antagonist program was the one most likely to fulfill this requirement and therefore, that we should concentrate all our available resources on making it happen. This inevitably produced trauma within the Research Institute, and it is very considerably to the credit of all our colleagues that they cooperated in this policy even though it inevitably led to the contraction, or annihilation, of their own favorite programs. These were not happy times... (Duncan and Parsons 1980, p. 621)

The UK research team invented the term 'H₂' in order to emphasize the difference between their objectives and those of their counterparts in the United States and of other companies which were looking for anti-secretory compounds (Duncan and Parsons 1980, pp. 621–2).[8] It can be said they set their domain not in the specific disease but in the specific approach, at least partly because of organizational reasons as regards their relationship with the US parent company.

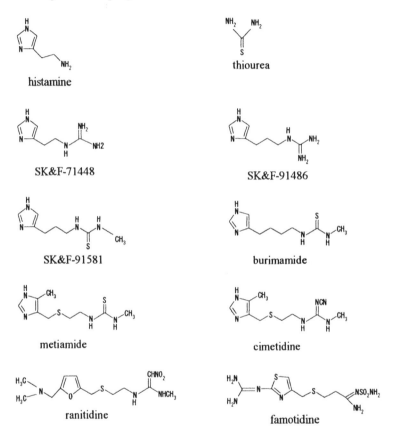

histamine

thiourea

SK&F-71448

SK&F-91486

SK&F-91581

burimamide

metiamide

cimetidine

ranitidine

famotidine

Figure 5.1: Various histamine H₂ antagonists and relevant chemicals

. In 1969, SK&F-91581, a thiourea analogue of SK&F-91486, was found not to act as a partial agonist, even though its activity as an antagonist was weaker than SK&F-91486. Further lengthening of the side chain of SK&F-91581 led to the discovery in 1970 of burimamide, which showed much stronger antagonist activity without stimulant activity. In total, about 700 compounds had been synthesized and tested before this discovery (Duncan and Parsons 1980, p. 622; Ganellin 1982, pp. 14–16).[9]

Burimamide demonstrated that there are histamine H_2 receptors and particular compounds that can antagonize the activity of the receptors. Confidence and morale in the research team became very high (Duncan and Parsons 1980, p. 622). However, burimamide was not active enough to be given orally; this meant that it could not be considered as a drug candidate (Ganellin 1982, p. 16). Further modification was necessary to find a practical candidate, but Black and Duncan decided that they should undertake single-dose experiments of burimamide in humans to confirm the transferability of the animal pharmacology to humans and that they should publish their data as early as possible (Duncan and Parsons 1980, p. 622). The experiments were conducted in 1971[10] and confirmed that burimamide inhibited acid secretion in humans as well as in animals. These findings were very important because they showed a key role for histamine in gastric secretion which had been controversial for a long time. The results were published in *Nature* in 1972, only a year after the Johnson's 'No Room for Histamine' paper. According to Duncan and Parsons (1980), this very early publication came from the intention to encourage other scientists to confirm their findings and to extend research in the area. It can be imagined that this also affected the valuation of this research by the management of the parent company.

After the discovery of burimamide, various modifications were examined systematically to increase potency. Based on the elegant, rational thinking of chemistry, sulphur was introduced in the side chain by Ganellin (Black personal communication, October 1999). This, together with the introduction of CH_3 in the ring system, made the compound about ten times more potent. This compound was synthesized in 1971 and named metiamide (Black *et al.* 1974; Ganellin 1982, pp. 16–23; 1985, pp. 106–11; Duncan and Parsons 1980, p. 623; Patrick 1995, pp. 294–8). Because it was effective even by oral administration, they believed that they had at last achieved their objective: a drug! Top priority was given to scaling-up the synthesis. The team was now expanded and about 150 scientists came to be involved in metiamide and other aspects of H_2 receptors. In March 1972, Duncan, Black and one of their American colleagues visited the Food and Drug Administration (FDA) in the United States to talk about burimamide and metiamide; this was the first of several meetings between SK&F and the FDA on the matter. In June 1972, an application was made to the Committee on Safety of Medicines (CSM) in the UK for a clinical trials certificate for metiamide and this was granted in April 1973 (Duncan and Parsons 1980, p. 623). The first international symposium on histamine H_2 receptor antagonists was held in London in October 1973.[11]

However, metiamide was not free from flaws. Even as early as March 1972, the research team regarded the presence of a thiourea group in the molecule as a potential disadvantage and started an effort to replace it with another structure. The pre-clinical development found that metiamide produced a granulocytopenia, a shortage in the normal number of granular leucocytes in the blood, in some dogs and some other side effects in rats and dogs. These effects were judged to be acceptable therapeutically when both the merits and demerits of metiamide were taken into account (Duncan and Parsons 1980, p. 623). However, of 700 patients treated with metiamide in the clinical trials, a few cases of granulocytopenia were reported (Ganellin 1982, p. 23). Because of these, the CSM recommended the suspension of the UK clinical trial certificates in June 1974; the FDA also took a similar action. The company had some meetings with the FDA and the CSM. In the UK the clinical trial certificate for metiamide was re-granted but for use only in seriously ill patients (Duncan and Parsons 1980, p. 624). Duncan and Parsons described how this matter, together with Black's resignation in 1973 to accept the chair of pharmacology at University College, London, depressed the research team (ibid.). They had already started work on modifying the structure of metiamide in March 1972, and eventually found that its nitroguanidine analogue and cyanoguanidine analogue were as potent as metiamide even without the thiourea group, which was regarded as the cause of the side effects of metiamide. The cyanoguanidine analogue was more potent and chosen as a successor of metiamide: this is cimetidine (Brimblecombe *et al.* 1975; Ganellin 1981, 1982, pp. 23–7; 1985, pp. 111–14; Patrick 1995, p. 281), which was synthesized in 1972 (Ganellin 1982, p. 33). It gradually became clear that cimetidine did not have the major side effect of metiamide. In 1974, cimetidine was administered to a patient who had agranulocytosis, serious granulocytopenia, caused by metiamide. The substitution of cimetidine for metiamide led to a rapid recovery from agranulocytosis: this was evidence that cimetidine is free from this side effect (Duncan and Parsons 1980, p. 624). After that, the development of cimetidine progressed rapidly. The drug was first marketed in the UK in 1976, in the US in 1977 and in over 100 countries by 1979 under the trade name Tagamet (Ganellin 1982, p. 33).

SmithKline and French intensively promoted cimetidine worldwide. In the statement of the chief executive officer in the 1976 annual report, the then chairman, Robert Dee, stated: '[w]e will devote a major share of our resources – people and money – to make 'Tagamet' available to patients throughout the world in 1977. ... The effective worldwide marketing of 'Tagamet' is a top priority' (SmithKline Corporation, *Annual Report* 1976, p. 3). The most important thing was to inform the medical market about the drug. They held the Second International Symposium on Histamine H_2-

Receptor Antagonists in London in October 1976 (SmithKline Corporation, *Annual Report* 1976, p. 9). Face-to-face promotion was also conducted, as the following extract shows:

> Because of the uniqueness of the H_2-antagonist concept, our sales representatives will be informing the world's physicians of a new method of treating gastrointestinal disorders. To prepare our people to do this, we have developed an intensive and comprehensive instruction program. The program includes training in the safety and efficacy profile of the compound, and also instruction in the concept of biochemical receptors and antagonists, which underlies the mode of action of 'Tagamet.' (SmithKline Corporation, *Annual Report* 1976, p. 9)

The following extract from the 1977 Annual Report of SmithKline Corporation shows how the company prepared for the worldwide market introduction of cimetidine:

> parallel strategic programs were implemented to assure that we had adequate chemical supplies and pharmaceutical production facilities, and the marketing capability to introduce the product effectively to the medical professions. Production facilities were expanded in the United Kingdom, Germany, France, Puerto Rico and a number of other countries. Sales forces were increased in several international markets, including Spain, Germany and Italy. (SmithKline Corporation, *Annual Report* 1977, p. 4)

The discovery and development of histamine H_2 antagonists has changed the view of the role of histamine in gastric secretion. It can be seen clearly when we compare the following statement in a recent textbook with that in 1968 cited above:

> Histamine is a major physiological mediator of HCl secretion. Cimetidine, a specific antagonist of H_2 receptors, blocks a large portion of acid secretion elicited by any known secretagogue. ... Gastrin is not as potent a direct stimulant of parietal cells as acetylcholine or histamine. The physiological response to elevated levels of gastrin in the blood is greatly attenuated by cimetidine. Thus a major component of the physiological response to gastrin may result from gastrin-stimulated release of histamine. (Berne and Levy 1996, pp. 466–7)

Black won a Nobel Prize in 1988 for his achievement in the discoveries of β-blockers and histamine H_2 antagonists.

5.3   RANITIDINE

5.3.1 Introduction

In 1968, David Jack, who was then research and development director at Allen & Hanbury, set up a research team for a gastrin antagonist after he had successfully achieved the discovery of salbutamol and BDP inhaler (see Chapter 4). The team leaders were Roy Brittain (pharmacology) and Barry Price (chemistry). They changed their target to histamine H_2 antagonists when burimamide appeared. They eventually discovered a new potent H_2 antagonist, ranitidine, in 1976. Ranitidine is a member of a new chemical class of H_2 antagonists in which the imidazole ring in burimamide, metiamide and cimetidine molecules is replaced by a furan ring carrying a basic substituent. Ranitidine was found to be more potent and more selective than cimetidine. Because of these superior characteristics as a drug and Glaxo's intensive global marketing efforts, it steadily displaced cimetidine after it was marketed in 1981 and became the world top-selling drug by 1988.

5.3.2 Shaping a World Best-selling Drug

Jack and his colleagues first considered the possibility of an improved treatment for peptic ulcer in 1968 (Jack personal communication, February 2000; Glaxo internal documents). Originally, this research team was directed towards the discovery of an antigastrin compound (Glaxo internal documents; Jack interview; Palmer interview).[12] This was found to be a very difficult task because gastrin is a relatively large peptide hormone whose cellular receptors were ill-defined (Jack personal communication). The project was about to be axed because it had been unsuccessful for almost four years (Palmer interview). In 1972, the research objective was abruptly changed to a new histamine H_2 antagonist when Black's work on histamine H_2 receptors was made public. Jack explained:

> Roy Brittain and I attended a lecture by James Black in Hatfield Polytechnic in which he revealed that burimamide, a simple derivative of histamine, inhibits not only histamine-induced acid secretion in animals and man but also that which follows ingestion of food. These results established beyond doubt the physiological role of histamine in acid secretion and gave our chemists a much easier starting point than gastrin analogues for their project. At that time, large molecules such as gastrin were 'bad news' for medicinal chemists because their chemistry and biology were more difficult and less well understood than that of small mediators like histamine. (Interview)

The SmithKline & French researchers probably believed that the imidazole ring, as in histamine, or an alternative basic aromatic ring system was essential in a potent histamine H_2 antagonist. This is evident in cimetidine and related compounds in the contents of their patent on H_2 antagonists (British Patent 1421792). The first objective of the Glaxo research team was, therefore, to find a potent H_2 antagonist that does not contain such a ring system, rather than to find a more selective drug (Jack interview and personal communication). Their starting point in 1972 was burimamide and later cimetidine. As Jack said:

> By 1976, we were looking for a drug as good as cimetidine. What we found was a better one. Ranitidine proved to be about five times more active than cimetidine as a histamine H_2 antagonist and to be more selectively acting because, unlike that drug, it does not inhibit cytochrome P450 processing enzymes in the liver or antagonize the actions of testosterone in man. We were very lucky to achieve this outcome because we were unaware of these shortcomings of cimetidine when ranitidine was first synthesized. (Interview)

The Glaxo team struggled unsuccessfully for nearly four years to circumvent the SK&F patents by replacing the imidazole ring by a variety of non-basic aromatic systems (Jack personal communication). The breakthrough came in 1976 when John Clithelow, a senior medicinal chemist, having made some poorly active furan analogues of potent H_2 antagonists, remembered that furan can be converted into a tertiary amine by a specific chemical procedure. The resultant compound retains the furan structure but it has a basic group *outside* the furan ring system (Jack personal communication).

The conversion was first carried out on the furan analogue of metiamide and yielded a modestly potent H_2 antagonist. Next came the dimethylaminomethyl furan analogue of cimetidine. It was found to be less active than cimetidine and to be toxic in animals. After a few modifications were tried in the side chain, the one that contains an unusual nitro-ethene grouping was found to be more active and less toxic than cimetidine. This was synthesized in 1976 and named ranitidine (Jack personal communication; technical booklet published by Glaxo Group Research titled *Ulcers*, p. 12). However, because ranitidine was a poorly soluble solid, it was replaced in the development programme by ranitidine hydrochloride in 1977.[13] Following extensive toxicity tests in animals, clinical trials of ranitidine started in 1978. Its efficacy and safety were confirmed in clinical trials. It was marketed in the UK in 1981 and in the US in 1983, under the trade name 'Zantac' (Jack personal communication; Brittain *et al.* 1981; Brittain and Jack 1983; Glaxo internal documents; Bradshaw *et al.* 1979; British Patent 1565966). Further research found that the furan ring system of ranitidine could be replaced by other base-substituted aromatic structures to yield a variety of potent, long-acting H_2-antagonists but none was found to be superior to ranitidine (Jack personal communication; Brittain and Jack 1983, p. 74; Brittain *et al.* 1981, pp. 311–12; Palmer interview).

Because they could obviously witness the success of cimetidine, it is easy to speculate that Glaxo was less uncertain and more confident about the success of ranitidine, which was gradually found to be better than cimetidine. This led the company to undertake the large investment in manufacturing and marketing; it also led the quite 'Commonwealth' orientated company to become a really international company operating in many countries, including other European countries, the United States and Japan. Documents published by the company described the situation:

> All available resources were swung behind the new compound. In the process, Glaxo began to break new ground in almost every department. Clinical trials were wider in scope and completed far more quickly than had ever been the case before. ... Marketing was approached in a totally new way, with co-promotion and licensing deals to achieve rapid penetration of markets. ... At the same time, greater-than-ever investment in production resources helped to meet the demand as it rose. In summary, Zantac was developed and brought to market in a single, worldwide programme, rather than locally and piecemeal as had always been the case in the past. (Glaxo 1987, p. 10)

Angela Palmer, who had worked closely with the research team, also described it:

> Ranitidine was first made chemically in 1976. Ranitidine hydrochloride ... was made in mid 1977. And large-scale production in a production plant at Montrose was commenced in October 1980. And certainly, a large amount of effort was put into the development. The company realized it's a good drug at the very early stage. (Interview)

John Wood, who had worked on the clinical trials since 1983, explained the internationalization as follows:

> We were a small-medium sized Commonwealth–English company. And we had a new product. We wanted to internationalize. Our chairman at the time, Sir Paul Girolami, decided this company needed to be internationalized, so we had to take a new drug, Zantac, and set up new companies in other countries, for example, America. ... Zantac was the opportunity. It was the new drug we would take into new countries. Now, I think that if we hadn't had Zantac, [we] might have been less encouraged to move other countries. (Interview)

In the course of this all-out and worldwide development of the drug, the approach that was taken was so-called 'development-in-parallel'. It was based on the idea that every month lost between synthesis and sales was potential revenue lost (Glaxo 1987, p. 11). This represents their confidence in the success of the drug in the market. Roy Brittain, the research director at Ware since 1983, stated: 'Had we done our tests strictly one after the other we could have lost a year or more in development time' (Glaxo 1987, p. 11). Richard Blythe, the secondary production controller at Glaxo Pharmaceuticals, said: 'We got going on production facilities before the clinical trails or even the animal trials were finished. If you wait until trials are over, you're eating all the time into your patent life' (ibid.).

The significance of communications between functions was emphasized. John Padfield, then pharmacy director at Glaxo Group Research, put it thus: 'We had to understand what was going on in development, of course. We had to talk constantly with the marketing people to discover what they wanted in terms of presentation, dosage forms, likely shelf lives and so on. We also had to understand the needs of the production people' (ibid., p. 12).

All these efforts towards worldwide, simultaneous development were based on the thought that market success would not just happen, but had to be planned. Sir Paul Giolami, the Group chief executive at the time, stated later: '[Zantac] did not just come out. It was made here in every respect – a whole team work, research, development' (Glaxo 1994, p. 8). Giolami also stated elsewhere, stressing the marketing function:

> Marketing has made that product as much as our research laboratories. For instance, in the United States where we had hardly started and in Germany and Japan where we were very small, we had to achieve two contradictory things: Make the most of Zantac and yet not hold back the development of our own company. That's when we came up with the idea of a co-marketing arrangement. We had the imagination and flexibility to hire a marketing team from a major company. (Glaxo 1987, p. 10)

The co-marketing arrangement was to promote the product jointly with marketing partners in other countries. Its rationale was explained to be that any dilution of income would be offset by faster market penetration. The partners were Menarini in Italy, Cancan in Germany, Fournier in France, Hoffmann-La-Roche in the US and Sankyo in Japan. Glaxo also had its own marketing subsidiaries in these countries though their strength in each market was varied (ibid., p. 17). These subsidiaries and the local partners in the same countries jointly promoted the drug. Even in the subsidiaries, local autonomy seemed to be regarded as important. John Wood said:

> I think the most important thing, this is a really important thing, is that our entire company was built on a human network of devolution, or decentralization. ... In this case, they were not told what to do. They were given the product, and they were allowed quite a lot of freedom to do differently in different countries. ...

The bosses of countries hired their people. ... Giolami's view was that the local people know best. (Interview)

The key role of marketing was shown by another activity, namely, persuading medical professionals. David Richards, then medical director at Glaxo Group Research, was reported as saying: 'By conducting clinical trials in all the main potential markets, we were able to create demand for the product among the opinion leaders before we actually launched' (Glaxo 1987, p. 11). Comparisons with cimetidine were fully utilized in the persuasion. It is easy to imagine that this tactic worked very well in taking the existing market from cimetidine. John Wood put it:

We've done a whole series of trials to compare ourselves with Tagamet. And we wrote many papers, to describe findings. And we were very fortunate because SmithKline had chosen a wrong dose. It's the dose which was not giving them the maximum effect. So we could use the dose of Zantac which gave a higher effect, both in ulcer healing and in maintenance. We had many chances to show that [the results] were repeated in other countries, and we showed that the lack of sexual side-effects [with Zantac], we showed that at high doses the side-effects got even worse with Tagamet. (Interview)

Wood also explained how they could take advantage of ranitidine's superior efficacy and duration to provide more convenient dosage compared with cimetidine:

Tagamet was being given four times a day. ... Two pills at bedtime to help you with acid over night. Five pills throughout a day. When we introduced Zantac, it was two pills, one in the morning, one at night. And then we did a whole series of big trials. And we made it converted to one pill a day, twice as big, at night, which worked just as well. ... And Tagamet tried to do that. They moved to 400 mg twice a day which was not as good as their original dose, but more convenient. Then they moved to 800 mg once a day, which was like a horse pill, and in that stage they were failing and losing. They had a big market share but we were taking more and more market share, as people learned the benefits of the product. (Ibid.)

Also Glaxo's internal documents stated: 'Zantac was marketed with the promotional messages, "Fast, Simple, Safe" which doctors interpreted as Faster, Simpler and Safer than Tagamet, although no such direct comparison was permitted in promotion.'[14] There were also many papers by medical doctors in which ranitidine and cimetidine were compared and the superiority of ranitidine was reported (Domschke *et al.* 1979; Zeldis *et al.* 1983; Strum 1983).

The application of the drug was expanded. In 1984, ranitidine was reported to have superior results in maintenance treatment, that is, there is a smaller chance of relapse when it is taken continuously (Gough *et al.* 1984; Silvis 1985; Glaxo 1987, p. 11). This can be accepted if the side effects of a drug are low enough. This maintenance treatment was used as the most important concept in competition with cimetidine. It is reported that Glaxo set out to persuade doctors that ulcers needed long-term, probably lifelong, maintenance treatment (Angelmar and Pinson 1991, p. 11 and Exhibit 22).

Many kinds of administration forms have also been developed. Wood said:

> We did a lot of different pharmaceutical forms, so, normal tablets, larger tablets, effervescent tablets, injections, soft gel capsules, and syrup, and those, ... finally, we got permission in the US to move it over the counter so that you didn't need to get doctor's prescription, you are just going to a shop in the US, a pharmacy shop or supermarket or garage and buy some Zantac. That's the lowest strength. And by that stage we had treated two hundred and forty million people. (Interview)

These developments after the first product launch were quite intensely promoted by the company. Wood, again:

> I think it's fair to say that the company started off investing more and more and more as we went along. And I've worked on this drug for 16 years, and I never had any restriction on the amount of money I could spend. Now, in other words, I wanted to do this trial, that trial, that trial, [and they said] just 'do it'. So I was never, ever [constrained]. (Ibid.)

As a result of these marketing efforts, ranitidine overtook Tagamet sales on an annual basis and became the highest-selling drug in the world in 1986. In 1988, its sales worldwide exceeded £1 billion and its sales in the US exceeded $1 billion (Glaxo internal documents).

5.4 FAMOTIDINE

5.4.1 Introduction

Famotidine was the third marketed histamine H_2 antagonist; it was developed by Yamanouchi, a Japanese pharmaceutical company. Famotidine is said to be much more active than cimetidine. The imidazole ring of cimetidine is replaced with a 2-guanidinothiazole ring and the side chain is also changed to contain a sulfonylamidine group (Patrick 1995, p. 309). This work was done by Isao Yanagisawa and his colleague at Yamanouchi's Central Research Laboratories. Famotidine was launched on the market in Japan in 1985 (Yanagisawa 1994, p. 167), in the US in collaboration with

Merck in 1986 (Angelmar and Pinson 1991, p. 12), and in about 80 countries by 1994. It has been the best-selling histamine H_2 antagonist in Japan since 1988 (*Gekkan Mikusu*, 24(14), 1996, p. 48). It was reported that in Japan famotidine enjoyed twice the sales of either ranitidine or cimetidine, but in the world its share was only about a third of that of ranitidine in 1993 and 1994 (*Scrip Yearbook*, 1995, vol. 1, p. 129).

5.4.2 Making the Top Histamine H_2 Antagonist in Japan

A group of researchers of Yamanouchi began the search for anti-peptic-ulcer drugs in the mid-1970s (Yanagisawa 1994, p. 162). They had studied the application of prostaglandins until then. One possible application area was anti-gastric-ulcer. Their interest focused on that area, and they began to look at other substances as well. Therefore, at the beginning, their search did not centre on histamine H_2 antagonists; rather, they included broad types of anti-acid substances, including prostaglandins, histamine H_2 antagonists and others (Yanagisawa interview).[15] Chemical synthesis and biological screening began in August 1976, after the investigation of patents and literature (Yanagisawa personal communication, September 1999). The research team consisted of four chemists, two pharmacologists, two assistants, and two researchers dedicated to the investigation of literature and patents, according to Yanagisawa (interview). Three lead compounds were chosen: one was discovered by Yamanouchi's researchers; the other was a compound originating from Schering; and the third was cimetidine, which was marketed and highlighted in the same year (interview). Because two of them were not H_2 antagonists, the pharmacological evaluation was done on both anti-acid activity and anti-histamine activity (Yanagisawa 1994, p. 162). The superiority of cimetidine was found in the course of the research in terms of potency and safety and it became the final lead compound (interview). They succeeded in replacing the cyanoguanidine part of the cimetidine molecule with cyano amidine and carbamoyl amidine parts[16] (Yanagisawa *et al.* 1984). Subsequently, they found that the compound containing the carbamoyl amidine had a histamine H_2 antagonist activity which is as strong as cimetidine. They also intended replacement of the imidazole ring of cimetidine; they tried many kinds of rings and discovered that the compounds with a 2-guanidinothiazole ring showed very strong H_2 antagonist activities. Eventually, they discovered that the compound that was the product of a combination of these two modifications was the most active among all the tested compounds (Yanagisawa *et al.* 1984; Yanagisawa 1989, 1994). However, this compound was not stable enough to be industrialized. This instability was thought to be due to the carbamoyl amidine part and its replacement was considered. Because they had already tried many kinds of amidine derivatives, and the carbamoyl amidine derivative had been the best of all, the ideas for further improvement almost ran out. A suggestion from the then director of the research laboratories to try sulfamoyl, which is slightly different from calbamoyl, opened the way to a solution. Yanagisawa was suspicious of the idea because sulfamoyl amidine derivative was supposed to be unstable as well and difficult to synthesize. Furthermore, the compound was not known in the existing literature. However, his team succeeded in the synthesis of the compound, and found that it was stable despite Yanagisawa's expectations (Yanagisawa 1994, pp. 165–6). This compound is famotidine (Yanagisawa *et al.* 1987; Yanagisawa 1989, pp. 208–10; Belgian Patent 882071, 1980), which was reported to be about 30–40 times more potent than cimetidine *in vivo* (Takagi *et al.* 1982; Friedman 1987). Before they reached famotidine, 424 compounds had been synthesized and screened (interview). After the toxicological and pharmacological characteristics were confirmed to be satisfactory in the pre-clinical studies, clinical trials of famotidine were started in 1980. The efficacy and safety of the drug were confirmed and it obtained approval for manufacturing in January 1985. There seemed to be no significant problems both in organizational authorization and in scaling-up after the synthesis to the launch, despite difficult production conditions and a modest estimation of market size, according to Yanagisawa (interview). International development was made by Merck (US), and it was marketed in the US in 1986 and in about 80 other countries by 1994 (Yanagisawa 1994).

Famotidine rapidly took the market from cimetidine and ranitidine in Japan. In 1986, its sales exceeded that of ranitidine, and in 1988 it superseded cimetidine as the highest-selling histamine H₂ antagonist in Japan (*Gekkan Mikusu*, 24(14), 1996, p. 48). In 1993–4, its share in the Japanese market was about twice as much as either that of ranitidine or of cimetidine.[17] There are several factors in the success of famotidine in the Japanese market. First, it was reported to be much more potent than cimetidine; this meant fewer doses, which is convenient for patients and for doctors who want to control their patients' dosing. Second, it has been seen as having fewer side effects than cimetidine. It is said that these two points have been thoroughly emphasized by Yamanouchi's representatives: these are similar to the marketing tactics Glaxo adopted against cimetidine. Third, the price of famotidine was set higher than that of cimetidine (*Gekkan Mikusu*, 24(14), 1996, p. 48).[18] This is beneficial for the company, given the quantity sold. Furthermore, unlike ordinary commodities, prescribed drugs can be sold in higher quantities despite being more expensive than rival products. In Japan, though the official prices, which are used for reimbursement by the various health insurance programmes, are set under the fee schedule scheme, the real prices applied to trade between hospitals and pharmaceutical companies are often lower than the official ones. The margin between the two prices (*yakka saeki*) constitutes a significant part of hospitals' and clinics' revenues (Campbell and Ikegami 1998, p. 148). Therefore, a higher price may be welcomed by doctors and may result in more frequent prescribing. This seems to be the case with famotidine compared with cimetidine, that is to say, the higher official price of famotidine seemed to stimulate doctors' preference for the drug (*Gekkan Mikusu*, 24(14), 1996, p. 48). These three factors explain the advantage of famotidine over cimetidine, but not over ranitidine. One possible reason why famotidine has surpassed ranitidine in the Japanese market share is the difference among sales forces. Yamanouchi regarded famotidine as the most important product to promote, while Nippon Glaxo, the main Japanese subsidiary of Glaxo, did not have such a large sales force, and Sankyo, the co-marketing partner of Glaxo in terms of ranitidine, had several other important drugs to promote at the time, including their own products, and could not concentrate sales efforts on ranitidine alone (ibid., p. 49).

The last point is interesting because it may also explain why famotidine was not very successful in overseas markets.[19] The overseas marketing of famotidine was conducted by Merck (US), but the world's largest pharmaceutical company also seemed unable to concentrate its promotional resources on famotidine because of internal competition with other, more profitable, drugs introduced around the same time (Angelmar and Pinson 1991, p. 12).

A few other factors have been reported as contributing to the success of famotidine in the Japanese market. One of them is that it was emphasized in promotion that famotidine reinforced a protection factor in the stomach mucous membrane (*Gekkan Mikusu*, 24(14), 1996, p. 49). This activity was identified by using a new instrument, namely, an ultrathin endoscope (Daneshmend *et al.* 1989). Another is that it has also had an injection formula from the beginning of its market launch, which has been welcomed by hospitals. Furthermore, because of frequent additions in application, dosage and form, the company has had many opportunities to meet doctors and explain the drug to them (*Gekkan Mikusu*, 24(14), 1996, p. 49). Thus, famotidine has been the top-selling histamine H_2 antagonist in Japan, but has had smaller sales than ranitidine in the world.

5.5   A BRIEF ANALYSIS

There are clear differences in the process of drug discovery and development between the case of cimetidine and those of ranitidine and famotidine. In the case of cimetidine, there was no exemplary drug other than its prototypes, burimamide and metiamide. The shaping of the compound was, therefore, more strongly linked with the shaping of organizational authorization. The powerful direction of the project leader with a track record, together with championing by research management, was necessary to overcome strong organizational resistance. In contrast, researchers involved in the projects of ranitidine and famotidine did not face such strong organizational resistance because they had a family of exemplary drugs: burimamide, metiamide and cimetidine. Their projects were institutionally limited by patents and strategically focused to create clear advantageous differences from the exemplars. The aspect of shaping compounds and of shaping markets played a central role for this purpose.

In the shaping of cimetidine, various human actors, non-human entities and institutional and structural factors were involved in the process of creating a credibility of the drug. In the shaping of the credible compound, actors including the project leader, chemists, biologists and research management played a significant role. Non-human entities such as bioassay systems also contributed to the process. Institutional and structural factors were also involved: the research institution distant from the headquarters, which preserved the project; the market which rationalized the substitution of metiamide for burimamide; the regulatory bodies which supported the substitution of cimetidine for metiamide; and the market competition which led to the development of different pharmaceutical forms. In the shaping of organizational authorization, the project leader and members, the local research management, the concept of histamine 'H₂' antagonism, the compounds which supported the concept, and the leading scientific journal which authorized the discovery of burimamide played an essential role. The concept, the compounds and relevant publications also played a crucial role in shaping the market. In addition, employees of the pharmaceutical company and allied companies, doctors, patients and regulators in various countries were involved in the process of shaping the drug's world. Clinical trials, symposia and business visits were also important in enhancing the credibility of the drug in the market.

In the cases of ranitidine and famotidine, various actors, entities and factors were also involved, but some elements were different from the case of cimetidine. The configuration of elements was also different. In the process of shaping ranitidine and famotidine as compounds, the roles of research management, chemists, the exemplary drugs such as burimamide, metiamide and cimetidine, rival companies' patents to be avoided, corporate strategy and external sources of knowledge were in particular significant. In the shaping of the market, another characteristic aspect in the shaping of ranitidine and famotidine, heterogeneous elements including employees of the pharmaceutical companies, those of allied companies in different countries, doctors, opinion leaders, patients, regulators, the compounds, bioassays, the ultrathin endoscope, production facilities, different drug forms, clinical trials, academic papers, business visits, advertisement, rhetoric, price systems and reimbursement systems were organized towards the creation of differences from existing drugs. Based on a network of these elements, better efficacy, safer properties, additional merits such as maintenance activity or protective activity, and other benefits for users were shaped. In addition, for swift and global marketing, development-in-parallel involving clinical development, production and marketing was promoted, and co-marketing among companies in different countries was arranged.

Thus, there is a clear contrast between the processes of shaping cimetidine and of ranitidine and famotidine. I name the former type of drug discovery and development paradigmatic innovation because it plays an exemplary role for drugs of the kind. The latter type is named modification-based innovation because distinguishable modification is regarded as essential. This type contributes to supporting and promoting existing theory and therapy, while the former type contributes to changing them. It should be noted that these types of innovation do not necessarily link to business performance.

The development from histamine, through burimamide and metiamide, to cimetidine has been regarded as one of the best examples of 'the rational approach' (Sneader 1985, p. 171; Patrick 1995, p. 281) of drug discovery. However, this does not seem to be the case when we examine the processes of discovery and development of these drugs in detail. The processes were characterized by trial and error, which resulted in hundreds of discarded compounds. The failure of metiamide was not anticipated but arose from clinical trials. In addition, without the successful political process inside and outside the pharmaceutical company, cimetidine could not have become a drug.

NOTES

1. However, there seemed to exist some researchers who continued to believe that histamine was significant in gastric secretion (for example, Code 1965).
2. There was also a concerted effort by researchers at Eli Lilly in the 1950s to find an antagonist of histamine-stimulated acid secretion (Ganellin 1982, p. 4).
3. Interviews with Sir David Jack and with Ms Angela Palmer. See note 12.
4. This interview with Sir James Black was conducted on 3 March 1999.
5. Later, but before the SmithKline & French team identify the histamine H_2 antagonist, Ash and Schild proposed in 1966 that the actions of histamine blocked by conventional antihistamine drugs should be defined as histamine H_1 receptors and that other actions not blocked by the antihistamines should be mediated by other receptors, or non-H_1 receptors (Ash and Schild 1966; Ganellin 1982, pp. 2–3; Duncan and Parsons 1980, p. 620).

6. Historically, this compound was first synthesized in 1928, but was reported to be devoid of interesting physiological activity (Ganellin 1985, p. 102).
7. α-methyl histidine 3,4-dichlorobenzene sulphonate.
8. Black did not like 'H₂' very much as the name of the receptor. In fact, there were people who read the title of the SK&F team's first paper as a new 'hydrogen receptor' antagonist! (Black personal communication, October 1999).
9. About the chemical modification from histamine to burimamide, see Ganellin (1985, pp. 102–6) and Patrick (1995).
10. The first volunteers were Duncan and Ganellin (Duncan and Parsons 1980, p. 622).
11. In the welcoming speech at the symposium, Duncan stated that in the drug industry potential new drugs were usually not discussed at such an early stage, that for various reasons nevertheless he had decided on the early disclosure of data and that one of the reasons was to improve its development (Duncan 1973). But, again, the symposium was also regarded as held at least partly because of the politics in academic, medical and business society. The social role of these kinds of symposia in the medical sciences is discussed by Thagard (1999, pp. 91–2, 185–98).
12. The interview with Sir David Jack was conducted on 27 April 1999. The interview with Dr John Wood and Ms Angela Palmer at GlaxoWellcome was conducted on 9 April 1999.
13. For convenience, hereafter I will refer to the compound simply as ranitidine instead of ranitidine hydrochloride.
14. In response to it, SmithKline & French promoted Tagamet as being 'Tried and Trusted', according to the same document. On the promotion battle between Zantac and Tagamet, see also Angelmar and Pinson (1991, pp. 7–8, 10–12, and Exhibit 19–23).
15. The interview with Dr Isao Yanagisawa was conducted on 22 January 1999.
16. Amidines were chosen because of their similarity to guanidines in terms of the chemical structure (Yanagisawa 1989, pp. 203–6).
17. Market shares of famotidine, ranitidine and cimetidine in Japanese anti-ulcer drugs in 1994 were reported to be 21 per cent, 10 per cent and 10 per cent respectively. The total share of these three histamine H₂ antagonists was only 42 per cent in Japan, whereas in the world their total comes to 58 per cent in 1994. This was because many kinds of traditional anti-ulcer drugs were still commonly used in the Japanese anti-ulcer drug market.
18. Prices of pharmaceutical drugs in Japan are set by the Central Social Insurance Medical Care Council (*Chuikyou*), an advisory committee to the Minister of Health and Welfare under the national fee schedule (*shinryo hoshu*) scheme. This scheme is universal and virtually compulsory in Japan (Campbell and Ikegami 1999, pp. 16–19, 145–50).
19. Worldwide market shares of famotidine, ranitidine and cimetidine in anti-ulcer drugs in 1994 were reported to be 12 per cent, 35 per cent and 11 per cent respectively. Market share of each in the US was 11 per cent, 48 per cent and 14 per cent respectively and in Europe 7 per cent, 40 per cent, 8 per cent respectively in the same year (data belonging to GlaxoSmithKline).

6. LHRH analogues

6.1 INTRODUCTION

The drugs that we examine in this chapter are called luteinizing hormone releasing hormone (LHRH) analogues, which are used for the treatment of prostate and breast cancer, endometriosis and some other sex-hormone-dependent diseases. LHRH is a hormone secreted from the hypothalamus in the brain, and it stimulates the secretion of luteinizing hormone (LH) from the pituitary gland. LH, in turn, stimulates the secretion of testosterone from the testes in males, or stimulates oestrogen production, ovulation and the development of the corpus luteum in females. Therefore, LHRH is a hormone that fundamentally regulates growth and activities of the gonads, so its analogues can be used for the treatment of various diseases in sex organs or the control of reproduction in human and other animals. The two LHRH analogues that we examine in detail here are leuprorelin acetate (hereinafter, leuprorelin), developed by an alliance between Takeda in Japan and Abbott in the US, and goserelin, developed by ICI Pharmaceuticals (now AstraZeneca) in the UK. They are the most successful LHRH analogues on the market in the world. Leuprorelin was synthesized in 1973 by a group of scientists at Takeda led by Masahiko Fujino. Goserelin was discovered in 1976 by Anand Dutta and Barry Furr at ICI Pharmaceuticals. However, what made these drugs highly successful in the market was the development of their depot preparations, which can release the drugs very slowly within the body. Frank Hutchinson and Barry Furr at ICI Pharmaceuticals achieved the development of the depot preparation[1] for goserelin in 1981. Yasuaki Ogawa and his colleagues at Takeda developed the equivalent for leuprorelin in 1984. Leuprorelin was first marketed with a preparation for daily injection in the United States in 1985; then its depot preparation was launched in the US in 1989 and in Japan in 1992. Goserelin was marketed as its depot preparation from the start. It was launched first in the UK in 1987, then in the US in 1990 and in Japan in 1991.

Table 6.1: Major events related to the discovery and development of
LHRH analogues

Year	Leuprorelin (Takeda=Abbott)	Goserelin (ICI)
1960	Discovery of LRF (LHRH)	
mid-1960s	Basic research starts (Abbott)	Basic research starts
1971	Research starts (Takeda)	
	Discovery of LHRH structure	
1972	TAP-31 discovered	
1973	Discovery of leuprorelin	
1975-6	Discovery of paradoxical effects	
1976		Discovery of goserelin
1979		Depot preparation research starts
1981	Depot preparation research starts	Depot preparation developed
1984	Depot preparation developed	
1985	Launch in the US (daily injection)	
1987		Launch in the UK
1989	Launch in the US (depot preparation)	
1990		Launch in the US
1991		Launch in Japan
1992	Launch in Japan	

6.2 DISCOVERY OF LHRH

The idea that the brain has an influence on the reproductive system via the pituitary gland was suggested in the 1930s. Since then, a number of scientists have done anatomical and physiological studies on the cerebral regulation of hormone secretion from the pituitary gland (Harris *et al.* 1966; Harris 1972; Schally *et al.* 1968; Burgus and Guillemin 1970). Geoffrey Harris in England was one of the leading researchers in this area. In 1947, he and J.D. Green proposed that this regulatory system worked by means of a humoral relay through the tiny vessels that link the hypothalamus in the brain with the pituitary gland (Green and Harris 1947). This idea was not immediately accepted (Wade 1978, p. 210). For example, Thomson and Zuckerman (1953) claimed that the vessels that Harris had reported did not

form the pathway of chemical transmitters. Harris argued back that
Zuckerman's experiment had flaws (Harris 1955, pp. 87–8). However, to
convince others of his idea, Harris had to find the substance which was
secreted from the hypothalamus and stimulated the release of hormones such
as luteinizing hormone (LH). Not only Harris but also some other
researchers in the world, including Samuel McCann, Roger Guillemin and
Andrew Schally in the United States, addressed this problem (Harris *et al.*
1966; Harris 1972; Schally *et al.* 1968; Burgus and Guillemin 1970; Wade
1978, pp. 210–11).

In 1960, McCann's research team in Pennsylvania reported that extracts
of a part of the hypothalamus stimulated the secretion of LH from the
pituitary gland in rats. They suggested the existence of an LH-releasing
factor in the hypothalamus (McCann *et al.* 1960; McCann 1962). At about
the same time, Harris's team independently found that extracts of a part of
the hypothalamus caused ovulation when infused into the pituitary gland in
rabbits. They concluded that the hypothalamus contained a specific
substance which stimulated the release of the gonadotrophic hormone such
as LH (Campbell *et al.* 1961; Harris *et al.* 1966, p. 268). Guillemin's team
confirmed these results in 1961 by using extracts of rat and sheep
hypothalamus (Guillemin 1964; Harris *et al.* 1966, p. 268). It was
speculated that the LH-releasing factor was polypeptide from its properties
as early as 1962 (McCann 1962; Guillemin 1964).

There was keen competition between McCann, Harris, Guillemin,
Schally and Karl Folkers for the isolation and molecular characterization of
the LH-releasing factor (Wade 1978, pp. 302–3, 1981, pp. 183–226). In
particular, Guillemin and Schally concentrated their efforts on obtaining the
molecular structure of the LH-releasing factor, whereas Harris and McCann
also paid attention to physiological aspects of the substance (Wade 1978, p.
358; Harris and Naftolin 1970; Latour and Woolgar 1986, pp. 117–19).
Guillemin and Schally had already engaged in severe competition for the
structure of another hypothalamic hormone called thyrotropin-releasing
factor (TRF; or thyrotropin-releasing hormone, TRH) from around 1962 to
1969, before they began to pour their full energy into the investigation of the
structure of the LH-releasing factor[2] (Latour and Woolgar 1986, pp. 105–50;
Wade 1978; Guillemin 1978; Schally 1978). In the previous competition
over TRF(H), Guillemin and Schally redefined the name of the game in
discovery of hypothalamic hormones. Discovery of a hormone was redefined
as the identification of its molecular structure by using methods acceptable
to peer scientists. To find a substance having an activity or to speculate on
its molecular structure without recognized methods became insufficient to
constitute the discovery of a hormone. This new rule was essential to the
practical use of these hormones in therapy, because the natural supply of

these hormones was very limited (only 250 micrograms of LH-releasing factor from 160,000 pig hypothalami[3]), so they had to be synthesized. What was also important was that this new definition of discovery changed the financial requirement for participating in the competition for discovery. It became necessary for each research team to buy expensive, sophisticated analytical equipment and obtain millions of animal hypothalami in order to compete effectively (Latour and Woolgar 1986, pp. 118–24, 134–43). It should be noted that it was unclear at that time whether the substance really existed or not, whether it was a polypeptide or not, and whether it was an unknown substance or not (ibid., pp. 116–17). Therefore, it was very risky to invest huge amounts of money into this competition to find the molecular structure. Probably, the uncertainty about the search for the structure of LHRH was considerably reduced after the identification of the structure of TRF(H), but this did not happen until 1969. Fortunately for Guillemin and Schally, both of them managed to obtain huge financial support from organizations such as the National Institutes of Health or the Veterans Administration, although this support considerably increased the pressure on them to hasten the research (Wade 1978, p. 221, 1981, p. 197; Latour and Woolgar 1986, p. 139). Because of these factors, Guillemin's and Schally's groups managed to take the lead in the competition, even though they began to concentrate on LHRH as late as 1969. Of course, they and their collaborators were creative and skilful researchers. However, Guillemin and Schally might not have overtaken the other groups without a combination of factors: the more demanding definition of hormone identification and characterization they had established; their research priority; their risk-taking attitude to the high uncertainty in the area; and their financial resources (Wade 1981, pp. 199, 220–4).

In 1971, Schally's team finally reported the molecular structure of the LH-releasing factor in pigs. Two Japanese chemists, Hisayuki Matsuo and Yoshihiko Baba, and a Japanese physiologist, Akira Arimura, crucially contributed to the discovery (ibid., pp. 204–14). It was a decapeptide, that is, it consisted of ten amino acids (Figure 6.1(a)) (Matsuo *et al.* 1971b). LHRH, which had been Schally's terminology (Schally *et al.* 1968), became widely accepted as the name of the substance. Soon after that, Guillemin's team confirmed an identical structure of LHRH in sheep (Burgus *et al.* 1972; Amoss *et al.* 1971). It is reported that shortage of the LH-releasing factor delayed Roger Burgus, Guillemin's chemist collaborator, in his efforts to determine the structure of the substance (Wade 1978, p. 302). Harris's team was also said to be close to discovering the structure at that time (Harris 1972, p. xiv; Gregory 1971, p. 21; Furr interview[4]). It was not only analytical chemistry but also synthetic chemistry that contributed to the discovery of the structure of LHRH. Synthesizing the replica of a speculated substance and then examining its biological activities was a major tool to reveal or confirm the molecular structure of the substance (Latour and Woolgar 1986, p. 144; Wade 1981, p. 212). Schally's group succeeded in the synthesis of LHRH, too, in 1971 (Matsuo *et al.* 1971a; Schally *et al.* 1971b). The research team of Karl Folkers, who was a former collaborator with Schally in his TRH project, also succeeded in synthesizing LHRH and confirming its biological activity, soon after Schally's announcement of the LHRH structure (Sievertsson *et al.* 1971).

(a) LHRH

pGly – His –Trp – Ser –Tyr – Gly – Leu – Arg – Pro – Gly – NH$_2$
   1   2   3   4   5   6   7   8   9   10

(b) TAP-031

pGly – His –Trp – Ser –Tyr – Gly – Leu – Arg – Pro – NHCH$_2$CH$_3$
   1   2   3   4   5   6   7   8   9   10

(c) Leuprorelin

pGly – His –Trp – Ser –Tyr – D-Leu – Leu – Arg – Pro – NHCH$_2$CH$_3$
   1   2   3   4   5   6   7   8   9   10

(d) Triprorelin

pGly – His –Trp – Ser –Tyr – D-Trp – Leu – Arg – Pro – Gly – NH$_2$
   1   2   3   4   5   6   7   8   9   10

(e) Goserelin

pGly – His –Trp – Ser –Tyr – D-Ser(Bu^t) – Leu – Arg – Pro – azaGly – NH$_2$
   1   2   3   4   5   6   7   8   9   10

(f) Buserelin

pGly – His –Trp – Ser –Tyr – D-Ser(Bu^t)– Leu – Arg – Pro – NHCH$_2$CH$_3$
   1   2   3   4   5   6   7   8   9   10

Note: The number under each amino acid indicates the position. Underlines indicate replacement.

Figure 6.1: LHRH and its analogues discussed in Chapter 6

Because LHRH was supposed to regulate the reproductive system, several pharmaceutical companies recognized its medical and commercial potential in the early stage of the research on LHRH. Two companies were involved in the discovery of LHRH: in England, ICI's Pharmaceuticals Division was in collaboration with Harris (Harris 1972, pp. xii–xiv; Gregory 1971); in the

United States, Wilfrid White at Abbott Laboratories collaborated with Schally in research on both follicle stimulating hormone-releasing hormone (FSH-RH) and LHRH[5] (Schally *et al.* 1968, pp. 537–8, 548–50, 1971a). In addition, researchers at Hoechst in Germany independently succeeded in synthesizing LHRH only three months after the first announcement of its structure (Geiger *et al.* 1971).

6.3. SYNTHETIC LHRH ANALOGUES: AN OVERVIEW

Even before the structure of LHRH was announced, analogues as well as LHRH itself began to be synthesized and examined by various research groups, including those involved in the competition for the structure of LHRH, in order to confirm the structure (Monahan *et al.* 1972; Chang *et al.* 1972; Schally *et al.* 1972; Geiger *et al.* 1972; Fujino *et al.* 1972a; Yanaihara *et al.* 1972). The early purpose of the synthesis of LHRH analogues was to understand the structure–activity relationship for the hormone and to create a synthetic antagonist of LH release (Schally *et al.* 1972, p. 366; Vale *et al.* 1972, p. 933; Monahan *et al.* 1973, pp. 4616, 4619), rather than to find a more potent agonist. This was because antagonists of LH release were thought to be useful for contraception, whereas LHRH itself could be used as a pro-fertility drug (Besser and Mortimer 1974, p. 178). However, when several analogues were found to be more potent than LHRH in these efforts, their clinical potential as pro-fertility agents began to attract more attention.

In 1972, Masahiko Fujino at the Central Research Division of Takeda Chemical Industries found that an analogue with modification at position 10 of the LHRH molecule (Figure 6.1(b)) was five times more potent than LHRH (Fujino *et al.* 1972b). In the next year, Michael Monahan and his colleagues at the Salk Institute, where Guillemin was leading the research, reported that several analogues with modification with D-amino acids (optical isomers) at position 6 had several times higher potency than LHRH (Monahan *et al.* 1973). In 1974, Fujino and his colleagues found that several analogues with modification at both position 6 and position 10 of the molecule were up to about a hundred times as potent as the original substance. One of these was leuprorelin (Figure 6.1(c)), the story of which we examine in detail in the following section (Fujino *et al.* 1974a, 1974b; Rippel *et al.* 1975). Schally's group reported similar results around the same time (Coy *et al.* 1974; Vilchez-Martinez *et al.* 1974). Coy and Schally (1978) estimated that about 700 analogues of LHRH had been synthesized by 1978; among them were four analogues marketed later: leuprorelin synthesized and developed by an alliance of Takeda and Abbott; triptorelin by Schally's group (Coy *et al.* 1975); goserelin by ICI (Dutta *et al.* 1978a);

and buserelin by Hoechst (Sandow *et al.* 1978) (Figure 6.1(d–f)). All but triptorelin are analogues modified at both position 6 and position 10 of the LHRH molecule.

These highly active analogues of LHRH, so-called 'super-active' agonists, were at first thought to be useful for stimulating fertility. However, when these compounds (including synthetic LHRH) were tested in laboratories and hospitals in the mid-1970s, it was found that they had a paradoxical effect: their repeated administration did not stimulate but eventually inhibited reproductive function in animals and humans (Oshima *et al.* 1975; Corbin and Beattie 1975; Banik and Givner 1975; Rippel and Johnson 1976; Happ *et al.* 1978). It was speculated that this was due to the phenomenon of 'desensitization' or 'down-regulation' of the physiological processes responsible for LHRH release (Hsueh *et al.* 1977; Belchetz *et al.* 1978; Rivier *et al.* 1978, p. 2303; Sandow 1983, pp. 571–5; Furr and Woodburn 1988, p. 535). This discovery of the paradoxical effect led researchers to alternative applications, including: treatment for breast cancer (Johnson *et al.* 1976), contraception (Beattie and Corbin 1977), treatment for prostate cancer (Redding and Schally 1981; Warner *et al.* 1981), treatment for idiopathic precocious puberty (Crowley *et al.* 1981), treatment for endometriosis (Meldrum *et al.* 1982), treatment for uterine fibroids (Filicori *et al.* 1983) and some other applications (Corbin 1982; Sandow 1983; Waxman 1984; Cutler *et al.* 1985; Furr and Woodburn 1988). These applications became much more important than the short-term pro-fertility use, which had originally been regarded as the main application. It should be noted that the development of these various applications was simultaneously conducted by different research groups with different analogues. We examine the development of applications of two analogues, leuprorelin and goserelin, in detail in the following sections. However, other analogues also contributed to the development of their various clinical applications. These include: buserelin (Jacobi and Wenderoth 1982; Faure *et al.* 1982; Waxman *et al.* 1983a, b: treatment for prostate cancer; Klijn and de Jong 1982: treatment for breast cancer; Lemay and Quesnel 1982: treatment for endometriosis; Labrie *et al.* 1984: combination therapy of prostate cancer with antiandrogens; Maheux *et al.* 1984: treatment for fibroids); triptorelin (Redding and Schally 1981; Tolis *et al.* 1982: treatment for prostate cancer; Redding and Schally 1983: treatment for breast cancer); and D-Trp^6- Pro^9-NEt-LHRH synthesized and developed by the Salk Institute (Rivier *et al.* 1978: contraception; Crowley *et al.* 1981: treatment for idiopathic precocious puberty; Meldrum *et al.* 1982: treatment for endometriosis; Filicori *et al.* 1983: treatment for fibroids; Comite *et al.* 1986: treatment for central precocious puberty).

Another important aspect in the development of LHRH analogues was the development of novel preparations (or formulations). Although 'super-active' LHRH analogues were longer acting than LHRH itself, it was necessary to give them daily in order to obtain the long-term paradoxical effect. Oral administration did not produce a clinically effective activity; therefore, daily injection was the first preparation of leuprorelin which was approved by the Food and Drug Administration in the US. Because of the lack of convenience of this preparation, in particular in countries where self-injection was not generally allowed, various other preparations were developed. The second preparation was a nasal spray preparation developed by Hoechst for buserelin. As the third preparation, ICI developed a biodegradable, sustained-release preparation in the early 1980s, which is described in detail in section 6.5 (Furr and Woodburn 1988, p. 536). The fourth preparation was one using biodegradable injectable microcapsules, adopted by Syntex for their LHRH analogue called nafarelin (Sanders *et al.* 1984), Schally's group for triptorelin (Reddings *et al.* 1984) and Takeda for leuprorelin (Ogawa *et al.* 1989). These biodegradable preparations were different from each other in composition and/or in production methods. All of these new preparations contributed greatly to the diffusion of these medicines. It should be noted that they were also developed by various research groups. However, due to limitation of space, in the following sections we look closely only at the processes of discovery, development of application and development of preparation in two highly successful LHRH analogues, leuprorelin and goserelin.

6.4 LEUPRORELIN

Leuprorelin (leuprolide in the US) is the first marketed LHRH analogue, discovered and developed by the alliance of Takeda Chemical Industries in Japan and Abbott Laboratories in the US. It was synthesized by a research team led by Masahiko Fujino at Takeda. Fujino, around 1965, studied the synthesis of peptides under D.N. Ward, one of Guillemin's co-workers, at the University of Texas. Fujino witnessed the keen competition between Guillemin and Schally over TRH there and was interested in hypothalamic hormones such as TRH and LHRH. He described the situation:

At that time, it was still very hard to synthesize peptides. If you had been able then to combine five amino acids, you would have been able to get a PhD. ... It was suggested to me [by a Japanese professor] that I do characterization and synthesis of TRF at Texas, but when I went there, it hadn't been isolated yet. So I couldn't do that. Instead, I worked on LH, luteinizing hormone, there. ...

> [Guillemin, Schally and McCann] were really fighting each other. ... I saw them spending enormous amounts of money. I saw a ceiling of the laboratory removed to set up huge columns for chromatography for the isolation [of the hypothalamic hormones]. I saw a number of excellent researchers really seriously working on the substances, and thought that something unusual must be going on. I felt that something extraordinary would happen when the substances were identified. I was really impressed. (Fujino interview[6])

After Fujino came back to Japan, he was involved in research on the synthesis of adrenocorticotrophic hormone (ACTH) and gastrin derivatives for a while (Fujino interview; Takeda 1983, p. 753). When the isolation and characterization of TRH was announced in 1969, he started research on the synthesis of TRH, because he had become interested in it as a result of his stay in Texas. The objective was to find a simple and economical way of synthesizing TRH. His team succeeded in synthesizing it on a large scale in 1974, and it was marketed in 1978 (Fujino 1992, p. 2; Fujino interview; Takeda 1983, pp. 743, 1006–7). This experience gave Fujino confidence in peptide research. He said:

> What I thought first was that [TRH] would become a drug if I could produce it at the level of kilograms. Because the substance was very active, we didn't need more. At that time, you could announce that you had made it if you could make only a few milligrams of it. ... So, when I succeeded in making TRH in kilograms, my confidence grew. I was convinced that I could make drugs from peptides. (Interview)

Meanwhile, in October 1970 Abbott proposed to Takeda that they collaborate in research on hypothalamic hormones. Abbott had been particularly interested in LHRH and its analogues. As mentioned above, the company had helped Schally's group to identify the molecular structure of LHRH. The company chose Takeda as its partner because Abbott's research staff, including Wilfred White, knew that Fujino and his colleagues at Takeda did good work on the synthesis of peptides; Fujino also knew White's work in the area. Takeda accepted the proposal and they made a research collaboration contract in August 1971. Shortly before that, the molecular structure of LHRH had been announced. The two companies at first agreed that Takeda would do the synthesis of LHRH analogues and Abbott would do biological tests of them. Although Takeda had excellent ability in synthetic chemistry, they did not have the *in vitro* assay for the hormone. However, each company learned the other's skill and later began to do both synthesis and biological tests. They exchanged information and material, but otherwise worked quite independently (Takeda 1983, p. 743; Fujino 1992, p. 3; Fujino interview; Kuwashima 1996, p. 119; Arnold *et al.* 1974).

Fujino's team started the synthesis of LHRH analogues around the end of 1971. The initial objective was to get a fertility stimulant. The methods they had developed for the synthesis of TRH were partly applied to this work and made it efficient. At first, replacement of every position of amino acid was tried (Fujino *et al.* 1972a, 1992, p. 4). However, the results were disappointing: all the early analogues were much less potent than LHRH. Then they tried the replacement of glycineamide (Gly-NH$_2$) at position 10 with various alkylamines, which have a similar size to glycineamide. Fujino focused on position 10 because it was speculated that an enzyme destroyed the LHRH molecule at that position. Fortunately for him, the method his team was using for the synthesis, the liquid-phase method, was suitable for this replacement, whereas the more commonly used solid-phase method was not (Fujino interview). Fujino had chosen the liquid-phase method because he had regarded it as better for producing a large quantity of peptide fragments, though there had been different opinions about the value of these methods at that time (Fujino personal communication, August 2000). Among them, an analogue (TAP-031), which was replaced by ethylamide, showed high potency, five times greater than LHRH in the ovulation-inducing assay (Fujino 1992, pp. 4–5; Fujino *et al.* 1972b, 1973a, 1973b; Rippel *et al.* 1973). This was the most potent LHRH analogue at that time and indicated to others that the replacement at position 10 was effective in enhancing the potency of LHRH analogues. TAP-031 was marketed later as a fertility stimulant for cattle, but failed to be a drug for humans because its administration for this purpose, the frequent injection, was not practicable (Fujino 1992, p. 5; Fujino interview; Takeda 1983, pp. 1035–6).

Fujino and his colleagues then tried replacement of amino acids at other positions, while keeping the modification of position 10. Fujino noticed glycine at position 6. He explained the reason:

> I noticed it because only glycine has no side chain. So, I thought that this was probably essential for the molecule to be bent. ... When we replaced it with another amino acid, the activity disappeared. I thought this was due to the bend of the molecule. So, I tried D-amino acids rather than ordinary L-amino acids to change the bend at position 6. Then, the activity remarkably increased. I've got it, I thought. (Interview)

Two episodes showing the serendipitous aspect of this discovery were also reported. First, when a young researcher was told by Fujino to link an ethylamide to position 10, he did it wrongly to position 9, but the resultant peptide showed a high potency. This made Fujino notice the replacement of position 10. Second, another young researcher simply replaced an amino acid at position 6 with another, and the resultant LHRH analogue showed astonishing activity. However, other skilled researchers failed to reproduce the experiment. Fujino did not ignore this occurrence: he made the researcher check every amino acid he had used. Then, it was found that the amino acid used at position 6 was not an L-amino acid but a racemic amino acid, which is a mixture of two optical isomers, an L-amino acid and its D counterpart. A racemic amino acid is the crude product of amino acid synthesis. The young researcher had used the crude synthetic amino acid, which should have been divided into the two isomers. However, this event turned Fujino's attention to the bend at position 6 (Ogawa and Fujino 1994, pp. 176–7).

As mentioned in section 6.3, Monahan at the Salk Institute found independently that the replacement of glycine at position 6 with a D-amino acid produced a several times more potent LHRH analogue (Monahan *et al.* 1973). However, when Fujino and his colleague combined the replacement at position 6 with the replacement at position 10, they obtained 50 to 80 times more potent analogues in ovulation-inducing activity in rats (Fujino *et al.* 1974a, 1974b; Fujino 1992, pp. 5–6). The activity of these analogues was not so remarkable *in vitro*: at most only several times more potent. Fujino explained the difference between *in vivo* and *in vitro*:

> You cannot know how strong the activity is, *in vitro*. You can know only whether the activity is strong. *In vitro*, the activity did not appear so strong. But in animals, it showed an outstanding activity. This is because its action lasted [in animals]. ... *In vitro*, you measure only one release. So, you cannot know [its whole activity]. (Interview)

Among the several analogues substituted at position 6 and position 10, the most potent one, [D-Leu^6, des-Gly-NH$_2$^{10}, Pro-ethylamide^9]-LHRH (TAP-144, leuprorelin), was chosen for the clinical development, aiming at the induction of ovulation in infertile women (Fujino *et al.* 1974b; Rippel *et al.* 1975; Fujino 1992, p. 6).[7] In the end, they synthesized about 150 LHRH analogues to obtain this one (Fujino 1992, p. 4).

However, in the process of pre-clinical studies, researchers at Abbott noticed the paradoxical effect of 'super-active' agonists, mentioned in section 6.3. When they gave a large dose of leuprorelin continuously to rats to examine its long-term toxicity, they found that it inhibited ovarian and uterine growth and that it caused atrophy of some sex organs such as the uterus and the epididymis (Rippel and Johnson 1976; Fujino interview). Several similar observations were reported outside the company at the time (Oshima *et al.* 1975; Corbin and Beattie 1975; Banik and Givner 1975). Knowing that the drug acted as if it were an antagonist in the long term, they began to look for alternative applications such as the treatment of sex hormone-related cancer. It was still possible to develop the drug as an ovulation-inducing drug. However, from the point of view of clinical usefulness and profitability, the anti-cancer application became the priority (Kuwashima 1996, p. 121). It had been known that the growth of breast cancer and of prostate cancer were dependent on the level of sex hormones in the blood (for example, Jensen *et al.* 1971; McGuire *et al.* 1974: on breast cancer; Huggins *et al.* 1941; Byar 1973: on prostate cancer). Because the drug could ultimately reduce the level, the researchers thought to use it for the treatment of breast cancer first. They confirmed that the drug led to mammary tumour regression in rats (Johnson *et al.* 1976). However, Fujino pointed out uncertainty in this area:

> It was not clear. At that time, it was said that too much steroid [sex] hormone caused breast cancer, but it didn't show up when measured. Also, patients with prostate cancer weren't necessarily rich in the male hormone. Anyway we tried. When we tried [leuprorelin], it surely worked in animals. ... So, there must be a relationship [between sex hormones and cancer]. But this isn't very clear even now, though it has become somewhat clearer after the advent of the inhibitory 'super-agonists'. (Interview)

The clinical trials of leuprorelin for the treatment of breast cancer failed to show very good results (Harvey *et al.* 1981). Fujino claimed that this was due to contextual reasons rather than to the efficacy of the drug itself:[8]

> Because surgical treatment was known to be quite effective in breast cancer, the drug was only able to be tested in patients with severe cancer who could not be treated by other means. It was because no one knew whether the drug was really effective in advance. No early-stage patient was willing to be given such a drug. I thought it was natural that the drug failed to show efficacy because it was given to the patients for whom no drug would work. (Interview)

Another target was prostate cancer, which was very common in the US and in European countries. There was no very effective treatment for this cancer in the advanced stage. Surgical castration was effective but often caused psychological trauma. Oestrogen therapy was also effective but with considerable side effects (Gittes 1991, pp. 241–2). Therefore, the potential market seemed to be promising. The development of leuprorelin for this use was first conducted by TAP Pharmaceuticals, a joint venture between Takeda and Abbott, in the US, where there were a large number of patients with the disease (Takeda 1983, p. 743; Fujino 1992, p. 8; Kuwashima 1996, p. 122). Kunio Takeda, then senior vice president of TAP Pharmaceuticals and a member of the Takeda family, championed the development of the drug (Fujino interview). The drug for this application was then tested in animals (Warner *et al.* 1981) and in patients (for example, Warner *et al.* 1982; Vance and Smith 1984; Santen *et al.* 1984a, 1984b; Smith *et al.* 1985). Comparative clinical trials with surgical castration or oestrogen therapy were also conducted (Warner *et al.* 1983; Leuprolide Study Group 1984; Winfield and Trachtenberg 1984). The drug went through clinical trials successfully and obtained approval for the treatment of prostate cancer from the FDA in the US in 1985. It was marketed there under the trade name Lupron®. As mentioned in section 6.3, the drug was at first given by daily injection, presupposing self-injection (Fujino 1992, p. 8).

However, the development of leuprorelin in Japan was slower. First, there were fewer patients with prostate cancer (Fujino interview). Second, because self-injection was not usually permitted in Japan, daily injection was difficult in practice there (Yamanaka *et al.* 1984, p. 558; Fujino interview). Third, as a result of these, there was a strong suspicion about marketability of the drug in Japan amongst the management and the marketing division of Takada. Fujino described the situation:

> In Japan, prostate cancer was not common at all. So, nobody thought of [leuprorelin] seriously. They said, 'This would not sell even 200 million yen at best.' Only Konishi-san [the then president of the company] stood by us, saying that this should be developed in Japan as well. But the others disregarded the drug, which is now the best selling drug in Takeda. ... I think if Konishi-san had not supported it, it might have been abandoned. So, its development in Japan was late. ... In Japan, self-injection wasn't permitted except insulin. So, they said, 'Daily injection can't sell in Japan. Who wants to go to the doctor everyday?' (Interview)

In this situation, researchers at Takeda sought a more convenient preparation. In the middle to late 1970s, Yasuaki Ogawa and his colleagues at the Pharmaceutics Laboratories of Takeda tried several preparations of leuprorelin such as a nasal spray, but failed to obtain stable absorption. Then, they turned back to injection, but this time, they thought of a slow-release preparation with the drug in biodegradable microcapsules, so that the patient would need only one injection a month, for example. Since the mid-1970s, a number of studies on using biodegradable materials for making slow-release preparations had been reported. However, most previous applications were for steroids, which were insoluble in water, and with tiny sticks of biodegradable polymer rather than microcapsules. Therefore, it was a difficult challenge for them to find out how to enclose the hydrophilic peptide in particles of hydrophobic biodegradable polymer and achieve an even distribution. They chose a co-polymer of lactic acids and glycolic acids (PLGA) as the biodegradable material. Around 1975, Ogawa had heard of this material from Tai Matsuzawa, who was a senior researcher at the Pharmaceutics Laboratories and was in the US at that time (Ogawa interview[9]). Matsuzawa, one of the earliest experts in biological pharmaceutics in Japan, was sending new concepts and information related to the area, including bio-availability (BA) and drug delivery systems

(DDS), from the United State to Japan; PLGA was part of that. This material was then well known as being biodegradable and was used in the United States, but the ratio of the mixture varied and needed optimization (Matsuzawa interview[10]).

The first task for Ogawa's team was to obtain the polymer. This was not easy, as Ogawa detailed:

> I asked various chemical companies in Japan for the polymer, but they said they didn't know about such material and didn't produce it. Then, I wrote to the American company that had published a book about the material, asking for it. They said they could supply it, but the price was $10,000 per 100 grams of the polymer. ... That was too expensive. So we gave up the idea of buying it and decided to make it, based on the patents. Because our company had a polymer group in the chemicals division, I went there first and asked. The man I asked was one of my peers employed in the same year and gave me an OK. However, when the plan went up to a higher rank, another man gave me a ring, asking, 'How much do you want?' When I said, 'Ten or twenty kilograms at most in a year,' he said, 'You should know that you need at least a ton if you want to order a chemical product. We can't do business on such a small scale. I don't know what your friend said, but we can't help you.'
>
> Then, we tried to synthesize the polymer by ourselves. But it was impossible for us to make it, referring only to the patents. So, there was nothing left for us but to look for a chemical company who could make the polymer for us. ... Fortunately, Wako Pure Chemical Industries in Osaka, which was producing cellulose polymers for pharmaceutical uses, took it seriously and sent a researcher to our laboratories. The researcher happened to be a two year junior of mine in the same course at the same university. ... The company agreed to synthesize the polymer for us, and we were able to start the research at last. That was in 1980 or 1981. (Interview)

Ogawa's team at Takeda and researchers at Wako made a joint effort to obtain a suitable polymer for the purpose. First, they developed a method of polymerization without using a heavy metal catalyst, because they were unable to get the material necessary for the conventional method, which uses a heavy metal catalyst. At the same time, the new method was better than the conventional one because the former was free from contamination by the heavy metal. Next, they tried to optimize the average molecular weight and the ratio of the mixture of lactic acid and glycolic acid. They synthesized seven or eight polymers with different ratios of mixture and examined their biodegrading and drug-releasing properties. The best ratio of lactic acid/glycolic acid for a month-long release was found to be 75/25. This work was completed in 1984 (Ogawa and Toguchi 1991, p. 22; Ogawa 1999).

In parallel with the development of the polymer, Ogawa and his colleagues also developed the method for producing microcapsules. First, they tried the phase separation method, which Syntex patented for a LHRH analogue preparation in 1982. However, they did not have a powerful mixer and, when they tried it with their less powerful one, they could not obtain proper microcapsules. Ogawa, an expert in emulsion research, next tried the in-water drying method, which produced microcapsules from a threefold water/oil/water emulsion of the drug. This method produced good microcapsules though the rate of capture of the drug was only 5 per cent. By differentiating the viscosity of the inside water solution including the drug and the outside water solution and by doing the process at a very low temperature, they managed to improve the rate of capture up to more than 95 per cent by the end of 1984. Again luckily for them, this method was later found to be more suitable for mass production than the phase separation method used by Syntex and Schally's group, because it did not need an organic solvent, which was potentially dangerous and difficult to remove completely from the product (Ogawa and Toguchi 1991, pp. 20–1, 23; Ogawa interview; Ogawa *et al.* 1989).

The sustained-release preparations, or the depot preparations, of LHRH analogues, like the one developed by Ogawa's team, were also being developed around the same time by other groups, including ICI, Syntex and Schally's group, all keenly competing with each other. All the groups adopted PLGA as the matrix material and all but the ICI group adopted microcapsules as the form (Sanders *et al.* 1984; Redding *et al.* 1984; Hutchinson and Furr 1985). Takeda was not always the front-runner. Ogawa wrote:

> I have experienced two serious shocks, which nearly made me quit the work. The first shock was the encounter with the Syntex patent. ... Their idea was the same as ours, and we were far behind. We just managed to produce microcapsules on a small scale. Although I was deeply disappointed, my boss encouraged me to catch up with them before commercialization. The second one was when I saw Dr Sanders' paper in the *Journal of Pharmaceutical Sciences* and Professor Schally's in *Proceedings of the National Academy of Sciences* in October 1984. I supposed, at first, that they were in clinical trials, and my shock then was even bigger than the first one. However, when I collected more information about them, I found that both were using the same method, which was originally created by Southern Research Institute, and neither had yet been tried clinically. I was convinced that I could catch up with them before commercialization because I knew that their method had problems. (Ogawa and Toguchi 1991, p. 23: translated by the author.)

By using a different method, Ogawa's group was able to avoid existing patents and file their own (Japanese Patent *Tokkai* 62-201816).

The next problem that Ogawa's team faced was to obtain the support of other divisions and the management of the company. Because the preparation was unfamiliar to everyone, there was a strong doubt within the organization about whether the regulator and doctors would accept it. Ogawa put it:

> When I proposed this, 99 per cent of people in the development division looked suspicious. 'What price are you proposing to the government?' 'How can doctors control the treatment?' 'Do you think doctors will be willing to leave their patients alone for a month?' Most opinions were like that. Only one, the then director of the development division, Dr Takahashi, supported us. Without him, this project might have been discarded. More accurately, only Dr Takahashi and Mr Konishi, who was then president, said that this was very interesting. Of course, people in the research division, including Dr Morita, then head of the division, supported us. But the rest in our company said that it would be hard to market such a drug. (Interview)

In 1984, the clinical development of the depot preparation managed to become a project, and was given a codename TAP-144-SR. At the beginning, its priority was still very low. However, when the company asked its allied overseas companies in the US and Europe which of its projects they found most interesting, all answers included TAP-144-SR. TAP Pharmaceuticals, which was about to launch the daily injection preparation of leuprorelin, promptly announced that they would also develop the depot preparation in the US. Soon after that, European partners also decided to develop it in European countries. This movement enhanced the priority of its development in Japan (Ogawa interview; Ogawa 1999).

In 1985, the depot preparation proceeded to clinical trials in Japan. However, there was another difficulty there. Kouji Sonoi, a manager at the Pharmaceutical Development Division of Takeda, said: 'Doctors in Japan at first regarded the drug as out of the question. ... They were unfamiliar with the concept of a one-month long-acting drug' (interview). Ogawa added: 'It was also difficult to make the protocol for the clinical trials, because the drug was an unprecedented one.' The protocol of clinical trials is usually made through discussion with the manufacturer of a new drug and doctors who conduct its trials. However, in the case of leuprorelin, doctors had no experience in clinical trials of this kind of drug. Here, it was fortunate for Takeda that the drug had already been marketed in the US with the preparation for daily injection, and that the clinical trials of its depot preparation also were more advanced in the US than in Japan. The experience in the US helped in the making of the protocol and reduced the anxiety of doctors about its efficacy and safety (Ogawa and Sonoi interview). The efficacy and the safety of the depot preparation were shown in clinical trials in various countries (for example, Sharifi *et al.* 1990; O'Brien and Hibberd 1990; Giraud 1990; Akaza *et al.* 1990; Bischoff and German Leuprorelin Study Group 1990; Niijima *et al.* 1990; Rizzo *et al.* 1990; Aso *et al.* 1991).

There was a problem in the manufacturing of the drug, too: how to ensure it was germ-free. This was essential in order to pass the inspection of the regulators. Because the drug was a peptide and contained in the delicate microcapsules, the easiest way, heating, was not available. Therefore, Takeda's engineers decided to make all the production processes germ-free, and this involved a great deal of trouble and effort. They achieved it by demonstrating that every element such as equipment and material was germ-free. It is reported that more than 1,000 documents were produced to validate the germ-freeness of each element of the production process (Toguchi *et al.* 1991, p. 407; Ogawa and Fujino 1994, p. 189; Ogawa interview).

The depot preparation of leuprorelin was first marketed in the US, France and Italy in 1989; the launch in Germany and the UK followed. In 1992, it was launched in Japan as Leuplin® (Ogawa 1999; Ogawa and Fujino 1994, p. 190). Meanwhile, other applications, such as the treatment for endometriosis, precocious puberty and uterine fibroids, were also clinically studied (see, for example, Dlugi *et al.* 1990; Lee *et al.* 1989; Parker and Lee 1989; Friedman *et al.* 1991). These were approved by regulators later (Ogawa 1999; Takeda internal documents). The sales of leuprorelin worldwide in 1994 were $425 million (Rickwood and Southworth 1995, p. 119).

The success of the depot preparation of leuprorelin brought organizational power to pharmaceutics researchers, the researchers working on pharmaceutical systems such as preparation and dosage forms, in Takeda. Ogawa explained:

> Before, pharmaceutics researchers were regarded as only blenders. Preparation was not necessarily regarded as a research area in the research division. [Since the success of the depot preparation] everyone has recognized that preparation is a research area. The company founded the DDS Research Laboratories. They also built a new building for the Pharmaceutics Laboratories. (Interview)

The drug also enhanced the significance of pharmaceutics amongst academics and bureaucrats in Japan. Ogawa said:

> I think that this was a major cause, though not the only cause, which made the concept of drug delivery system important in the Japanese society of pharmaceutical sciences. Leuplin is now ... recognized by academics as textbook stuff. Another thing is that the Ministry of Health and Welfare has recognized these products, maybe because [Leuplin] worked very well. They gave us quite a reasonable price for the drug. (Interview)

Sonoi added that the depot preparation of leuprorelin by injection contributed to establishing an advantageous differentiation of the product from the most significant rival product, goserelin, which adopted a different form of depot preparation and was marketed a little earlier than the leuprorelin depot preparation (Sonoi interview).

6.5 GOSERELIN

The Pharmaceuticals Division of Imperial Chemical Industries (ICI) had a research tradition in sex hormone-related medicines for humans and animals (Sneader 1985, pp. 198–9; Furr interview). Tamoxifen citrate (Nolvadex®) was one of the products from this tradition. The drug, discovered by Arthur Walpole and his colleagues, was an effective anti-oestrogen and marketed for the treatment of breast cancer in 1973 (Sneader 1985, p. 199; Kennedy 1993, pp. 133–4, 175). Walpole also collaborated with Geoffrey Harris at Oxford on research on LHRH from 1966 (Furr 1991; see section 6.2). Barry Furr, one of the key researchers who discovered goserelin, described their position in the area at that time:

> ICI Pharmaceuticals worked with Harris, trying to isolate that factor. And at the time that Schally and Guillemin described their deca-peptide, ICI had three possible structures for LHRH. One of which was the same, two of which were different. So we were very close behind Schally and Guillemin. And this work was done by Arthur Walpole, Geoffrey Harris and an outstanding peptide/protein chemist called Harry Gregory. (Interview)

Furr succeeded Walpole in some of his responsibility in the reproductive biology unit at ICI's Pharmaceuticals Division in the mid-1970s. By that time, a number of research groups in the world had begun to synthesize and examine LHRH analogues to find a drug. ICI's team also started the search for effective LHRH analogues for pro-fertility and anti-cancer uses. Furr said:

> Initially, we were looking for agents that were the same as LHRH but more potent and more stable, and our concept was that we could use these to stimulate reproduction. At the same time, we were looking for LHRH antagonists, and our view was that these would inhibit reproduction. And these were the ones that we believed to be useful in breast and prostate cancer and in sex hormone-dependent gynaecological conditions. So we had a concept that: LHRH agonists would be pro-fertility, and then LHRH antagonists would inhibit fertility. That was the overall view. (Interview)

Based on the information that replacement of amino acids at position 6 and at position 10 was important for obtaining the potency and the stability of LHRH analogues, Anand Dutta and his fellow chemists at ICI tried not only D-amino acids, as others were doing, but also α-aza-amino acids, whose derivatives were rather unexploited. This was because they thought that both types of amino acids were more resistant to peptide-destroying enzymes (Dutta and Morley 1975; Dutta and Giles 1976; Dutta *et al.* 1993, pp. 11–12). Furr described the situation:

> When LHRH agonists were being developed, there was a recognition that they were rapidly broken down in blood and tissues by enzymes, and they were cleaved between positions 6 and 7, and 9 and 10. ...
> We tried primarily D-amino acids and aza-amino acids. And we tried them in various positions, we tried two azas, one aza in 6 and one in 10, we tried D-amino acid in 6 and aza in 10, and that was the combination that gave us the best results in terms of intrinsic potency, potency at the level of the pituitary gland and also stability from attack by the enzymes. (Interview)

ICI researchers also had to work outside the patents of other companies. However, this was not the starting point of their research. Again, Furr's explanation:

> We chose to put an aza-glycine in, which gave us, we believe, a better quality product. So there was an element of avoidance although, at the time we were doing it, there was a lot of overlap, because other people were working at the same time. So we weren't always sure what other people were doing. It only became clear later. (Interview)

The ICI research team thus synthesized more than a hundred analogues. Among them the one that showed best total performance in terms of efficacy and duration of action was chosen to be developed in 1976.[11] This was goserelin, which substituted a D-amino acid, D-Serine (Bu^t), at position 6 and azaglycine at position 10 (Figure 6.1(e)). Goserelin showed 100 times higher ovulation-inducing activity in rats (British Patent 1524747; Dutta *et al.* 1976, 1978a, 1978b, 1979a, 1979b, 1993, pp. 11–13; Furr 1998, p. 118; Furr interview).

When Furr and his colleagues examined goserelin, they encountered the paradoxical effect of LHRH analogues, as did other researchers working on them (Dutta *et al.* 1993, pp. 13–15; Furr 1998, p. 119). Furr described it:

> We realized this was not a paradox but a well-known effect, which was described by physiologists as desensitization of tissue, by pharmacologists as tachyphylaxis, and then by molecular biologists and by biochemists as receptor down-regulation, which was describing the mechanism of action. So it was a well-appreciated phenomenon. But because endocrinologists rather than pharmacologists worked on it, it was initially a surprise ... (Interview)

When Furr noticed the paradoxical effect, he switched the target of goserelin to the one for LHRH antagonists, the treatment of sex hormone-dependent diseases such as breast cancer and prostate cancer (Dutta *et al.* 1993, p. 15; Furr 1998, p. 119; Furr interview). The use of goserelin for stimulating fertility was not impossible, but it required practitioners to administer the drug every 90 minutes. Furr thought that this could not be a major use (Furr interview). Therefore, he and his colleagues investigated the possibility of using the drug for the treatment of breast cancer, which they were familiar with through the prior development of tamoxifen. They tested the drug in rats and found that it had an anti-tumour activity against a certain kind of mammary tumour (Nicholson and Maynard 1979; Furr and Nicholson 1982). However, there was concern about the strategic positioning of goserelin when they already had tamoxifen citrate, an effective drug for the treatment of breast cancer. Furr put it:

> One of the problems I had ... was that we also had Nolvadex [tamoxifen], which was very good in breast cancer, and that was an orally available drug with a reasonable side effect profile. So, I was not clear how we could develop Zoladex [goserelin] to be commercially successful as a daily injection in breast cancer when we had a good competitor, which was Nolvadex. It was in the same company but even if it had been in another company it would still have been a difficult competitor, to argue a case. (Interview)

Furr and his colleagues changed the primary target of goserelin to the treatment for advanced prostate cancer, which had a few alternative treatments such as surgical castration and oestrogen administration but none were without problems, as mentioned above (see section 6.4). They did not give up its use for the treatment of breast cancer, but the priority was put on the treatment of prostate cancer (Furr interview). Clinical studies of goserelin for the treatment of prostate cancer started in the early 1980s, and three early studies with about 10 patients claimed the efficacy of the drug in the treatment (Allen *et al.* 1983; Walker *et al.* 1983; Ahmed *et al.* 1983). Another report claimed that the drug failed to show long-term efficacy in the treatment of 15 patients (Kerle *et al.* 1984). However, later studies with the depot preparation of goserelin did not support this report. The failure was interpreted as being probably due to the variation of patients, based on a study with 29 patients (Grant *et al.* 1986, p. 542), or perhaps due to insufficient dosage and less than ideal preparation form, based on a study with 27 patients (Murphy *et al.* 1987). Trials with a larger number of patients did not demonstrate the therapeutic failure again (Debruyne *et al.* 1988; Peeling 1989; Soloway *et al.* 1991).

Meanwhile, a depot preparation of goserelin was developed. Although daily injection could be used and was used in the early studies, it was thought that the preparation would limit its acceptance by medical practitioners and reduce patient compliance with the treatment. They began to investigate alternative ways of administering of the drug. Nasal administration was examined, but found to be unsuitable because the absorption rate was low and too variable. Next a depot preparation with a biodegradable material was considered (Dutta *et al.* 1993, p. 15). Here, Furr's human network contributed to the solution. He explained it:

> I had some very good fortune with Zoladex in that I had worked with a formulation scientist, called Frank Hutchinson, and we together developed slow release formulations of prostaglandins for dogs. ... So I said one day to Frank, 'We have an LHRH agonist, which is a peptide, and we need to deliver this as a monthly depot so that we don't have to give daily injection. And ideally, we want something that's biodegradable so that there will be no depot left at the end of the month. It's no good having to cut pieces of plastic out of a patient. Can you do it?' And he had the concept that he could by using polymers of lactic acid and glycolic acid. So, he said he could do it, and a lot of people said, 'This would be impossible because how can you encapsulate a biodegradable peptide in a biodegradable matrix and expect to get activity?' But he had all sorts of reasons why he could do it. And he did it. And I tested the materials he made and they worked. (Interview)

Suspicion was not only about the feasibility of such a preparation but also about the absence of immune rejection response to the material used (Furr 1998, p. 119). However, Hutchinson began to attack the target in 1979 (Furr interview). In the development process, a serendipitous event saved the project. Furr talked about the episode:

> [The preparation] seemed to work for a very short period, ... a period of about a week. But we couldn't ... get longer periods of action. Then, I went on holiday, and the person who was collecting the samples continued to collect them for a much longer period than we normally did. And when I came back, I analysed the results. What had happened was that we got our usual seven days worth of activity, then we lost activity for between seven and twenty days, and then the activity returned. Frank Hutchinson then realized, when he saw these data, that there were two phases of release of the drug. ... He realized there was a diffusional phase of release, followed by a degradation phase of release. So then he could change the characteristics of the polymer of lactide and glycolide to overlap diffusion and degradation, and then you got a smooth release of the drug. So, it was a bit of good fortune that I'd gone on holiday, because we might not have realized that there was a secondary phase, because normally we stopped the experiment when we lost the activity. (Interview)

The first depot preparation of an LHRH analogue, a tiny rod of PLGA matrix containing the drug for implanting, was thus developed in 1981 (Furr 1998, p. 119; Dutta *et al.* 1993, pp. 15–21; Hutchinson and Furr 1985).

Soon, clinical trials of the depot preparation of goserelin started in which the drug was compared with existing endocrinological treatments, surgical castration, oestrogen therapy and even the daily injection of the same drug. It was shown that the preparation was as effective as surgical castration and oestrogen, safer than oestrogen, and more effective than the daily injection of goserelin (Grant *et al.* 1986; Van Cangh *et al.* 1986; Namer *et al.* 1986; Murphy *et al.* 1987; Emtage *et al.* 1987; Peeling 1989; Soloway *et al.* 1991).

There were several problems to be solved in the process of clinical development. First, ICI workers had to explain the mode of action to the medical and regulatory authorities because they expected that goserelin would have a stimulatory effect but it had an inhibitory effect (Furr interview). Second, 'super-active' LHRH analogues in fact had an acute stimulatory effect, often called the 'flare-up' phenomenon (Waxman *et al.* 1985). They were able to demonstrate that this phenomenon was not serious to patients unless they had an imminent risk of spinal collapse (Furr interview; Grant *et al.* 1986, p. 542; Murphy *et al.* 1987, p. 189; Beacock *et al.* 1987, pp. 440–1; Chrisp and Goa 1991, p. 281). This phenomenon was observed in every 'super-active' LHRH analogue, and it was proposed that the combination therapy with anti-androgens could avoid the exacerbation of symptoms caused by the phenomenon (Labrie *et al.* 1984; Klign *et al.* 1985; Gittes 1991, p. 242). Some other side effects also had to be explained and shown to be practically insignificant. Third, establishment of its production was a very difficult task. Producing the peptide on a large scale with a high degree of quality and stability was another unprecedented achievement and required a lot of skills and effort (Furr interview). These problems were resolved by organizational integration, in particular, through a multi-disciplinary team, consisting of chemists, biologists, pharmacists, pharmacologists, toxicologists, production managers and project coordinators (Furr interview).

Goserelin was first launched in the UK in 1987 for the treatment of prostate cancer under the trade name Zoladex®. It was then marketed in the US in 1990 and in Japan in 1991. Meanwhile, applications for the treatment of pre-menopausal breast cancer, endometriosis and fibroids were also clinically developed (Williams *et al.* 1986; Zeneca 1999a: breast cancer; Shaw and Zoladex Endometriosis Study Team 1992; Candiani *et al.* 1990; Zeneca 1999b: endometriosis and fibroids). Goserelin was launched in the UK for endometriosis and breast cancer in 1992 and for fibroids in 1996 (Furr personal communication, July 2000). The sales of goserelin worldwide were estimated to be $321 million in 1994 (Rickwood and Southworth 1995, p. 119).

6.6   A BRIEF ANALYSIS

In the aspect of shaping the compound, Leuprorelin needed a project leader with expertise in hormone synthesis, skilled researchers, external knowledge and skill in bioassay obtained from the linkage with Abbott, strategic research alliance, external scientific knowledge developed by various research teams in the world and diffused by academic journals and conferences, research materials and instruments, and serendipities. The depot preparation of leuprorelin needed another leader with skill in emulsion engineering, know-how in biodegradable polymers from the collaboration with Wako, scientific information from patents, scientific papers, various polymers, mixers and other apparatus. Goserelin also needed a project leader with expertise, skilled researchers, internal scientific assets accumulated by a research tradition in hypothalamic hormones, external scientific knowledge, and research materials and instruments. In addition, each process of shaping the compound was also restricted by institutional factors such as patents owned by other organizations, and by techno-economic factors such as medical efficacy and production efficiency.

In the aspect of shaping the applications, activities of different research teams, alliances between them, the 'externality' of their competition in knowledge diffusion, various academic media supporting the externality, patient population, alternative treatments and corporate product lines affecting the marketability and profitability of the new drugs, and the serendipitous discovery of the paradoxical effect were involved. Material elements including the compounds, bodies of experimental animals and human bodies were also involved in the shaping of applications.

The shaping of organizational authorization was in particular significant in the development of leuprorelin in Japan. Because of the smaller number of patients with prostate cancer, the restriction of self-injection, and the general unfamiliarity with LHRH analogues and their biodegradable preparations, many people at Takeda were doubtful about the marketability and profitability of leuprorelin and its depot preparation. Leadership of the project leader, championing by top management, and high evaluation by allied overseas companies contributed to the shaping of organizational authorization. It was also necessary that the physical and biological properties of the compound and its preparation should support the usefulness of leuprorelin in the proposed medical applications.

In the shaping of the market, clinical trials played an essential role. Comparative studies with alternative treatments were devised to convince doctors and regulators of the effectiveness of the LHRH analogues. Explanation of the mode of action and demonstration of the safety of the drugs were also provided. In the case of goserelin, there was a report of clinical trials failing to show efficacy; then, the counterevidence with a larger sample and the explanation of the failure contributed to the shaping of the market. In the case of leuprorelin, experience in the US and other overseas countries in clinical trials and practices significantly helped the shaping of its market in Japan, where doctors were suspicious about the new type of drug. Academic papers played an important role as medium. The development of depot preparations contributed to the diffusion of the LHRH analogues because of its convenience. The addition of more applications also contributed to the expansion of the market in both cases. The establishment of high-quality mass production was also crucial to securing the market.

In the previous chapter, I identified two different patterns of drug discovery and development: paradigmatic innovation and modification-based innovation. The process of shaping LHRH analogues seems to be paradigmatic innovation. There was high uncertainty surrounding the process; in particular, people at Takeda were at first unfamiliar with leuprorelin and showed their suspicion of it. Strong championing by top management was needed to shape organizational authorization. However, the exemplary role of the drug was not clear. Keen competition was observed throughout the process of shaping LHRH analogues: in the discovery of LHRH, in the synthesis of its analogues, in the development of clinical applications, in the development of preparations, and in clinical trials. Various LHRH analogues were simultaneously developed by different organizations. Leuprorelin was the first LHRH analogue with modifications at position 6 and position 10, while goserelin was the first LHRH analogue with the depot preparation. Both played an exemplary role in a particular aspect among the class of drugs, but neither was an absolute exemplar. Development processes of different LHRH analogues affected each other. Thus, various LHRH analogues collectively made a paradigm. In the next chapter, we examine three more cases of drug discovery and development in Japan in detail to confirm the different types of drug innovation which arose in this and previous chapters.

NOTES

1. The word 'formulation' in place of 'preparation' is often used among experts in the area.
2. Guillemin and Schally 'independently' determined the structure of TRF(H) in 1969. Both of them won the Nobel Prize in Physiology or Medicine in 1977 in recognition of their contribution to research on hypothalamic hormones.
3. Wade (1981, p. 205).
4. The interview with Dr Barry Furr, one of the discoverers of goserelin at ICI Pharmaceuticals Division (now AstraZeneca), was conducted on 21 July 1999.
5. The two hypothalamic hormones were found to be identical later (Schally *et al.* 1971a, 1973, p. 344; Matsuo *et al.* 1971b; Besser and Mortimer 1974, p. 176).

6.   The interview with Dr Masahiko Fujino was conducted on 28 January 1999.
7.   [D-Ala^6, des-Gly-NH$_2$^{10}, Pro-ethylamide^9]-LHRH was about as potent as leuprorelin, but the latter was better from the viewpoint of production (Fujino personal communication, August 2000).
8.   Leuprorelin succeeded in obtaining approval from the Japanese regulator for the treatment of pre-menopausal breast cancer in 1996, four years after its marketing for the treatment of prostate cancer in the country (Takeda internal document).
9.   The interview with Dr Yasuaki Ogawa, who developed the depot preparation of leuprorelin, and Mr Kouji Sonoi, who was involved in the clinical development of leuprorelin, was conducted on 27 January 1999.
10. The interview with Dr Tai Matsuzawa was conducted on 8 February 1999.
11. According to Dr Furr, easiness of synthesis on a large scale may have been also taken into consideration (Furr personal communication, July 2000).

7. Three case studies of pharmaceutical innovation in Japan

7.1 INTRODUCTION

In this chapter, we examine three cases of drug discovery and development which took place in Japan, in order to confirm the existence of different types of drug innovation and to understand the properties of each. The first case is that of mevastatin, the first, exemplary drug among a class of drugs called HMG-CoA reductase inhibitors or statins. Although this drug itself was not brought to market, it provides us with a rare case of paradigmatic innovation in Japan. The second case is cefotiam, a cephalosporin antibiotic, which can be regarded as a modification-based innovation. The third is the case of tamsulosin, a drug called an α_{1c}-blocker which is used for the treatment of urination disorder accompanying benign prostate hypertrophy. This drug is chemically one of the drugs called α-blockers, which was not unfamiliar to experts, but it was the first one used for urination disorder. This drug, therefore, can be regarded as a modification-based innovation as a compound, but can be regarded as a paradigmatic innovation as a therapy. In each case, the detailed process of innovation inside the company is examined.

7.2 MEVASTATIN

7.2.1 Introduction

The drugs called HMG-CoA reductase inhibitors, including lovastatin, pravastatin and simvastatin, are used for the treatment of hypercholesterolemia. Hypercholesterolemia refers to the presence of an abnormally large amount of cholesterol, especially LDL-cholesterol, in the circulating blood, and it may cause such diseases as arteriosclerosis and coronary heart disease. HMG-CoA reductase is the rate-limiting enzyme in the synthesis of cholesterol in the body. HMG-CoA reductase inhibitors antagonize the action of the enzyme and reduce the amount of LDL-cholesterol in the blood. HMG-CoA reductase inhibitors appeared on the market in the late 1980s and have been remarkably successful. The sales of lovastatin (Mevacor®) and pravastatin (Mevalotin®) became 'blockbusters' with more than $1 billion annual sales in the mid-1990s. Simvastatin (Zocor®) is more successful. Its worldwide sales surpassed those of lovastatin by 1994 and amounted to $3.6 billion in 1997. Simvastatin was probably the top selling drug in the world in the late 1990s (Yakugyo Jihou 1999, p. 131).

Lovastatin, pravastatin and simvastatin are all analogues of a drug, mevastatin (ML-236B; compactin), the first HMG-CoA reductase inhibitor discovered by Akira Endo at Sankyo Co. in Japan in 1973. However, the development of mevastatin ceased in 1980. Meanwhile, Merck Co. (US) obtained experimental data and samples of mevastatin from Sankyo, discovered lovastatin in 1978 and marketed it in 1987. Merck also chemically synthesized simvastatin from lovastatin, and launched it in 1988. Sankyo re-examined analogues of mevastatin just after giving up the development of mevastatin, and decided to develop pravastatin, which had already been discovered by Sankyo's researchers in 1979. Pravastatin was launched in the market in 1989. In contrast with the enormous success of these analogue drugs, the story of the discovery and development of mevastatin, the prototype drug, is full of hardships. Although mevastatin failed to be a drug, its discoverer, Endo still believes that mevastatin could have been as successful as its analogues if it had been marketed.

7.2.2 Discovery, Development and Failure of Mevastatin

Akira Endo was a senior researcher in the Fermentation Research Laboratories at Sankyo, the dedicated laboratories for the discovery of useful substances from microbes, when he started research on anti-cholesterol drugs in 1971. Before that, from 1966 to 1968, he had stayed in New York to study the biochemistry of phospholipid and cholesterol (Endo interview;[1] Endo 2001). At that time, scientists were close to understanding the synthesizing process of cholesterol in the body (Bloch 1965) and had identified HMG-CoA reductase as the enzyme that plays a central role in controlling the process (Bucher *et al.* 1960; Siperstein and Fagan 1966; Siperstein 1970; Dietschy and Wilson 1970). The relationship between the amount of cholesterol in the blood and the frequency of coronary heart disease was also well known through the Framingham study (Emerson Thomas *et al.* 1966; Dawber and Kannel 1966). People in the United States had become very conscious of the amount of fat in their diet because a great number of people there died of heart diseases, though this had not necessarily been the case in Japan at that time. However, there was no truly effective and safe anti-cholesterol drug even in the US. At first, Endo's interest was in the biochemistry of phospholipid and cholesterol, but later he became interested in the discovery of an anti-cholesterol drug, after learning about cholesterol-related diseases (Endo interview).

Table 7.1: Major events related to the discovery and development of mevastatin

Year	Sankyo	Merck
1971	Research started	
1973	Discovery of mevastatin	
1974	Turndown of mevastatin by the Central Research Laboratories	
1976	Discovery of mevastatin's effectiveness in hens	
1977	Pre-clinical study of mevastatin started	
	Controversy on the safety of mevastatin in the company	
1978	Clinical trials of mevastatin by Yamamoto at Osaka University	Discovery of lovastatin
	Organizational authorization of clinical development of mevastatin	
1979	Discovery of pravastatin	
1980	Suspension of the development of mevastatin	
1981	Pre-clinical study of pravastatin started	Discovery of simvastatin
1984	Clinical trials of pravastatin started	
1987		Launch of lovastatin
1988		Launch of simvastatin
1989	Launch of pravastatin	

After coming back to Japan in autumn 1968, Endo was involved in research on antibiotics for a while. Simultaneously, he studied the literature on cholesterol to find a way to the discovery of an anti-cholesterol drug. Three approaches were considered for lowering the amount of cholesterol in the blood: blocking the intestinal absorption of cholesterol from the diet; inhibiting the synthesis of cholesterol in the body; and promoting its excretion (Kuwashima 1998, p. 461; Endo 1992, p. 1570). Inhibiting biosynthesis seemed the most effective of the three alternatives because biosynthesis was regarded as contributing most to the amount of cholesterol

(Siperstein 1970). Furthermore, he learned from the literature that the activity of HMG-CoA reductase is closely related to the overall rate of cholesterol synthesis (Endo 1992; Siperstein and Fagan 1966; Siperstein 1970; Dietschy and Wilson 1970). By autumn 1970, he was convinced that he could reduce the amount of cholesterol in the blood if he could inhibit the activity of HMG-CoA reductase in some way (Endo 1999). At the time, however, his idea was only an hypothesis without any 'hard' evidence.

Endo subsequently decided to search for a substance able to inhibit HMG-CoA reductase from microbes, rather than from chemical syntheses. This choice was based on his interests and expertise. He was familiar with and interested in microbes, especially moulds and fungi, from his childhood in a farming family. He studied them at the Department of Agriculture, Touhoku University, and continued researching them to find useful substances for medicine and agriculture after he joined Sankyo (Endo interview; Endo 1999). He also speculated that some microbes would produce HMG-CoA reductase inhibitors as a weapon to fight against other microbes that required sterols such as cholesterol for growth (Endo 1992, p. 1570). Since 1969, he had been at the Fermentation Research Laboratories, which was newly established to reinforce the search for antibiotics and other drugs from microbes. About 80 researchers at the laboratories were involved in the search for antibiotics; a half of the rest, about 10 researchers including Endo, were seeking drugs such as various enzyme inhibitors. Therefore, he was in a position which was organizationally suited to him searching for HMG-CoA reductase inhibitors from microbes (Endo interview; Kuwashima 1998, pp. 460–1).

Endo, with Masao Kuroda, devised an assay system using rat liver enzymes to identify inhibitors of the biosynthesis of cholesterol. A more specific assay system, which could detect only HMG-CoA reductase inhibitors by using [^{14}C] HMG-CoA, was also available, but it was too expensive to use for screening thousands of samples. The method they chose was less focused: it could not distinguish the inhibition of HMG-CoA reductase from any other inhibition in the early stages of the cholesterol synthetic pathway (Endo 1992, p. 1570). However, it was less expensive and so they could afford it. To obtain further savings, they improved the existing assay system and achieved 20 to 40 times higher efficiency (Endo 2001; Kuwashima 1998).

In April 1971, Endo and Kuroda began the screening of samples extracted from various microbes. For more than two years, approximately 6,000 microbial strains were tested for their ability to inhibit cholesterol synthesis. As the result of the screening, two strains of moulds were found to produce active substances. One was *Pythium ultimum*, which produces citrinin, a substance known as a mycotoxin; however, they gave up the development of citrinin as an HMG-CoA reductase inhibitor because it was too toxic (Endo interview; Endo 1992, p. 1570). The other was a strain of *Penicillium citrinum*, which produces mevastatin (formerly called ML-236B or compactin), ML-236A and ML-236C. Neither ML-236A nor ML-236C was as active as mevastatin. Mevastatin was discovered in July 1973 and its structure was determined by a combination of spectroscopic, chemical and X-ray crystallographic methods three months later (Endo *et al.* 1976b; Endo 1992, p. 1570). Later it was also identified that mevastatin is an HMG-CoA reductase inhibitor (Endo *et al.* 1976a). It took Endo more than two years, and came as he was reaching the limits of his patience:

> I was prepared to give up this approach if we were unable to gain a feeling of hit after two years. The feeling is that we will likely hit a target if we keep trying a little more. Without such readiness in mind, a search for drugs tends to get bogged down. This is unlike a lottery, which must includes prizes. [In a search of drug,] no one knows if there is a prize. ... It is like a battle, in which we have a limited variety of and a limited number of forces. If we have no prospects of victory after a two-year-long battle, we should retreat. (Endo interview)

In early 1974, Endo's team handed over mevastatin to the *in vivo* assay team at the Central Research Laboratories, where the efficacy and safety of drugs are preliminarily tested in animals (Endo 1992, p. 1573; Kuwashima 1998, p. 462). Mevastatin cleared acute safety tests but, unexpectedly, it was found in March 1974 that the substance did not lower plasma cholesterol in rats. These were used predominantly in the first stage of *in vivo* tests; other animals such as rabbits, dogs and monkeys were occasionally used, but only after the tests in rats because the former were more expensive. Rats were the first living 'filter' for screening out inappropriate substances; mevastatin was screened out there (Endo interview; Endo 1992; Kuwashima 1998, p. 463).

Endo did not give up. Mevastatin was the product of his hard work of almost three years. Furthermore, he was not convinced that ineffectiveness in rats truly indicated ineffectiveness in humans. He and his team members decided to conduct *in vivo* tests themselves (Endo interview; Kuwashima 1998, p. 463). At the time, he belonged to the non-antibiotic research groups at the Fermentation Research Laboratories. This research institute was still a young organization and, in particular, the non-antibiotic research groups there were regarded as 'play' groups, which were not expected to bring immediate products to the company. Therefore, his research proposal about anti-cholesterol drugs was readily approved when he submitted it to the director in April 1974 (Endo interview). Endo and his colleagues gave mevastatin to rats by injection and tried the substance in mice instead of rats, but failed to obtain any good results. The only hope was that the substance reduced the amount of cholesterol in the blood when they administered it to the disease-model rats (that is, the rats with artificially induced hypercholesterolemia) (Endo 1987, 1992, p. 1574). They also conjectured that the cholesterol-inhibiting action of mevastatin could be antagonism against HMG-CoA reductase because of the structural similarity between an HMG-CoA molecule and a mevastatin molecule. This mechanism of action was in principle very suitable for a drug (Endo interview; Endo 1992, p. 1571). However, their work continued for two years without good results (Endo interview).

In the meantime, Endo learned of the work by Goldstein and Brown which showed that the activity of HMG-CoA reductase is suppressed by a particular class of lipoprotein known as LDL and that HMG-CoA reductase in cells from patients with familial hypercholesterolemia (FH) is not suppressed by LDL. Goldstein and Brown proposed the existence of LDL receptors and the deficiency of them in FH patients (Brown *et al.* 1973; Brown and Goldstein 1974).[2] Their studies of cholesterol metabolism strongly helped Endo's study in both experimental techniques and in the general idea of developing HMG-CoA reductase inhibitors (Endo 1992, p. 1572). Endo wrote to Goldstein in October 1975 and his study interested the American researcher. Goldstein agreed with Endo's idea that mevastatin might work in disease cells, and he also proposed that they conduct joint research. Endo acquired cells from FH patients from the United States and tested mevastatin in those and other mammalian cells by using the techniques Goldstein and Brown developed. As a result, he confirmed that mevastatin strongly inhibited synthesis of cholesterol in (cultured) human and other mammalian cells (Endo 1992, p. 1572, 1987, 1991).

In early 1976, Endo decided that he would change the animals used in the experiments from rats to other animals with high levels of HMG-CoA reductase in their livers. He happened to talk with a senior researcher at the Central Research Laboratories, who was doing the toxicity tests of agricultural chemicals with hens, and asked the researcher to try mevastatin in the hens that had been used in other experiments and were going to be killed: Endo thought hens were appropriate since the eggs they lay every day are rich in cholesterol. Because the talk between Endo and the researcher was an informal one in a bar, the idea was realized without any organizational resistance. Endo has speculated that the tests in hens might not have been realized if they had been formally proposed to the Central Research Laboratories, which had turned mevastatin down two years before (Endo interview). The tests were conducted in spring 1976, and Endo and his colleagues found that the amount of cholesterol in the hens was reduced by as much as 50 per cent. Because hens are not mammals, the data were not acceptable for drug development. However, the remarkable results in hens opened up an opportunity to conduct tests in dogs and monkeys (Endo interview; Endo 1992, p. 1574). When they administered mevastatin to dogs, the amount of cholesterol in the blood was reduced by 45 per cent; it also showed remarkable potency in monkeys (Tsujita *et al.* 1979; Kuroda *et al.* 1979). Thus, Endo was convinced that mevastatin would be effective in humans even though it had no effect in rodents such as rats and mice (Endo interview; Endo 1992, p. 1575). Sankyo decided to develop mevastatin as a drug in August 1976. It was also decided that the project would be a joint undertaking between the Fermentation Research Laboratories, the Central Research Laboratories and the Laboratory Animal Science and Testing Center, with Endo as the project leader (Endo interview). Until then, he had experienced a lot of criticism in the company. He put it thus:

> There were a lot of [unpleasant] experiences. Some people said to me, for example, 'Stop such research.' Others said, 'You waste young people,' because I used several young researchers. Especially, our efforts probably made some people in the Central Research Laboratories irritated. You know, they were not happy, because they had turned [mevastatin] down but I tackled it persistently. ... At that time, the Central Research Laboratories was the centre of the drug development. Our Lab was only peripheral. (Interview)

The patent of mevastatin was publicized in Belgium and Japan in December 1975. Having learned of this substance from the patents, Merck Sharp & Dohme Research Laboratories proposed joint research on mevastatin to Sankyo in the spring of 1976. The two companies made a disclosure agreement, and Sankyo sent the related data, experimental methods and a sample of mevastatin to Merck (Endo interview; Endo 1994, 1987). Although Merck did not give an immediate positive valuation to mevastatin at that time (Endo 1994, p. 125), the company's approach drew the attention of the senior research managers at Sankyo to the substance.

Formal pre-clinical tests started in January 1977. In toxicological tests in rats, another problem arose in the spring of 1977. Toxicologists at the Laboratory Animal Science and Testing Center found tiny, unfamiliar crystals within the liver cells of the rats that were given a massive amount of mevastatin. They were very concerned about this phenomenon because mevastatin would be given to patients for a very long time. A subtle debate was held between Endo and the toxicologists. At that time, it was impossible for them to analyse the crystals directly. Using a variety of indirect evidence, Endo argued that the crystals were cholesterol ester, which should be resoluble (Endo interview; Endo 2001, Endo 1994, pp. 124–5). The toxicologists and pathologists at the Laboratory Animal Science and Testing Center did not readily agree with him. Endo described the subtle character of the debate:

> When [the toxicologists] doubted the safety of a substance, its project would usually be abandoned. I have witnessed a lot of such cases. However, [the toxicologists] didn't used to say 'no'. It was because they didn't want to take the responsibility of stopping the project. They didn't want to incur our ill will. So, they asked us what we thought about the unfavourable results of their tests, instead of saying 'no' straightforwardly. We answered it, but they were not convinced by our answer. We offered another answer, and so on. They just waited for us to give up the substance. This is a very Japanese way, isn't it? (Interview)

Endo also put it thus:

> It is a matter of course that unfamiliar phenomena are observed when we test an unfamiliar substance. [The crystal] was an example of such phenomena. Whether they can develop a unique drug or not is dependent on how they deal with such phenomena. I analysed the crystal and identified it as cholesterol. Even though I explained the phenomena logically, even though I showed evidence to the pathologists and toxicologists, they were not convinced. ... The story would have been completely different if there had been a precedent. If a company in America, Britain or elsewhere outside Japan had found the same thing and had insisted it's OK, there might have been no problem. (Interview)

About the same time, a group of chemists at the Central Research Laboratories was conducting the synthesis of analogues of mevastatin (Sato *et al.* 1980). They also biologically tested one of them, RWX-163 (R-163), without informing Endo's team. The first presentation about RWX-163 in the company was given on 22 and 23 June 1977. In December 1977, the promoters of RWX-163 insisted that the compound did not produce any crystals in the liver cells of rats; they also claimed that it reduced the amount of cholesterol in rats. The proposal to replace mevastatin with RWX-163 was discussed at the project-coordinating meeting on 10 January 1978. Unfortunately for Endo's team, Kou Arima, who was then director of the Fermentation Research Laboratories and a main supporter of the mevastatin project in the company, was absent from the meeting. The proposal won the consensus of the major members and was to be finally approved by Arima, who was also the director of the Central Research Laboratories. It was very hard for him to ignore the consensus at the meeting without a convincing reason.[3] Mevastatin was thus about to be turned down again (Endo interview and personal communication).[4] However, Endo and Arima did not give up mevastatin. Endo explained the reasons:

> The compound had only two hundred times less potency than mevastatin. This means patients would have to take it two hundred times more than mevastatin at a dose. Such a compound can't become a drug. However, for the chemists at the Central Research Laboratories, this was an opportunity for taking an initiative.

Moreover, this was favourable for the pathologists and toxicologists at the Laboratory Animal Science and Testing Center because there would be no problem in their jurisdiction. Their interests coincided here. This resulted in one versus two. And, you know, it was the pathologists who were regarded as responsible finally for the safety of a substance. Therefore, if they didn't say 'yes', a substance compound couldn't be a drug. (Interview)

Endo and Arima tried to find a way outside the company to save mevastatin from being dumped. Before then, in the autumn of 1977, Akira Yamamoto at the Osaka University Hospital had asked Endo for mevastatin to try it with one of his patients who had serious familial hypercholesterolemia (FH). Yamamoto had come to know Endo through the latter's paper on the work of Goldstein and Brown. Yamamoto proposed that he should take the initiative with the tests: this proposal was genuinely attractive to Endo. Soon after the project coordinating meeting on 10 January 1978, Endo went to see Yamamoto and arranged the tests. In Sankyo, only Endo and Arima knew of this plan.[5] The tests began on 2 February 1978. Arima later let the head of toxicology at Sankyo know about the plan for the tests; it caused turmoil within the organization. However, there was no way for others in the company to stop the tests, because the doctor took the initiative. Doctors, especially those belonging to universities, had great power over pharmaceutical companies at that time in Japan. At the next project coordinating meeting on 9 February 1978, the direction shown at the last meeting was reversed and the development of mevastatin was approved (Endo interview and personal communication).

The tests of mevastatin by Yamamoto's team at first did not show very good results. The amount of cholesterol in the blood was reduced but by less than expected. Furthermore, side effects such as muscular weakness were observed. The tests were ceased. However, Yamamoto was intuitively convinced that mevastatin would work when he listened to the patient's neck and found that 'vascular bruit (noise)' was impressively reduced after the use of the drug: the side effect was regarded as due to an overdose. In addition, the patient had a particular kind of hypercholesterolemia, called homozygous FH. Although his professor told him to give up the drug, he tried it again with alterations in dosages and targets (Yamamoto 2000, p. 78). Yamamoto treated nine other patients with primary hypercholesterolemia with lower doses of mevastatin. These tests produced remarkable results (Yamamoto *et al.* 1980; Endo 1992, p. 1575, 1994, p. 125). In May 1978, the development of mevastatin was formally authorized at the corporate meeting at Sankyo headquarters. In November of the year, formal clinical trials (Phase I) began. However, Endo left Sankyo and moved to Tokyo Noko University in December 1978 (Endo 2001).

In the summer of 1979, clinical trials of mevastatin proceeded to Phase II and the drug was administered to many patients with serious hypercholesterolemia by over 10 groups in Japan. The results showed that mevastatin was effective for all kinds of hypercholesterolemia except homozygous FH. Some of the results of clinical trials were presented at the International Symposium on Drugs Affecting Lipid Metabolism in June 1980 (Endo 1994, p. 126). However, most of these clinical trials were suddenly suspended soon after that symposium, because of the report that mevastatin showed toxic effects in some dogs at high doses in a long-term toxicity study (Endo 1992, p. 1575). Endo criticized the study thus:

> [The tests] committed three errors. First, doses were too much. About 1,000 times higher doses than the effective doses in man were given to the dogs. Second, a long-term toxicity study usually lasts for a year. However, in this case, it was extended to two years because there had been nothing wrong after 39-week-long administration. I can't understand why they made such a decision. ... Third, it was a matter of course that toxicity was observed. But the dose was 1,000 times higher. They should have analysed the phenomenon logically, because there was nothing wrong in 50 times higher doses. Any drug would show toxicity if it was taken to the amount of 1,000 times higher than ordinary doses. Therefore, such tests are total nonsense. (Interview)[6]

When Endo was at the company, he insisted that the long-term toxicity tests should be done with doses 50 times higher than the effective doses in humans.[7] However, his insistence was not accepted. The much higher doses were adopted together with lower doses; it was because even the highest doses had not produced serious toxic effects in the middle-term toxicity tests conducted before. There was also an opinion that toxicity tests should be conducted with doses high enough to produce some toxic effects (Endo 1991, p. 721). Endo generalized the problem here thus:

> If there had been an exemplar, it would have been all right. If an American company or a company elsewhere had done [a long-term toxicity study] with only 50 times higher doses, the Japanese company would have done with 50 times higher. But there was no such exemplar. [Mevastatin] was very safe. They thought that's OK because they didn't find toxic effects in the sub-acute toxicity tests [with the same amount of doses]. So easy. Their thinking wasn't based on theories. Very intuitive. I think this is a Japanese way of thinking. They are not good at thinking logically and analytically. (Interview)

Although the results of the test might have been different if they had chosen lower doses and a shorter period of time, which was a practical option at the first trial, these sorts of experiment cannot be redone. Even if the second trial had showed that mevastatin was safe, doubts among people could not have been wiped out completely (Endo 1991, pp. 721–2). As a result,

Sankyo virtually ceased the development of mevastatin in the summer of 1980. Sankyo mentions this incident only briefly in its official story of mevastatin and pravastatin: '[pravastatin] was selected because of its advantage in the balance of efficacy and safety' (Sankyo, 1996, p. 10). Although mevastatin failed to be a drug, it was used in some medical studies even after that. In August 1981, Hiroshi Mabuchi and his colleagues at Kanazawa University reported on the effectiveness of mevastatin in seven patients with FH (Mabuchi *et al*. 1981). The team also reported in March 1983 that mevastatin was very effective in combination with another drug for the treatment of FH without any side effects (Mabuchi *et al*. 1983). Yamamoto's team confirmed these results. These studies appeared to accelerate greatly the development of HMG-CoA reductase inhibitors in the 1980s (Endo 1992, p. 1576; Brown and Goldstein 1981, p. 516). Mevastatin provided 'hard' evidence to support theories of cholesterol synthesis in the body. Brown and Goldstein acknowledged the contribution of mevastatin in the editorial of a major medical journal as follows:

> Many hurdles must be overcome before compactin [mevastatin] and mevinolin [lovastatin] can be accepted as a 'penicillin' for hypercholesterolemia. ... Yet, the studies with the parent compounds compactin and mevinolin have established a general principle: interference with cholesterol synthesis can trigger an increase in LDL receptors, thereby reducing LDL levels in plasma without depleting vital body stores of cholesterol. This is indeed encouraging news. (Brown and Goldstein 1981, p. 517)

Endo was awarded the Twelfth Annual Warren Alpert Foundation Prize together with Brown and Goldstein in 2000 for the discovery of mevastatin, the first HMG-CoA reductase inhibitor.

7.2.3 Lovastatin, Simvastatin and Pravastatin: the Offspring

Discovery and development of lovastatin and simvastatin by Merck
Merck obtained a sample of mevastatin and unpublished data related to it from Sankyo under a disclosure agreement in July 1976. The contract between Merck and Sankyo did not include a clause that prohibited Merck from conducting improved inventions for a fixed period (Endo interview). Researchers at Merck began their own screening tests and discovered lovastatin from a strain of mould in November 1978 (Alberts *et al*. 1980; Alberts 1988; Endo 1994, p. 125).[8] It is reported that clinical trials of lovastatin were once interrupted because of the suspension of the development of mevastatin. However, Merck gradually resumed the clinical trials after the studies by Yamamoto and by Mabuchi which indicated the effectiveness of mevastatin for the treatment of FH (Endo 2001; Endo 1994,

pp. 126–7). As to the survival of the project, the fact that the then president of the Merck Sharp & Dohme Research Laboratories, P. Roy Vagelos, was a famous researcher in the biochemistry of lipids and cholesterol should be noted here (Galambos and Sewell 1995, p. 125; Endo 2001). Lovastatin cleared clinical trials and was approved by the FDA in the autumn of 1987 (Hoeg *et al.* 1986; Lovastatin Study Group II 1986; Havel *et al.* 1987; Grundy 1988, p. 25). In the course of clinical trials of lovastatin, the detailed action mechanism of HMG-CoA reductase inhibitors was explained (Bilheimer *et al.* 1983; Grundy 1988). Side effects which occurred in animal tests at very high dosage levels were also successfully explained and did not inhibit the project (MacDonald *et al.* 1988). In the early 1980s, Merck synthesized simvastatin by modifying lovastatin chemically (Hoffman *et al.* 1986). The company developed it in parallel with lovastatin. In 1988, Merck marketed simvastatin, which became the second HMG-CoA reductase inhibitor to be marketed (Todd and Goa 1990, pp. 586–7).

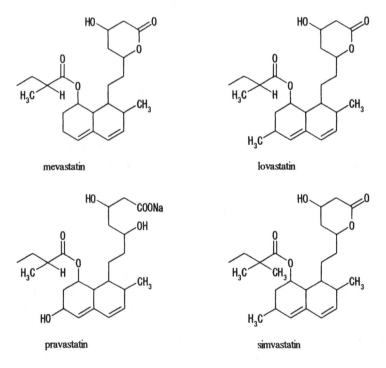

Figure 7.1: HMG-CoA reductase inhibitors discussed in Chapter 7

Discovery and development of pravastatin by Sankyo

In parallel with the development of mevastatin, researchers at Sankyo had searched for a better HMG-CoA reductase inhibitor by screening natural substances and synthesized compounds. This work linked with the investigation of the mechanism, activities and the structure–activity relationship of mevastatin; that is, in order to understand mevastatin, it was necessary to examine related substances and compounds as well. Masao Kuroda, who was one of the main researchers involved in the HMG-CoA reductase inhibitor project at the Fermentation Research Laboratories, described this process thus: 'In real laboratories, things don't proceed so neatly as "We have established the assay system. Now, let's begin the screening with it." In reality, we are building an assay system with trials and errors' (interview).[9] One of the substances discovered to be active in these efforts was pravastatin. This substance was first found in 1979 when Sankyo researchers examined the metabolites in the urine of dogs that were given mevastatin (Kuroda interview; Serizawa *et al.* 1983a, p. 604; Sankyo 1996, p. 10). Although the substance was found to be active when it was first discovered, the researchers could not identify its chemical structure because the quantity was too small. Because it was a metabolite, the researchers speculated that it could be a hydroxyl derivative of mevastatin. They tried to produce it by chemical modification and microbial transformation: the latter approach was found to be more efficient. Then, they matched the physical chemistry properties of the substance thus produced with those of the metabolite and at last identified the structure of the substance named pravastatin. It was in fact a hydroxyl derivative of mevastatin. Establishment of large-scale production was also essential for them to conduct various pre-clinical tests and clinical trials. However, pravastatin did not become a candidate for the development immediately after the discovery, but many other substances were examined as well (Kuroda interview; Kuroda 1994, pp. 76–7; Serizawa *et al.* 1983a, 1983b, 1983c, 1983d).

Soon after the failure of the development of mevastatin in the summer of 1980, Sankyo's researchers began reviewing 'hundreds of' these analogues of mevastatin (Kuroda interview; Kuwashima 1998, p. 463). The standard of potency was mevastatin, and the new candidate substance had to be better than it. Pravastatin was the survivor of the screening. Kuroda described the situation at that time thus:

> The problem was that we were the first to develop an HMG-CoA reductase inhibitor in the world. In such a case, there were objections and scepticism that such a mechanism of action would not result in a drug. It was our pride as the first research team who had discovered such kind of compounds that persistently led us to the development of pravastatin. (Interview)

Despite some expressions of suspicion within the company, Sankyo decided to develop pravastatin in 1981 (Kuroda personal communication, April 2000; Kuwashima 1998). Sankyo stated that the choice was made because of stronger effectiveness and less toxicity (Sankyo 1996, p. 10). The company attributed these advantages to the tissue-selectivity (that is, the ability to inhibit cholesterol synthesis selectively in livers and intestines) of pravastatin (Tsujita *et al.* 1986; Koga *et al.* 1990; Sankyo 1996, p. 10; Tsujita 1993, pp. 627–9). Researchers at Sankyo also made a considerable effort to develop a more efficient microbiological production method for pravastatin and succeeded in obtaining one using a strain of Australian microbe (Serizawa *et al.* 1983a, 1983c; Matsuoka *et al.* 1989; Sankyo 1996, p. 10). Clinical trials of pravastatin in Japan started in February 1984 and were cleared rapidly with good results (Nakaya *et al.* 1987; Mabuchi *et al.* 1987; Kuroda 1994, pp. 82–3). It was approved for manufacture by the Ministry of Health and Welfare and marketed in Japan in 1989. It also went through clinical trials in the US and European countries and obtained favourable results (Hunninghake *et al.* 1990; Hoogerbrugge *et al.* 1990). By 1996, it was being sold in 69 countries (Kuwashima 1998).

The remarkable successes in the market of these three analogues of mevastatin, namely, lovastatin, simvastatin and pravastatin, have already been noted in the introduction to this section. There are three other HMG-CoA reductase inhibitors marketed today which are also highly successful in the market: atorvastatin (Lipitor®) marketed by Warner and Lambert; cerivastatin[10] (Lipobay®) marketed by Bayer; and fluvastatin (Lescol®) marketed by Novartis. Although these three compounds share the key structure with mevastatin, they are less similar to mevastatin than lovastatin, simvastatin or pravastatin.

7.3   CEFOTIAM

7.3.1 Introduction

Cefotiam is an antibiotic synthesized and developed by Takeda Chemical Industries in Japan. This drug is classified into a subgroup of antibiotics called cephalosporins. Cephalosporins are analogues of cephalosporin C, originated in Italy but identified and investigated in the UK. Cephalosporins have a similar chemical structure to penicillins: both subgroups of antibiotics possess the structure called β-lactam. Therefore, they are also broadly called β-lactam antibiotics together with some other antibiotics with the same structure. Cefotiam was synthesized in 1974 (Takeda 1983, p. 743) and launched in Japan in 1981. Cefotiam is classified as one of so-called second-generation cephalosporins, which have a broader spectrum of activity than first-generation ones, but in general lesser antibacterial activity against Gram-negative bacteria than third-generation ones (Webber and Wheeler 1982, p. 377; Donowitz and Mandell 1988, p. 490). However, this does not mean that the second-generation cephalosporins became obsolete after the advent of third-generation ones. This is because doctors do not always use third-generation cephalosporins for fear of making bacteria resistant to antibiotics. In Japan, the increase of antibiotic-resistant bacteria has been a major medical problem since the 1980s (Hiramatsu 1999, p. 114). A narrower spectrum of activity has the advantage of preventing a broad range of bacteria from becoming antibiotic-resistant unnecessarily (Silver and Bostian 1993, p. 378). Therefore, cefotiam has sold very well in Japan even after the advent of third-generation cephalosporins. Its sales in Japan were estimated to be about 22 billion yen (about £110 million) in 1998; it was the second best selling antibiotic for injection use (*Yakuji Handobukku* 1999).

Table 7.2: Major events related to the discovery and development of cefotiam

Year	Events
1945	Discovery of *Cephalosporium acremonium*
1953	Discovery of cephalosporin C
1962	Synthesis of the first marketed cephalosporin, cephalothin
1971	Start of the cephalosporin project at Takeda
1974	Synthesis of SCE-785 and SCE-963
1975	Stop of the development of SCE-785; start of the development of SCE-963
1976	Start of the clinical trials of SCE-963 (cefotiam)
1980	Approval for manufacture of cefotiam
1981	Launch of cefotiam

7.3.2 Discovery and Early Progress of Cephalosporins

Giuseppe Brotzu, a professor at the Institute of Hygiene of Cagliari in Italy conjectured that self-purification of seawater might be partly due to microbial antagonism. In 1945, he sampled seawater near a local sewage outfall and discovered a species of mould, *Cephalosporium acremonium*, which produced a substance with a wider antibacterial activity than penicillin. He published his finding in a pamphlet in 1948, which had only a small circulation and attracted little attention in the country. He then sent a copy to his friend in London, Blyth Brooke, and suggested that English researchers should take up the work to isolate the active substances, which would be beyond his resources. Based on the suggestion of the Medical Research Council, Brooke wrote to Sir Howard Florey at the Sir William Dunn School of Pathology at Oxford. Florey gladly agreed to take up further investigation and Brotzu sent a culture of his mould to Florey in September 1948 (Abraham and Loder 1972, pp. 3–5; Selwyn 1980, pp. 39–40).

At Oxford, Edward Abraham and H.S. Burton found an antibiotic, named cephalosporin P, from the organic solvent extract of Brotzu's culture by 1949, but this had only a narrow spectrum of antibacterial activity. In August 1949, they found another substance from the culture fluids. The substance, which was hydrophilic and had a broader spectrum of activity as described by Brotzu, was at first named cephalosporin N. This was later renamed penicillin N because it had the same nucleus of molecular structure as penicillin. In the process of isolating cephalosporin N, Abraham and G.G.F. Newton found the third antibiotic as a contaminant from crude cephalosporin N preparations in 1953. This substance, named cephalosporin C, was found to have a similar range of activity to cephalosporin N but to be much less active. However, this new antibiotic had some unique properties such as non-toxicity, stability and, in particular, resistance to penicillinase, a class of enzymes produced by bacteria. These enzymes destroy penicillins including cephalosporin N (Newton and Abraham 1955, 1956; Abraham and Loder 1972, pp. 5–7; Sneader 1985, pp. 316–17).

The production of cephalosporin C in quantity was difficult at the time. The Oxford researchers helped the Medical Research Council's Antibiotic Research Station to produce the substance on a larger scale. The National Research Development Corporation (NRDC) secured patents related to the production of cephalosporin C (Abraham and Loder 1972, pp. 7–9; Selwyn 1980, p. 46). The Antibiotic Research Station had been founded to avoid a repetition of the situation that had arisen when British companies had to pay large royalties to produce penicillin by deep fermentation processes, which were developed in the US. NRDC had been established in 1949 to exploit discoveries made in Britain, which had, again, not been achieved in the case of penicillin (Sneader 1985, pp. 316–17). NRDC asked all British pharmaceutical companies with fermentation facilities to help in the production of cephalosporin C, but only Glaxo showed serious interest. In 1956, NRDC began to organize meetings between Glaxo, the researchers at Oxford and the Antibiotic Research Station. By 1957, 100 mg of cephalosporin had been produced by Glaxo, contributing to the work to confirm the chemical structure of the substance (Abraham and Loder 1972, p. 10).

Several foreign companies contacted NRDC and signed licensing agreements with the corporation related to cephalosporin C: Squibb and Eli Lilly in the US in 1959; Merck, Pfizer, SmithKline & French (all in the US), Ciba (Switzerland), Farmitalia (Italy) in 1960; and Fujisawa in Japan in 1961. However, the possibility of developing cephalosporin C itself as a drug in practice disappeared when methicillin, a potent semi-synthetic penicillin, showed resistance to penicillinase in 1960 (Abraham and Loder 1972, p. 10). Fortunately, the patient research on cephalosporins at Oxford, which was supported by the accumulation of intellectual and material assets obtained from their research on penicillin since the mid-1930s, provided cephalosporins with a future. By 1960, the researchers at Oxford had identified the chemical structure of cephalosporin C (Abraham and Newton 1961; Hodgkin and Maslen 1961), and found that 7-aminocephalosporanic acid (7-ACA), which could be obtained in small amounts from cephalosporin C by using a particular method, was a rich source of derivatives that had much higher potency than cephalosporin C (Loder *et al.* 1961; Abraham and Loder 1972, pp. 9, 11–15; Selwyn 1980, p. 46). This meant, in principle, that it should be possible to produce a lot of potent semi-synthetic cephalosporins from 7-ACA in the same way as semi-synthetic penicillins were then being obtained from 6-aminopenicillamic acid (Sneader 1985, p. 318). The critical problem in exploiting the commercial potential of cephalosporins was to discover a method for producing 7-ACA on a large scale (Abraham and Loder 1972, pp. 10–11).

In 1960, Robert Morin and his colleagues at the Lilly Research Laboratories devised a more efficient procedure for converting cephalosporin C into 7-ACA (Morin *et al.* 1962; Abraham and Loder 1972, p. 11; Selwyn 1980, p. 47). By that time, both Eli Lilly and Glaxo had achieved large-scale production of cephalosporin C by fermentation. Thus, 7-ACA became available in larger quantities, and a number of derivatives were synthesized and examined in the search for potent antibiotics. At Eli Lilly, Robert Chauvette and his colleagues prepared a series of 7-ACA derivatives, and cephalothin was selected for clinical trials from them (Chauvette *et al.* 1962). This was marketed in 1964, becoming the first marketed cephalosporin (Griffith and Black 1964; Selwyn 1980, p. 47). Shortly after that, Glaxo also succeeded in making a marketable semi-synthetic cephalosporin, cephaloridine, which was marketed in 1964 (Muggleton *et al.* 1964; Selwyn 1980, p. 47). Both cephalothin and cephaloridine were claimed to have a broader spectrum of activity than penicillins, to be active against some penicillin-resistant bacteria, and to be free from serious side effects. Safety for patients with penicillin allergy was also reported (Griffith and Black 1964; Muggleton and O'Callaghan 1967). Eli Lilly then synthesized the first orally active cephalosporin, cephaloglycin, by adopting the same side-chain as ampicillin, a semi-synthetic penicillin developed by Beecham a little earlier. Shortly after, however, this drug was replaced by a better-absorbed oral cephalosporin named cephalexin, which was synthesized independently by Eli Lilly and Glaxo and marketed in 1967 (Wick 1967; Newall 1985, p. 215; Selwyn 1980, p. 47; Sneader 1985, pp. 318–19). In 1970, Chauvette and his colleagues at Eli Lilly developed a new chemical process for converting penicillin into cephalexin. This production process could be applied to other cephalosporins, and made the production of 7-ACA more efficient (Chauvette *et al.* 1971; Selwyn 1980, p. 47). By 1971, several cephalosporins with similar properties became clinically available, including cefazolin (Fujisawa), cephapirin (Bristol), and cephacetrile (Ciba-Geigy) (Hewitt 1973; Numata 1981, p. 19). These cephalosporins were later called first-generation cephalosporins; they were more active against Gram-positive bacteria such as staphylococci and streptococci (non-resistant ones), but less active[11] against Gram-negative bacteria such as *E. coli*, *Klebsiellia* and *Pr. mirabilis* than second-generation cephalosporins such as cefamandol, cefaclor (Eli Lilly) and cefuroxime (Glaxo), which had been marketed since around 1972 (Donowitz and Mandell 1988; Numata 1981, pp. 41–5). Cefotiam, developed by Takeda, was one of the second-generation cephalosporins. When they started research on cephalosporins in 1970, first-generation cephalosporins were their exemplars and the targets to be superseded in the search for a new drug (Numata 1981, p. 20).

7.3.3 The Beginning of Takeda's Research on Cephalosporin

Takeda Chemical Industries is one of the oldest pharmaceutical companies in Japan, and also has decades of history of pharmaceutical research, including prodrugs of vitamin B_1 (Arinamin®) which were major products of the company for a long time (Morita 2000, pp. 173–5). In the 1960s and 1970s, antibiotics became the leading drugs that brought substantial profits into pharmaceutical companies in Japan (Nihon Yakusi Gakkai 1995, pp. 119–23). In this area, however, Takeda had no competitive products until the end of the 1960s. In 1967 Takeda started research on semi-synthetic penicillin and succeeded in synthesizing sulbenicillin disodium by 1968, which was marketed in 1973 (Lilacillin®) (Takeda 1983, pp. 755–6). The company also started preliminary research on cephalosporins in 1967. In order to discover a new cephalosporin, however, they had to establish the supply of 7-ACA, which was not generally available. In November 1970, Takeda agreed with Ciba-Geigy to cooperate on cephalosporin research. Under this agreement, in 1971 Takeda started intensive research on cephalosporins with 7-ACA supplied by Ciba-Geigy. Results of the research would be shared between both companies (Takeda 1983, pp. 743, 764). Takeda also started research on production of cephalosporin C in 1970. This research resulted in the invention of a new production process for deacetylcephalosporin C (DCPC) in 1973, which it was later found could be used as an alternative material for production of cephalosporins (Takeda 1983, p. 765). The sales force of Takeda, however, could not just wait for the birth of their new cephalosporin. Immediately after the agreement with Ciba-Geigy, the company developed a new production process for cephalexin, and marketed its generic product in 1973 under the process patent system in Japan.[12] In addition, Takeda and Ciba-Geigy cooperated on clinical trials and marketing of Ciba's cephalosporin, cephacetrile, in Japan. This was marketed in Japan in 1978 (ibid., p. 818).

The earliest attempt at synthesizing a new cephalosporin at Takeda was conducted by the research group that had created sulbenicillin disodium, a semi-synthetic penicillin. In May 1970, they began to synthesize new cephalosporins on a small scale, with the agreement with Ciba-Geigy in prospect. They found that one of them, SCE-20, which had the same side chain as sulbenicillin disodium, had an activity against a particular group of Gram-negative bacteria called *Pseudomonas aeruginosa*.[13] This interested the researchers because existing antibiotics were largely ineffective against these bacteria. In 1971, with a supply of 7-ACA from Ciba-Geigy, they synthesized further analogues of SCE-20, and found that two of them, SCE-120 and SCE-129, were much more active against the bacteria than SCE-20 though they were not very active against other bacteria. Although there was doubt about its marketability, Takeda decided to develop SCE-129 in 1973 because of its unique activity against *Pseudomonas aeruginosa*. Researchers at Ciba-Geigy and academic specialists in infectious disease supported Takeda's decision (ibid., p. 971; Numata 1981, pp. 11–16). SCE-129 was named cefsulodin and launched in 1981 (Takesulin®). From the beginning, however, it was obvious that this would not cover the requirements of the sales division of the company, because of the drug's narrow range of antibacterial activity. They needed a cephalosporin with a much broader range (Hiramatsu interview[14]) Although these early attempts did not earn much income, it should be noted that they earned trust from Ciba-Geigy and ensured a further supply of 7-ACA, which helped further cephalosporin research at Takeda (Takeda 1983, p. 971). The research group that produced cefsulodin did not belong to the Central Research Division, but to the Manufacturing Division. They were somewhat peripheral as researchers in Takeda (Numata interview). The search for a broader cephalosporin, which the company truly needed, was conducted by the 'mainstream' of Takeda's research division (Takeda 1983, p. 973).

7.3.4 Discovery of Cefotiam

Takeda charged the First Chemical Research Department at the Central Research Division led by Katsura Morita with research to discover a new cephalosporin in 1971. Morita described this project as 'a life-betting gamble' for the company and for himself. The project was created by the strategic needs of the company, and the project team had to achieve the goal though they had no experience in synthesizing cephalosporins. If they failed, they would have to take responsibility for the failure, and the company would have lost out in the Japanese antibiotic market (Morita interview;[15] Morita 2000, pp. 207–8). Two of the staff of the Investigation Department also participated in the project team. They investigated almost all related patents and literature, and mapped the situation of cephalosporin research in the world, including chemical structures and antibacterial properties of all cephalosporins available. There were pessimistic opinions expressed by the team, when they looked at the chart (Morita interview; Morita 2000, pp. 208–9). He persuaded his team members:

> I said, 'There were only several thousand compounds. Despite this, no existing cephalosporin had stronger activity [against Gram-positive bacteria] than penicillins. In addition, penicillins were cheaper than cephalosporins. So, we can catch up [with leading companies]. Moreover, penicillin has only one place to be modified. But cephalosporin has two places. That means hundreds of thousands of compounds in principle can be synthesized. Not the level of several thousand. So, we have a chance.' (Interview)

This persuasion was successful. Morita also faced the question of which approach to adopt: random searching or rational searching. He thought about his available resources and chose the latter. He put it:

> It was a divergence which was better: to make as many compounds as possible without thinking until coming across a hit, like blind shooting; or to make a working hypothesis first, then begin to synthesize compounds based on the hypothesis. I was afraid we would not tolerate the former choice. I thought we should make a hypothesis about why cephalosporins were active, what kind of mechanism killed bacteria, and what structure should be designed. The hypothesis had to be unique, which others did not share. I thought we should make such a hypothesis by ourselves. My staff agreed with me. (Interview)

The hypothesis was made based on knowledge of organic chemistry in the related area (for example, Sweet and Dahl 1970) and investigation of the structure–activity relationship of existing cephalosporins. Morita and his colleagues conjectured that an 'active hydrogen' in the side chain at position 7 of a cephalosporin molecule (Figure 7.2) was linked with antibacterial activity of the drug by enhancing the chemical reactivity of the molecule to the cell-wall-making enzyme of bacteria (Morita *et al.* 1980, pp. 17–8, 2000, pp. 209–12; Morita interview). Not all team members were fully convinced by the hypothesis; a few researchers did not adhere to it (Morita interview). It is still unclear if the hypothesis is correct (Numata interview). Most researchers were, however, convinced that they would work with it. Based on this hypothesis, they considered putting a particular atomic group called β-ketoacid into the side chain in order to produce an 'active hydrogen' (Figure 7.3). This structure was chosen because it was unique and not protected by patents of other companies (Numata 1981, p. 22: Morita *et al.* 1980, p. 17; Numata interview). However, it was clear that this was a hard task because β-ketoacid was very unstable (Morita 2000, pp. 212–13; Numata 1981, p. 26).

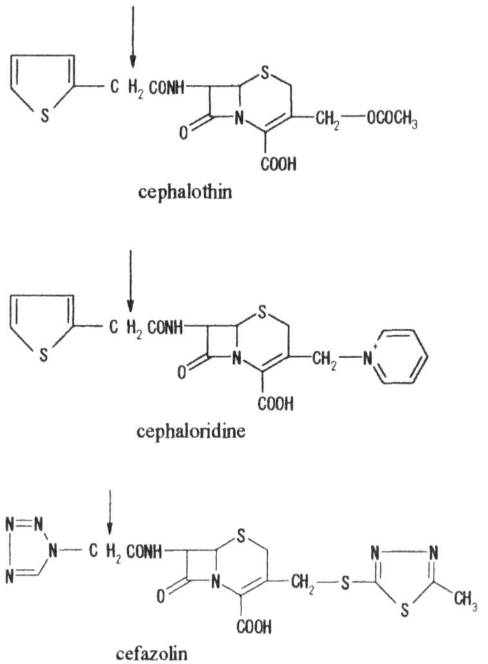

cephalothin

cephaloridine

cefazolin

Note: Arrows point to the 'active hydrogen'.

Figure 7.2:   First generation cephalosporins and the 'active hydrogen'

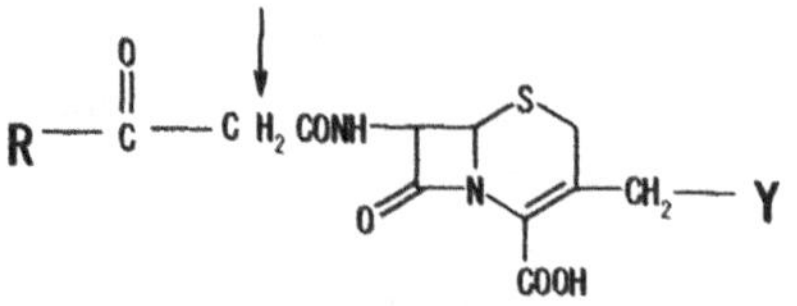

Notes: 'R' and 'Y' mean variable chemical groups.
      The arrow points to an 'active hydrogen'.

Figure 7.3: Target compounds with the β-ketoacid side chain

Morita thought that this project should be completed in at most three years (Morita 2000, p. 208); and he organized five dedicated research groups. This was an exceptionally concentrated deployment of a research force. Three of the groups were charged with chemical synthesis; one was in charge of pharmacological study; the other one was in charge of the supply of β-ketoacids (Morita interview; Numata interview). Morita mixed 'lay researchers,' that is, researchers who were not specialized in the area, into the research groups. He put it:

'Cephalosporins are more expensive than penicillins.' 'Cephalosporins are less active than penicillins.' People who were familiar with antibiotics and penicillins tended to say such words to me. I did not want those people in my project team. I preferred ignorant people without such prejudice. Ignorant people can act boldly, take drastic measures and find something unexpected. ... Indeed, after all, they did produce excellent results. (Interview)

Mitsuo Numata, the leader of the winning research group in this project, was one of the 'lay researchers'. He shared Morita's opinion:

[A success point is] that [Morita] did not use specialists only, but mixed lay people with specialists. ... If the team members had been specialists only, their view would have been much narrower. The team needed someone with foolishness enough to challenge what specialists believed to be impossible. Of course, lay people only would not have produced any better results. Mixture was important. (Interview)

There was keen competition between the research groups. Numata, one of the group leaders, and Kenji Okonogi, who conducted the biological study of the compounds synthesized by all research groups, described the situation at that time lightheartedly:

Hara: Was there exchange of information between the research groups?
Numata: No. Rarely. Because we were fighting each other [laugh]. Members of each group spoke ill of other groups at Okonogi's laboratory. He was a good listener.

Okonogi: Yes. I can confess it now. To be honest, it was a very hard job to be fair to every group [laugh].
Numata: I asked him, for example, not to give this information to Dr Ochiai [laugh]. All of us had a strong sense of rivalry. However, Morita had the ability to control this situation. (Interview)

Morita made careful efforts to control conflicts inside his research organization. He described an example of his efforts:

I did not become a co-author of papers produced by the researchers in my department after I became the Head. I even declined to be mentioned in acknowledgements. ... If I had allowed them to put my name into their papers, I could not have promoted competition in my organization. If I had become a co-author of one research group, I would have had to become a co-author of another research group, in order to be neutral between them. But if I had done this, it would have made me look indifferent and somewhat irresponsible. (Interview)

In the first year of the project, SCE-150, which did not include β-ketoacids in its structure, was synthesized by one of the research groups. Although SCE-150 was as potent as the most potent cephalosporin available at that time, Morita gave up its development because he believed that it would become obsolete before it appeared on the market several years later (Morita interview).

The research group led by Numata succeeded in putting β-ketoacids into cephalosporin molecules at the position 7 side chain and synthesized many compounds. Most of them showed only disappointing activity. However, when they introduced an atom group called methyl-thio-methyl to the β-ketoacid side chain, the resultant compound showed fairly high potency (Numata *et al.* 1978a, 1978b; Numata 1981, pp. 25–6; Morita *et al.* 1983, p. 19). This result encouraged them to make further analogues of this compound. Serendipitous discovery occurred in the process: when they tried to combine another related atom group called thiocyanate with the side chain, the nuclear magnetic resonance analyser in their laboratories was broken; because of this, the compound was left for a week. After the machine was repaired, a young researcher of the group analysed the compound and found that it was different from what they expected. They examined the unknown compound and found that the atomic group at the end of the side chain had become a cyclic structure. Moreover, this new compound possessed remarkable antibacterial activity which was stronger than any existing cephalosporin, particularly against Gram-negative bacteria. This showed the way to what they were looking for. When they used thiourea, another related chemical group, in place of thiocyanate, a similar reaction, namely 'cyclization', occurred immediately and produced a cephalosporin with a unique side chain called 2-aminothiazol-4-ylacetyl with good yields (Figure 7.4). They then made an effort to optimize another side chain at position 3. The consequent cephalosporin, codenamed SCE-785 (Figure 7.5), satisfied the requirements for a competitive cephalosporin in future market. Takeda decided to develop SCE-785 in July 1974, five months after its synthesis (Numata *et al.* 1978c, pp. 1262–3; Numata 1981, pp. 27-30; Morita *et al.* 1983, p. 19; Takeda 1983, p. 973; Numata interview). The unique structure of SCE-785, 2-aminothiazol-4-yl, later became a standard component structure: most third-generation cephalosporins developed later adopted it (Takeda 1983, p. 973; Webber and Wheeler 1982, pp. 379, 389–90).

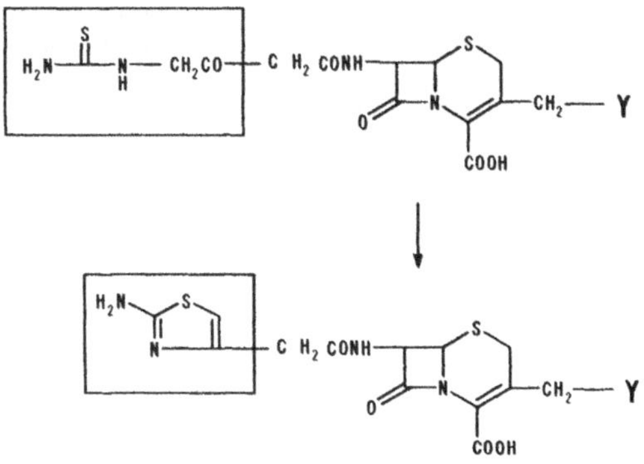

Figure 7.4: The 'cyclization' of the β-ketoacid side chain resulting in formation of 2-aminothiazol-4-ylacetyl side chain

SCE-785 was pre-clinically tested for about a year and its efficacy was confirmed (Takeda 1983, p. 973). However, tiny deposits were observed in the kidneys and the bladders of rabbits to which a lot of SCE-785 was administered. This was believed to be due to the low solubility of the compound in water. Morita insisted on continuing its development because results in humans might be different from those in rabbits, but toxicologists at Takeda argued that they should wait for a better drug (Morita 2000, p. 214; Morita interview). SCE-785 proceeded to clinical trials with healthy volunteers, but one of them showed side effects. This was also believed to be due to the low solubility of the compound in water (Numata interview; Takeda 1983, p. 973). Thus, the development of SCE-785 was stopped in December 1975 (Takeda 1983, p. 973).

Along with the development of SCE-785, the search for a better cephalosporin was continued in Morita's department. This time, Morita concentrated researchers' efforts on improving 2-aminothiazol-4-ylacetyl cephalosporins, that is to say, analogues of SCE-785 (Morita 2000, p. 213;

Morita interview). At this stage, he made Numata's group open up their information to other researchers in order to promote competition among them (Morita interview). Numata was transferred to the Manufacturing Division to help development of the production process of SCE-785 (Numata interview). In Morita's department, further efforts were made to optimize the side chain at position 3. Okonogi, who was involved in assaying these compounds, described how busy he was at that time, dealing with the compounds which were synthesized one after another:

> We examined about 30 compounds a week. We divided them into two sessions. It took three days to assay compounds: plant bacteria on the first day; put compounds into the culture next day; then observe results on the third day. By that time, our company had adopted a five-day working week. ... So we had two sessions: Monday to Wednesday and Wednesday to Friday. We continued this for weeks. (Interview)

As a result, 154 compounds were synthesized. When the development of SCE-785 was stopped, several compounds that had higher solubility in water were chosen from the newly synthesized compounds. After detailed examination of these compounds, in December 1975 Takeda decided to develop one of them, SCE-963, in place of SCE-785. This compound, named cefotiam (Figure 7.5), also had a broad range of activity and was in particular more active against some of Gram-negative bacteria than existing antibiotics at that time. Cefotiam quickly passed through pre-clinical tests and proceeded into clinical trials in August 1976 (Takeda 1983, pp. 973–4; Numata *et al.* 1978c; Morita *et al.* 1983, pp. 19–20; Tsuchiya *et al.* 1978).

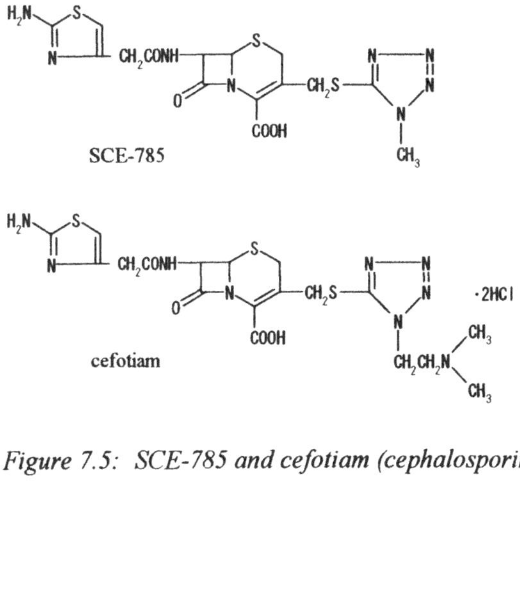

Figure 7.5: SCE-785 and cefotiam (cephalosporins)

7.3.5 Development of Cefotiam

Development of an efficient production process for cephalosporins proceeded concurrently with chemical syntheses and biological studies of the compounds (Takeda 1983, p. 973). Production costs of cephalosporins had been a critical problem for the commercialization of the drugs. Penicillins were much cheaper than cephalosporins at that time, and this produced obstacles to research and development of cephalosporins. Morita faced such criticism when he led the cephalosporin project at Takeda. He put it:

> One of my senior colleagues asked me, 'Morita, I hear you have begun to research cephalosporins. But do you know the prices of penicillins and cephalosporins?' I said, 'I don't know exactly, but cephalosporins seem expensive.' He said, 'Ten times as expensive. I mean, costs of raw materials. In addition, penicillins are fast in fermentation. Moreover, it is easy to extract penicillins into butanol, but cephalosporins are hydrophilic and insoluble in butanol. How could you succeed?' (Interview)

In order to reduce the costs of cephalosporins, Takeda had made efforts early on in their research. As I mentioned above, they developed a new production process of deacetylcephalosporin C (DCPC) in 1973. They then invented a new route to produce semi-synthetic cephalosporins such as cefotiam from DCPC in good yields and on a large scale; this reduced production costs to an acceptable level (Takeda 1983, p. 974; Tsushima *et al.* 1979). It should be noted, however, that this problem of the cost of cephalosporins was also related to patents secured by other companies. Numata explained:

> At that time, only members of the syndicate [organized by NRDC] could use [the raw material, 7-ACA]. ... When we thought about methods of its production, we found more patents protected them. So, only DCPC enabled us to circumvent those patents. ... So, we at first made DCPC and use it as the raw material of cephalosporins. Later, those patents expired one by one, and it became more economical to use 7-ACA available on the market than to use DCPC made by us. (Interview)

Takeda also had to design a unique preparation to make cefotiam suitable for practical use. Because of the production route of cefotiam and in order to maintain stability of the compound, the company decided to market cefotiam as a salt with two moles of hydrochloric acid. When this salt alone was dissolved in water, however, the solution was too acidic to be appropriate for clinical use. Therefore, they prepared sodium carbonate with the drug to neutralize the acid. Then, they reduced the pressure in the phials containing the preparation to control the carbon dioxide generated when water was added to them. To produce the phial, they also had to develop new equipment for packaging (Takeda 1983, p. 974). Fortunately for them, however, the good solubility of the prescription was highly appreciated by medical practitioners including doctors and nurses, according to Nobuyoshi Hiramatsu who was involved in the marketing of cefotiam (interview). This is because medical practitioners often face cases in which they have to administer an antibiotic to patients immediately (Numata personal communication, June 2000).

Clinical trials of cefotiam went ahead smoothly. In February 1977, it proceeded to Phase II. Its double-blind trials with cefazolin, a highly potent first-generation cephalosporin developed in Japan, were conducted from November 1977. The results of these Phase III trials were presented at the annual conference of the Japan Society of Chemotherapy in June 1978. The efficacy and safety of cefotiam were supported there (Shimizu *et al.* 1979; various papers in *Chemotherapy*, 27, supplement 3, April 1979). Based on these data, Takeda and its development partner Ciba-Geigy (Japan) obtained approval for manufacturing cefotiam from the Ministry of Health and Welfare in 1980. Takeda launched cefotiam under the trade name Pansporin® in February 1981 (Takeda 1983, p. 974). Cefotiam was also marketed in several foreign countries including Germany, but its sales abroad were limited.[16]

Two institutional factors contributed to the relatively rapid development of cefotiam in Japan. First, because antibiotics were used to cure acute diseases, its long-term side effects were regarded as less important than those of drugs for chronic diseases such as hypertension and hypercholesterolemia. Rather, the regulatory body sought to approve any better antibiotic as soon as possible (Hiramatsu interview). Second, there was a well-organized society of specialist doctors in the chemotherapy area in Japan, the Japan Society of Chemotherapy, which was practice-orientated rather than basic-research-orientated: it focused on evaluation of drugs rather than research about infectious diseases (Japan Society of Chemotherapy website[17]). This society had its own routine for managing clinical trials. When pharmaceutical companies asked the society to do clinical trials, it organized and arranged them; then, they proceeded steadily under the initiative of the society. This system strongly promoted the development of antibiotics in Japan (Hiramatsu interview).

Cefotiam was profitable because it was more active against bacteria than existing drugs at that time. This was not only because the drug was sold better than other drugs, but also because its price was fixed by the regulatory body at a higher level than other drugs. In Japan, the official price of a drug is fixed in comparison with those of other equivalent drugs, or of most similar drugs if there is no equivalent drug. Because cefotiam was almost twice as active as existing drugs, it succeeded in gaining the same price as others for only a half quantity: in other words, it won almost double the price per gram compared with existing drugs (Hiramatsu interview).

7.4 TAMSULOSIN

7.4.1 Introduction

Tamsulosin is a drug that is a remedy for the urination disorder that accompanies benign prostatic hypertrophy (Japanese Patent WO 95/02419, 1995). It was discovered by a research team led by Toichi Takenaka in 1980 at first as a potential anti-hypertension drug. However, its new application in the urological area was later recognized and it was clinically developed for this. In addition, the drug was developed at first in its racemic mixture (Yamanouchi 1994; Takenaka, *et al.* 1995), that is to say, in a 50:50 mixture of two stereoisomers that have a mirror-image relationship. A racemic mixture is symbolized as ($\pm$), while each of the stereoisomers is expressed as (+) or (–). It was later switched to be the single (–)-isomer only. Tamsulosin (Harnal®) was marketed in Japan in 1993 (Yamanouchi 1994), in European countries in 1995 and in the US in 1997 (Takenaka interview).[18] It had sales in Japan of about £150 million and its overseas sales were about £50 million in 1997 (Nihon Sougou Kenkyusyo 1998, p. 274).

Table 7.3: Major events related to the discovery and development of tamsulosin

Year	Events
1976	Research started
1980	Discovery of YM-12617 (a racemic mixture of tamsulosin)
1982	Organizational authorization
1983	Clinical trials started
1986	Switch to the single (–)-isomers (tamsulosin)
1993	Launch in Japan

7.4.2 Synthesis of Tamsulosin

Benign prostatic hypertrophy (BPH) often arises when men age. It causes some difficulties in urination such as retarded urination, frequent urination and residual urine. It is said that a fifth of men over 55 years old suffer from the disease (Yamanouchi 1994a). Although it is not a fatal disease, it seriously damages the quality of life of patients. BPH had previously been treated by traditional Chinese medicine or hormone preparations; surgery was the only treatment that was more effective. Furthermore, most patients were unwilling to go to urogenital clinics, partly because of their negative image, especially in Japan, and partly because the disease was not fatal (Takenaka interview). It was common for sufferers to buy over-the-counter (OTC) drugs based on traditional Chinese medicine to relieve the difficulty.

Tamsulosin was not synthesized at first as a drug for the treatment of urination disorder. Researchers at Yamanouchi had been involved in research on α and β adrenergic receptors since 1965. As outcomes of this research, they discovered a β-blocker for the treatment of heart diseases and hypertension, indenolol, in 1968, a β-stimulant for the treatment of asthma, formoterol, in 1972, and an $\alpha\beta$-blocker for the treatment of hypertension, amosulalol, in 1976 (Yamanouchi 1994a; Takenaka *et al.* 1995). The discovery of tamsulosin stemmed from the research on amosulalol.[19] From the research on differences in the receptor selectivity of various $\alpha\beta$-blockers, researchers found the (+)-isomer of amosulalol to be more potent in blocking α_1 receptors, a subtype of α receptors, and the (−)-isomer to be more potent in blocking β_1 receptors, a subtype of β receptors. They synthesized the derivatives of amosulalol to obtain more potent α_1 blockers without β_1 blocking activity. They found that sulfamoylphenethylamines constituted a structurally new type of potent α_1 blockers. YM-12617 (the racemic mixture of tamsulosin), synthesized in 1980, was found to be the most potent compound of all (Takenaka *et al.* 1984, 1995) and became a candidate for development (Figure 7.6). Therefore, tamsulosin was synthesized as an α_1 blocker, without a specific application of the compound. Toichi Takenaka explained why he turned his attention to α_1 blockers:

> I was interested in α receptors, because at that time a new theory emerged that there were two subtypes of α receptors, namely, α_1 receptors and α_2 receptors. Then, I was keen to know what kinds of roles each subtype played. So, we examined their distribution and related properties. I remained in this area of research because of my intellectual curiosity, and expected to lead studies and experiments, such as one on which subtypes govern the prostate and the urethra, to academic publication. (Interview)

The synthesis of the compound, in other words the modification from amosulalol to the compound, was said to have been done quite rationally and relatively smoothly. Takenaka put it thus:

> The drug design went smoothly, because the lead compound was our own and we had experience of amosulalol. And in our own research, we had been involved in research on the sympathetic nervous system for a long time, since around 1965. So, we had already, in our company, developed concepts, methods for experiments and whatever related to the drug. (Interview)

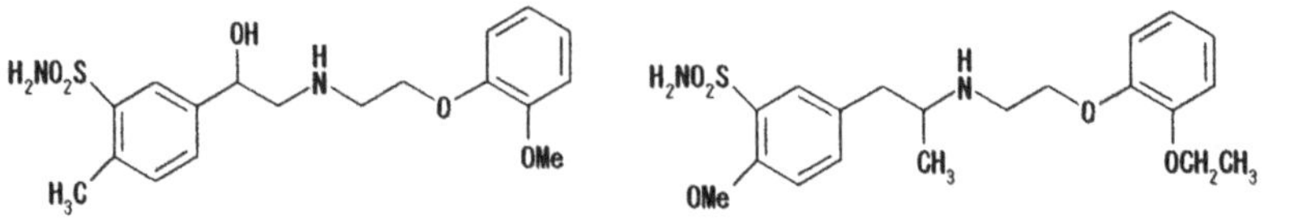

Figure 7.6: Amosulalol (αβ-blocker) and tamsulosin (α$_{1c}$-blocker)

7.4.3 Discovery of the Application

At first, α$_1$ blockers were considered for use in treating anti-hypertension. However, Yamanouchi had already developed indenolol, nicardipine (Ca^{++} blocker) and amosulalol for anti-hypertension and intra-company competition between these drugs existed. Therefore, the researchers started the search for an application of the new α$_1$ blocker (Yamanouchi 1994a).

They turned their attention to the area of urology. There were at least three reasons for this. First, they considered the research of Raz and Caine (1972), suggesting that α receptors played a predominant role in urethral contraction, though they had not identified which subtype of α receptors was related to the activity (Yamanouchi 1994a; Takenaka *et al*. 1995). This led Takenaka and his colleagues to conduct their own investigation of the distribution of the subtypes, as described in his statement above. Takenaka's connection with a urologist was the turning point of his work. He put it thus:

> An unexpected enquiry about whether our company was dealing in a classic α blocker came from a urologist friend of mine when we were doing the research. ... Because I couldn't understand why he was interested in such a drug, I went to ask him. Then, I found that he wanted to try the drug to improve his patients' urination because the Israeli [Raz and Caine's] research said it could do this. ... I answered him that I couldn't provide any immediately but that I would likely be able to provide the drug soon. Therefore, just at that time, the lead compound, the concept and the idea of its application came together. (Interview)

Second, the area of urology had not been well-developed as a market for the pharmaceutical industry. The competition was not considered to be fierce and a good business opportunity was expected there. Third, Yamanouchi staff had established a connection with urologists through the development and marketing of an antibiotic for urinary tract infection: the area was a new and strategically important market for them; they were able to hear urologists' views and exchange information with them through their medical representatives (Takenaka interview).

The research team found that the receptors that mediate contraction of the smooth muscle in the lower urinary tract and prostate gland of the rabbit are α_1 receptors (Honda *et al.* 1985; Takenaka *et al.* 1995). Their subsequent study, in collaboration with urologists at the University of Tokyo, showed that the human urinary bladder base and prostatic urethra are also mediated by α_1 receptors (Kunisawa *et al.* 1985).[20] This opened the way to applying YM-12617 to the treatment of urination disorder accompanying BPH.

7.4.4 Acquisition of Internal Authorization

Yamanouchi decided in 1982 to develop YM-12617 as a drug for the treatment of urination disorder accompanying BPH. There were several other similar candidate compounds, but YM-12617 was chosen because it was believed that its overall record in potency, pharmacokinetic properties and costs was best of all.

The acquisition of approval from the company management for the development of YM-12617 was the most crucial barrier facing the research team on the path to turning their discovery into an innovation.[21] The management was full of doubts about the marketability of the drug.[22] First, there was a doubt as to whether BPH could really be considered to be a disease. Second, this drug would reduce the necessity of surgery for the treatment of BPH;[23] there were questions about whether the drug would be accepted by practitioners and how it would coexist with surgery. There was also the problem of how high a price should be set to balance the anticipated decrease in doctors' income from surgery.[24] Third, there was a problem of estimating the potential market size for this drug, because many patients with BPH at the time were unwilling to go to urogenital clinics.

The connection and communication with urologists played an essential role in sweeping away these concerns. Takenaka, the project leader, had an interest in medical needs and actively investigated this with the marketing staff. They found that a group of urologists at Gunma University had been doing studies on BPH for a long time in a village in Gunma Prefecture. These data provided Takenaka's team with a valuable basis for estimating the number of potential patients. Market information obtained from urologists like this enabled Takenaka to prepare evidence good enough to persuade the management (Takenaka interview).

Economic reviews were conducted systematically by the company even after the approval for development had been given by the management. An expert department of the company assessed the project at least three times: before Phase I, before Phase III and before the application for governmental approval. They estimated the market size and sales, development and production investments and operational costs. It was their policy to proceed as fast as possible when the results were good, therefore the economic review had a significant influence on the speed of development (Takenaka interview). Because the company had at first estimated that the number of patients for the drug would be 50,000, the priority given to the project was not very high until 1985. Because of an improvement in the technology used in the medical check-up for the disorder, the estimated number of the patients was corrected to 150,000. After that, the priority of the project rose steeply (Nihon Sougou Kenkyusyo 1998).

7.4.5 Technological Changes in the Development Process

In 1983, Yamanouchi started clinical trials of the drug, following its pre-clinical tests which had started in the previous year (Nihon Sougou Kenkyusyo 1998). There was no practical problem in Phase I and Phase II. However, it was known that YM-12617 was a racemic mixture and that only its (–)-isomer was clinically active. An American consultant of Yamanouchi suggested to the company that the racemic property of the drug might become a significant problem in marketing in the United States and European countries.[25] The company knew that the single isomers of the drug would be at most twice as active as its racemic mixture and that it would cost a lot to produce the single isomers, together with the loss of time and money that they had already spent on the clinical trials of YM-12617. Nevertheless, the company decided 'with tears' to switch the drug to the single (–)-isomers because they wanted to use the drug strategically as a decisive step in the company's globalization. They restarted clinical trials of the (–)-isomers of YM-12617, now named tamsulosin, from Phase I in 1986 (Takenaka interview).[26]

Another problem was the control of a minor side effect. Although tamsulosin was selective to the receptors at the prostate and the urethra, it also had a weak influence on blood pressure. This can cause orthostatic hypotension: dizziness felt on standing up. In order to avoid this disorder, the Takenaka group at first tried to increase the dosage of the drug gradually so that the body could get accustomed to it. This method was, however, very bothersome for doctors and patients. Therefore, they considered making a sustained release preparation of the drug to avoid the side effect. They succeeded in realizing this and achieved oral, once-a-day administration in 1986 (Takenaka interview; Fukai 1995, p. 489; Yamanouchi 1994a; Takenaka *et al.* 1995). This was also commercially important. Takenaka put it thus:

> We chose a sustained release preparation for the drug and this was another key factor in the success. This was done intentionally. We considered the business aspect very much at that stage. We had many talks with doctors and heard them

say, 'Sustained release is better', 'Yes, this is good', and comments like that. (Interview)

Commercial consideration was also seen in Yamanouchi's efforts to establish an economical large-scale production system for the drug. They considered the abandonment of the other isomers, namely, (+)-isomers, to be a waste. They succeeded in recycling the isomers to turn them into (–)-isomers and reduced the production costs enough for them to be acceptable (Takenaka interview).

7.4.6 Clinical Trials and Promotion

In the clinical trials of tamsulosin, the cooperative attitudes of doctors toward the trials were important. For example, doctors could use placebos in the clinical trials. But it was, and it has probably always been, extremely difficult for them to use placebos in clinical trials under the practice of informed consent in Japan. However, a comparison with placebos is the most convincing way of showing the efficacy and safety of a drug. Yamanouchi succeeded in obtaining doctors' cooperation to use placebos in Phase II and Phase III of the clinical trials of the drug. They also succeeded in obtaining doctors' agreement to conduct more detailed dosage response tests. Moreover, they persuaded doctors to apply the US guidelines, which were stricter than the Japanese counterparts, to the trials. With the cooperation of doctors, they achieved high-quality clinical trials, which confirmed the efficacy and safety of the drug (Takenaka interview; Kawabe *et al.* 1990).[27]

The market was shaped partly by the company and partly by other actors in Japanese society. Takenaka put it thus in my interview with him:

Takenaka: Social needs in the treatment of BPH changed and influenced [the development of the drug] positively. More men went to urogenital clinics. Doctors wrote about the urination disorder in newspapers, and people recognized it.
Hara: As a disease?
Takenaka: Yes, luckily. We promoted it intentionally to some extent, but there was a limit to what we could do. After all, society did it. And the concept of QOL [quality of life] penetrated deeply in society. You wake up frequently at night for urination, so you can't have a good sleep, and this is a bad quality of life. We need a drug to improve the situation. It was time such thoughts emerged.

Scientific and technological progress also affected the progress of the development and sales of the drug. In 1987, subtypes of α_1 receptors were pharmacologically found and named α_{1A} receptors and α_{1B} receptors (Morrow and Creese 1987; Minneman *et al.* 1988). Lepor *et al.* (1993)

showed that the α_1 receptors which mediate the contraction of the prostatic smooth muscle are the α_{1A} subtype. Later, by using molecular biology, three subtypes of α_1 receptors were found to exist, renamed α_{1a} receptors, α_{1b} receptors and α_{1c} receptors (Schwinn *et al.* 1990; Lomasney *et al.* 1991). Price *et al.* (1993), using techniques of molecular biology, identified that the α_1 receptors which predominantly exist in the prostate are the α_{1c} receptors (which encode for the pharmacological α_{1A} receptors).[28] Several studies showed that the affinity of tamsulosin to the pharmacological α_{1A} receptors and the cloned α_{1c} receptors is greater than that to the α_{1B} receptors (Abrams *et al.* 1995). These studies showed that tamsulosin is selective in the prostate because of its high affinity to the α_{1c} receptors (or the pharmacological α_{1A} receptors). According to Takenaka, 'this completed the scientific concept of the drug' (interview). He described how this worked in the marketing of the drug:

> The influence [of the concept of the α_{1A} blocker] was enormous. In particular, when the word 'selectivity' appeared, I could announce that I had discovered a selective drug. It was a scientific achievement. I could write many papers on it and become famous. This made the marketing of the drug very easy. 'How is it different from existing drugs?' 'Doctor, this is α_{1A} selective.' 'What's α_{1A}?' 'Well, you don't know? α_{1A} is the one that is widespread in the prostate.' 'A-ha! So it works on BPH.' Like that. We could give a very simple explanation. (Interview)

Tamsulosin was launched in Japan in August 1993 under the trade name of Harnal. As I have already mentioned, it was also launched in the US and European countries later. The drug was exclusively developed by Yamanouchi. There were approaches from several companies about co-development but Yamanouchi declined them all (Nihon Sougou Kenkyusyo 1998). The experience of the international development of the drug was a crucial step in the globalization of the company[29] (interview). To my question of what was the most important factor in the success, Takenaka mentioned leadership and teamwork and emphasized their previous experience of success in drug discovery and development (Takenaka interview; Nihon Sougou Kenkyusyo 1998). He put it thus:

> While I was researching receptors, I had also made several drugs from the research. Some of them succeeded commercially, others not. But when I researched something, I made a drug from the research and led it to the market. I did Pulsan, then I did Perdipine, and then Lowgan, and this Harnal. Then Hypoca.[30] I materialized and commercialized research as drugs, so the management looked at me positively.
> ... After all, to be trusted is important. If you are trusted, you can do things as you like, to some extent. Then, you can take some risks. It's important to have

experience of success. People who have experience of success can do something radical. (Interview)

7.5　A BRIEF ANALYSIS

There were differences in the pattern of drug discovery and development process between the three cases in this chapter. The process of shaping mevastatin clearly demonstrates the properties of the paradigmatic innovation discussed in the previous chapters. This compound played an exemplary role. It demonstrated the idea of lowering the cholesterol level in the blood by inhibiting HMG-CoA reductase and showed what kind of compound could achieve it. Because of this novelty, scientific and technological uncertainty was very high. Organizational resistance based on unfamiliarity arose in the company. For the survival of the project, Endo showed strong leadership. He mobilized various resources, including scientific explanations, the hens for experiment which were obtained through informal friendship, academic authorities such as Goldstein and Yamamoto, and experimental data.

In contrast, in the case of cefotiam, scientific and technological uncertainty was not so high, because there were several exemplary cephalosporins. What the Takeda researchers had to do was to modify molecular structure in order to obtain significantly better properties. However, existing patents, access to the raw material and technical opportunity limited the process of modification. Morita, the project leader, organized researchers and added an element of competition to the process. The company made organizational efforts to make change to existing cephalosporins in various aspects: efficacy, the range of target, safety, production costs, and convenient preparations. Thus, the case of cefotiam clearly demonstrates the properties of modification-based innovation.

The case of tamsulosin was ambivalent. The compound itself was not so novel as in paradigmatic innovation, because α blockers were well-known compounds; that is, the drug had exemplars as compounds. However, it had novelty in its application; that is, the treatment for urination disorder accompanying BPH. People inside and outside the organization were doubtful about this application. Takenaka defended the project by providing evidence, including the potential market size of the drug. In this process of shaping a new application, the linkage with doctors in the urological area was particularly important: they provided Takenaka and his company with the idea, the evidence and the concept. However, without the heterogeneous engineering conducted by Takenaka, the idea could not have been materialized. In the shaping of market, the company promoted the drug by using the concept of α_{1c} blockage. In this way, the case of tamsulosin has mixed properties of paradigmatic innovation and modification-based innovation. This ambiguity can be attributed to its novelty in application and familiarity with its molecular structure. Therefore, I propose to regard the shaping of tamsulosin as belonging to another type of innovation, named application innovation. Thus, three different patterns of drug discovery and development can be identified from the case studies in this chapter.

These cases also reveal how a pharmaceutical company is not a monolithic organization. In the case of mevastatin, there was interpretative flexibility about the efficacy and safety of mevastatin. The pharmacologists at the Central Research Laboratories thought that the drug was not effective because it did not work in rats, whereas Endo thought that it failed because the model animal was not appropriate. The toxicologists believed that mevastatin was not safe enough because they observed unknown deposits in the liver cells of the rats, whereas Endo believed that it was safe because the deposits were resoluble cholesterol ester. On the toxicity study that led to the suspension of its development, the company considered that mevastatin was not safe enough because the long-term tests demonstrated its potential toxicity, whereas Endo considered it was safe because the tests had flaws in the choice of dosage. In the case of cefotiam, there was also interpretative flexibility about the safety of SCE-785, its prototype. Morita thought that the compound should be examined in humans because humans were not the same as the rabbits that showed its toxicity, whereas toxicologists thought that it should be abandoned because the rabbit body probably represented the human body. In addition, there were other kinds of divergence of opinions in the companies. In the case of cefotiam, there were doubts about the possibility of further improvement of cephalosporins and about the profitability of the new cephalosporin. In the case of tamsulosin, there were also different views about marketability and profitability.

This divergence of opinions required a closure mechanism to shape organizational authorization. Various resources were mobilized for this. In the case of mevastatin, animals, data, explanations and the linkage with external medical authorities played an important role in obtaining organizational authorization. In the case of tamsulosin, the track record of the project leader, the linkage with external medical academics and social awareness of the quality of life were significant. In the case of cefotiam, although the project team obtained the support of management from the beginning, they had to demonstrate the feasibility and profitability of the specific compound in order to sweep away doubts within the company. Thus, obtaining organizational authorization was important in any type of innovation, though to a different degree, and various human actors, non-human entities and institutional and structural factors had to be mobilized to achieve this.

The heterogeneity of elements involved in the process of drug discovery and development were also seen in the other aspects of shaping. In the shaping of mevastatin, cefotiam and tamsulosin as compounds, human actors (for example, project leaders, various researchers, external academics, corporate management, doctors, patients), non-human entities (such as microbes, bioassay systems, different animals, spectroscopes, X-ray crystallography), and institutional and structural factors (for example, external academic linkages, organizational structure, informal human networks, organizational assets, product lines, corporate strategies, competitive position, regulatory systems) were involved. In the shaping of the application of tamsulosin, the project leader, project team members, external medical experts, the linkage between these, the compound itself, the assay system, potential medical needs, project evaluation systems, corporate strategy, product lines and complementary assets played a significant role. In the shaping of markets, the corporate workers, the doctors, the patients, the regulators, the compounds, the drug preparations, clinical trials, toxicological studies, academic papers, conferences, advertisements, business visits, scientific concepts, data on efficacy and safety, and production costs affected the process.

In particular, the three cases in this chapter reveal the influence of Japan-specific structural and cultural factors on the innovation process of pharmaceuticals. The case of mevastatin shows the importance of consensus in the Japanese organization. The project-coordinating meeting played a decisive role, and the project could not go ahead without the agreement of toxicologists and pathologists. It also demonstrates the power of academic clinicians at universities in Japan. But for the offer of clinical trials from Yamamoto at Osaka University, the project of mevastatin would have been axed earlier. In the case of cefotiam, the policy of the regulatory body in Japan and the support system of the Japan Society of Chemotherapy were highlighted. In the case of tamsulosin, the unwillingness of Japanese people to go to urogenital clinics in Japan was indicated.

NOTES

1. The interview with Dr Akira Endo was conducted on 5 November 1999.
2. Goldstein and Brown won the Nobel Prize in 1985 for these achievements.
3. Arima was regarded somewhat as an outsider in the research laboratories because he had worked in other departments for a long time before he became the director (Endo personal communication, April 2000).

4. It should be noted that experimental results about mevastatin were presented in academic societies in 1977 but the responses of scientists were not very favourable. Goldstein's team and Yamamoto's team were rare exceptions (Endo 1987, p. 652; Endo 1994, p. 125).

5. Before the tests in Japan, Endo had planned a similar attempt in the US, based on a proposal of Goldstein to try mevastatin in his patients with serious FH in May 1977. However, this attempt was not realized because of the lack of sufficient safety tests and the objection from a domestic medical authority (Endo interview; Endo 1991, p. 721).

6. About the details of the doses of the tests, see Endo (1992, p. 1575) and Endo (1994, p. 126).

7. Even the doses Endo had insisted on at that time were later found to be 250 times higher than the ordinarily effective doses (Endo personal communication).

8. Endo independently discovered lovastatin from another mould in early 1979 and named it monacolin K (Endo 1979; Brown and Goldstein 1981, p. 516). The application for patents of monacolin K by Endo was before that of lovastatin, but because of the difference of principle in US patent law and its counterparts in most countries in the world including Japan (priority on invention versus priority on application), the patent of lovastatin became valid in the US only and the patent of monacolin K, which was handed over to Sankyo by Endo, became valid in the rest of the world. Therefore, Merck did not market lovastatin in Japan but did market simvastatin later (Endo 2001; Endo 1987, p. 652).

9. Interview with Dr Masao Kuroda was conducted on 24 March 2000.

10. Cerivastatin was withdrawn from the market in 2001 because of side effects when used in combination with another anti-cholesterol drug (*The Financial Times*, 8 August 2001).

11. First-generation cephalosporins were in general more active against Gram-negative bacteria than penicillins (Hewitt 1973, p. S314).

12. Japan's patent system was reformed to be the product patent system in 1976. See Howells and Neary (1995, pp. 145–9).

13. *Pseudomonas aeruginosa* is a typical opportunistic pathogen and can cause various infectious diseases, including sepsis, osteomyelitis, airways infection and urinary tract infection, particularly in patients who do not have a normal level of immunity. It is resistant to commonly used antiseptics and antibiotics and may cause hospital infection.

14. The interview with Dr Mitsuo Numata, who was the leader of the key research group in the synthesis of cefotiam, Dr Kenji Okonogi, who was involved in the biological study on cefotiam and other antibiotics, and Mr Nobuyoshi Hiramatsu, who was involved in the development of antibiotics at Takeda, was conducted on 26 January 1999.

15. This interview with Dr Katsura Morita was conducted on 8 February 1999.

16. It was said that Ciba-Geigy gave up its launch in Switzerland because of its small sales prospects. In the US, its launch was not fulfilled because the delay in obtaining an approval from the regulatory body eroded its competitiveness (Okonogi personal communication, June 2000).

17. http:// www03.u-page.so-net.ne.jp/jc4/karyo/index.htm, May 2000.

18. The interview with Dr Toichi Takenaka was conducted on 22 January 1999.

19. The research on tamsulosin was a continuation of the research on amosulalol. Therefore, it is almost impossible to identify the starting point on the research of tamsulosin. In this chapter, I define the starting point as being 1976, just after the discovery of amosulalol. See Fukai (1995, p. 489).

20. The collaboration with the university was a key to the unprecedented research because animal experiments did not guarantee the same results in human beings and because the company could not do experiments with human tissues on its own, according to Takenaka (interview).

21. This paragraph is based on the interview with Dr Takenaka.

22. The procedure for decision making had already been institutionalized in Yamanouchi in the 1980s. First, a research group leader would propose the development of the drug to the assessment meeting inside R&D. Then, if the proposal were approved by the assessment meeting, it would be proposed in the management meeting. The decision of the management meeting would be final (Takenaka interview).

23. This is a common problem in the cases of histamine H_2 antagonists and of anti-prostate cancer drugs. See Chapters 5 and 6 of this book.

24. A higher drug price implies a higher income for doctors in the conventional Japanese health care system. This is because of the margin between the official price and the amount actually paid to purchase the drug. See sub-section 5.4.2 of this book.
25. There was also the same opinion in academia from the viewpoint of drug safety, and Yamanouchi was aware of this (Takenaka *et al.* 1995, p. 778; Ariens 1984).
26. The establishment of an economical, large-scale synthetic procedure was also reported to promote the switch (Fukai 1995, p. 489).
27. The size and the format of clinical trials of tamsulosin were praised by both editors of the *Journal of Urology* (Wein 1990; Lepor 1990).
28. The pharmacological classification of α_1 receptors and their molecular biological classification was not consistent until recently (Forray *et al.* 1994; Kirby and Pool 1997).
29. Yamanouchi has bitter experience of the co-marketing of famotidine. See section 5.4.
30. Pulsan®, Perdipine®, Lowgan® and Hypoca® are the trade names of indenolol, nicardipine, amosulalol and barnidipine, respectively.

8. The process of drug discovery and development

In the previous chapters, we examined the process of drug discovery and development in Japan and the United Kingdom in four different therapeutic areas: namely, cardiovascular diseases, bronchial asthma, peptic ulcer and prostate cancer. In addition, we also investigated three more cases in Japan. The processes may appear to be linear if we look only at their formal aspects. However, close examination of them reveals that they were much more complex. In this chapter I highlight three major findings from the analysis of the cases: heterogeneous and interactive process of drug shaping; the different types of pharmaceutical innovation; and the features of Japanese pharmaceutical innovation.

8.1 FOUR ASPECTS OF DRUG SHAPING: HETEROGENEITY AND INTERACTIONS

To analyse the process of drug discovery and development, I have distinguished four aspects of shaping a drug: namely, the shaping of the compound, of its application, of organizational authorization, and of the market. Each aspect can be characterized by different human actors, non-human entities, and institutional and structural factors involved. In this section, I first examine the elements involved in each aspect and the relationship between them. Then I discuss how a drug is shaped through the interaction between different aspects.

8.1.1 The Shaping of the Compound

The first aspect of the shaping process of a drug is the shaping of the compound. The compound here refers to the material aspect of a drug. The core of the compound is a chemical believed to have a profile of biological activities of clinical use. Therefore, this aspect includes the process of drug discovery and biological/clinical tests. It also includes the modification of molecular structure and the creation of preparation (formulation) and other material devices for its practical use. Several actors, entities and factors play a significant role in this aspect. Let us examine them one by one.

First, in the shaping of the compound, the primary player is the leader of the research project, whose interest and expertise orientates the direction of and limits the range of the search for the compound. James Black's interest and expertise in beta-blocker and H_2 antagonists, David Jack's in anti-asthma drugs, Masahiko Fujino's and Barry Furr's in LHRH analogues, Akira Endo's in HMG-CoA reductase inhibitors, Toichi Takenaka's in receptor-based drugs, and Katsura Morita's in cephalosporins were the driving forces of their research projects, which eventually led to the discovery of drugs. They also play the role of heterogeneous engineer (Law 1987), who links up the heterogeneous elements necessary for the shaping of compounds.

Second, the knowledge and skills of the research team and the company also limit the area of research. Their expertise often guides the research in a specific direction. Glaxo's intellectual assets in steroids, Takeda's and ICI's in peptide synthesis, Sankyo's in fermentation, Yamanouchi's in adrenergic receptor-based drugs and Takeda's in antibiotics, which were embodied in researchers and supporting staff, seemed to facilitate research in specific areas. However, the activity of shaping compounds also contributed to the accumulation of the intellectual assets, in turn. It was seen in the pairs of innovation in the same organization, such as propranolol and atenolol, salbutamol and salmeterol, BDP and fluticasone propionate, and mevastatin and pravastatin. This interaction between the intellectual assets of the organization and the shaping of the compound is consistent with the discussion of technological trajectories advocated by evolutionary economists, and also that of core capabilities in the resource-based firm theory (Nelson and Winter 1977; Dosi 1982; Prahalad and Hamel 1990; Leonard-Barton 1995; Teece *et al.* 1997; Hodgeson 1999, pp. 247–75).

Third, the material conditions of the organization constrain the research. This is closely related to the intellectual assets described above. Intellectual assets are often accompanied by specific non-human entities: for example, assay systems, model animals and special experimental equipment. These entities make some research areas easy but others hard to accomplish. For example, Glaxo had patented steroids when Jack looked for anti-inflammatory substances, and this probably affected his choice. In contrast, mice used in tests could have prevented mevastatin from becoming a drug, because it showed the ineffectiveness of the drug. Hens, dogs and monkeys, however, helped Endo to overturn the previous belief about mevastatin's ineffectiveness. Of course, strictly speaking, the material does not intend to prove or disprove the belief and it is people who believe or disbelieve the proof,[1] but compounds can never be shaped without the material, and material conditions significantly affect the process of shaping compounds.

Fourth, linkage with relevant science and technology outside the organization is also important. Researchers often obtain new knowledge from their external networks. In particular, in Japanese cases such as the discoveries of leuprorelin and mevastatin, links with state-of-the-art science in the US played a crucial role: providing the leading researchers with specific research interests and skills. In contrast, in British cases, their intellectual sources seemed to be more domestic. Some key researchers including Black and Furr had worked as academic researchers before they joined pharmaceutical companies. However, as discussed below, the range of the external network is relatively narrower in this aspect than in others: usually, it does not include clinicians and engineers. Knowledge transfers were normally conducted through literature. However, when a research organization does not possess the relevant tacit knowledge, research collaboration with an external organization may be conducted (Collins 1992, pp. 51–78). This is observed in the case of nicardipine in which researchers were sent to universities to learn the necessary techniques for experiments, and in the case of leuprorelin in which the research team was in collaboration with other companies in order to obtain the bioassay system for LHRH analogues and to develop the biodegradable polymer for its depot preparation.

Fifth, the strategy of the company sometimes affects the properties of the compound. In the case of cefotiam, Takeda's strategy to enter the cephalosporin market was the starting point of research. In the case of ranitidine and famotidine, Glaxo and Yamanouchi were looking for anti-peptic ulcer drugs when Black discovered H_2-antagonists. Their previous strategic choice of the therapeutic area probably encouraged the Glaxo and Yamanouchi researchers to conduct their own research on H_2-antagonists. In the case of tamsulosin, strategically Yamanouchi wanted the drug to be internationally competitive. Because overseas regulatory bodies preferred purer compounds, Yamanouchi chose to switch from the racemic mixture of the drug to the single isomers that were effective, even though they had to spend a lot of money and time over the change.

Sixth, market needs also sometimes affect the properties of the compound. Here, the notion of reverse salients (Hughes 1983, pp. 79–105) seems to be useful. In the case of anti-asthmatic drugs in Glaxo, two approaches, bronchial dilation and anti-inflammation, were adopted for the treatment of bronchial asthma. When bronchial dilation was achieved by salbutamol, anti-inflammation became the reverse salient. When it was solved by BDP, the short duration of action of salbutamol became the next reverse salient because other companies launched longer-acting bronchodilators. Then, salmeterol eliminated the reverse salient. Finally, fluticasone propionate resolved another reverse salient after BDP, namely moderate potency and insufficient selectivity. It is important to notice that these reverse salients emerged not only when relevant technologies or therapies advanced but also when rival companies launched competing products. Perceived demand also explains why LHRH analogues such as leuprorelin and goserelin appeared on the market as their depot preparation. The inconvenience of daily injection urged the Takeda and ICI researchers to develop more convenient forms of the drugs. A similar example is also seen in the case of the development of the preparation of cefotiam.

Seventh, the regulatory system significantly affects the properties of the compound. It is obvious that the level of acceptable toxicity and efficacy of the compound are defined by the regulation. The quality and purity of the compound are also conditioned by the regulation. For example, tamsulosin was switched late on in its R&D process from a racemic mixture to the single isomer. This was because regulators preferred purer compounds. In the case of leuprorelin, it was in practice impossible for Takeda to sell the drug for daily injection because the Japanese regulator did not permit self-injection. This encouraged the development of the depot preparation of the drug.

Eighth, competitors have an influence on the shaping of the compound: their patents limit the opportunity. When researchers at Glaxo or Yamanouchi tried to modify the molecular structure of existing H_2 antagonists, they had to avoid infringing relevant patents of SmithKline & French. This led them to the somewhat unique molecular structures of ranitidine and famotidine. LHRH analogues and their preparations were different because each company had to avoid the existing patents of rivals. On the other hand, competitors also have a positive influence. Their patents and other publications may help the search for a new drug. The work of researchers at SmithKline & French Laboratories gave the concept of an H_2-antagonist to researchers at Glaxo and Yamanouchi. A similar intellectual spill-over between rivals was also seen in the case of LHRH analogues.

Ninth, serendipity sometimes plays an important role. For example, cardio-selective β-blockers, the paradoxical effect of LHRH analogues, two phases of release of goserelin depot preparation and the cyclization of the side chain of cephalosporins were all serendipitously discovered. This implies the role of non-human entities in the shaping of the compound. Although serendipity includes cognitive and social activities as well, without the independent activities of non-human entities it would not have happened. The shaping of the compound is a complex process in which not only human actors but also non-human entities play an active role.

Tenth, production costs may also affect the choice of the compound. As is suggested in the cases of leuprorelin and goserelin, production costs seem to be significant in the choice of compound when there are several compounds with similar properties.

Thus, in the shaping of the compound, different human actors are involved: including the project leader, team members with different fields of expertise, the management who creates strategy, external academics who provide knowledge and authority, competitors who affect the range of opportunity, doctors and patients who constitute the market, and regulators. Non-human entities including chemicals, bioassays, animals, and experimental instruments are also involved in the process. In addition, institutional and structural factors such as organizational assets, corporate strategy, academic networks, market properties, competitive structure, regulatory systems, patents and the techno-economic structure of production also affect the shaping of the compound. The process of shaping compounds can be regarded as heterogeneous engineering (Law 1987).

8.1.2 The Shaping of the Application

The second aspect of the shaping process of a drug is the shaping of the application. This is, in other words, the shaping process of the meanings of the compound in practice. The compound often has various biological activities. The same hormone or neurotransmitter often plays various roles in the body because its receptors at different places cause different reactions. For example, β adrenergic receptors not only dilate bronchi but also increase heart rate when they are stimulated by adrenaline. This is also the case in drugs mimicking the activity of naturally occurring hormones and neurotransmitters. That is to say, the compound often has plural potential activities.

The first two factors that limit the application of a compound are, therefore, potential activities of the compound and therapeutic needs. This is why an H_1-antagonist cannot become an anti-peptic ulcer drug and why 'β_2-blockers' do not appear on the medical market. Normally, the range of potential activities and the range of therapeutic needs narrow the feasible application of the compound to only one or a few relevant ones. In some cases, however, quite different potential applications may exist. When these plural potential applications are unrelated to each other and one of them is chosen for a clinical use, the others may cause side effects. For example, when isoprenaline is used for dilating the bronchi, its cardinal activity constitutes a serious side effect. In such cases, the ambiguity of the compound is normally what should be eliminated. This should be done in the shaping of the compound. Drugs with selectivity such as β_2-stimulants and β_1-blockers were results of ambiguity reduction. However, when side effects of this sort are not serious and can be controlled, one of the potential applications may be selected for strategic reasons without eliminating the ambiguity; such cases are not common, but tamsulosin and LHRH analogues are examples. In these cases, the shaping of the application is particularly important.

The third factor affecting the shaping of the application is the cognitive ability of the project leader and other researchers to explore the potential applications of the compound. Researchers working on LHRH analogues at first thought that the main application of the drugs was fertility promotion. However, when they came across the 'paradoxical effect' of LHRH analogues, the researchers turned their attention to sex hormone dependent diseases such as breast cancer and prostate cancer. This was possible because they had broad knowledge about potential therapeutic areas. Thus, the broad knowledge of researchers in therapeutic areas is an important factor in the shaping of the application; in other words, the intellectual capability of the organization across a range of therapeutic areas conditions the search for applications. This is also consistent with the discussion of evolutionary economics and that of the resource-based view of organizations.

The fourth factor is an external network: in particular amongst clinicians from whom the researchers collect information about how to use the drug. In the case of tamsulosin, the key researcher heard of the possible new application of α blockers from a urologist. Without the linkage between the drug researcher and the clinician, the researcher could not have obtained such information and tamsulosin might not have appeared as a drug for the treatment of the urination disorder. Therefore, network linking to clinicians, who play an equivalent role to the 'lead users' (von Hippel 1988), is important for the shaping of the application.

The fifth factor is the competition in R&D. As with the shaping of the compound, the behaviour of competitors has a spill-over effect. In the case of LHRH analogues, their makers entered the same therapeutic areas one after another.

The sixth factor is the size of the potential market of the drug. In the case of tamsulosin, if its market for urination disorder had been regarded as being much smaller than its hypertension market, Yamanouchi might have chosen the application for anti-hypertension rather than for the treatment of urination disorder. In the cases of LHRH analogues, Takeda, Abbott and ICI recognized that the prostate cancer area would be a safer market than other areas such as contraception and gynaecological disorders, which had effective alternative means of treatment. It should be noticed that the potential market is what is recognized as being able to be shaped as the real market; that is, the recognition of the potential market of a drug overlaps with the shaping of its real market. In other words, the recognition of the potential market is a mental simulation of the shaping of the real market. Therefore, the relationship between the shaping of application and the shaping of market is interactive. Researchers' speculation about how much they will be able to expand the market is reflected in their recognition of the size of the potential market, which affects the shaping of the application. The shaping of the application, in turn, has a great influence on the shaping of the market.

The process of shaping applications is also heterogeneous engineering. It includes human actors such as researchers, board members, clinicians and competitors, non-human entities such as compounds, telephones and calculators, and institutional and structural factors such as organizational assets, market needs, market size, external human network and competition.

8.1.3 The Shaping of Organizational Authorization

The shaping of organizational authorization means the persuasion of people inside the company, in particular the management. In the case studies, we can see that even people in the same organization may resist the development of a new drug when the concept of the drug is novel and unfamiliar to them. The background of this is the conflict between groups within a company over its limited resources. The clinical development of a drug costs a huge amount, as explained in Chapter 2, and its failure seriously damages the financial situation of the company. The shaping of organizational authorization can be regarded as the 'micro' political aspect of drug shaping. In fact, in many cases, including nicardipine, salmeterol, burimamide, leuprorelin, mevastatin, tamsulosin and cefotiam, organizational resistance was observed. It was necessary for the researchers to obtain organizational authorization to realize the development of their drugs. Several factors play an important role in the shaping of organizational authorization.

The main player is the project leader. Endo gathered evidence for the efficacy of mevastatin by himself when the researchers at the Central Research Laboratories had denied it. He also arranged clinical trials to reverse the decision of the company to abandon his project. Takenaka provided the management with evidence for the marketability and profitability of tamsulosin. It was reported that Duncan at SmithKline & French Laboratories in England also made a lot of effort to prevent the American parent company from cutting off Black's project. To convince people within the company, not only evidence but also the track record of the project leader was important: Black and Takenaka had such reputations.

The position and power of the project leader in the company are also important. Jack, in the case of salmeterol, was the director of research and development at Glaxo at that time, and he could tell people to work on the drug instead of persuading them persistently.

The management is the counter player. Their decision of 'go or no-go' (Kuwashima 1998; Pisano 1997, p. 97) is an essential element in shaping organizational authorization. Unless they recognize the significance of the project, the discovery of a drug will not lead to an innovation. When they champion the project, the shaping of organizational authorization can be seen as being almost completed. In the case of leuprorelin, Shinbei Konishi, who was then president of Takeda, and Kunio Takeda, then vice-president of TAP Pharmaceuticals and a member of the Takeda family, supported the development of the drug in Japan and the US. Also, in the case of cefotiam, the top management of Takeda backed the project in a somewhat top-down manner. In the case of nicardipine, Masuo Murakami, then director of the central laboratory of Yamanouchi and a powerful figure in the company, gave Takenaka his approval.

Third, evidence for the future of the drug, such as the properties of the compound, estimation of marketability and profitability, and the distinguishable concept of the drug, is important. Estimation of marketability and profitability is a simulation of the shaping of the market and is conditioned by the shaping of the application. The potential size of market, the expected situation of competition and the estimated price of the drug are important in the estimation. In many cases, however, the forecasting of these parameters was extremely difficult because drug development is accompanied with high uncertainty and takes a very long time. Rather, the concepts of drugs like 'H_2', 'α_{1c} selective' and 'third generation' may be more convincing than the uncertain estimation of sales and profits. However, if the R&D assessment system is strictly institutionalized, as is seen in the case of tamsulosin, the estimation can be more critical. The assessment system plays a similar role to clinical trials in the shaping of market and restricts the behaviours of proponents, opponents and decision makers. Internal workers involved in the estimation of the market are likely to gain more power in this case.

Fourth, linkage with external experts, in particular clinicians, often plays an important role in supplying evidence and authority. In the case of mevastatin, Endo used his network amongst worldwide researchers including Goldstein and Brown and domestic clinicians including Yamamoto at Osaka University Hospital in order to enhance the credibility of his argument. Yamamoto's active proposal for clinical trials of the drug overturned the previous trends of opinion within the company. Takenaka and his colleagues used the data they obtained from clinicians at universities in order to prepare convincing evidence of the marketability and profitability of tamsulosin. Academic journals also seem to play an important role by supplying credibility, as was seen in the case of cimetidine.

Fifth, corporate strategy affects the decision of go or no-go. Glaxo had a strategic interest in the anti-asthma area because of the size of its potential market. Both Glaxo and Yamanouchi regarded the anti-peptic ulcer area as strategically important. Takeda aimed at the establishment of its domain in the cephalosporin antibiotics area. Strategy thus promoted the projects of anti-asthma drugs and ranitidine in Glaxo, famotidine in Yamanouchi and cefotiam in Takeda. If the companies had had a strategy focusing on other therapeutic areas, the progress of the projects might have been delayed or thrown away. In fact, in the cases of leuprorelin and goserelin, it was said that the projects were not given high priority at first.

Sixth, organizational capability in recognizing the value of new drugs is also important. Employees belonging to other divisions of the company, including toxicological studies, clinical development, finance, production, marketing and sales, may become opponents of the project. Their understanding of the concept of the new drug and their insights into pharmaceutical business significantly affect the intensity of organizational resistance. The newer the concept of the drug is, the more difficult for people outside the project team to understand its value. The organizational resistance in the case of cimetidine seemed to be much stronger than in the case of ranitidine or famotidine.

Seventh, changes in social values seem to have an influence on decision making. For example, the rise in awareness of the quality of life in Japanese society possibly affected the approval of tamsulosin by the Yamanouchi management. The recent emergence of 'lifestyle drugs', which improve the quality of life and alleviate the physical disorders of old age ('Losing the drugs war', *The Financial Times*, 13 April 1999), may reflect the similar worldwide change in social values. Today, the project leaders working on drugs of this kind find it easier to obtain organizational authorization than in the past. Pharmaceutical companies are also sensitive to negative public response (Clarke and Montini 1993, p. 54). They may abandon their research in a particular area if the general public criticizes it, as was seen in the case of genetically modified crops ('Monsanto drops GM "terminator"', *Guardian*, 5 October 1999).

It is clear that the shaping of organizational authorization is also heterogeneous engineering. Human actors including the project leader, the management, other employees, clinicians and the general public, non-human entities including compounds and material assets of the organization, and institutional and structural factors including organizational structure, organizational capability, corporate strategy, routines for the evaluation of projects, external network of the organization and social values, are all involved in the process of shaping organizational authorization.

8.1.4 The Shaping of the Market

The fourth aspect of the shaping process of a drug is the shaping of the market. The main activities of this aspect include clinical trials, regulatory approval and marketing. More heterogeneous actors, particularly outside the company, are involved in this aspect. This can be regarded as the 'macro' social aspect of drug shaping and is the aspect that is most closely investigated by other sociological works on drug development (see Chapter 2). In this sub-section, we shall examine what kinds of actor are generally involved in the shaping process of the market of a drug, though there are probably more relevant actors in specific cases (see, for example, Clarke and Montini 1993).

The first actor is the company, which defines the target market of the drug and tries to seize it. The definition of the target market has been mainly conducted in the shaping of the application and in the shaping of organizational authorization, though the company can redefine it in the process of clinical trials and marketing. The ability of the company to identify the potential market restricts the range of their real market. This is a strategic as well as a cognitive issue. They have to decide their therapeutic and geographic domains. They also have to forecast the future of their business conditions and their own position. Their organizational capability also limits their future market. Unless they can secure sufficient money, production capability, cooperation of clinicians and patients, necessary sales force, expertise in legal and regulatory affairs, and management ability to organize these heterogeneous factors, the shaping of the market is unlikely to be achieved. Glaxo, in the case of ranitidine, most remarkably demonstrated its organizational capability to achieve the quick shaping of its worldwide market.

The second actor is the regulator, who officially approves the manufacturing and marketing of the drug within its jurisdiction. It provides the drug with a kind of social authorization, and there is a similarity between the shaping of regulatory approval and the shaping of organizational authorization. Values and criteria are probably different between the two. Safety, quality, efficacy and cost-effectiveness of the drug should be more important for the regulator than marketability and profitability, which are essential for the company. However, in practice, the difference may be little, because without regulatory approval the drug cannot be marketed, and the values and the criteria of regulators are likely to be reflected in the decisions of companies. In the case of leuprorelin, the restriction on self-injection ruled by the Japanese regulator prevented the drug from development until its depot preparation had been developed. As is seen in the case of practolol, the regulator may limit the market of a drug after its launch. In addition, regulators in some countries including Japan determine the price of drugs. This also affects the size of the market in terms of value.

The third actor is the doctor, who conducts clinical trials and prescribes the drug after its launch. Doctors directly constitute the drug market; therefore, their evaluation is crucial for the establishment and expansion of its market. The leading clinicians in the therapeutic area of the drug play a particularly important role: their support and collaboration are essential in the clinical trials. They often have interests in clinical trials and in the publication of results. The collaboration between the company and the doctors often results in the high quality of clinical trials, which in turn enhances the value of the drug amongst doctors and government officials. The opinions of leading clinicians on the drug also affect its valuation. In particular, in the highly hierarchical medical society in Japan (Campbell and Ikegami 1998, p. 67), leading clinicians at universities have a very strong influence over other doctors. This was typically observed in the case of procaterol.

Therefore, two activities are in particular important to involve doctors in the shaping of the market: clinical trials and promotion. Clinical trials are the core evidence of efficacy and safety. Clinicians participating in clinical trials learn the properties of the drug while they conduct its clinical trials. They transfer their evaluation to other clinicians, regulators and other relevant people. However, as many scholars indicate (Marks 1997; Abraham 1995; Epstein 1996; Richards 1988; Bodewitz *et al.* 1987), the results of clinical trials are not free from controversy. The occurrence of such controversy was observed in the cases of β stimulants and LHRH analogues. In these cases, the closure of controversy was not achieved by 'crucial' clinical trials but by the redefinition of the problem or by the accumulation of experience (both tests and uses) over a considerable time. This observation is consistent with the discussion of the social construction of technology (Pinch and Bijker 1987). In addition, because the properties of the compound are ultimately based on belief (MacKenzie 1996b), they are not always stable. It is possible that the efficacy and safety of the compound described earlier may become problematic in the process of clinical trials and practical use. For example, the safety of practolol became doubtful when the reports about its side effects appeared, and the drug lost the market. Mevastatin also failed in the shaping of the market when its safety became problematic, and the company gave up its development rather than try to re-establish belief in its safety.

After the launch of the drug, the pharmaceutical company promotes it to doctors. New drug concepts such as 'Ca antagonists' and 'H$_2$ antagonists' attract doctors' interests. Drug properties such as 'new generation', 'more selective' and 'longer acting' also appeal to them. The latter was seen in the cases of latecomer drugs such as procaterol, ranitidine, famotidine and cefotiam. Ease of use can also become a good reason for choice; the case of cefotiam demonstrates this. Thus, the shaping of the compound and its application strongly affects the shaping of the market. However, it is also important for the company to inform doctors about these properties. The means of information consist of clinical trials, academic papers, symposia, conferences, advertisements and visits by medical representatives. In addition, the financial opportunity for doctors is important. If doctors suffer a significant decrease in income because of the substitution of a drug for an existing treatment, the drug is unlikely to be accepted by them. In the cases of tamsulosin and LHRH analogues, some people in the companies were afraid of this.

The fourth are academics who create knowledge, skills and artefacts related to the drug. Their activities may construct or destroy the market of the drug. For example, Fleckenstein's concept 'Ca antagonism' and Ito's classification 'the third-generation β_2-stimulant' helped the shaping of the markets of these kinds of drugs. A new technique using biotechnology identified subtypes of α_1 receptors, which explained the mode of action of tamsulosin and promoted its marketing. In contrast, as in a case study provided by Richards (1988), the 'randomized, controlled, double-blinded' method in clinical trials destroyed the market of vitamin C as an anti-cancer drug.

The fifth are rival companies that have competitive products in the same therapeutic area. They have both advantageous and disadvantageous effects in the shaping of the market. The advantageous effect was seen in the cases of LHRH analogues and nicardipine. The simultaneous clinical development of the same type of drug by different companies facilitated learning by doctors and regulators about the drugs. The disadvantageous effect is more obvious: patients are limited in number, so companies must divide the market. Competition also affects the price of the drug, though its effect on the price seems to be complicated because of regulation.

The sixth to eighth actors are patients, their families and carers, and activists. The number of patients who give their informed consent to clinical trials is essential for the development of the drug. This factor seems to explain partially the delay in the development of leuprorelin in Japan. In the tamsulosin case, it was necessary to make the BPH patients aware of the disease and drive them to visit clinics. Articles and lectures by opinion leaders, the advice of family doctors and advertisements by the company contributed to this. Patients, together with their families, carers and activists, may actively request the development and marketing of particular drugs, as was seen in the case studies of anti-AIDS agents and thalidomide (Epstein 1996; Timmermans and Leiter 2000; see also Clarke and Montini 1993).

Thus, various human actors take part in the process of shaping the market of drugs. It is obvious that non-human entities and institutional and structural factors are also involved in the process: the former includes compounds, bioassay systems, animals, devices for drug administration, means of communication and production facilities, while the latter includes organizational capabilities, clinical trials, the structure of the medical society, the regulatory system, the market structure, academic papers, conferences and social values. That is to say, the shaping of the market is also heterogeneous engineering.

8.1.5 Interaction Between the Different Aspects of Drug Shaping

Through examination of the four aspects of shaping drugs, we can obtain two important findings about the process of drug discovery and development. First, the shaping of drugs is the process of heterogeneous engineering. Various human actors, non-human entities and institutional and structural factors are involved in the process. In some cases, we can see interpretative flexibility about the properties of compounds, a diversity of candidate drugs and different closure mechanisms. This is consistent with the argument of the social construction of technology (see sub-section 2.1.2). With regard to non-human entities, various things, including compounds, animals, scientific instruments and production equipment, restrict or facilitate the process of drug shaping. As advocates of actor-network theory insist, actors are not naked (Strum and Latour [1987] 1999). Without non-human entities, humans cannot shape a drug. In addition, actors are not isolated from wider and quite stable social relationships. Institutions and structures such as organizational structures, organizational capabilities, corporate strategies, external human networks, academic societies, medical systems, regulatory systems, clinical trials, patent systems, production economies and market structures affect the process of shaping drugs. This is consistent with the key argument of the social shaping of technology (MacKenzie and Wajcman 1999, pp. 3–27; Williams and Edge 1996, p. 867). Cultural factors such as social values also have an influence on the shaping of drugs.

The second finding is that the four aspects of drug shaping interact with each other. The compound limits the shaping of the application. The compound and its proposed application are key factors for the project leader to persuade management. Therefore, they limit the shaping of organizational authorization. They are also key factors for the company to apply for regulatory approval and to promote the drug amongst doctors. Therefore, the compound and its application limit the shaping of the market. The shaping of the application can be also regarded as the cognitive simulation of the shaping of the market. The organizational authorization of the compound conditions the shaping of its market. Without organizational authorization, it is obvious that the compound cannot become a drug.

There are also influences in the opposite direction. The application sometimes affects the shaping of the compound. For example, LHRH analogues should be given to patients continuously to obtain the paradoxical effect for the treatment of prostate cancer. For this, depot preparations had to be developed. Organizational authorization limits the choice of the compound and its application. It is unlikely that researchers would choose a compound or an application that seems to bring no beneficial outcome to their organization. The market also affects all aspects of the shaping of a drug. It restricts the organizational authorization. When the possibility of successfully shaping the market seems to be slim, the project probably fails to obtain approval by management. The needs of the market in turn have an influence on the shaping of the compound and its application. Two things, however, should be noted: first, the market is not clear in advance; second, the market is what can be constructed. Therefore, on the one hand, the cognitive and interpretative processes of project leaders and of management members mediate the influences of the market on the shaping of the compound, the application and the organizational authorization. On the other hand, the capabilities of the company to intervene in the shaping of the market also condition these influences, though there are other contingent factors such as regulation, medical societies and social movement. The constructed nature of the market is in accordance with the discussion of the social shaping of technology (Williams and Edge 1996, p. 877).

Thus, the four aspects of drug shaping are interactive. They are not sequential, but overlapping and co-evolving. The interactions include not only explicit and observable ones but also implicit and cognitive ones. Because human actors speculate about the results of actions, speculative results sometimes play a role in the shaping process. This anticipative behaviour of actors involved in the innovation process, such as scientists and companies, is consistent with the arguments of Webster (1991, pp. 48–50, 59) and McKelvey (1996, p. 226). Market constituencies such as doctors, patients and regulators also speculate on the results of accepting a drug in shaping. The four aspects are also interdependent. If one aspect becomes unstable, all the others also become unstable. For example, if the safety of the compound becomes problematic, its application, its organizational authorization and its market also become questionable. If the market of a class of drugs dwindles, a new compound of the class for the conventional application is unlikely to appear; even if it happened to appear, the management would probably axe the project. In sum, a drug emerges only when all its four aspects are successfully shaped and being shaped. The compound, the application, the organizational authorization and the market collectively support drug innovation. Figure 8.1 schematizes the interactive relationships between the four aspects.

The shaping of the compound	⟷	The shaping of the application
↕	⤡⤢	↕
The shaping of the organizational authorization	⟷	The shaping of the market

Figure 8.1:   Interactions between the four aspects of drug shaping

It should be noted that the inter-reflection is neither perfect nor exclusive. There are always contingencies and actual results of any action are not exactly the same as anticipated ones. They are interdependent but not self-contained. The shaping of drugs is a network consisting of various human actors, non-human entities, institutional and structural factors, and connecting/disconnecting between them. A new element can enter the network at any time and transform or even dissolve it. Newly arriving non-human entities may change the network without intention. Humans can intentionally transform or scrap the network. A wider structural change can also alter it against wills of the actors involved in it. Therefore, the shaping of drugs is a networking activity, similar to the one that actor-network theorists describe. The transformation of the networks surrounding drug discovery and development also seems to share a lot of points with the discussion of Galambos and Sewell (1995) about dynamic networking related to vaccine development.

Finally, it should be noted that the products of the process of shaping drugs are not only the drugs but also the various sub-products. For example, paradigmatic drug innovations such as propranolol and cimetidine changed the theory of the relevant receptors. In other words, the shaping process of these drugs produced a theory: science plays a role in the shaping of a drug and vice versa. Potent β stimulants caused controversy with regard to their safety and guidelines for their use were set up: regulations condition the shaping of a drug and vice versa. Glaxo earned a huge income from the marketing of ranitidine and became one of the giant pharmaceutical companies in the world: pharmaceutical companies create drugs and vice versa. In addition to them, many kinds of elements are produced from the process: experimental materials, experimental methods, the cognitive ability of researchers, the cognitive ability of the management, knowledge about a new therapeutic area, a new linkage with external specialists, a new strategy, the reputation of the company among doctors, patients and investors, and so on. Thus, the process of shaping drugs is also a process of co-creating materials, knowledge and institutions.

8.2   TYPES OF DRUG INNOVATION

When we compare the shaping processes of the various drugs described in this study, we can find differences between them. In some cases, the concept of a new drug has no exemplar. Most people inside and outside the organization are unfamiliar with the concept and wary of it. Therefore, the project leader and co-workers must first persuade people in their company to obtain organizational authorization. Then if the company decides to develop it, they must persuade outside people such as doctors and regulators. In other cases, the concept of a new drug has an exemplar and few people are suspicious about its efficacy and safety. However, there might be another kind of suspicion amongst people in the company: concerning its profitability. Doctors and regulators may ignore the drug, failing to find any advantage over existing drugs of a similar kind. Therefore, the researchers must seek to create advantageous characteristics which are enough to differentiate their drug from others. The company must promote the characteristics amongst doctors and regulators. Thus, the difference in familiarity with the concept of a drug induces distinct patterns as to the shaping of drugs.

We can divide the situation of the shaping of drugs into three types in terms of familiarity: the case in which both the compound and its application are unfamiliar; that in which the compound is familiar but its application is unfamiliar; and that in which both of them are familiar.[2] Corresponding with this classification, we can identify three types of innovation in the pharmaceutical industry. I name them paradigmatic innovation, application innovation and modification-based innovation, respectively, as in Table 8.1.

Table 8.1:   Three types of pharmaceutical innovation

Type of innovation	Compound	Application	Examples	Relevant chapter	Origins
Paradigmatic	Unfamiliar	Unfamiliar	Propranolol	Ch. 3	British
			Salbutamol	Ch. 4	British
			Cimetidine	Ch. 5	British
			Leuprorelin	Ch. 6	Japanese–American
			Goserelin depot	Ch. 6	British
			Mevastatin	Ch. 7	Japanese, failed
Application	Familiar	Unfamiliar	BDP	Ch. 4	British
			Tamsulosin	Ch. 7	Japanese
Modification-based	Familiar	Familiar	Atenolol	Ch. 3	British
			Nicardipine	Ch. 3	Japanese
			Salmeterol	Ch. 4	British
			Fluticasone propionate	Ch. 4	British
			Procaterol	Ch. 4	Japanese
			Ranitidine	Ch. 5	British
			Famotidine	Ch. 5	Japanese
			Cefotiam	Ch. 7	Japanese

8.2.1 Paradigmatic Innovation

The first type is paradigmatic innovation, in which neither the compound nor the application is familiar before being shaped. Because the concept of the drug does not have an exemplar but itself constitutes one, I name this type paradigmatic innovation, based on the analogy of Kuhn's terminology (Kuhn 1970). Propranolol, salbutamol, cimetidine, leuprorelin, the depot preparation of goserelin and mevastatin can be classified into this type.

Following their advent, drugs with similar molecular structure and the same mode of action were developed.

Several characteristics of paradigmatic innovation can be extracted from the case studies of these drugs. First, the level of uncertainty is very high. All kinds of uncertainty are involved: scientific, technological, business and regulatory. In the case of burimamide, metiamide and cimetidine, the existence of H_2 receptors and their effects on gastric acid secretion were unknown when the search for the compound was conducted, nor was the assay system to identify such a compound fully established. It was also unclear whether the practitioners would accept such a drug in place of surgical treatment. In the case of pronethalol and propranolol, the receptor theory was not widely believed when they were looking for drugs based on it. In the case of mevastatin, the existence of HMG-CoA reductase inhibitor was uncertain, and so was the safety of mevastatin. In the cases of leuprorelin and goserelin, their paradoxical effect was unknown. It was also uncertain whether doctors and regulators would accept these drugs.

Second, because of very high uncertainty, the level of doubt about the drug is also very high among people both inside and outside the company. To shape organizational authorization, the project leader must persuade the management and other relevant staff in the company. Strong, dauntless leadership is necessary. Endo, for example, did not give up when he faced negative responses from inside the company: he found a way out of adverse circumstances by himself or with help from outside the company. Black did not make a compromise with the idea of developing a drug which was not the H_2-antagonist he had been looking for: his track record and reputation contributed to keep the project alive. Such organizational resistance to innovation and the need for strong leadership seem to be conformable to Donald Schon's argument about the product champion (Schon 1963). However, leaders in drug innovation are probably more properly named project champions than product champions, because they have to be active before any product is invented. In addition to leadership, clear profiles of the drug are important. In particular, the basic properties of the drug, namely clear efficacy and acceptable safety, are essential.

Third, the project leaders and co-workers must do heterogeneous engineering (Law 1987, pp. 113–16) to connect up heterogeneous actors, entities, and institutional and structural factors in order to achieve the shaping of the compound, the application and organizational authorization. Endo and his co-workers devised an assay system by themselves, procured animals for experiments, established the linkage with top world scientists in the field, and arranged the preliminary clinical trials. The shaping of the market also requires heterogeneous engineering, which is often conducted organizationally. For example, to shape a market for goserelin, ICI's workers developed its depot preparation, supported its clinical trials, demonstrated its advantages over surgical treatment or other kinds of drugs, explained its mode of action, showed that the 'flare-up' phenomenon was not serious, established its production process, obtained approvals for marketing from the regulators of various countries, set up its marketing and distributing organizations in these countries, and informed doctors about how to use its unique preparation. To achieve this, they had to link a huge number of heterogeneous actors, entities, institutions and structures with each other. Thus, the process of paradigmatic innovation can be regarded as the shaping of a new network for innovation.

Fourth, paradigmatic innovation transforms major factors including science, therapy and business. The discovery of pronethalol and propranolol destroyed the then dominant 'sympathin' theory and established the receptor theory as a paradigm. The discovery of salbutamol demonstrated the subtypes of adrenergic β receptors. The discovery of burimamide, metiamide and cimetidine also evidenced the existence of H_2 receptors. LHRH analogues led to the discovery of the paradoxical effect and contributed to the relevant research. Mevastatin also played a role in providing evidence of the theory of cholesterol regulation in the body which had been advanced by Joseph Goldstein and Michael Brown. Thus, paradigmatic innovation transforms scientific theories. It also changes therapies: cimetidine transformed the mainstream treatment for peptic ulcer from surgery to internal medicine; LHRH analogues also created a new option for the treatment of prostate cancer; mevastatin made the high level of cholesterol in the blood a therapeutic area that could be treated by drugs. This transformation in science and therapy in turn changes business in the pharmaceutical industry in terms of the research strategy, the approaches and targets of research projects, the organization and approaches of marketing, and the conditions of competition.

8.2.2 Application Innovation

The second type is application innovation, in which the profile of the compound is familiar but its application is not. Because it is the application of the drug that is innovative, we name this type application innovation. BDP as inhaled steroid for the treatment of bronchial asthma and tamsulosin for the treatment of urination disorder are examples. These drugs are or can be used in other areas. BDP is used in the dermatological area. Tamsulosin can be developed as a drug for the treatment of hypertension. However, the companies developed new applications for strategic reasons.

There are several characteristics of application innovation. First, the level of uncertainty is still high, especially in the shaping of the application, organizational authorization and the market. On the shaping of the application, in the case of BDP there were various doubts: about efficacy, fear of causing infection, and side effects. On organizational authorization, in the case of tamsulosin, the management had doubts about whether the urination disorder would be regarded as a disease, whether doctors would accept the drug, whether patients would go to urogenital clinics to receive such a treatment, and whether the government would give it a price good enough to be accepted by doctors. On the shaping of the market, doctors and regulators tend to be at first doubtful about the advantage of the new drug, mainly because the mode of action is unfamiliar to them. This was seen in the case of tamsulosin, where doctors initially asked how the drug differed from others.

Second, high uncertainty causes suspicion among people in application innovation, as in paradigmatic innovation. Persuasion of these people is important here, too. It is the role of the project leader to obtain organizational authorization; evidence of feasibility, marketability and profitability is necessary. Jack, the leader of the BDP project, conducted animal experiments and demonstrated that BDP would work as an inhaled glucocorticoid. Takenaka, the project leader of tamsulosin, himself actively investigated the medical needs for the drug with the marketing staff and obtained convincing data about the potential size of the market. For the successful shaping of the market, it is essential that the clinical trials of the drug demonstrate its high efficacy and acceptable safety in the proposed therapeutic area. In addition to this, the company must actively promote the drug. Takenaka and his colleagues mobilized the α_{1c} receptors, which had just been discovered by using biotechnology, to establish the concept of tamsulosin and promote the drug.

Third, heterogeneous engineering is necessary to shape a new application, organizational authorization and the market. For example, a broad range of different actors, entities, and institutional and structural factors had to be connected with each other to accomplish the shaping of these aspects of tamsulosin: the project leader, clinicians, physiologists, corporate chemists and biologists, toxicologists, an assay system, experimental animals and instruments, epidemic studies, marketing staff, a system for market estimation, the management, the consultant, the regulatory body, chemical engineers, techniques for the separation of isomers, economical production systems, pharmaceutics experts, a slow-release preparation of the drug, clinical trials, patients, patient education, the change in social values, biotechnology, various means of promotion, and so on. Application innovation is a process of shaping a network including old elements related to the familiar compound and new elements related to the unfamiliar application.

Fourth, application innovation also significantly transforms relevant factors, especially therapy and market. BDP introduced inhaled steroids into the treatment of bronchial asthma. Tamsulosin created a new market for the medicinal treatment of the urination disorder accompanying benign prostatic hypertrophy. They also changed the business of the companies. With the introduction of BDP, Glaxo obtained full coverage of the treatment for bronchial asthma; the respiratory area became one of their major business areas. Yamanouchi also established its network in the area of urology with tamsulosin.

8.2.3 Modification-based Innovation

If both the profiles of the compound and its application are familiar to relevant people, the innovation of the drug is classified into the third type. We name it modification-based innovation because profiles of the drug can be seen as modifying those of an exemplary drug. Examples include atenolol, nicardipine, procaterol, salmeterol, fluticasone propionate, ranitidine, famotidine and cefotiam. However, modification-based innovation is not the same as incremental innovation, which is often discussed in the literature on innovation. Incremental innovation is characterized by bit-by-bit, cumulative improvement, particularly in components of the technological system. This does not include major change in organizational competences (Abernathy and Utterback 1978; Tushman and Anderson 1986; Henderson and Clark 1990). Modification-based innovation is not a bit-by-bit kind of innovation: it takes about ten years to develop even a modified drug. It is also difficult to identify components of the product in the pharmaceutical industry as is seen in assembled products. There may not be a need for major change in skills, abilities and knowledge in the organization when the company already has experience in developing the same kind of drug, as in the case of atenolol. However, it is not the case when the company first develops a modified drug, the exemplar of which was developed by another company, as in the cases of nicardipine, procaterol, ranitidine, famotidine and cefotiam. Thus, modification-based innovation is not the same as incremental innovation. It is perhaps closer to the original notion of normal science (Kuhn 1970) than incremental innovation. Modification-based innovation is based on past scientific achievement and existing therapeutic approaches and does not challenge them. However, this does not mean either that modification-based innovation is not an organizational challenge, or that it is devoid of radical process change.

Modification-based innovation has several characteristics. First, the level of uncertainty is generally lower than in paradigmatic innovation or application innovation especially in terms of technical feasibility. However, business uncertainty still remains. Existing patents have to be circumvented. In addition, the condition of competition and the valuation by the regulator are uncertain. Therefore, doubts about the patentability, marketability and profitability of the drug may arise. In the case of cefotiam, there was a doubt within the company that it was too late to enter the area. Whether the company can develop a drug which has a distinct advantage over existing drugs is essential for a successful marketing and regulatory application. In other words, the construction of differences is crucial in modification-based innovation. Secondary properties such as selectivity, duration of action and convenient forms of dosage are important, in addition to sufficient efficacy and safety. The cases of atenolol, procaterol and ranitidine well demonstrate this characteristic.

Second, because the main uncertainty springs from business conditions, the decision of the management plays a key role. The strategic, top-down approach is often adopted in modification-based innovation. In this approach, systematic and intensive mobilization of resources in the organization is carried out. Clinical trials, production process development, the development of preparations and the establishment of the marketing and distributing system are often conducted simultaneously. This is because the speed of development is crucial: rival companies also see the same business opportunity. The keys to the accomplishment of fast development are organizational assets and strategic integration. The case of ranitidine and that of cefotiam well illustrate such an organizational capability.

Third, heterogeneous engineering for the construction of differences is an important activity in modification-based innovation. As we discussed above, the company often conducts a considerable part of this activity in a systematic and organizational way. In order to demonstrate the differences between the new drug and existing ones, various kinds of elements including new concepts such as 'cardio-selectivity', 'longer-acting' and 'the third generation β stimulants', a close relationship with leading clinicians, more convenient preparations, a richer variety of drug forms, papers on comparative clinical trials, instruments and techniques for measurement and analysis, catch phrases like 'Fast, Simple, Safe', and cost performance are mobilized, as was seen in the cases classified in this type of innovation. If the company has experience in the development of a drug in the same area, the network of heterogeneous elements is, for the most part, an existing one. How much the company can exploit the network for the shaping of the drug seems to be the main question in this case. But if the company does not have such experience, the construction of a new network for the company will be required.

Fourth, influences of modification-based innovation on relevant factors are in general more limited than with other types of innovation. Modification-based innovation does not challenge existing paradigms of science and therapy: rather, it maintains them. However, it may transform market structure and conditions to a great extent. The drugs produced by modification-based innovations often commercially supersede existing drugs including the paradigmatic original, as was demonstrated in the cases of ranitidine and famotidine. Thus, modification-based innovation may provide the company with more money than paradigmatic innovation. This income changes the organization and the strategy of the company; it also provides resources for further R&D. Therefore, modification-based innovation may transform not only the market but also the relevant organization.

In sum, we can distinguish three types of pharmaceutical innovation classified in terms of familiarity with the concept of a drug, namely paradigmatic innovation, application innovation and modification-based innovation. In other words, the pattern of drug discovery and development is neither identical nor totally different. Therefore, it is rational to consider the management of the drug-shaping process, though 'the one best way' of management of the process does not exist. In addition, it should be noted again that any type could result in market success. The theoretical and practical implications of the different types of drug innovation will be discussed in the next chapter.

8.3   DISTINCTIVE FEATURES OF DRUG DISCOVERY AND DEVELOPMENT IN JAPAN

When we look at Table 8.1 from the viewpoint of Japanese–British comparison, we find that most cases of Japanese pharmaceutical innovation belong to modification-based innovation rather than to paradigmatic innovation whereas its British counterparts are distributed in a better balanced way. This is not due to my choice of cases; other researchers also indicate the same point using a larger number of samples (Hawkins and Reich 1992). On the contrary, I chose mevastatin because it is a rare paradigmatic innovation in Japan. Leuprorelin may also be an exception. However, leuprorelin is probably better regarded as a half-Japanese and half-American innovation, because it is unlikely that the drug would have been shaped successfully without the contribution of workers at Abbott and TAP Pharmaceuticals in the United States. Mevastatin was not completed as an innovation because it was discarded halfway through the development. Thus, there is no case in our study that can be seen as an unconditional example of paradigmatic innovation shaped in Japan. This is consistent with the view that is generally held about Japanese pharmaceutical innovation (Kneller 1999, p. 422; Odagiri and Goto 1996, p. 246; Reich 1990, p. 134). It is probable that some historical, structural and cultural factors are related to the tendency of Japanese pharmaceutical companies towards modification-based innovation. The case studies of the two 'almost' paradigmatic innovations involving Japanese companies, namely leuprorelin and mevastatin, are particularly useful in identifying such factors.

8.3.1 Level of Science and Technology

As a latecomer amongst industrial countries, Japan has a history of importing scientific knowledge and technology from Western countries (Odagiri and Goto 1996). Although Japan has made some unique contributions to the progress of science and technology in the pharmaceutical area, it seems that its level of science and technology in the area was considerably lower than its British and American counterparts at least until the 1970s, the period when most of the drugs examined in this study were discovered. Many Japanese industrial researchers in this study, including Fujino and Matsuzawa in the case of leuprorelin and Endo in the case of mevastatin, studied in the United States. Their experience there led them to the research that resulted in the discovery and development of the drugs. All other concepts of the drugs in this study, namely β blockers, Ca antagonists, β_2 stimulants, H_2 antagonists and cephalosporin antibiotics, came from British, German or American scientists. Although α_{1c} antagonists seemed to be first named by Yamanouchi's researchers, it was overseas scientists who discovered α_{1c} receptors. These examples indicate that the level of the scientific basis in the pharmaceutical area in Japan was in general lower than in such countries as the UK, the US and Germany. This was the case not only in academia but also in industry. It was only after 1960 that most large Japanese pharmaceutical companies began to establish their full-scale research laboratories to discover new drugs (Nihon Yakushi Gakkai 1995, p. 123). There was an insufficient accumulation of scientific knowledge and technology within pharmaceutical companies in the 1970s: they had to send their researchers to foreign and domestic universities to obtain the necessary knowledge and skills. An example of technology transfer from domestic universities to pharmaceutical companies can be seen in the case of nicardipine, in which the techniques for experiments were transferred. Thus, the insufficient level of science and technology in the pharmaceutical area in Japan may be one of the factors explaining the lack of paradigmatic innovation in the country.

8.3.2 Collectiveness and Conservatism of the Organization

Consensus, interdependence, group-based, overlapping, intensive communication and the sharing of information and knowledge are the concepts that are often used to characterize the Japanese corporate organization (Porter *et al.* 2000, pp. 69–76; Nonaka and Takeuchi 1995, pp. 75–83, 198–9; Clark and Fujimoto 1991, pp. 215–28). Here, for convenience, I express these characteristics with one word: collectiveness. The collectiveness of Japanese organizations probably contributes to the integration of resources in the organization, but may enhance the strength of organizational resistance when it combines with the conservative, risk-averting attitude of its members to unfamiliar ideas and uncertain plans. In the case of mevastatin, Endo, the project leader, faced strong organizational resistance, which came from biologists at the Central Research Laboratories, toxicologists, pathologists and many others in the company. They were doubtful because there was no exemplar drug of the kind. Without their consensus at the project-coordinating meeting, the project could not survive. Actually, mevastatin was once abandoned at the meeting, but Endo, borrowing the authoritative power of an academic clinician in Japan, succeeded in reversing the decision. However, after Endo left the company, the mevastatin project was terminated, and its successor drug, pravastatin, came after Merck's lovastatin. Thus, the collectiveness of the organization, combined with the conservatism of organizational members, delayed the shaping of the new type of drug. The lack of an exemplar also caused doubts within the company in the case of leuprorelin and became one of the reasons for the delay of its development in Japan. Organizational resistance was observed in other cases of the pharmaceutical innovation in Japan, including nicardipine, tamsulosin and cefotiam. In the case of tamsulosin, the track record of the project leader contributed to the shaping of organizational authorization; in other cases, a powerful member of the management backed the project so that it could survive. Thus, the collectiveness of the Japanese organization and the risk-averting tendency of its members may be another factor that hinders the shaping of paradigmatic innovation.

8.3.3 Highly-regulated, Well-organized Conservative Market

Several characteristics of the Japanese pharmaceutical market may affect the tendency towards modification-based innovation in Japan. First, regulation matters. It is said that the pharmaceutical industry in Japan was nurtured and promoted through a highly regulated market with government-set prices (Reich 1990, p. 125). In Japan, it was common until recently for doctors not only to prescribe drugs but also to dispense them. Though the separation of dispensaries and clinics has proceeded, most hospitals still dispense drugs. The prescriptions dispensed by doctors are reimbursed based on the price lists set by the Ministry of Health, Labour and Welfare (MHLW; until December 2000 it was MHW). The margin between the purchase price and the reimbursement price, called '*yakka saeki*', has been an important source of income for hospitals and doctors. Since 1981, the MHW has reduced the reimbursement price of drugs (Campbell and Ikegami 1998, p. 158). This has had an unintended impact on the shaping of drugs: doctors responded to the price cuts by shifting their prescription patterns to new drugs, which have higher profit margins; it in turn stimulated pharmaceutical companies to introduce new drugs frequently. However, these new drugs did not have to be truly innovative drugs (Reich 1990, p. 137). Modification-based new drugs such as famotidine, procaterol and cefotiam obtained sound prices. In contrast, as was seen in the case of leuprorelin, paradigmatic new drugs are accompanied with uncertainty about the price because price setting is normally based on the prices of the existing drugs in the same area. It is only since 1989 that the MHW has distinguished between innovative drugs, called '*picashin*', and less innovative drugs, called '*zoroshin*', and began to promote the former (Howells and Neary 1995, p. 126). Before then, the policy of the regulatory body had unintentionally promoted modification-based innovation rather than paradigmatic innovation. In the case of cefotiam, an explicit government policy for modification-based innovation in the antibiotic area was also observed.

Second, the structure of Japanese medical society may affect the tendency towards modification-based innovation. In Japan, doctors, in particular those at universities, have almost decisive power in the shaping of drug market, because medical society in Japan is well organized hierarchically and professors of medicine are at the top of the pyramid. They were more powerful in the 1960s and 1970s than at present, and it is said that pharmaceutical companies at the time regarded them as if they were 'kings' (Low *et al.* 1999, pp. 175–6, 178–80; Reich 1990, p. 132; Campbell and Ikegami 1998, pp. 27–9, 31–2, 129–31; Howell and Neary 1995, pp. 28–9, 54–5). This authoritative power of academic clinicians was seen in the cases of procaterol and mevastatin. In the area of antibiotics, academic clinicians organize the Japanese Society of Chemotherapy, which has established the routine to manage clinical trials, as was seen in the case of cefotiam. The institution has significantly promoted frequent modification-based innovation in the area.

Third, market response to something new may have a significant influence on innovation. People who constitute the Japanese market, namely doctors, patients and regulatory agents in the country, seem to have had a conservative, risk-averting tendency, as did people in Japanese pharmaceutical companies. This is demonstrated in the words of the project leader of nicardipine that people at that time did not trust any Japanese work until someone with authority announced that it was all right. In the case of leuprorelin, it was experience in clinical development in the US that made the acceptance of the drug among Japanese doctors and regulatory agents easier. Japanese patients also seem to be conservative. As discussed in the case of tamsulosin, clinical trials under the practice of informed consent are not easy in Japan. Thus, the conservatism of doctors, patients and regulators in Japan, together with strong price regulation and the well-organized medical society, seem to promote modification-based innovation rather than paradigmatic innovation in the society.

In conclusion, the relatively low level of relevant science and technology, the collectiveness and conservatism of the organization, and the highly-regulated, well-organized conservative pharmaceutical market probably contributed to the tendency towards modification-based innovation, rather than paradigmatic innovation, in Japan. In addition, as Reich (1990) argues, it is likely that the well-protected nature of the Japanese pharmaceutical market limited the incentive of Japanese companies to seek internationally competitive drugs until recently. It should be noted, however, that these conditions will probably not last long because they result from social shaping. If any relevant actor regards it as a problem and acts to resolve it, the situation is likely to change. This seems to be what is in progress.

In this chapter, we analyse our cases of the process of drug discovery and development in the previous chapters both in an integrated way and in a comparative way. As a result, we understand that the process of shaping drugs is an interactive one in which heterogeneous human actors, non-human entities and institutional and structural factors are networked. Four aspects of drug shaping, namely the shaping of the compound, of the application, of organizational authorization, and of the market also interact with and are interdependent on each other. We also find three different patterns of drug discovery and development, namely paradigmatic innovation, application innovation and modification-based innovation. They involve different kinds of heterogeneous engineering or networking. In terms of the British–Japanese comparison, we identify the tendency towards modification-based innovation in the past Japanese pharmaceutical industry. The lower level of science and technology in the biomedical area, the collectiveness and conservatism of organizations, and the highly-regulated, well-organized conservative pharmaceutical market in Japan seem to affect the shaping of that tendency. Based on these findings about the process of drug discovery and development, I shall discuss several theoretical and practical implications of this study in the next, concluding chapter.

NOTES

1. Relevant discussion about this issue is found in MacKenzie (1996a, pp. 13–16) and Collins and Yearley (1992).
2. The application in this classification does not mean the therapeutic area itself but the idea of using a compound for the treatment of a specific therapeutic area. For example, in the case of cimetidine, people knew about peptic ulcer and wanted an effective drug for it, but no one in advance knew that a class of drugs such as cimetidine could be used for the treatment of peptic ulcer.

9. Conclusion

In this chapter, I conclude the book by discussing the theoretical and practical implications of each issue found in this study. The issues include the heterogeneous, interactive networking of the drug-shaping process, the importance of non-human entities, the different types of drug innovation, and the differences in historical, structural and cultural context between Japanese and British pharmaceutical innovation. Then the uniqueness and generality of the results of this study among different industrial sectors is discussed. Finally, I indicate the effectiveness of the approach of the social shaping of technology as a theoretical framework for technology management and innovation policy.

9.1 HETEROGENEITY, INTERACTIVITY AND NETWORKING

The linear model of technological change has been mainly criticized on three points. First, there are two-way flows of knowledge between science and technology (see, for example, Faulkner and Senker 1995, pp. 206–11). Second, there are also two-way influences between science and technology on the one hand, and the economy and markets on the other (for example, Kline 1985). Third, heterogeneous actors are involved in these interactive relationships (see, for example, McKelvey 1996; Pinch and Bijker 1987).

Our findings about the process of shaping drugs are consistent with these three criticisms of the linear model. Science affects the shaping of drugs, while the shaping of drugs may change science. The process of drug innovation neither moves from the shaping of compounds to the shaping of the market, nor does it from the latter to the former. The four aspects of a drug, namely the compound, the application, the organizational authorization and the market, are shaped interactively and simultaneously. They are also interdependent. Heterogeneous human actors, non-human entities and institutional and structural factors are involved in the process of drug shaping. Different groups of human actors often interpret the same compound differently, as the advocates of the social construction of technology argue. This causes conflicts between different actors which result in organizational and market resistance. Non-human entities are crucial for the justification and the empowerment of the actors. Institutional and structural factors inhibit some behaviours of actors while promoting others. In sum, the process of drug discovery and development can be seen as the interactive process of linking up these heterogeneous elements in order to shape the drug. It is the activity of heterogeneous engineering or networking. Thus, although some practitioners and academics hold a view that the innovation process of pharmaceuticals is exceptionally subject to the linear model, our study demonstrates that this is not the case. The innovation process is not linear *even* in the pharmaceutical area. The linear model has lost its last bastion!

The interactive feature of the process of shaping drugs means that the process at the same time shapes various relevant elements including theories, cognitive abilities, skills, instruments, materials, profits, regulations, authorities and social linkages. In other words, the process of shaping drugs is also the process of co-shaping materials, knowledge and institutions related to the drug. This essentially supports the view of Callon (1986, p. 20) that technological change is the co-evolution of 'society', technological artefacts and knowledge of nature. This also seems to be consistent with the argument of the evolutionary view of innovation (Nelson and Winter 1982; McKelvey 1996).

Thus, the interactive process of shaping drugs seems to be better described by the 'pinball' model (Webster 1991, p. 47) than by the linear model. However, if we incorporate the heterogeneity and networking of the process into the model, our 'pinball' will become different from the familiar one: first, there are many various 'balls' (elements of drug technology) which are simultaneously bouncing off many various 'pins' (shapers of drug technology); second, the 'balls' can combine together and split; third, the 'pins' are movable; fourth, some 'pins' (human 'pins') have their intentions but others not; fifth, there is no strict distinction between 'balls' and 'pins'; sixth, there is no external player and it is human 'pins' that bring 'balls'; seventh, some 'pins' may exit and others may enter. It could be also described as football with various sticky balls, played between numerous teams at the same time in a rain forest!

The heterogeneity and interactivity of the drug-shaping process has several practical implications. In order to promote innovation in the pharmaceutical industry, financial and material support in research must help but is not sufficient. The shaping of drugs requires networking heterogeneous elements inside and outside the organization. Therefore, building communicative channels between researchers and other corporate members, and between corporate workers and external actors such as academics, doctors, patients and regulators, is essential for mobilizing the necessary elements or resources to achieve innovation.

Organizational capabilities to integrate heterogeneous resources are also important. As the advocates of evolutionary economics and the resource-based firm theory argue, such organizational capabilities are not obtained from market transactions but from learning by doing and using (Nelson and Winter 1982; Teece *et al.* 1997; Hodgson 1999). Organizational capabilities for integration contribute to making the process of shaping a drug efficient and effective when the project obtains organizational authorization successfully. However, if not, integrated organization creates strong resistance against the project. External organizations related to the market, such as governmental bodies and medical societies, also have their capabilities to promote or inhibit particular projects of drug development. Therefore, it is essential to mobilize the capabilities of relevant organizations for the project through in-house politics and negotiations with external actors such as doctors and regulators, in order to achieve drug shaping.

However, because organizations have specific, historically obtained routines, it might be difficult for them to evaluate an entirely new project. In such a case, its linkages with external actors, again, may help to provide different visions and evaluate the new project properly (Nelson and Winter 1982; Fransman 1990). This also supports the arguments of various scholars that external networking is important for pharmaceutical innovation, particularly in the era of biotechnology, the age of change (Whittaker and Bower 1994; Faulkner and Senker 1995; Gambardella 1995; Powell *et al.* 1996).

Thus, to promote drug innovation, we (namely researchers, managers, policy makers, doctors, patients, and the rest of us who want better drugs) should pay attention not only to economic but also to the various social activities such as channelling, integrating and negotiating. Leaders for innovation should be both open-minded and dauntless, though it is difficult. Without efforts in these activities, innovation-promoting campaigns in the pharmaceutical industry will be less efficient and less effective.

9.2   THE MATERIAL MATTERS

In the process of shaping drugs, the activities of human actors are central, as was discussed in the previous section, but non-human entities such as compounds, bioassay systems, scientific instruments, production facilities and various material media for communication also play an indispensable, though not decisive, role. They are an important part of the heterogeneous elements involved in the process of drug discovery and development, and are combined with other elements to shape a drug. Human actors cannot conduct any activity for drug shaping without non-human elements. This demonstrates what I call the material imperative, the concept that non-humans significantly restrict all our activities though their restriction is not deterministic. The findings of this study basically support the key claim of actor-network theory on the essential role of non-humans in the shaping of technology, though I believe that the influence of humans and that of non-humans on technological change is qualitatively different.

The material imperative implies that the distribution of physical resources (such as scientific apparatus, or disease-model animals) among economic organizations affects the shaping of drugs. Therefore, financial and material support for research does matter in the promotion of drug innovation, though it is just one condition of many. It also implies that the material infrastructure, including a stable energy supply, high-quality materials, excellent production equipment and efficient transportation, also matters in the shaping of new drugs. In particular, it was seen in our case studies that the level of such technologies as scientific instruments and production equipment is essential for the shaping not only of compounds but also of their organizational status (in terms of acceptable production costs) and market (as regards demonstrating their efficacy and safety). It should be also noted that the shaping process of drugs itself produces new material conditions. Thus, many kinds of relevant industrial sectors should be nurtured together with the pharmaceutical industry to promote drug innovation.

9.3   DIFFERENT TYPES OF DRUG INNOVATION

The processes of shaping drugs are neither the same nor completely different. We found three distinguishable patterns in terms of familiarity with the compound and its application, namely paradigmatic innovation, application innovation and modification-based innovation. In paradigmatic innovation, both the compound and its application are unfamiliar, and uncertainty is high in all aspects of drug shaping. In application innovation, in which the compound is familiar but its application is unfamiliar, uncertainty is high in all aspects except the shaping of the compound. In modification-based innovation, in which both the compound and its application are familiar, uncertainty is moderate but possibly high in the aspects of shaping organizational authorization and market, in terms of patentability, marketability and profitability.

These three types of drug innovation have different characteristics in the shaping process. Paradigmatic innovation is characterized by strong resistance within the organization and suspicion outside it. Therefore, it needs strong leadership to accomplish innovation. Leaders have to combine heterogeneous factors inside and outside the organization to construct all aspects of the drug. In application innovation, linkage with clinicians in different therapeutic areas is particularly important in order to identify new applications. Strong leadership can be also required to overcome considerable resistance inside and outside the company against the unfamiliar use of a familiar compound. The networking of heterogeneous elements including those in the new therapeutic area is needed. In modification-based innovation, with several rivals of the same kind, the creation of distinctive features is the key task. It also requires swift development, because the opportunity cost due to delay is clearer. An organizational capability to conduct systematic and intensive development is in particular essential. There are also differences in the degree of impact of innovation on relevant actors, entities and factors among the different types of innovation. The impact of innovation seems to be most significant in paradigmatic innovation and least significant in modification-based innovation. However, it should be noted that any type is not in particular linked with market success. Ranitidine seemed to be more successful on the market than cimetidine, though it was a modification-based innovation. But this is not the case for every modification-based innovation.

From the practical point of view, different types of drug innovation require different activities to promote them. To encourage paradigmatic innovation, the reduction of organizational, regulatory and professional resistance to unfamiliarity seems to be the key. However, this resistance is necessary to protect the company and society from the undesirable results that might come from the development of inappropriate drugs. Proper assessment of projects is required. For this, the fusion of external and internal knowledge seems particularly significant. It seems effective to encourage communication, particularly between academic/clinical experts and corporate and regulatory workers, in addition to communication within each organization. The management, the regulator and clinicians should be also aware of the constructed nature of scientific knowledge. Even though dominant scientific knowledge is inconsistent with the concept of a new drug, it can be possible that existing scientific knowledge has flaws. Of course, strong direction by the project leader is essential. The leader should know that innovation is the process of heterogeneous engineering and requires his/her own activities to link up heterogeneous elements including organizational and market power. Efficacy and safety of the drug is pivotal, but is not enough.

To promote application innovation, in particular with regard to the discovery of new applications, the communication between corporate researchers and clinicians in various therapeutic areas seems important. Communication among researchers in different areas and between researchers and marketing staff in various therapeutic areas also seems to be helpful. With regard to the proper assessment of projects, corporate managers and regulatory agents should establish linkage with various clinical experts, though they should also be aware that scientific knowledge is a system of constructed beliefs, including errors. In order to overcome organizational and market resistance, project leaders and champions should recognize that they have to link up heterogeneous elements to convince the relevant people of the effectiveness of the drug in the new application.

To promote modification-based innovation, building the integrated organization is crucial so that the development of a distinguishable drug can be swiftly achieved. Various functions in the organization, including research, intellectual property management, pre-clinical tests, clinical development, production, pharmaceutics and marketing and sales, should move in parallel in order to minimize the opportunity costs due to delay. Communication with medical practitioners and patients seems to be helpful to identify the needs for improvement and the room for differentiation of the drug. However, to secure resources from unnecessary modification-based innovation, a proper system to evaluate cost-effectiveness seems to be necessary both in companies and in society.

Thus, different types of innovation require different ways of management. There is no 'one best way' of management of drug innovation. However, because there are also similarities among different types of drug innovation, the ways of management do not seem to be completely different from each other: rather, the differences seem to be a matter of emphasis. In addition, it should be noted that it is difficult, and perhaps unwise in terms of risk 'portfolio', for a drug company to pursue exclusively any one of the types of drug innovation, given that there is keen competition among companies in the same therapeutic areas and that it takes about ten years to develop a drug. Although you have sought for paradigmatic innovation, part-way through the process you might find that your rival is also shaping a similar drug. In such a case, you should think of changing the way of management. Pursuing only paradigmatic innovation seems too risky, but relying entirely on modification-based innovation seems too passive and perhaps unfavourable in the long run for the corporate and national economy. Therefore, corporate executives and policy makers should consider a proper mix of drug R&D projects belonging to different types of innovation, each of which should be managed suitably and flexibly.

9. 4 DRUG DISCOVERY AND DEVELOPMENT IN JAPAN

As was discussed in the previous chapter, when we compare the Japanese cases of drug discovery and development with the British ones, the proportion of modification-based innovation is higher in the former than in the latter. Historical, cultural and structural factors, namely the relatively lower level of science and technology in the biomedical area in Japan, the collectiveness and conservatism of Japanese organizations, and the highly regulated, well-organized but conservative Japanese pharmaceutical market, seem to contribute to the orientation of Japanese companies toward modification-based innovation.

This finding supports the arguments of the social shaping of technology that the historical and structural context should be examined to understand technological change though its influence is less explicit than those from directly involved actors. This study demonstrates that the comparison among different countries is useful to identify the historical and structural context. Attention to that context contributes to bridging a gap between the relatively microscopic examination of drug-shaping process and the more macroscopic discussion of industrial policy.

In fact, the finding of this study is compatible with the argument that the national innovation system, which includes companies, governmental bodies, universities as core institutions (Nelson 1996, pp. 274–301; Fransman 1999, pp. 155–66), exists and affects innovation processes. However, this study also reveals that the national system of innovation seems to be partly different among different industries, and even the common features of the system may affect the innovation process differently when the configuration of the system is different. For example, the collectiveness of Japanese organizations seems to be unfavourable to paradigmatic innovation in the pharmaceutical industry, whereas it is argued to be favourable to innovation in other industries such as automobiles and electronics (Clark and Fujimoto 1991; Odagiri and Goto 1993; Nonaka and Takeuchi 1995; Porter *et al.* 2000). It is probably due to the differences in the level and stability of relevant science and technology, the dominant innovation type, and the structure of markets among those industries: in the automobile or electronics industry, the technical base is relatively stable, incremental innovation is dominant, and the market is less controlled. The orientation of the Japanese pharmaceutical industry towards modification-based innovation rather than paradigmatic innovation has made their presence modest in the global market, though Japanese companies have enjoyed sound profits thanks to the naturally specific industrial environment (Reich 1990). In contrast, British pharmaceutical companies have faced international competition since the late 1940s and have had to develop internationally competitive drugs (Owen 1999, pp. 371–2). Of course, even modification-based innovation can be internationally successful if the drug has a clear advantage and the company demonstrates it effectively to overseas customers, but lacking strong international marketing networks of their own, Japanese companies seem to have failed to exploit overseas markets, at least until recently. This seems to be the main reason why the Japanese pharmaceutical industry is less successful in the world market than its British counterpart.

From the practical point of view, the involvement of historical, cultural and structural factors in drug innovation suggests that broader transformations of society may be required in order to change the pattern of innovation. For example, to promote paradigmatic innovation in Japan, it may be necessary to transform the structure and the culture of science, technology, organizations and market of the country. For example, relevant scientific and technological jobs in Japan should be made more attractive to young people and foreign people with ability in order to enhance the level of science and technology. The research infrastructure should also be improved. To make organization more progressive, flows of knowledge between public sector researches and industries should be promoted. Heterogeneity and heterodoxy in organization should be allowed. Unfamiliar things should be tried rather than being avoided. The Japanese pharmaceutical market should also enhance its tolerance of the risk accompanying unfamiliar concepts. Strengthening international activities of academics, business people and policy makers may help to transform the attitude to something unfamiliar. Thus, it is obvious that these transformations require more than the effort of pharmaceutical companies alone. Scientists, engineers, educators, managers, investors, doctors, patients, regulators, policy planners and all citizens should each play their role. In other words, because everybody is, indeed, to some extent involved in the shaping process of drugs, no one is immune from responsibility. If we want better medicines, each of us should be aware of this, think about his/her role, and play the role.

9. 5   BEYOND THE PHARMACEUTICAL INDUSTRY

Innovation in the pharmaceutical industry has several distinct features. First, it is more strongly linked with science and with regulation than innovation in such industries as automobiles and electronics, which have been the empirical bases of major innovation studies, for example, Abernathy (1978), Whipp and Clark (1986), Clark and Fujimoto (1991), Fransman (1990), Henderson and Clark (1990), Christensen (1997) and Iansiti (1998). As was seen in case studies in this book, the linkage with external sources of scientific knowledge has a direct influence on the process of innovation in the pharmaceutical industry. This is consistent with the arguments of different works dealing with innovation in the biomedical area, including Faulkner and Senker (1995), Gambardella (1995) and Powell *et al.* (1996). Our case studies also confirm that regulation has a crucial impact on the shaping of drugs. Regulation in the pharmaceutical industry extends to all kinds of activities including R&D, production, selling, prices and patents. It strictly conditions what can be made, what can be sold and what can be profitable. Therefore, the influence of regulation on the innovation process in the pharmaceutical industry is explicit in the shaping of compounds and markets, and implicit in the shaping of applications and organizational authorization. Thus, all aspects are affected by regulation.

Second, with regard to the typology of innovation, the traditional distinction between radical innovation and incremental innovation may be inappropriate for the pharmaceutical industry. In particular, incremental innovations characterized by bit-by-bit and cumulative improvement do not fit minor innovations in pharmaceuticals, which normally take a very long time, occur much less frequently and often significantly affect the technological and organizational systems of the company. In this book, therefore, I propose a different typology of innovation which is specific to the pharmaceutical industry. The typology, namely paradigmatic innovation, application innovation and modification-based innovation, seems to be more appropriate in the analysis of technological change in the pharmaceutical industry than the traditional one.

Third, the structural and cultural context of the pharmaceutical industry seems different from that of other industries. In such industries as automobiles and electronics, in which the relevant scientific base is relatively stable, market needs are better articulated and incremental innovations are dominant, strongly integrated organizations are probably most suitable for innovation. However, in the pharmaceutical industry, in particular for paradigmatic innovation and application innovation, such coherent organizations may not be favourable because few members can accept the unfamiliar concept accompanying these types of innovation. Rather, more heterogeneous organization with networks linking various external knowledge sources seem to be more appropriate for balanced innovation management in the pharmaceutical industry.

Although innovations in the pharmaceutical industry possess these differences, I think they are not completely unique. On the contrary, some of these characteristics may become more common among other industries. The finer the technology of an industry becomes, the closer together the technology and scientific frontiers will become. Then, more and more industries should strengthen their linkage with external research institutions. On the other hand, globalization and standardization of business currently in progress will make the influence of industrial activities on our lives much more significant. Our lives will become probably more vulnerable to their influences. In such a situation, as the consciousness of quality of life among us grows, regulations governing business activities in various industries are likely to be required to protect and improve our lives. Thus, more and more industries may become strongly related both to science and to regulation. The theoretical framework and practical implications of this study may also be useful to such industries.

9.6 THE SOCIAL SHAPING OF TECHNOLOGY AND THE MANAGEMENT OF TECHNOLOGY

This book demonstrates that the social shaping of technology (SST) is an extremely useful framework for the analysis of technological change. The approach emphasizes the heterogeneous and interactive process of technological change; in addition, it also notices the historical and structural context surrounding it. Thus, the approach provides a set of painting materials to produce the richest picture of technological change including both microscopic and macroscopic phenomena. However, we cannot produce a meaningful painting only with a set of painting materials: we also need a subject to paint. This book chooses the process of drug discovery and development as its subject. Given the subject, the framework of the SST works actively. It demonstrates how heterogeneous, how interactive and how contingent the process of shaping drugs is. At the same time, it shows us several practical implications about how we can intervene in the process of drug discovery and development. It suggests different ways of the management of drug innovation in different settings. Thus, we can see that the SST approach is a useful theoretical base for technology management and industrial policy.

Based on the SST approach, the picture this book provides may be criticized for being too comprehensive to focus and too specific to generalize. I admit it partly; but, if the reality of technological change is in fact complex, it seems, at least to me, worth trying to tolerate impurity, contingency and complexity in order to obtain more grounded and effective implications. Simplification is certainly needed, but excessive simplification may be at the cost of important details necessary to manage technology in a concrete situation. In addition, a specific phenomenon includes something general as well as something unique. I hope that this book can show it to some extent.

Bibliography

Abel, J. J. and S. Kubota (1919), 'On the Presence of Histamine (β-Imidazolyl-Ethylamine) in the Hypophysis Cerebri and Other Tissues of the Body and its Occurrence among the Hydrolytic Decomposition Products of Proteins', *Journal of Pharmacology and Experimental Therapeutics*, **13**, 243–300.

Abernathy, W. J. (1978), *The Productivity Dilemma: Roadblock to Innovation in the Automobile Industry*, Baltimore, MD: Johns Hopkins University Press.

Abernathy, W. J. and J. M. Utterback (1978), 'Patterns of Industrial Innovation', *Technology Review*, **80**, 41–7.

Abraham, E. P. and P. B. Loder (1972), 'Cephalosporin C', in E. H. Flynn (ed.), *Cephalosporins and Penicillins: Chemistry and Biology*, New York: Academic Press, pp. 1–26.

Abraham, E. P. and G. G. F. Newton (1961), 'The Structure of Cephalosporin C', *Biochemical Journal*, **79**, 377–93.

Abraham, J. (1995), *Science, Politics and the Pharmaceutical Industry: Controversy and Bias in Drug Regulation*, London: UCL Press.

Abrams, P., C. C. Schulman, S. Vaage and the European Tamsulosin Study Group (1995), 'Tamsulosin, a Selective α_{1c}-Adrenoceptor Antagonist: a Randomized, Controlled Trial in Patients with Benign Prostatic "Obstruction"', *British Journal of Urology*, **76**, 325–36.

Achilladelis, B. (1993), 'The Dynamics of Technological Innovation: the Sector of Antibacterial Medicines', *Research Policy*, **22**, 279–308.

Achilladelis, B. and N. Antonakis (2001), 'The Dynamics of Technological Innovation: the Case of the Pharmaceutical Industry', *Research Policy*, **30**, 535–88.

Ahlquist, R. P. (1948), 'A Study of the Adrenotropic Receptors', *American Journal of Physiology*, **153**, 586–600.

Ahlquist, R. P. (1973), 'Adrenergic Receptors: a Personal and Practical View', *Perspectives in Biology and Medicine*, **17**, 119–22.

Ahmed, S. R., P. J. C. Brooman, S. M. Shalet, A. Howell, N. J. Blacklock and D. Rickards (1983), 'Treatment of Advanced Prostatic Cancer with LHRH Analogue ICI 118630: Clinical Response and Hormonal Mechanisms', *Lancet*, **2**, 415–18.

Akaza, H., Y. Aso, K. Koiso, H. Fuse, K. Isurugi, K. Okada, M. Usami, T. Kotake, T. Ohashi, T. Ueda, T. Niijima and TAP-144-SR Study Group (1990), 'Leuprorelin Acetate Depot: Results of a Multicentre Japanese Trial', *Journal of International Medical Research*, **18** (supplement 1), 90–102.

Alberts, A. W. (1988), 'Discovery, Biochemistry and Biology of Lovastatin', *American Journal of Cardiology*, **62** (Supplement), 10J–15J.

Alberts, A. W., J. Chen, G. Kuron, V. Hunt, J. Huff, C. Hoffman, J. Rothrock, M. Lopez, H. Joshua, E. Harris, A. Patchett, R. Monaghan, S. Currie, E. Stapley, G. Albers-Schonberg, O. Hensens, J. Hirshfield, K. Hoogsteen, J. Liesch and J. Springer (1980), 'Mevinolin: a Highly Potent Competitive Inhibitor of Hydroxymethylglutaryl-coenzyme A Reductase and a Cholesterol-lowering agent', *Proceedings of the National Academy of Sciences (USA)*, **77**: 3957–61.

Alexander, D. L. (1996), 'R&D Productivity and Global Market Share in the Pharmaceutical Industry', in R. B. Helms (ed.), *Competitive Strategies in the Pharmaceutical Industry*, Washington, D.C.: AEI Press, pp. 130–54.

Alexander, D. L., J. E. Flynn and L. A. Linkins (1995), 'Innovation, R&D Productivity and Global Market Share in the Pharmaceutical Industry', *Review of Industrial Organization*, **10**, 197–207.

Allen, J. M., J. P. O'Shea, K. Mashiter, G. Williams and S. R. Bloom (1983), 'Advanced Carcinoma of the Prostate: Treatment with a Gonadotrophin Releasing Hormone Agonist', *British Medical Journal*, **286**, 1607–9.

Alleyne, G. A. O., C. J. Dickinson, A. C. Dornhorst, R. M. Fulton, K. G. Green, I. D. Hill, P. Hurst, D. R. Laurence, T. Pilkington, B. N. C. Prichard, B. Robinson and M. L. Rosenheim (1963), 'Effect of Pronethalol in Angina Pectoris', *British Medical Journal*, **2**, 1226–9.

Amoss, M., R. Burgus, R. Blackwell, W. Vale, R. Fellows and R. Guillemin (1971), 'Purification, Amino Acid Composition and N-Terminus of the Hypothalamic Luteinizing Hormone Releasing Factor (LRF) of Ovine Origin', *Biochemical and Biophysical Research Communication*, **44**, 205–10.

Angelmar, R. and C. Pinson (1991), *Zantac*, Fontainebleau, France: INSEAD.

Ariëns, E. J. (1984), 'Stereochemistry: a Basis for Sophisticated Nonsense in Pharmacokinetics and Clinical Pharmacology', *European Journal of Clinical Pharmacology*, **26** (6), 663–8.

Arnold, W., G. Flouret, R. Morgan, R. Rippel and W. White (1974), 'Synthesis and Biological Activity of Some Analogs of the Gonadotropin Releasing Hormone', *Journal of Medicinal Chemistry*, **17**, 314–19.

Ash, A. S. F. and H. O. Schild (1966), 'Receptors Mediating Some Actions of Histamine', *British Journal of Pharmacology and Chemotherapy*, **27**, 427–39.

Aso, Y., T. Niijima and TAP-144-SR Study Group (Japan) (1991), 'Clinical Phase III Study on TAP-144-SR, an LH-RH Agonist Depot Formulation, in Patients with Prostatic Cancer', *Hinyou Kiyou*, **37**, 305–20. (in Japanese)

Association of the British Pharmaceutical Industry (1997), *Pharma Facts and Figures*, London: Association of the British Pharmaceutical Industry.

Åström, H. and H. Vallin (1974), 'Effect of a New Beta-adrenergic Blocking Agent, ICI 66082, on Exercise Haemodynamics and Airway Resistance in Angina Pectoris', *British Heart Journal*, **36**, 1194–200.

Baba, M., Y. Nakayama, H. Shiota, S. Matsumoto, Y. Sakiyama, Y. Wagatsuma, K. Togashi, N. Nemoto, Y. Yamaguchi, W. Yamada, M. Ayuse, K. Tateno, T. Akasaka, R. Tochigi, Y. Arai, N. Kobayashi, H. Hayakawa, K. Shiraki, F. Komota, C. Otaki, T. Mukoyama, Y. Tomita, H. Sugimoto, Y. Iikura, T. Nagakura, K. Shirai, C. Naito, A. Nakajima, Y. Teramichi, T. Nemoto, T. Hirao, S. Torii, M. Yoshida, M. Ueda, H. Mikawa, K. Shinomiya, K. Seyama, S. Nishima and F. Nakajima (1981), 'Syouni Kikanshi Zensoku ni Taisuru Shin β_2 Jyuyoutai Shigekisei Kikanshi Kakucyouyaaku Procaterol no Yakkou Hyouka, 2' (A Study on Efficacy of Procaterol, a New β_2-Receptor Stimulant Bronchodilator in Children's Bronchial Asthma, 2), *Igaku no Ayumi*, **118**, 241–53. (in Japanese)

Babkin, B. P. (1934), 'The "Chemical" Phase of Gastric Secretion and its Regulation', *American Journal of Digestive Diseases and Nutrition*, **1**, 715–21.

Ball, D. I., R. A. Coleman, L. H. Denyer, A. T. Nials and K. E. Sheldrick (1987), '*In Vitro* Characterisation of the β-Adrenoceptor Agonist, Salmeterol', *British Journal of Pharmacology*, **92**, 591P.

Ball, D. I., R. T. Brittain, R. A. Coleman, L. H. Denyer, D. Jack, M. Johnson, L. H. C. Lunts, A. T. Nials, K. E. Sheldrick and I. F. Skidmore (1991), 'Salmeterol, a Novel, Long-Acting β_2-Adrenoceptor Agonist: Characterization of Pharmacological Activity *In Vitro* and *In Vivo*', *British Journal of Pharmacology*, **104**, 665–71.

Banik, U. K. and M. L. Givner (1975), 'Ovulation Induction and Anti-fertility Effects of an LH-RH Analogue (AY-25, 205) in Cyclic Rats', *Journal of Reproduction and Fertility*, **44**, 87–94.

Barger, G. and H. H. Dale (1910), 'Chemical Structure and Sympatho-mimetic Action of Amines', *Journal of Physiology*, **41**, 19–59.

Barnes, B. (1982), 'The Science–Technology Relationship: a Model and a Query', *Social Studies of Science*, **12**, 166–72.

Barnes, B. and D. Edge (1982), 'The Interaction of Science and Technology,' in B. Barnes and D. Edge (eds), *Science in Context*, Milton Keynes: Open University Press.

Barnes, B., D. Bloor and J. Henry (1996), *Scientific Knowledge: A Sociological Analysis*, London: Athlone.

Barns, N. C., G. Maronee, G. U. Di Maria, S. Visser, I. Utama and S. L. Payne (1993), 'A Comparison of Fluticasone Propionate, 1 mg Daily, with Beclomethasone Dipropionate, 2 mg Daily, in the Treatment of Severe Asthma', *European Respiratory Journal*, **6**, 877–84.

Barrett, A. M. (1971), 'The Pharmacology of Practolol', *Postgraduate Medical Journal*, **47** (Supplement 2), 7.

Barrett, A. M. (1977), 'The Pharmacology of Atenolol', *Postgraduate Medical Journal*, **53** (Supplement 3), 58–64.

Barrett, A. M., J. Carter, J. D. Fitzgerald, R. Hull and D. Le Count (1973), 'A New Type of Cardioselective Adrenoceptive Blocking Drug', *British Journal of Pharmacology*, **48**, 340P.

Bartley, M. (1990), 'Do We Need a Strong Programme in Medical Sociology?', *Sociology of Health & Illness*, **12**, 371–90.

Bayer (Japan) Co. Ltd (1994), 'Doitsu de umare Nihon de sodatta Ca Kikkouyaku Nifedipine' (a Ca Antagonist which was born in Germany and brought up in Japan), *Yakushigaku Zassi*, **29**, 279–80. (in Japanese)

Beacock, C. J., A. C. Buck, R. Zwinck, W. B. Peeling, R. W. M. Rees, A. Turkes, K. Walker and K. Griffiths (1987), 'The Treatment of Metastatic Prostatic Cancer with the Slow Release LH-RH Analogue Zoladex ICI 118630', *British Journal of Urology*, **59**, 436–42.

Beattie, C. W. and A. Corbin (1977), 'Pre- and Postcoital Contraceptive Activity of LH-RH in the Rat', *Biology of Reproduction*, **16**, 333–9.

Beevers, D. G. and G. A. MacGregor (1999), *Hypertension in Practice*, 3rd edn, London: Martin Dunitz.

Belchetz, P. E., T. M. Plant, Y. Nakai, E. J. Keogh and E. Knobil (1978), 'Hypophysial Responses to Continuous and Intermittent Delivery of Hypothalamic Gonadotropin-releasing Hormone', *Science*, **202**, 631–3.

Berne, R. M. and M. N. Levy (1996), *Principles of Physiology*, 2nd edn, St Louis, MO: Mosby.

Besser, G. M. and C. H. Mortimer (1974), 'Hypothalamic Regulatory Hormones: a Review', *Journal of Clinical Pathology*, **27**, 173–84.

Bierly, P and A. Chakrabarti (1996), 'Technological Learning, Strategic Flexibility, and New Product Development in the Pharmaceutical Industry', *IEEE Transactions on Engineering Management*, **43**, 368–80.

Bijker, W. E. (1995), *Of Bicycles, Bakelites, and Bulbs: Toward a Theory of Sociotechnical Change*, Cambridge, MA: MIT Press.

Bijker, W. E., T. P. Hughes and T. Pinch (eds) (1987), *The Social Construction of Technological Systems*, Cambridge, MA: MIT Press.

Bilheimer, D. M., S. C. Grundy, M. S. Brown and J. L. Goldstein (1983), 'Mevinolin and Colestipol Stimulate Receptor-mediated Clearance of Low Density Lipoprotein from Plasma in Familial Hypercholesterolemia Hetrozygotes', *Proceedings of the National Academy of Sciences (USA)*, **80**, 4124–8.

Bischoff, W. and German Leuprorelin Study Group (1990), '3.75 and 7.5 mg Leuprorelin Acetate Depot in the Treatment of Advanced Prostatic Cancer: Preliminary Report', *Journal of International Medical Research*, **18** (supplement 1), 103–13.

Black, J. W. (1976), 'Ahlquist and the Development of Beta-Adrenoceptor Antagonists', *Postgraduate Medical Journal*, **52** (Supplement 4), 11–13.

Black, J. W. and J. S. Stephenson (1962), 'Pharmacology of a New Adrenergic Beta-Receptor-Blocking Compound (Nethalide)', *Lancet*, **2**, 311–14.

Black, J. W., A. F. Crowther, R. G. Shanks, L. H. Smith and A. C. Dornhorst (1964), 'A New Adrenegic Beta-Receptor Antagonist', *Lancet*, **1**, 1080–1.

Black, J. W., W. A. M. Duncan, D. J. Durant, C. R. Ganellin and E. M. Parsons (1972), 'Definition and Antagonism of Histamine H_2-receptor', *Nature*, **236**, 385–90.

Black, J. W., G. J. Durant, J. C. Emmett and C. R. Ganellin (1974), 'Sulphur-Methylene Isosterism in the Development of Metiamide, a New Histamine H2-Receptor Antagonist', *Nature*, **248**, 65–7.

Black, J., V. P. Gerskowitch and P. Leff (1982), 'Reflections on the Classification of Histamine Receptors', in C. R. Ganellin and M. E. Parsons (eds), *Pharmacology of Histamine Receptors*, Bristol: Wright, pp. 1–9.

Blauw, G. J. and R. G. J. Westendorp (1995), 'Asthma Deaths in New Zealand: Whodunnit?', *Lancet*, **345**, 2–3.

Bloch, K. (1965), 'The Biological Synthesis of Cholesterol', *Science*, **150**, 19–28.

Bloor, D. (1991), *Knowledge and Social Imagery*, 2nd edn, Chicago, IL: University of Chicago Press.

Bloor, D. (1999), 'Anti-Latour', *Studies in History and Philosophy of Science*, **30A**, 81–112.

Bodewitz, H. J. H. W., H. Buurma and G. H. de Vries (1987), 'Regulatory Science and the Social Management of Trust in Medicine,' in W. E. Bijker, T. P. Hughes and T. Pinch (eds), *The Social Construction of Technological Systems*, Cambridge, MA: MIT Press, pp. 243–59.

Bogner, W. C. and H. Thomas (1996), *Drug to Market: Creating Value and Advantage in the Pharmaceutical Industry*, New York: Pergamon.

Bossert, F. and W. Vater (1971), 'Dihydropyridine, eine neue Gruppe stark wirksaamer Coronartherapeutika' (Dihydropyridine, a New Group of Strongly Effective Drug for Coronary Care), *Naturwissenschaaften*, **58**, 578. (in German)

Boulet, L. P. (1994), 'Long- versus Short-acting β_2-Agonists: Implications for Drug Therapy', *Drugs*, **47**, 207–22.

Bowles, M. J., V. Barasubramanian, N. S. Khurmi, A. B. Davies and E. B. Raftery (1981), 'Efficacy of a New Calcium Channel Blocking Agent, Nicardipine, in Chronic Stable Angina', *British Journal of Clinical Pharmacology*, **13**, 590P.

Bradshaw, J., R. T. Brittain, J. W. Clitherow, M. J. Daly, D. Jack, B. J. Price and R. Stables (1979), 'Ranitidine (AH 19065): a New Potent, Selective Histamine H_2-Receptor Antagonist', *British Journal of Pharmacology*, **66**, 464P.

Bradshaw, J., R. T. Brittain, R. A. Coleman, D. Jack, I. Kennedy, L. H. C. Lunts and I. F. Skidmore (1987), 'The Design of Salmeterol: a Long-Acting Selective β_2-Adrenoceptor Agonist', *British Journal of Pharmacology*, **92**, 590P.

Braunwald, E. (1966), 'Symposium on Beta Adrenergic Receptor Blockade: an Editorial Introduction to the Symposium', *American Journal of Cardiology*, **18**, 303–7.

Braverman, H. (1974), *Labour and Monopoly Capital: The Degradation of Work in the Twentieth Century*, New York: Monthly Review Press.

Brick, I., K. J. Hutchison, D. G. McDevitt, I. C. Roddie and R. G. Shanks (1968), 'Comparison of the Effects of ICI 50172 and Propranolol on the Cardiovascular Responses to Adrenaline, Isoprenaline and Exercise', *British Journal of Pharmacology*, **34**, 127–40.

Brimblecombe, R. W., W. A. M. Duncan, G. J. Durant, C. R. Ganellin, M. E. Parsons and J. W. Black (1975a), 'The Pharmacology of Cimetidine, a New Histamine H_2-Receptor Antagonist', *British Journal of Pharmacology*, **53**, 435P–6P.

Brimblecombe, R. W., W. A. M. Duncan, G. J. Durant, J. C. Emmett, C. R. Ganellin and M. E. Parsons (1975b), 'Cimetidine: a Non-Thiourea H_2-Receptor Antagonist', *Journal of International Medical Research*, **3**, 86–92.

British Medical Journal (1975), 'Side Effects of Practolol', *British Medical Journal*, **2**, 577–8.

British Thoracic Society, British Paediatric Association, Research Unit of the Royal College of Physicians of London, King's Fund Centre, National Asthma Campaign, Royal College of General Practitioners, General Practitioners in Asthma Group, British Association of Accident and Emergency Medicine and British Paediatric Respiratory Group

(1993), 'Guidelines on the Management of Asthma', *Thorax*, **48** (Supplement), S1–S24.

British Thoracic Society, National Asthma Campaign, Royal College of Physicians of London, General Practitioners in Asthma Group, British Association of Accident and Emergency Medicine, British Paediatric Respiratory Society and Royal College of Paediatrics and Child Health (1997), 'The British Guidelines on Asthma Management: 1995 Review and Position Statement', *Thorax*, **52** (Supplement 1), S1–S21.

Brittain, R. T. (1982), 'Discovery and Evolution of Ranitidine', in A. J. Riley and P. R. Salman (eds), *Ranitidine: Proceedings of an International Symposium held in the Context of the Seventh World Congress of Gastroenterology*, Amsterdam: Excerpta Medica, pp. 5–14.

Brittain, R. T. and D. Jack (1983), 'Histamine H_2-Antagonists: Past, Present and Future', *Journal of Clinical Gastroenterology*, **5** (Supplement 1), 71–9.

Brittain, R. T., J. B. Farmer, D. Jack, L. E. Martin and W. T. Simpson (1968), 'α-[(t-Butylamino)methyl]-4-hydroxy-m-xylene-α^1, α^3-diol (AH. 3365): a Selective β-Adrenergic Stimulant', *Nature*, **219**, 862–3.

Brittain, R. T., D. Jack and A. C. Ritchie (1970), 'Recent β-Adrenoceptor Stimulants,' in N. J. Harper and A. B. Simmonds (eds), *Advances in Drug Research*, vol. 5, London: Academic Press, pp. 197–253.

Brittain, R. T., D. Jack and B. J. Price (1981), 'Recent Developments in Histamine H_2-Receptor Antagonists', *Trends in Pharmacological Sciences*, **2**, 310–13.

Brittain, R. T., D. Jack and M. J. Sumner (1988), 'Further Studies on the Long Duration of Action of Salmeterol, a New, Selective Beta$_2$-Stimulant Bronchodilator', *Journal of Pharmacy and Pharmacology*, **40** (Supplement), 93P.

Britton, M. G., J. S. Earnshaw, J. B. D. Palmer, on behalf of a European Study Group (1992), 'A Twelve Month Comparison of Salmeterol with Salbutamol in Asthmatic Patients', *European Respiratory Journal*, **5**, 1062–7.

Brogden, R. N. and D. Faulds (1991), 'Salmeterol Xinafoate: a Review of Its Pharmacological Properties and Therapeutic Potential in Reversible Obstructive Airways Disease', *Drugs*, **42**, 895–912.

Brown, M. S. and J. L. Goldstein (1974), 'Familial Hypercholesterolemia: Defective Binding of Lipoproteins to Cultured Fibroblasts Associated with Impaired Regulation of 3-Hydroxy-3-Methylglutaryl Coenzyme A Reductase Activity', *Proceedings of the National Academy of Sciences (USA)*, **71**, 788–92.

Brown, M. S. and J. L. Goldstein (1981), 'Lowering Plasma Cholesterol by

Raising LDL Receptors', *New England Journal of Medicine*, **305**, 515–17.

Brown, M. S., S. N. Dana and J. L. Goldstein (1973), 'Regulation of 3-Hydroxy-3-Methylglutaryl Coenzyme A Reductase Activity in Human Fibroblasts by Lipoproteins', *Proceedings of the National Academy of Sciences (USA)*, **70**, 2162–6.

Bucher, N. L. R., P. Overath and F. Lynen (1960), 'β-Hydroxy-β-Methylglutaryl Coenzyme A Reductase, Cleavage and Condensing Enzymes in Relation to Cholesterol Formation in Rat Liver', *Biochimica et Biophysica Acta*, **40**, 491–501.

Buist, A. S., P. G. J. Burney, A. R. Feinstein, R. I. Horwitz, S. F. Lanes, A. S. Rebuck and W. O. Spitzer (1989), 'Fenoterol and Fatal Asthma', *Lancet*, **1**, 1071.

Bunney, R. (1993), 'Study Too Small to Detect Increase in Deaths', *British Medical Journal*, **306**, 1610.

Burgus, R. and R. Guillemin (1970), 'Hypothalamic Releasing Factors', *Annual Review of Biochemistry*, **39**, 499–526.

Burgus, R., M. Butcher, M. Amoss, N. Ling, M. Monahan, J. Rivier, R. Fellows, R. Blackwell, W. Vale and R. Guillemin (1972), 'Primary Structure of the Ovine Hypothalamic Luteinizing Hormone-releasing Factor (LRF)', *Proceeding of the National Academy of Sciences USA*, **69**, 278–82.

Butchers, P. R., C. J. Vardey and M. Johnson (1991), 'Salmeterol: a Potent and Long-acting Inhibitor of Inflammatory Mediator Release from Human Lung', *British Journal of Pharmacology*, **104**, 672–6.

Byar, D. P. (1973), 'The Veterans Administration Cooperative Urological Research Group's Studies of Cancer of the Prostate', *Cancer*, **32**, 1126–30.

Cadogan, J. (1997), 'From Pure Science to Profit', *Chemistry & Industry*, 1 December 1997, pp. 937–9.

Caldwell, I. W., S. P. Hall-Smith, R. A. Main, P. J. Ashurst, V. Kirton, W. T. Simpson and G. W. Williams (1968), 'Clinical Evaluation of a New Topical Corticosteroid Beclomethasone Dipropionate', *British Journal of Dermatology*, **80**, 111–17.

Callon, M. (1986), 'The Sociology of an Actor-Network: the Case of the Electric Vehicle,' in M. Callon, J. Law and A. Rip (eds), *Mapping the Dynamics of Science and Technology*, Basingstoke, Hants.: Macmillan, pp. 19–34.

Callon, M. (1987), 'Society in the Making: the Study of Technology as a Tool for Sociological Analysis,' in W. E. Bijker, T. P. Hughes and T. Pinch (eds), *The Social Construction of Technological Systems*, Cambridge, MA: MIT Press, pp. 83–103.

Callon, M. and B. Latour (1992), 'Don't Throw the Baby Out with the Bath School! A Reply to Collins and Yearley', in A. Pickering (ed.), *Science as Practice and Culture*, Chicago: University of Chicago Press, pp. 343–68.

Campbell, H. J., G. Feuer, J. Garcia and G. W. Harris (1961), 'The Infusion of Brain Extracts into the Anterior Pituitary Gland and the Secretion of Gonadotrophic Hormone', *Journal of Physiology*, **157**, 30P–31P.

Campbell, J. C. and N. Ikegami (1998), *The Art of Balance in Health Policy: Maintaining Japan's Low-cost, Egalitarian System*, Cambridge: Cambridge University Press.

Candiani, G. B., P. Vercellini, L. Fedele, L. Arcaini, S. Bianchi and M. Candiani (1990), 'Use of Goserelin Depot, a Gonadotropin-Releasing Hormone Agonist, for the Treatment of Menorrhagia and Severe Anemia in Women with Leiomyomata Uteri', *Acta Obstetrica et Gynecologica Scandinavica*, **69**, 413–15.

Cannon, W. B. and A. Rosenblueth (1933), 'Studies on Conditions of Activity in Endocrine Organs', *American Journal of Physiology*, **104**, 557–74.

Cantor, D. (1992), 'Cortisone and the Politics of Drama, 1949–55,' in J. V. Pickstone (ed.), *Medical Innovations in Historical Perspective*, London: Macmillan, pp. 165–84.

Carey, R. A., A. M. Harvey, J. E. Howard and W. L. Winkenwerder (1950), 'The Effect of Adrenocorticotropic Hormone (ACTH) and Cortisone on the Course of Chronic Bronchial Asthma', *Bulletin of the Johns Hopkins Hospital*, **87**, 387–414.

Castle, W., R. Fuller, J. Hall and J. Palmer (1993), 'Serevent Nationwide Surveillance Study: Comparison of Salmeterol with Salbutamol in Asthmatic Patients Who Require Regular Bronchodilator Treatment', *British Medical Journal*, **306**, 1034–7.

Chang, J-K., R. H. Williams, A. J. Humphries, N. G. Johansson and K. Folkers (1972), 'Luteinizing Releasing Hormone, Synthesis and Arg^8-Analogs and Conformation–Sequence–Activity Relationships', *Biochemical and Biophysical Research Communication*, **47**, 727–32.

Chapman, K. R., S. Kesten and J. P. Szalai (1994), 'Regular vs As-needed Inhaled Salbutamol in Asthma Control', *Lancet*, **343**, 1379–82.

Chatterjee, S. S. and A. E. Perry (1971), 'Salbutamol: Clinical Application as Pressure-packed Aerosol', *Postgraduate Medical Journal*, **47** (Supplement), 53–5.

Chauvette, R. R., E. H. Flynn, B. G. Jackson, E. R. Lavagnino, R. B. Morin, R. A. Mueller, R. P. Pioch, R. W. Roeske, C. W. Ryan, J. L. Spencer and E. Van Heyningen (1962), 'Chemistry of Cephalosporin Antibiotics. II:

Preparation of a New Class of Antibiotics and the Relation of Structure to Activity', *Journal of the American Chemical Society*, **84**, 3401–2.

Chauvette, R. R., P. A. Pennington, C. W. Ryan, R. D. G. Cooper, F. L. José, I. G. Wright, E. M. Van Heyningen and G. W. Huffman (1971), 'Chemistry of Cephalosporin Antibiotics. XXI: Conversion of Penicillins to Cephalexin', *Journal of Organic Chemistry*, **36**, 1259–67.

Chiesa, V. (1996), 'Separating Research from Development: Evidence from the Pharmaceutical Industry', *European Management Journal*, **14**, 638–47.

Choo-Kang, Y. F. G., W. T. Simpson and I. W. B. Grant (1969), 'Controlled Comparison of the Bronchodilator Effects of Three β-Adrenergic Stimulant Drugs Administered by Inhalation to Patients with Asthma', *British Medical Journal*, **2**, 287–9.

Chrisp, P. and K. L. Goa (1991), 'Goserelin', *Drugs*, **41**, 254–88.

Christensen, C. M. (1997), *The Innovator's Dilemma: When New Technologies Cause Great Firms to Fail*, Boston, MA: Harvard Business School Press.

Chung K. F. (1993), 'The Current Debate Concerning β-Agonists in Asthma: a Review', *Journal of the Royal Society of Medicine*, **86**, 96–100.

Clark, K. B. and T. Fujimoto (1991), *Product Development Performance: Strategy, Organization, and Management in the World Auto Industry*, Boston, MA: Harvard Business School Press.

Clark, T. J. H. (1972), 'Effect of Beclomethasone Dipropionate Delivered by Aerosol in Patients with Asthma', *Lancet*, **1**, 1361–4.

Clark, T. J. H. (1991), 'β₂-Agonists in Asthma', *Lancet*, **337**, 44–5.

Clarke, A. and T. Montini (1993), 'The Many Faces of RUC486: Tales of Situated Knowledges and Technological Contestations', *Science, Technology & Human Values*, **18**, 42–78.

Cockburn, I. and R. Henderson (1994), 'Racing to Invest? The Dynamics of Competition in Ethical Drug Discovery', *Journal of Economics & Management Strategy*, **3**, 481–519.

Code, C. F. (1956), 'Histamine and Gastric Secretion', in G. E. W. Wolstenholme and C. M. O'Connor (eds), *CIBA Foundation Symposium Jointly with the Physiological Society and the British Pharmacological Society on Histamine*, London: J. & A. Churchill, pp. 189–219.

Code, C. F. (1965), 'Histamine and Gastric Secretion: a Later Look, 1955–1965', *Federation Proceedings*, **24**, 1311–21.

Collins, H. M. (1981), 'Stages in the Empirical Programme of Relativism', *Social Studies of Science*, **11**, 3–10.

Collins, H. M. (1992), *Changing Order: Replication and Induction in Scientific Practice*, 2nd edn, Chicago: University of Chicago Press.

Collins, H. M. and S. Yearley (1992). 'Epistemological Chicken', in A. Pickering (ed.), *Science as Practice and Culture*, Chicago: University of Chicago Press, pp. 301–26.

Comanor, W.S. (1986), 'The Political Economy of the Pharmaceutical Industry', *Journal of Economic Literature*, **24**, 1178–1217.

Comite, F., F. Cassorla, K. M. Barnes, K. D. Hench, A. Dwyer, M. C. Skerda, D. L. Loriaux, G. B. Cutler and O. H. Pescovitz (1986), 'Luteinizing Hormone Releasing Hormone Analogue Therapy for Central Precocious Puberty', *Journal of the American Medical Association*, **255**, 2613–16.

Conolly, M. E., D. S. Davies, C. T. Dollery and C. F. George (1971a), 'Resistance to β-Adrenoceptor Stimulants (A Possible Explanation for the Rise in Asthma Deaths)', *British Journal of Pharmacology*, **43**, 389–402.

Conolly, M. E., D. A. Warrel, J.A. Newton Howes, J. W. Paterson, L. J. Beilin, D. G. Robertson and C. T. Dollery (1971b), 'A Comparison of the Cardiorespiratory Effects of Isoprenaline and Salbutamol in Patients with Bronchial Asthma', *Postgraduate Medical Journal*, **47** (Supplement), 77–81.

Constant, E. W. (1980), *The Origins of the Turbojet Revolution*, Baltimore, MD: Johns Hopkins University Press.

Coombs, R., P. Saviotti and V. Walsh (1987), *Economics and Technological Change*, Totowa, NJ: Rowman & Littlefield.

Corbin, A. (1982), 'From Contraception to Cancer: a Review of the Therapeutic Applications of LHRH Analogues as Antitumor Agents', *Yale Journal of Biology and Medicine*, **55**, 27–47.

Corbin, A and C. W. Beattie (1975), 'Post-coital Contraceptive and Uterotrophic Effects of Luteinizing Hormone-releasing Hormone', *Endocrinological Research Communication*, **2**, 445–58.

Coy, D. R. and A. V. Schally (1978), 'Gonadotrophin Releasing Hormone Analogues', *Annals of Clinical Research*, **10**, 139–44.

Coy, D. H., E. J. Coy, A. V. Schally, J. Vilchez-Martinez, Y. Hirotsu and A. Arimura (1974), 'Synthesis and Biological Properties of [D-Ala-6, des-Gly NH_2-10]-LH-RH Ethylamide, a Peptide with Greatly Enhanced LH- and FSH-Releasing Activity', *Biochemical and Biophysical Research Communication*, **57**, 335–40.

Coy, D. H., F. Labrie, M. Savary, E. J. Coy and A. V. Schally (1975), 'LH-releasing Activity of Potent LH-RH Analogs *in Vitro*', *Biochemical and Biophysical Research Communication*, **67**, 576–82.

Crane J., N. Pearce, A. Flatt, C. Burgess, R. Jackson, T. Kwong, M. Ball and R. Beasley (1989), 'Prescribed Fenoterol and Death from Asthma in New Zealand, 1981–1983: Case-control Study', *Lancet*, **1**, 917–22.

Crane, J., C. Burgess, R. Beasley and N. Pearce (1991), 'β_2-Agonists in Asthma', *Lancet*, **337**, 44.

Crane, J., N. Pearce, C. Burgess and R. Beasley (1995a), 'Asthma and the β-Agonist Debate', *Thorax*, **50** (Supplement 1), S5–S10.

Crane, J., N. Pearce, C. Burgess and R. Beasley (1995b), 'Asthma Morbidity and Mortality in New Zealand', *Thorax*, **50**, 1020.

Crompton, G. K. (1991), 'β_2-Agonists in Asthma', *Lancet*, **337**, 43–4.

Crompton, G. K. (1993), 'Regular Treatment with β Agonists Remains Unevaluated', *British Medical Journal*, **306**, 1610.

Crowe, M. J., H. E. Counihan and K. O'Malleey (1985), 'A Comparative Study of a New Selective β_2-Adrenoceptor Agonist, Pracaterol and Salbutamol in Asthma', *British Journal of Clinical Pharmacology*, **19**, 787–91.

Crowley, W. F., F. Comite, W. Vale, J. Rivier, D. L. Loriaux and G. B. Cutler (1981), 'Therapeutic Use of Pituitary Desensitization with a Long-acting LHRH Agonist: a Potential New Treatment for Idiopathic Precocious Puberty', *Journal of Clinical Endocrinology and Metabolism*, **52**, 370–2.

Crowther, A. F. and L. H. Smith (1968), 'β-Adrenergic Blocking Agents. II: Propronolol and Related 3-Amino-1-naphthoxy-2-propanols', *Journal of Medicinal Chemistry*, **11**, 1009–13.

Crowther, A. F., D. J. Gilman, B. J. McLoughlin, L. H. Smith, R. W. Turner and T. M. Wood (1969), 'β-Adrenergic Blocking Agents. V: 1-Amino-3-(substituted phenoxy)-2-propanols', *Journal of Medicinal Chemistry*, **12**, 638–42.

Cruickshank, J. M. and B. N. C. Prichard (1987), *Beta-blockers in Clinical Practice*, Edinburgh: Churchill Livingstone.

Cullum, V. A., J. B. Farmer, D. Jack and G. P. Levy (1969), 'Salbutamol: a New, Selective β-Adrenoceptive Receptor Stimulant', *British Journal of Pharmacology*, **35**, 141–51.

Cutler, G. B., A. R. Hoffman, R. S. Swerdloff, R. J. Santen, D. R. Meldrum and F. Comite (1985), 'Therapeutic Applications of Luteinizing-hormone-releasing Hormone and its Analogs', *Annals of Internal Medicine*, **102**, 643–57.

Dahl, R. (1991), 'β_2-Agonists in Asthma', *Lancet*, **337**, 43.

Dale, H. H. and P. P. Laidlaw (1910), 'The Physiological Action of β-Imidazolyl-Ethylamine', *Journal of Physiology*, **41**, 318–44.

Daneshmend, T. K., P. J. Prichard, N. K. Bhaskar, P. J. Millns and C. J. Hawkey (1989), 'Use of Microbleeding and Ultrathin Endoscope to Assess Gastric Mucosal Protection by Famotidine,' *Gastroenterology*, **97**, 944–9.

Davenport-Hines, R. P. T. and J. Slinn (1992), *Glaxo: A History to 1962*,

Cambridge: Cambridge University Press.

David, P. (1985), 'Clio and the Economics of QWERTY', *American Economic Review*, **75**, 332–7.

Davis, P. (1997), *Managing Medicines: Public Policy and Therapeutic Drugs*, Buckingham: Open University Press.

Davson, H. and M. G. Eggleton (eds) (1968), *Starling and Lovatt Evans: Principles of Human Physiology*, 14th edn, London: J. & A. Churchill.

Dawber, T. R. and W. B. Kannel (1966), 'Editorial: The Framingham Study, an Epidemiological Approach to Coronary Heart Disease', *Circulation*, **34**, 553–5.

Debruyne, F. M. J., L. Denis, G. Lunglmayer, C. Mahler, D. W. W. Newling, B. Richards, M. R. G. Robinson, P. H. Smith, E. H. J. Weil and P. Whelan (1988), 'Long-term Therapy with a Depot Luteinizing Hormone-releasing Hormone Analogue (Zoladex) in Patients with Advanced Prostatic Carcinoma', *Journal of Urology*, **140**, 775–7.

della Valle, F. and A. Gambardella (1993), ' "Biological" Revolution and Strategies for Innovation in Pharmaceutical Companies', *R&D Management*, **23**, 287–302.

Dietschy, J. M. and J. D. Wilson (1970), 'Regulation of Cholesterol Metabolism', *New England Journal of Medicine*, **282**, 1128–38, 1179–83, 1241–9.

Dlugi, A. M., J. D. Miller, J. Knittle and Lupron Study Group (1990), 'Lupron Depot (Leuprolide Acetate for Depot Suspension) in the Treatment of Endometriosis: a Randomized Placebo-controlled, Double-blind Study', *Fertility and Sterility*, **54**, 419–27.

Domschke, W., G. Lux and S. Domschke (1979), 'Gastric Inhibitory Action of H_2-Antagonists Ranitidine and Cimetidine', *Lancet*, **1**, 320.

Donowitz, G. R. and G. L. Mandell (1988), 'Beta-lactam Antibiotics' (second of two parts), *New England Journal of Medicine*, **318**, 490–500.

Dornhorst, A. C. and B. F. Robinson (1962), 'Clinical Pharmacology of a Beta-adrenergic-blocking Agent (Nethalide)', *Lancet*, **2**, 314–17.

Dosi, G. (1982), 'Technological Paradigms and Technological Trajectories', *Research Policy*, **11**, 147–62.

Dosi, G. (1988), 'The Nature of the Innovation Process,' in G. Dosi, C. Freeman, R. Nelson, G. Silverberg and L. Soete (eds), *Technical Change and Economic Theory*, London: Frances Pinter, pp. 221–38.

Duncan, W. A. M. (1973), 'Welcome from SmithKline & French', in C. J. Wood and M. A. Simkins (eds), *International Symposium on Histamine H_2-receptor Antagnoists*, London: SmithKline & French Laboratories.

Duncan, W. A. M. and M. E. Parsons (1980), 'Reminiscences of the Development of Cimetidine', *Gastroenterology*, **78**, 620–5.

Dunlop, D. and R. Shanks (1968), 'Selective Blockade of Adrenoceptive

Beta Receptors in the Heart', *British Journal of Pharmacology and Chemotherapy*, **32**, 201–18.

Dutta, A. S. and M. B. Giles (1976), 'Polypeptides. Part XIV: a Comparative Study of the Stability towards Enzymes of Model Tripeptides Containing α-Aza-Amino-Acids, L-Amino-Acids and D-Amino Acids', *Journal of the Chemical Society, Perkin Transactions*, **I**, 244–8.

Dutta, A. S. and J. S. Morley (1975), 'Polypeptides. Part XIII: Preparation of α-Aza-Amino-Acid (Carbazic Acid) Derivatives and Intermediates for the Preparation of α-Aza-Peptides', *Journal of the Chemical Society, Perkin Transactions*, **I**, 1712–20.

Dutta, A. S. and J. S. Morley (1976), 'α-Aza-Analogues of Biologically-active Peptides', in *Peptides 1976: Proceedings of the Fourteenth European Peptide Symposium*, Brussels: Editions de l'Université de Bruxelles.

Dutta, A. S., B. J. A. Furr, M. B. Giles and B. Valcaccia (1978a), 'Synthesis and Biological Activity of Highly Active α-Aza Analogues of Luliberin', *Journal of Medicinal Chemistry*, **21**, 1018–23.

Dutta, A. S., B. J. A. Furr, M. B. Giles and J. S. Morley (1978b), 'Synthesis and Biological Activity of α-Azapeptide: α-Aza-Analogues of Luteinizing Hormone Releasing Hormone', *Clinical Endocrinology*, **5** (Supplement), 291S–298S.

Dutta, A. S., B. J. A. Furr, M. B. Giles, B. Valcaccia and A. L. Walpole (1978c), 'Potent Agonist and Antagonist Analogues of Luliberin Containing an Azaglycine Residue in Position 10', *Biochemical and Biophysical Research Communication*, **81**, 382–90.

Dutta, A. S., B. J. A. Furr and M. B. Giles (1979a), 'Polypeptides. Part 15: Synthesis and Biological Activity of α-Aza-Analogues of Luliberin Modified in Position 6 and 10', *Journal of the Chemical Society, Perkin Transactions*, **I**, 379–88.

Dutta, A. S., B. J. A. Furr and M. B. Giles (1979b), 'Polypeptides. Part 16: Synthesis and Biological Activity of α-Aza-Analogues of Luliberin with High Antagonist Activity', *Journal of the Chemical Society, Perkin Transactions*, **I**, 389–94.

Dutta, A. S., B. J. A. Furr and F. G. Hutchinson (1993), 'The Discovery and Development of Goserelin (Zoladex®)', *Pharmaceutical Medicine*, **7**, 9–28.

Ebashi, S. (1988), 'Historical Overview: Calcium Ion and Contractile Proteins', *Annals of New York Academy of Sciences*, **522**, 51–9.

Edkins, J. S. (1906), 'The Chemical Mechanism of Gastric Secretion', *Journal of Physiology*, **34**, 133–44.

Elks, J. and G. H. Phillipps (1985), 'Discovery of a Family of Potent Topical

Anti-inflammatory Agents', in S. M. Roberts and B. J. Price (eds), *Medicinal Chemistry: The Role of Organic Chemistry in Drug Research*, London: Academic Press, pp. 167–88.

Elston, M. A. (1997), 'Introduction: The Sociology of Medical Sciences and Technology,' in M. A. Elston (ed.), *The Sociology of Medical Sciences and Technology*, Oxford: Basil Blackwell, pp. 1–27.

Emerson Thomas, H., W. B. Kannel, T. R. Dawber and P. M. McNamara (1966), 'Cholesterol–Phospholipid Ratio in the Prediction of Coronary Heart Disease: The Framingham Study', *New England Journal of Medicine*, **274**, 701–5.

Emtage, L. A., C. Trethowan, C. Hilton, D. G. Arkell, D. M. A. Wallace, M. A. Hughes, D. J. Farrar, C. Young, M. Jones, A. M. Hay, A. R. E. Blacklock, A. D. Rowse, and G. R. P. Blackledge (1987), 'A Randomised Trial Comparing Zoladex 3.6 mg Depot with Stilboestrol 3 mg/day in Advanced Prostate Cancer: Patient Characteristics, Response and Treatment Failures', *European Journal of Cancer and Clinical Oncology*, **23**, 1239.

Endo, A. (1975), 'Shin Seiri Kassei Bussitsu no Seizo-hou' (Methods for the production of a new bioactive substance), *Japanese Patent (Tokukai)* 50-155690, Tokyo: Patent Office. (in Japanese)

Endo, A. (1979), 'Monacolin K, a New Hypocholesterolemic Agent that Specifically Inhibits 3-Hydroxy-3-Methylglutaryl Coenzyme A Reductase', *Journal of Antibiotics*, **33**, 334–6.

Endo, A. (1987), 'Inhibitors of Cholesterol Biosynthesis Are Coming Soon', *Bio Industry*, **4**, 651–8. (in Japanese)

Endo, A. (1991), 'Memoirs of the Development of HMG-CoA Reductase Inhibitors', *Igaku no Ayumi*, **157**, 720–2. (in Japanese)

Endo, A. (1992), 'The Discovery and Development of HMG-CoA Reductase Inhibitors', *Journal of Lipid Research*, **33**, 1569–82.

Endo, A. (1994), 'Past, Present and Future of HMG-CoA Reductase Inhibitors', *Lipid*, **5**, 122–9. (in Japanese)

Endo, A. (1999), 'A Scientist's Dream, Microbes, and Discovery of A Miracle Drug "Statin" ', mimeo.

Endo, A. (2001), 'Details of the Discovery of HMG-CoA Reductase Inhibitors "Statins" ', *Doumyaku Kouka*, **28**, 111–14. (in Japanese)

Endo, A., M. Kuroda and K. Tanzawa (1976a), 'Competitive Inhibition of 3-Hydroxy-3-Methylglutaryl Coenzyme A Reductase by ML-236A and ML-236B Fungal Metabolites, Having Hypocholesterolemic Activity', *FEBS Letters*, **72**, 323–6.

Endo, A., M. Kuroda and Y. Tsujita (1976b), 'ML-236A, ML-236B and ML-236C, New Inhibitors of Cholesterogenesis Produced by *Penicillium Citrinum*', *Journal of Antibiotics*, **29**, 1346–8.

Endo, A., Y. Tsujita, M. Kuroda and K. Tanzawa (1977), 'Inhibition of Cholesterol Synthesis *in Vitro* and *in Vivo* by ML-236A and ML-236B, Competitive Inhibitors of 3-Hydroxy-3-Methylglutaryl-Coenzyme A Reductase', *European Journal of Biochemistry*, 77, 31–6.

Epstein, S. (1996), *Impure Science: AIDS, Activism and the Politics of Knowledge*, Berkeley and Los Angeles: University of California Press.

Ernst, P. (1998), 'Long Acting β_2 Agonists and the Risk of Life Threatening Asthma', *Thorax*, 53, 1–2.

Ernst, P. and S. Suissa (1995), 'End of New Zealand Asthma Epidemic', *Lancet*, 345, 384.

Faulkner, W. and J. Senker (1995), *Knowledge Frontiers: Public Sector Research and Industrial Innovation in Biotechnology, Engineering Ceramics, and Parallel Computing*, Oxford: Clarendon Press.

Faure, N., F. Labrie, A. Lemay, A. Bélanger, Y. Gourdeau, B. Laroche and G. Robert (1982), 'Inhibition of Serum Androgen Levels by Chronic Intranasal and Subcutaneous Administration of a Potent Luteinizing Hormone-releasing Hormone (LH-RH) Agonist in Adult Men', *Fertility and Sterility*, 37, 416–24.

Filicori, M., D. A. Hall, J. S. Loughlin, J. Rivier, W. Vale and W. F. Crowley (1983), 'A Conservative Approach to the Management of Uterine Leiomyoma: Pituitary Desensitization by a Luteinizing Hormone-releasing Hormone Analogue', *American Journal of Obstetrics and Gynecology*, 147, 726–7.

Fitzgerald, J. D. (1977), 'Why Another Beta-Antagonist?', *Postgraduate Medical Journal*, 53 (Supplement 3), 52–7.

Fitzgerald, J. D. (1982), 'The Effect of Different Classes of Beta-Antagonists on Clinical and Experimental Hypertension', *Clinical and Experimental Hypertension: Theory and Practice*, A4 (1–2), 101–23.

Fitzgerald, J. D. (1992), 'Technology Transfer Issues in Licensing Pharmaceutical Products', *R&D Management*, 22, 199–208.

Fleck, J. (1996), 'Models of Innovation', in *XIII Congreso de Estudios Vascos: Ciencia, Tecnologia y Cambio Social en Euskal Herria = Zientzia, teknologia eta gizarte aldaketa Euskal Herrian* (13. 1995. Zamudio), Donostia: Eusko Ikaskuntza, pp. 13–16.

Fleckenstein, A. (1977), 'Specific Pharmacology of Calcium in Myocardium, Cardiac Pacemakers, and Vascular Smooth Muscle', *Annual Review of Pharmacology and Toxicology*, 17, 149–66.

Fleckenstein, A. (1988), 'Historical Overview: the Calcium Channel of the Heart', *Annals of the New York Academy of Sciences*, 522, 1–15.

Fleckenstein, A., H. Tritthart, H. J. Döring and K. Y. Byon (1972), 'BAY a 1040 – ein hochaktiver Ca^{++}-antagonistischer Inhibitor der elektromechanischen Koppelungsprozesse im Warmblüter-Myokard' (BAY a

1040: A Highly Active Ca^{++} Antagonistic Inhibitor of the Electro-mechanical Coupling Processes in the Warm-blooded Myocardium), *Arzneimittel Forschung (Drug Research)*, **22**, 22–33. (in German)

Folkow. B., K. Hæger and G. Kahlson (1948), 'Observations on Reactive Hyperaemia as Related to Histamine, on Drugs Antagonizing Vaso-dilation Induced by Histamine and on Vasodilator Properties of Adreno-sinetriphosphate', *Acta Physiologica Scandinavica*, **15**, 264–78.

Forray, G., J. A. Bard, J. H. Wetzel, G. Chiu, E. Shapiro, R. Tang, H. Lepor, P. R. Hartig, R. L. Weinshank, T.A. Branchek and C. Gluchowski (1994), 'The α_1-Adrenergic Receptor that Mediates Smooth Muscle Contraction in Human Prostate Has the Pharmacological Properties of the Cloned Human α_{1c} Subtype', *Molecular Pharmacology*, **45**, 703–8.

Fransman, M. (1990), *The Market and Beyond: Information Technology in Japan*, Cambridge: Cambridge University Press.

Fransman, M. (1999), *Visions of Innovation: The Firm and Japan*, Oxford: Oxford University Press.

Freeman, C. and L. Soete (1997), *The Economics of Industrial Innovation*, 3rd edn, London: Frances Pinter.

Friedman, A. J., D. I. Hoffman, F. Comite, R. W. Browneller and J. D. Miller (1991), 'Treatment of Leiomyomata Uteri with Leuprolide Acetate Depot: a Double-blind Placebo-controlled, Multicenter Study', *Obstetrics and Gynecology*, **77**, 720–5.

Friedman, G. (1987), 'Famotidine', *American Journal of Gastroenterology*, **82**, 504–6.

Fujimura, J. H. (1996), *Crafting Science: A Sociohistory of the Quest for the Genetics of Cancer*, Cambridge, MA: Harvard University Press.

Fujino, M. (1992), *Leuplin® Kenkyu Kaihatsu Monogatari* (The Research and Development of Leuplin®) Osaka: Takeda Chemical Industries. (in Japanese)

Fujino, M., S. Kobayashi, M. Obayashi, T. Fukuda, S. Shinagawa, I. Yamazaki, R. Nakayama, W. F. White and R. H. Rippel (1972a), 'Synthesis and Biological Activities of Analogs of Luteinizing Hormone-releasing Hormone (LH-RH)', *Biochemical and Biophysical Research Communication*, **49**, 698–705.

Fujino, M., S. Kobayashi, M. Obayashi, S. Shinagawa, T. Fukuda, C. Kitada, R. Nakayama, I. Yamazaki, W. F. White and R. H. Rippel (1972b), 'Structure–Activity Relationships in the C-Terminal Part of Luteinizing Hormone-releasing Hormone (LH-RH)', *Biochemical and Biophysical Research Communication*, **49**, 863–9.

Fujino, M., S. Shinagawa, I. Yamazaki, S. Kobayashi, M. Obayashi, T. Fukuda, R. Nakayama, W. F. White and R. H. Rippel (1973a), '[Des-Gly-NH_2^{10}, Pro-ethylamide⁹]-LH-RH: a Highly Potent Analog of

Luteinizing Hormone-releasing Hormone', *Archives of Biochemistry and Biophysics*, **154**, 488–9.

Fujino, M., S. Shinagawa, M. Obayashi, S. Kobayashi, T. Fukuda, I. Yamazaki, R. Nakayama, W. F. White and R. H. Rippel (1973b), 'Further Studies on Structure–Activity Relationships in the C-Terminal Part of Luteinizing Hormone-releasing Hormone', *Journal of Medicinal Chemistry*, **16**, 1144–7.

Fujino, M., I. Yamazaki, S. Kobayashi, T. Fukuda, S. Shinagawa, R. Nakayama, W. F. White and R. H. Rippel (1974a), 'Some Analogs of Luteinizing Hormone-releasing Hormone (LH-RH) Having Intense Ovulation-inducing Activity', *Biochemical and Biophysical Research Communication*, **57**, 1248–56.

Fujino, M., T. Fukuda, S. Shinagawa, S. Kobayashi, I. Yamazaki, R. Nakayama, J. H. Seely, W. F. White and R. H. Rippel (1974b), 'Synthetic Analogs of Luteinizing Hormone-releasing Hormone (LH-RH) Substituted in Position 6 and 10', *Biochemical and Biophysical Research Communication*, **60**, 406–13.

Fukai, S. (1988), *Konnichi no Shinyaku* (New Drugs Today), 5th edn, Tokyo: Yakugyo Jihou Sya. (in Japanese)

Fukai, S. (1995), *Konnichi no Shinyaku* (New Drugs Today), 6th edn, Tokyo: Yakugyo Jihou Sya. (in Japanese)

Fuller, R., W. Castle, J. Hall and J. Palmer (1993), 'Authors' Reply', *British Medical Journal*, **306**, 1611.

Furr, B. (1991), 'History of Zoladex', a document given by Dr Barry Furr.

Furr, B. (1998), 'Exploiting the Unexpected', *Biologist*, **45**, 117–21.

Furr, B. J. A. and R. I. Nicholson (1982), 'Use of Analogues of Luteinizing Hormone-releasing Hormone for the Treatment of Cancer', *Journal of Reproduction and Fertility*, **64**, 529–39.

Furr, B. J. A. and J. R. Woodburn (1988), 'Luteinizing Hormone-releasing Hormone and its Analogs: a Review of Biological Properties and Clinical Uses', *Journal of Endocrinological Investigation*, **11**, 535–57.

Galambos, L. and J. E. Sewell (1995), *Networks of Innovation: Vaccine Development at Merck, Sharp & Dohme, and Mulford, 1895–1995*, Cambridge and New York: Cambridge University Press.

Gambardella, A. (1995), *Science and Innovation: The US Pharmaceutical Industry During the 1980s*, Cambridge and New York: Cambridge University Press.

Ganellin, C. R. (1981), 'Medicinal Chemistry and Dynamic Structure–Activity Analysis in the Discovery of Drugs Acting at Histamine H_2 Receptors', *Journal of Medicinal Chemistry*, **24**, 914–20.

Ganellin, C. R. (1982), 'Cimetidine,' in J. S. Bindra and D. Lednicer (eds), *Chronicles of Drug Discovery*, vol. 1, New York: John Wiley, pp. 1–38.

Ganellin, C. R. (1985), 'Discovery of Cimetidine', in S. M. Roberts and B. J. Price (eds), *Medicinal Chemistry: The Role of Organic Chemistry in Drug Research*, London: Academic Press, pp. 93–118.

Garnett, J., J. Kolbe, G. Richards, T. Whitlock and H. Rea (1995), 'Major Reduction in Asthma Morbidity and Continued Reduction in Asthma Mortality in New Zealand: What Lessons Have Been Learned?', *Thorax*, **50**, 303–11.

Gavin, G., E. W. McHenry and M. J. Wilson (1933), 'Histamine in Canine Gastric Tissues', *Journal of Physiology*, **79**, 234–8.

Geiger, R., W. König, H. Wissmann, K. Geisen and F. Enzmann (1971), 'Synthesis and Characterisation of a Decapeptide Having LH-RH/FSH-RH Activity', *Biochemical and Biophysical Research Communication*, **45**, 767–73.

Geiger, R., H. Wissmann, W. König, J. Sandow, A. V. Schally, T. W. Redding, L. Debeljuk and A. Arimura (1972), 'Synthesis and Biological Evaluation of 4-Alanine-Luteinizing Hormone-releasing Hormone ([Ala^4] LH-RH)', *Biochemical and Biophysical Research Communication*, **49**, 1467–73.

Gelman J., R. L. Feldman, K. F. Cremer, E. Scott and C. J. Pepine (1983), 'Nicardipine, a New Calcium Blocker, in Patients with Rest Angina and Coronary Spasm', *Circulation*, **68** (4), III-401.

Gillam, P. M. S. and B. N. C. Prichard (1965), 'Use of Propranolol in Angina Pectoris', *British Medical Journal*, **2**, 337–9.

Gillam, P. M. S. and B. N. C. Prichard (1976), 'Beta-blockade and Hypertension', *Postgraduate Medical Journal*, **52** (Supplement 4), 70–5.

Giraud, B. (1990), 'Interim Report of a Large French Multicentre Study of Efficacy and Safety of 3.75 mg Leuprorelin Depot in Metastatic Prostatic Cancer', *Journal of International Medical Research*, **18** (supplement 1), 84–9.

Gittes, R. F. (1991), 'Carcinoma and the Prostate', *New England Journal of Medicine*, **324**, 236–45.

Glaxo Holdings plc (1987), 'Zantac: the Catalyst of Change', *Glaxo World*, no. 4, pp. 9–18.

Glaxo Holdings plc (1994), 'End of an Era as Sir Paul Steps Down', *Glaxo World*, no. 25, pp. 6–8.

Glossman, M. I., C. Robertson and C. E. Rosiere (1952), 'The Effect of Some Compounds Related to Histamine on Gastric Acid Secretion', *Journal of Pharmacology and Experimental Therapeutics*, **104**, 277–83.

Gough, K. R., M. G. Korman, K. D. Bardhan, F. I. Lee, J. P. Crowe, P. I. Reed and R. N. Smith (1984), 'Ranitidine and Cimetidine in Prevention of Duodenal Ulcer Relapse: a Double-blind, Randomised, Multicentre, Comparative Trial', *Lancet*, **2**, 659–62.

Grabowski, H. and J. Vernon (1990), 'A New Look at the Returns and Risks to Pharmaceutical R&D', *Management Science*, **36**, 804–21.

Grabowski, H. G. and J. M. Vernon (1994), 'Returns to R&D on New Drug Introductions in the 1980s', *Journal of Health Economics*, **13**, 383–406.

Grabowski, H. G., J. M. Vernon and L. G. Thomas (1978), 'Estimating the Effects of Regulation on Innovation: an International Comparative Analysis of the Pharmaceutical Industry', *Journal of Law and Economics*, **21**, 133–63.

Grainger, J., K. Woodman, N. Pearce, J. Crane, C. Burgess, A. Keane and R. Beasley (1991), 'Prescribed Fenoterol and Death from Asthma in New Zealand, 1981–1987: a Further Case-control Study', *Thorax*, **46**, 105–11.

Grant, I. W. B. (1983), 'For Debate: Asthma in New Zealand', *British Medical Journal*, **286**, 374–7.

Grant, J. B. F., S. R. Ahmed, S. M. Shalet, C. B. Costello, A. Howell and N. J. Blacklock (1986), 'Testosterone and Gonadotrophin Profiles in Patients on Daily or Monthly LHRH Analogue ICI 118630 (Zoladex) Compared with Orchiectomy', *British Journal of Urology*, **58**, 539–44.

Graves, S. B. and N. S. Langowitz (1993), 'Innovative Productivity and Returns to Scale in the Pharmaceutical Industry', *Strategic Management Journal*, **14**, 593–605.

Green, J. D. and G. W. Harris (1947), 'The Neurovascular Link between the Neurohypophysis and Adrenohypophysis', *Journal of Endocrinology*, **5**, 136–49.

Greenacre, J. K., P. Schofield and M. E. Collony (1978), 'Desensitization of the β-Adrenoceptor of Lymphocytes from Normal Subjects and Asthmatic Patients *in Vitro*', *British Journal of Clinical Pharmacology*, **5**, 199–206.

Greenberg, M. J. and A. Pines (1967), 'Pressurized Aerosols in Asthma', *British Medical Journal*, **1**, 563.

Greening, A. P., P. W. Ind, M. Northfield and G. Shaw, on behalf of Allen & Hanburys Limited UK Study Group (1994), 'Added Salmeterol versus Higher-dose Corticosteroid in Asthma Patients with Symptoms on Existing Inhaled Corticosteroid', *Lancet*, **344**, 219–24.

Gregory, H. (1971), 'The Chemistry of the Releasing Factors', in D. T. Baird and J. A. Strong (eds), *Control of Gonadal Steroid Secretion*, Edinburgh: Edinburgh University Press.

Gregory, R. A. and H. J. Tracy (1964), 'The Constitution and Properties of Two Gastrins Extracted from Hog Antral Mucosa', *Gut*, **5**, 103–17.

Gregory, R. A., P. M. Hardy, D. S. Jones, G. W. Kenner and R. C. Sheppard (1964), 'Structure of Gastrin', *Nature*, **204**, 931–3.

Griffith, R. S. and H. R. Black (1964), 'Cephalothin – a New Antibiotic',

Journal of the American Medical Association, **189**, 823–8.

Grove, A. and B. J. Lipworth (1995), 'Bronchodilator Subsensitivity to Salbutamol after Twice Daily Salmeterol in Asthmatic Patients', *Lancet*, **344**, 219–24.

Grundy, S. M. (1988), ' HMG-CoA Reductase Inhibitors for Treatment of Hypercholesterolemia', *New England Journal of Medicine*, **319**, 24–33.

Guillemin, R. (1964), 'Hypothalamic Factors Releasing Pituitary Hormones', *Recent Progress in Hormone Research*, **20**, 89–121.

Guillemin, R. (1978), 'Pioneering in Neuroendocrinology 1952–1969', in J. Meites, B. T. Donovan and S. M. McCann (eds), *Pioneers in Neuroendocrinology II*, New York: Plenum Press, pp. 221–39.

Hamada, A., T. Shida, J. Kabe and T. Miyamoto (1986), 'Kikanshi Zensoku ni Taisuru Procaterol Kyuunyuuyaku no Rinshou Hyouka' (Clinical Evaluation of Procaterol Aerosol in Bronchial Asthma), *Igaku no Ayumi*, **137**, 939–57. (in Japanese)

Hamlin, C. (1992), 'Reflexivity in Technology Studies: Toward a Technology of Technology (and Science)?', *Social Studies of Science*, **22**, 511–44.

Happ, J., P. Scholz, T. Weber, U. Cordes, P. Schramm, M. Neubauer and J. Beyer (1978), 'Gonadotropin Secretion in Eugonadotropic Human Males and Postmenopausal Females under Long-term Application of a Potent Analog of Gonadotropin-releasing Hormone', *Fertility and Sterility*, **30**, 674–8.

Hara, T. (1997), 'Industrial Technological Trajectories and Corporate Technology Traditions: the Development of Antibacterial Drugs in Japan', *Annals of the School of Business Administration, Kobe University*, **41**, 1–18.

Harden, T. K. (1983), 'Agonist-induced Desensitization of the β-Adrenergic Receptor-linked Adenylate Cyclase', *Pharmacological Reviews*, **35**, 5–32.

Harper, A. A. (1946), 'The Effect of Extracts of Gastric and Intestinal Mucosa on the Secretion of HCl by the Cat's Stomach', *Journal of Physiology*, **105**, 31P.

Harris, G. W. (1955), *Neural Control of the Pituitary Gland*, London: Edward Arnold.

Harris, G. W. (1972), 'Humours and Hormones', *Journal of Endocrinology*, **53**, ii–xxii.

Harris, G. W. and F. Naftolin (1970), 'The Hypothalamus and Control of Ovulation', *British Medical Bulletin*, **26**, 3–9.

Harris, G. W., M. Reed and C. P. Fawcett (1966), 'Hypothalamic Releasing Factors and the Control of Anterior Pituitary Function', *British Medical Bulletin*, **22**, 266–72.

Hartley, D., D. Jack, L. H. C. Lunts and A. C. Ritchie (1968), 'New Class of

Selective Stimulants of β-Adrenergic Receptors', *Nature*, **219**, 861–2.

Harvey, H. A., A. Lipton, R. J. Santen, M. S. Hershey, G. C. Escher, M. A. Hardy, L. M. Glode, A. Segaloff, R. L. Landau, H. Schneir and D. T. Max (1981), 'Phase II Study of a Gonadotropin-releasing Hormone Analogue (Leuprolide) in Postmenopausal Advanced Breast Cancer Patients', *Proceedings of the American Association for Cancer Research*, **22**, 444.

Harvey, J. E. and A. E. Tattersfield (1982), 'Airway Response to Salbutamol: Effect of Regular Salbutamol Inhalations in Normal, Atopic, and Asthmatic Subject', *Thorax*, **37**, 280–7.

Havel, R. J., D. B. Hunninghake, D. R. Illingworth, R. S. Lees, E. A. Stein, J. A. Tobert, S. R. Bacon, J. A. Bolognese, P. H. Frost, G. E. Lamkin, A. M. Lees, A. S. Leon, K. Gardner, G. Johnson, M. J. Mellies, P. A. Rhymer and P. Tun (1987), 'Lovastatin (Mevinolin) in the Treatment of Heterozygous Familial Hypercholesterolemia', *Annals of Internal Medicine*, **107**, 609–15.

Hawkins, E. S. and M. R. Reich (1992), 'Japanese-originated Pharmaceutical Products in the United States from 1960 to 1989: an Assessment of Innovation', *Clinical Pharmacology and Therapeutics*, **51**, 1–11.

Heel, R. C., R. N. Brogden, T. M. Speight and G. S. Avery (1979), 'Atenolol: a Review of its Pharmacological Properties and Therapeutic Efficacy in Angina Pectoris and Hypertension', *Drugs*, **17**, 425–60.

Heino, M. (1994), 'Regularly Inhaled β-Agonists with Steroids Are Not Harmful in Stable Asthma', *Journal of Allergy and Clinical Immunology*, **93**, 80–4.

Hench, P. S., E. C. Kendall, C. H. Slocumb and H. F. Polley (1949), 'The Effect of a Hormone of the Adrenal Cortex (17-Hydroxy-11-Dehydrocorticosterone: Compound E) and of Pituitary Adreno-corticotropic Hormone on Rheumatoid Arthritis', *Proceedings of the Staff Meetings of the Mayo Clinic*, **24**, 181–97.

Henderson, R. and I. Cockburn (1995), 'Scale, Scope and Spillovers: the Determinants of Research Productivity in Ethical Drug Discovery', *MIT Sloan School of Management Working Paper*, 3738-94.

Henderson, R. M. and K. B. Clark (1990), 'Architectural Innovation: the Reconfiguration of Existing Product Technologies and the Failure of Established Firms', *Administrative Science Quarterly*, **35**, 9–30.

Hewitt, W. I. (1973), 'The Cephalosporins – 1973', *Journal of Infectious Diseases*, **128** (Supplement), S312–19.

Hill, R. C. and P. Turner (1969), 'Preliminary Investigations of a New Beta-Adrenoceptive Receptor Blocking Drug, LB46, in Man,' *British Journal of Pharmacology*, **36**, 368–72.

Himori, N. and N. Taira (1977), 'Assessment of the Selectivity of OPC-

2009, a New β_2-Adrenoceptor Stimulant, by the Use of the Blood-perfused Trachea *in Situ* and of the Isolated Blood-perfused Papillary Muscle of the Dog', *British Journal of Pharmacology*, **61**, 9–17.

Hiramatsu, K. (1999), *Kousei-bussitsu ga Kikanai* (Lost Antibiotics), Tokyo: Syueisya. (in Japanese)

Hodgkin, D. C. and E. N. Maslen (1961), 'The X-ray Analysis of the Structure of Cephalosporin C', *Biochemical Journal*, **79**, 393–402.

Hodgson, G. M. (1999), *Evolution and Institutions: On Evolutionary Economics and the Evolution of Economics*, Cheltenham, UK and Northampton MA: Edward Elgar.

Hoeg, J. M., M. B. Maher, L. A. Zech, K. R. Bailey, R. E. Gregg, K. J. Lackner, S. S. Fojo, M. A. Anchors, M. Bojanovski, D. L. Sprecher and H. B. Brewer (1986), 'Effectiveness of Mevinolin on Plasma Lipoprotein Concentrations in Type II Hypercholesterolemia', *American Journal of Cardiology*, **57**, 933–9.

Hoffbrand, B. I. (ed.) (1977), 'Atenolol', *Postgraduate Medical Journal*, **53**, Supplement 3.

Hoffman, W. F., A. W. Alberts, P. S. Anderson, J. S. Chen, R. L. Smith and A. K. Willard (1986), '3-Hydroxy-3-Methylglutaryl-coenzyme A Reductase Inhibitors. 4: Side Chain Ester Derivatives of Mevinolin', *Journal of Medicinal Chemistry*, **29**, 849–52.

Högger, P. and P. Rohdewald (1994), 'Binding Kinetics of Fluticasone Propionate to the Human Glucocorticoid Receptor', *Steroids*, **59**, 597–602.

Holgate, S. T., C. J. Baldwin and A. E. Tattersfield (1977), 'β-adrenergic Agonist Resistance in Normal Human Airways', *Lancet*, **2**, 375–7.

Holliday, S., D. Faulds and E. M. Sorkin (1994), 'Inhaled Fluticasone Propionate: a Review of its Pharmacodynamic and Pharmacokinetic Properties, and Therapeutic Use in Asthma', *Drugs*, **47**, 318–31.

Honda, K., A. Miyata-Osawa and T. Takenaka (1985), 'α_1-Adrenoceptor Subtype Mediating Contraction of the Smooth Muscle in the Lower Urinary Tract and Prostate of Rabbits', *Naunyn-Schmiedeberg's Archives of Pharmacology*, **330**, 16–21.

Hoogerbrugge, N., M. J. T. M. Mol, J. J. Van Dormaal, C. Rustemeijer, E. Muls, A. F. H. Stalenhoef and J. C. Birkenhäger (1990), 'The Efficacy and Safety of Pravastatin, Compared to and in Combination with Bile Acid Binding Resins, in Familial Hypercholesterolemia', *Journal of Internal Medicine*, **228**, 261–6.

Howe, R. (1969), 'β-Adrenergic Blocking Agents. VI: Pronethalol and Propranolol Analogs with Alkyl Substituents in the Alkanol Side Chain', *Journal of Medicinal Chemistry*, **12**, 642–6.

Howe, R. and B. S. Rao (1968), 'β-Adrenergic Blocking Agents. III: The

Optical Isomers of Pronethalol, Propranolol, and Several Related Compounds', *Journal of Medicinal Chemistry*, **11**, 1118–21.

Howe, R. and R. G. Shanks (1966), 'Optical Isomers of Propranolol', *Nature*, **210**, 1336–8.

Howe, R., A. F. Crowther, J. S. Stephenson, B. S. Rao and L. H. Smith (1968), 'β-Adrenergic Blocking Agents. I: Pronethalol and Related N-Alkyl and N-Aralkyl Derivatives of 2-Amino-1-(2-naphthyl)ethanol', *Journal of Medicinal Chemistry*, **11**, 1000–8.

Howe, R., B. J. McLoughlin, B. S. Rao, L. H. Smith and M. S. Chodnekar (1969), 'β-Adrenergic Blocking Agents. IV: Variation of the 2-Naphthyl Group of Pronethalol [2-Isopropylamino-1-(2-naphthyl)ethanol],' *Journal of Medicinal Chemistry*, **12**, 452–7.

Howells, J. and I. Neary (1995), *Intervention and Technological Innovation: Government and the Pharmaceutical Industry in the UK and Japan*, London: Macmillan.

Hsueh, A. J. W., M. L. Dufau and K. J. Catt (1977), 'Gonadotropin-induced Regulation of Luteinizing Hormone Receptors and Desensitization of Testicular 3':5'-cyclic AMP and Testosterone Responses', *Proceeding of the National Academy of Sciences USA*, **74**, 592–5.

Huggins, C., R. E. Stevens and C. V. Hodges (1941), 'Studies on Prostatic Cancer. II: The Effects of Castration on Advanced Carcinoma of the Prostate Gland', *Archives of Surgery*, **43**, 209–23.

Hughes, T. (1983), *Networks of Power*, Baltimore, MD, and London: Johns Hopkins University Press.

Hughes, T. P. (1987), 'The Evolution of Large Technological System', in W. E. Bijker, T. P. Hughes and T. Pinch (eds), *The Social Construction of Technological Systems*, Cambridge, MA: MIT Press, pp. 51–82.

Hughes, T. (1988), 'The Seamless Web: Technology, Science, et Cetera, et Cetera', in B. Elliott (ed.), *Technology and Social Process*, Edinburgh: Edinburgh University Press, pp. 9–19.

Hunninghake, D. B., R. H. Knopp, G. Schonfeld, A. C. Goldberg, W. V. Brown, E. J. Schaefer, S. Margolis, A. S. Dobs, M. J. Mellies, W. Insull and E. A. Stein (1990), 'Efficacy and Safety of Pravastatin in Patients with Primary Hypercholesterolemia. I: A Dose-response Study', *Atherosclerosis*, **85**, 81–9.

Hutchinson, F. G. and B. J. A. Furr (1985), 'Biodegradable Polymers for the Sustained Release of Peptides', *Biochemical Society Transactions*, **13**, 520–3.

Iansiti, M. (1998), *Technology Integration*, Boston, MA: Harvard Business School Press.

Iliopoulou, A., P. Turner and S. J. Warrington (1983), 'Acute Haemodynamic Effects of a New Calcium Antagonist, Nicardipine, in Man: a Comparison with Nifedipine', *British Journal of Clinical Pharmacology*, **15**, 59–65.

Inman, W. H. W. (1993), 'Manufacturers Underestimate Mortality from Asthma', *British Medical Journal*, **306**, 1610.

Inman, W. H. W. and A. M. Adelstein (1969), 'Rise and Fall of Asthma Mortality in England and Wales in Relation to Use of Pressurised Aerosols', *Lancet*, **2**, 279–85.

Ivy, A. C. (1930), 'The Rôle of Hormones in Digestion', *Physiological Review*, **10**, 282–335.

Iwanami, M., T. Shibamura, M. Fujimoto, R. Kawai, K. Tamazawa, T. Takenaka, K. Takahashi and Masuo Murakami (1979), 'Synthesis of New Water-soluble Dihydropyridine Vasodilators', *Chemical and Pharmaceutical Bulletin*, **27**, 1426–40.

Jack, D. (1989), 'The Challenge of Drug Discovery', *Drug Design and Delivery*, **4**, 167–86.

Jack, D. (1990), 'Safety by Design', *Drug Safety*, **5** (Supplement 1), 4–23.

Jack, D. (1991), 'A Way of Looking at Agonism and Antagonism: Lessons from Salbutamol, Salmeterol and Other β-Adrenoceptor Agonists', *British Journal of Clinical Pharmacology*, **31**, 501–14.

Jack, D. (1996), 'The Use of Inhaled β_2-Adrenergic Bronchodilators and Anti-inflammatory Steroids in Asthma', *Journal of Pharmaceutical Medicine*, **6**, 5–16.

Jack, D. (1998), 'Selective Adrenergic and Glucocorticoid Treatments for Asthma', in P. Leff (ed.), *Receptor-based Drug Design*, New York: Marcel Dekker, pp. 135–72.

Jackson, R. T., R. Beaglehole, H. H. Rea and D. C. Surtherland (1982), 'Mortality from Asthma: a New Epidemic in New Zealand', *British Medical Journal*, **285**, 771–4.

Jacobi, G. H. and U. K. Wenderoth (1982), 'Gonadotropin-releasing Hormone Analogues for Prostatic Cancer: Untoward Side Effects of High-dose Regimens Acquire a Therapeutic Dimension', *European Urology*, **8**, 129–34.

Japan Pharmaceutical Manufacturers Association (1997), *Data Book 1997–98*, Tokyo: Japan Pharmaceutical Manufacturers Association.

Jenkins, M. M., C. J. Hilton, J. C. de Kock and J. B. D. Palmer (1991), 'Exacerbations of Asthma in Patients on Salmeterol', *Lancet*, **337**, 913–14.

Jenne, J. W., T. W. Chick, R. D. Strickland and F. J. Wall (1977), 'Subsensitivity of Beta Responses during Therapy with a Long-acting Beta-2 Preparation', *Journal of Allergy and Clinical Immunology*, **59**, 383–90.

Jensen, E. J. (1987), 'Research Expenditures and the Discovery of New

Drugs', *Journal of Industrial Economics*, **36**, 83–95.

Jensen, E. V., G. E. Block, S. Smith, K. Kyser and E. R. DeSombre (1971), 'Estrogen Receptors and Breast Cancer Response to Adrenalectomy', *National Cancer Institute Monograph*, **34**, 55–70.

Johnson, E. S., J. H. Seely, W. F. White and E. R. De Sombre (1976), 'Endocrine-dependent Rat Mammary Tumor Regression: Use of a Gonadotropin-releasing Hormone Analog', *Science*, **194**, 329–30.

Johnson, L. R. (1971), 'Control of Gastric Secretion: No Room for Histamine?', *Gastroenterology*, **61**, 106–18.

Jorpes, J. E., O. Jalling and V. Mutt (1952), 'A Method for the Preparation of Gastrin', *Biochemical Journal*, **52**, 327–8.

Kaplan, N. M. (1998), *Clinical Hypertension*, 7th edn, Baltimore, MD: Williams & Wilkins.

Kaufer, E. (1990), 'The Regulation of New Product Development in the Drug Industry', in G. Majone (ed.), *Deregulation or Re-regulation?: Regulatory Reform in Europe and the United States*, London: Frances Pinter.

Kawabe, K., A. Ueno, Y. Takimoto, Y. Aso, H. Kato and YM617 Clinical Study Group (1990), 'Use of an α_1-Blocker, YM617, in the Treatment of Benign Prostatic Hypertrophy', *Journal of Urology*, **144**, 908–11.

Kawai, M., K. Kawakatsu and M. Takeyama (1987), 'β Shigekiyaku' (β Stimulants), *Gendai Iryou*, **19**, 1433–43. (in Japanese)

Kennedy, C. (1993), *ICI: The Company that Changed Our Lives*, 2nd edn, London: Paul Chapman.

Kerle, D., G. Williams, H. Ware and S. R. Bloom (1984), 'Failure of Long Term Luteinising Hormone Releasing Hormone Treatment for Prostatic Cancer to Suppress Serum Luteinising Hormone and Testosterone', *British Medical Journal*, **289**, 468–9.

Kirby, R. S. and J. L. Pool (1997), 'Alpha Adrenoceptor Blockade in the Treatment of Benign Prostatic Hyperplasia: Past, Present and Future', *British Journal of Urology*, **80**, 521–32.

Klijn, J. G. M. and F. H. de Jong (1982), 'Treatment with a Luteinising-Hormone-releasing-hormone Analogue (Buserelin) in Premenopausal Patients with Metastatic Breast Cancer', *Lancet*, **1**, 1213–16.

Klign, J. G. M., H. J. De Voogt, F. H. Schröder and F. H. De Jong (1985), 'Combined Treatment with Buserelin and Cyproterone Acetate in Metastatic Prostatic Carcinoma', *Lancet*, **2**, 493.

Kline, S. J. (1985), 'Innovation Is Not a Linear Process', *Research Management*, **28**, 36–45.

Kneller, R. (1999), 'University–Industry Cooperation in Biomedical R&D in Japan and the United States: Implications for Biomedical Industries', in L. M. Branscomb, F. Kodama and R. Florida (eds), *Industrializing*

Knowledge: University–Industry Linkages in Japan and the United States, Cambridge, MA: MIT Press, pp. 410–38.

Koch, F. C., A. B. Luckhardt and R. W. Keeton (1920), 'Gastrin Studies. V: Chemical Studies on Gastrin Bodies', *American Journal of Physiology*, **52**, 508–20.

Koga, T., Y. Shimada, M. Kuroda, Y. Tsujita, K. Hasegawa and M. Yamazaki (1990), 'Tissue-selective Inhibition of Cholesterol Synthesis *in Vivo* by Pravastatin Sodium, a 3-Hydroxy-3-Methylglutaryl Coenzyme A Reductase Inhibitor', *Biochimica et Biophysica Acta*, **1045**, 115–20.

Komarov, S. A. (1938), 'Gastrin', *Proceedings of the Society for Experimental Biology and Medicine*, **38**, 514–16.

Konzett, H. (1940a), 'Neuw broncholytisch hochwirksame Körper der Adrenalinreihe' (New Highly Active Bronchodilating Substance of Adrenalin Series), *Naunyn-Schmiedeberg's Archiv für Experimentelle Pathologie und Pharmakologie*, **197**, 27–40. (in German)

Konzett, H. (1940b), 'Neues zur Athmatherapie' (News for the Asthma Therapy), *Klinische Wochenschrift*, **19**, 1303–6. (in German)

Kuhn, T. S. (1970), *The Structure of Scientific Revolutions*, 2nd edn, Chicago: University of Chicago Press.

Kunisawa, Y., K. Kawabe, T. Niijima, K. Honda and T. Takenaka (1985), 'A Pharmacological Study of Alpha Adrenergic Receptor Subtypes in Smooth Muscle of Human Urinary Bladder Base and Prostatic Urethra', *Journal of Urology*, **134**, 396–8.

Kuroda, M. (1994), 'A Drug Lowering Cholesterol: Mevalotin', in H. Iwamura, S. Ogino, K. Matsumoto and Y. Yamada (eds), *Ima Wadai no Kusuri* (Drugs in the News), Tokyo: Gakkai Syuppan Center, pp. 69–85.

Kuroda, M., Y. Tsujita, K. Tanzawa, and A. Endo (1979), 'Hypolipidemic Effects in Monkeys of ML-236B, a Competitive Inhibitor of 3-Hydroxy-3-Methylglutaryl Coenzyme A Reductase', *Lipids*, **14**, 585–9.

Kuwashima, K. (1996), 'Senryakuteki Teikei' (Strategic Alliance), in N. Takahashi (ed.), *Mirai Keisya Genri* (the Principle of Leaning on Future), Tokyo: Hakutou Syobou, pp.107–30. (in Japanese)

Kuwashima, K. (1998), 'Patterns of New Product Development in Japan's Pharmaceutical Industry: the Case of "Mevalotin" ', in E. Geisler and O. Heller (eds), *Management of Medical Technology: Theory, Practice and Cases*, Boston, MA: Kluwer Academic Publishers, pp. 459–68.

Labrie, F., A. Dupont, A. Bélanger, J. Emond and G. Monfette (1984), 'Simultaneous Administration of Pure Antiandrogens, A Combination Necessary for the Use of Luteinizing Hormone-releasing Hormone Agonists in the Treatment of Prostate Cancer', *Proceeding of the National Academy of Sciences USA*, **81**, 3861–3.

Lal, S., D. M. Harris, K. K. Bhalla, S. N. Singhal and A. G. Butler (1972),

'Comparison of Beclomethasone Dipropionate Aerosol and Prednisolone in Reversible Airways Obstruction', *British Medical Journal*, 3, 314–17.

Lambert, C. R., J. A. Hill, W. W. Nichols, R. L. Feldmon and C. J. Pepine (1985), 'Coronary and Systemic Hemodynamic Effects of Nicardipine', *American Journal of Cardiology*, 55, 652–6.

Lancet (1975), 'More and More Beta-blockers', *Lancet*, 1, 961–2.

Lancet (1990), 'β_2 Agonists in Asthma: Relief, Prevention, Morbility', *Lancet*, 336, 1411–12.

Lands, A. M., A. Arnold, J. P. McAuliff, F. P. Luduena and T. G. Brown (1967), 'Differentiation of Receptor Systems Activated by Sympathomimetic Amines', *Nature*, 214, 597–8.

Larsson, S., N. Svedmyr and G. Thiringer (1977), 'Lack of Bronchial Beta Adrenoceptor Resistance in Asthmatics During Long-term Treatment with Terbutaline', *Journal of Allergy and Clinical Immunology*, 59, 93–100.

Latour, B. (1987), *Science in Action: How to Follow Scientists and Engineers through Society*, Cambridge, MA: Harvard University Press.

Latour, B. [1992] (1999), 'One More Turn After the Social Turn', in M. Biagioli (ed.), *The Science Studies Reader*, New York: Routledge, pp. 276–89.

Latour, B. (1999a), 'For David Bloor ... and Beyond', *Studies in History and Philosophy of Science*, 30A, 113–29.

Latour, B. (1999b), 'On Recalling ANT', in J. Law and J. Hassard (eds), *Actor Network Theory and After*, Oxford: Blackwell, pp. 15–25.

Latour, B. and S. Woolgar (1986), *Laboratory Life: The Construction of Scientific Facts*, Princeton, NJ: Princeton University Press.

Law, J. (1987), 'Technology and Heterogeneous Engineering: the Case of Portuguese Expansion', in W. E. Bijker, T. P. Hughes and T. Pinch (eds), *The Social Construction of Technological Systems*, Cambridge, MA: MIT Press, pp. 111–34.

Law, J. (1999), 'After ANT: Complexity, Naming and Topology', in J. Law and J. Hassard (eds), *Actor Network Theory and After*, Oxford: Blackwell, pp. 1–14.

Le Count, D. J. (1982), 'Atenolol', in J. S. Bindra and D. Lednicer (eds), *Chronicles of Drug Discovery*, vol. 1, New York: John Wiley, pp. 113–32.

Lee, P. A., J. G. Page and Leuprolide Study Group (1989), 'Effects of Leuprolide in the Treatment of Central Precocious Puberty', *Journal of Pediatrics*, 114, 321–4.

Le Fanu, J. (1999), *The Rise and Fall of Modern Medicine*, London: Little, Brown.

Lemay, A. and G. Quesnel (1982), 'Potential New Treatment of Endometriosis: Reversible Inhibition of Pituitary–Ovarian Function by Chronic Intranasal Administration of a Luteinizing Hormone-releasing Hormone (LH-RH) Agonist', *Fertility and Sterility*, **38**, 376–9.

Leonard-Barton, D. (1995), *Wellsprings of Knowledge*, Boston, MA: Harvard Business School Press.

Lepor, H. (1990), 'Editorial Comments', *Journal of Urology*, **144**, 912.

Lepor, H., R. Tang, S. Meretyk and E. Shapiro (1993), 'Alpha₁ Adrenoceptor Subtypes in the Human Prostate', *Journal of Urology*, **149**, 640–2.

Leuprolide Study Group (1984), 'Leuprolide versus Diethylstilbestrol for Metastatic Prostate Cancer', *New England Journal of Medicine*, **311**, 1281–6.

Lewis, A. A. G. (ed.) (1971), 'Advances in Adrenergic Beta-Receptor Therapy', *Postgraduate Medical Journal*, **47**, Supplement 2.

Lewis, P. (1976), 'Essential Action of Propranolol in Hypertension', *American Journal of Medicine*, **60**, 837–52.

Lish, P. M., J. H. Weikel and K. W. Dungan (1965), 'Pharmacological and Toxicological Properties of Two New β-Adrenergic Receptor Antagonists', *Journal of Pharmacology and Experimental Therapeutics*, **149**, 161–73.

Loder, B., G. G. F. Newton and E. P. Abraham (1961), 'The Cephalosporin C Nucleus (7-Aminocephalosporanic Acid) and Some of its Derivatives', *Biochemical Journal*, **79**, 408–16.

Loev, B. and K. M. Snader (1965), 'The Hantzsch Reaction. I: Oxidative Dealkylation of Certain Dihydropyridines', *Journal of Organic Chemistry*, **30**, 1914–16.

Loev, B., S. J. Ehrreich and R. E. Tedeschi (1972), 'Dihydropyridines with Potent Hypotensive Activity Prepared by the Hantzsch Reaction', *Journal of Pharmacy and Pharmacology*, **24**, 917–18.

Löfdahl, C. G. and N. Svedmyr (1991), 'Beta-Agonists – Friends or Foes?', *European Respiratory Journal*, **4**, 1161–5.

Lomasney, J. W., S. Cotecchia, R. J. Lefkowitz and M. G. Caron (1991), 'Molecular Biology of α₁-Adrenergic Receptors: Implications for Receptor Classification and for Structure–Function Relationships', *Biochimica et Biophysica Acta*, **1095**, 127–39.

Lovastatin Study Group II (1986), 'Therapeutic Response to Lovastatin (Mevinolin) in Nonfamilial Hypercholesterolemia', *JAMA*, **256**, 2829–34.

Low, M., S. Nakayama and H. Yoshioka (1999), *Science Technology and Society in Contemporary Japan*, Cambridge: Cambridge University Press.

Lundback, B., M. Alexander, J. Day, J. Herbert, R. Holzer, R. Van Uffelen,

S. Kesten and A. L. Jones (1993), 'Evaluation of Fluticasone Propionate (500 μg day⁻¹) Administered Either as Dry Powder via a Diskhaler® Inhaler or Pressurized Inhaler and Compared with Beclomethasone Dipropionate (1000 μg day⁻¹) Administered by Pressurized Inhaler', *Respiratory Medicine*, **87**, 609–20.

Lunts, L. H. (1985), 'Salbutamol: a Selective β₂ Stimulant Bronchodilator', in S. M. Roberts and B. J. Price (eds), *Medicinal Chemistry: The Role of Organic Chemistry in Drug Research*, London: Academic Press, pp. 49–67.

Mabuchi, H., T. Haba, R. Tatami, S. Miyamoto, Y. Sakai, T. Wakasugi, A. Watanabe, J. Koizumi and R. Takeda (1981), 'Effects of an Inhibitor of 3-Hydroxy-3-Methylglutaryl Coenzyme A Reductase on Serum Lipoproteins and Ubiquinone-10 Levels in Patients with Familial Hypercholesterolemia', *New England Journal of Medicine*, **305**, 478–82.

Mabuchi, H., T. Sakai, Y. Sakai, A. Yoshimura, A. Watanabe, T. Wakasugi, J. Koizumi and R. Takeda (1983), 'Reduction of Serum Cholesterol in Heterozygous Patients with Familial Hypercholesterolemia, Additive Effects of Compactin and Cholestyramine', *New England Journal of Medicine*, **308**, 609–13.

Mabuchi, H., N. Kamon, H. Fujita, I. Michishita, M. Takeda, K. Kajinami, H. Itoh, T. Wakasugi and R. Takeda (1987), 'Effect of CS-514 on Serum Lipoprotein Lipid and Apolipoprotein Levels in Patients with Familial Hypercholesterolemia', *Metabolism*, **36**, 475–9.

MacDonald, J. S., R. J. Gerson, D. J. Kornbrust, M. W. Kloss, S. Prahalada, P. H. Berry, A. W. Alberts and D. L. Bokelman (1988), 'Preclinical Evaluation of Lovastatin', *American Journal of Cardiology*, **62** (Supplement), 16J–27J.

MacKenzie, D. (1988), ' "Micro" versus "Macro" Sociologies of Science and Technology', *Edinburgh PICT Working Paper* no.2, Edinburgh: Research Centre for Social Science, University of Edinburgh.

MacKenzie, D. (1990), *Inventing Accuracy: A Historical Sociology of Nuclear Missile Guidance*, Cambridge, MA: MIT Press.

MacKenzie, D. (1996a), *Knowing Machines: Essays on Technical Change*, Cambridge, MA: MIT Press.

MacKenzie, D. (1996b), 'How Do We Know the Properties of Artefacts? Applying the Sociology of Knowledge to Technology', in E. Fox (ed.), *Technological Change*, Amsterdam: Harwood Academic Publishers, pp. 247–63.

MacKenzie, D. and J. Wajcman (1985), 'Introductory Essay', in D. MacKenzie and J. Wajcman (eds), *The Social Shaping of Technology*, Milton Keynes: Open University Press, pp. 2–25.

MacKenzie, D. and J. Wajcman (1999), 'Introductory Essay: the Social

Shaping of Technology', in D. MacKenzie and J. Wajcman (eds), *The Social Shaping of Technology*, 2nd edn, Buckingham: Open University Press, pp. 3–27.

Maheux, R., C. Guilloteau, A. Lemay, A. Bastide and A. T. A. Fazekas (1984), 'Regression of Leiomyomata Uteri Following Hypoestrogenism Induced by Repetitive Luteinizing Hormone-releasing Hormone Agonist Treatment: Preliminary Report', *Fertility and Sterility*, **42**, 644–6.

Makino, S., K. Koshou and T. Miyamoto (eds.) (1998), *Zensoku Yobou, Kanri Guideline 1998* (The Guideline of Asthma Prevention and Management 1998), Tokyo: Kyouwa Tsushin Kikaku. (in Japanese)

Mann, R. D. (1994), 'Results of Prescription Event Monitoring Study of Salmeterol', *British Medical Journal*, **309**, 1018.

Marks, H. (1997), *The Progress of Experiment: Science and Therapeutic Reform in the United States, 1900–1990*, Cambridge: Cambridge University Press.

Marks, H. M. (1992), 'Cortisone, 1949: a Year in the Political Life of a Drug', *Bulletin of the History of Medicine*, **66**, 419–39.

Marx, L. and M. R. Smith (1994), 'Introduction', in M. R. Smith and L. Marx (eds), *Does Technology Drive History? The Dilemma of Technological Determinism*, Cambridge, MA: MIT Press, pp. ix–xv

Matsuo, H., A. Arimura, R. M. G. Nair and A. V. Schally (1971a), 'Synthesis of the Porcine LH- and FSH-Releasing Hormone by the Solid-phase Method', *Biochemical and Biophysical Research Communication*, **45**, 822–7.

Matsuo, H., Y. Baba, R. M. G. Nair, A. Arimura and A. V. Schally (1971b), 'Structure of the Porcine LH- and FSH- Hormone. I: The Proposed Amino Acid Sequence', *Biochemical and Biophysical Research Communication*, **43**, 1334–9.

Matsuoka, T., S. Miyakoshi, K. Tanzawa, K. Nakahara, M. Hosobuchi and N. Serizawa (1989), 'Purification and Characterization of Cytochrome P-450$_{sca}$ from *Streptomyces Carbophilus*', *European Journal of Biochemistry*, **184**, 707–13.

Maxwell, R. A. and S. B. Eckhardt (1990), 'Propranolol', in *Drug Discovery: A Casebook and Analysis*, Clifton, NJ: Humana Press, pp. 3–19.

McCann, S. M. (1962), 'A Hypothalamic Luteinizing-hormone-releasing Factor', *American Journal of Physiology*, **202**, 395–400.

McCann, S. M., S. Taleisnik and H. M. Friedman (1960), 'LH-Releasing Activity in Hypothalamic Extract', *Proceeding of the Society for Experimental Biology and Medicine*, **104**, 432–4.

McGuire, W. L., G. C. Chamness, M. E. Costlow and R. E. Shepherd (1974), 'Hormone Dependence in Breast Cancer', *Metabolism*, **23**, 75–100.

McIntosh, F. C. (1938), 'Histamine as a Normal Stimulant of Gastric Secretion', *Quarterly Journal of Experimental Physiology and Cognate Medical Sciences*, **28**, 87–98.

McIntyre, A. M. (1999), *Key Issues in the Pharmaceutical Industry*, Chichester, Sussex: John Wiley.

McIvor, R. A., E. Pizzichini, M. O. Turner, P. Hussack, F. E. Hargreave and M. R. Sears (1998), 'Potential Masking Effects of Salmeterol on Airway Inflammation in Asthma', *American Journal of Respiratory and Critical Care Medicine*, **158**, 924–30.

McKelvey, M. D. (1996), *Evolutionary Innovations: The Business of Biotechnology*, Oxford: Oxford University Press.

McKenzie, A. W. and R. B. Stoughton (1962), 'Method for Comparing Percutaneous Absorption of Steroids', *Archives of Dermatology*, **86**, 608–10.

Meldrum, D. R., R. J. Chang, J. Lu, W. Vale, J. Rivier and H. L. Judd (1982), ' "Medical Oophorectomy" Using a Long-acting GnRH Agonist: a Possible New Approach to the Treatment of Endometriosis', *Journal of Clinical Endocrinology and Metabolism*, **54**, 1081–3.

Mikawa, H., S. Ito, M. Baba, T. Mukoyama, Y. Iikura, T. Obata, Y. Teramichi, T. Nemoto, Y. Arai and S. Nishima (1986), 'Syouni Kikanshi Zensoku ni Taisuru Syouni Procaterol Kyuunyuuyaku no Yakkou Hyouka' (Efficacy Evaluation of Procaterol Aerosol for Children in Children's Bronchial Asthma), *Igaku no Ayumi*, **138**, 297–313. (in Japanese)

Minette, M. (1971), 'Ventilatory Results and Side-effects of Salbutamol Given by Different Routes in Coalminers with Reversible Broncho-obstruction', *Postgraduate Medical Journal*, **47** (Supplement), 55–61.

Ministry of Health and Welfare (Japan) (1996), *Sinyaku Shounin Sinsei Handobukku* (The Handbook of Application for Approval of New Drugs), Tokyo: Yakugyo Jihou Sya. (in Japanese)

Minneman, K. P., C. Han and P. W. Abel (1988), 'Comparison of α_1-Adrenergic Receptors Subtypes Distinguished by Chlorethylclonidine and WB 4101', *Molecular Pharmacology*, **33**, 509–14.

Mol, M. J. T., D. W. Erkelens, J. A. Gevers Leuven, J. A. Schouten and A. F. H. Stalenhoef (1986), 'Effects of Synvinolin (MK-733) on Plasma Lipids in Familial Hypercholesterolemia', *Lancet*, **2**, 936–9.

Monahan, M. W., J. Rivier, W. Vale, R. Guillemin and R. Burgus (1972), '[Gly^2] LRF and des-His^2-LRF: the Synthesis, Purification and Characterization of Two LRF Analogues Antagonistic to LRF', *Biochemical and Biophysical Research Communication*, **47**, 551–6.

Monahan, M. W., M. S. Amoss, H. A. Anderson and W. Vale (1973),

'Synthetic Analogs of the Hypothalamic Luteinizing Hormone Releasing Factor with Increased Agonist or Antagonist Properties', *Biochemistry*, **12**, 4616–20.

Moran, N. C. and M. E. Perkins (1958), 'Adrenergic Blockade of the Mammalian Heart by a Dichloro Analogue of Isoproterenol', *Journal of Pharmacology and Experimental Therapeutics*, **124**, 223–37.

Morin, R. B., B. G. Jackson, E. H. Flynn and R. W. Roeske (1962), 'Chemistry of Cephalosporin Antibiotics. I: 7-Aminocephalosporanic Acid from Cephalosporin C', *Journal of the American Chemical Society*, **84**, 3400–1.

Morita, K. (2000), *Sin-yaku ha Koushite Umareru* (New Drugs Are Born in This Way), Tokyo: Nihon Keizai Shinbun Sya. (in Japanese)

Morita, K., H. Nomura, M. Numata, M. Ochiai and M. Yoneda (1980), 'An Approach to Broad-spectrum Cephalosporins', in *Penicillin Fifty Years after Fleming: A Royal Society Discussion*, London: Royal Society, pp. 15–24.

Morrelli, H. F. (1973), 'Propranolol', *Annals of Internal Medicine*, **78**, 913–17.

Morrow, A. L. and I. Creese (1987), 'Characterization of α_1-Adrenergic Receptor Subtypes in Rat Brain: a Reevaluation of [^{3}H]WB 4104 and [^{3}H]Prazosin Binding', *Molecular Pharmacology*, **29**, 321–30.

Morrow Brown, H., G. Storey and W. H. S. George (1972), 'Beclomethasone Dipropionate: a New Steroid Aerosol for the Treatment of Allergic Asthma', *British Medical Journal*, **1**, 585–90.

Muggleton, P. W. and C. H. O'Callaghan (1967), 'The Antibacterial Activities of Cephaloridine: Laboratory Investigation', *Postgraduate Medical Journal*, **43** (Supplement), 17–22.

Muggleton, P. W., C. H. O'Callaghan and W. K. Stevens (1964), 'Laboratory Evaluation of a New Antibiotic – Cephaloridine (Ceporin)', *British Medical Journal*, **2**, 1234–7.

Mullen, M., B. Mullen and M. Carey (1993), 'The Association between β-Agonist Use and Death from Asthma', *Journal of the American Medical Association*, **270**, 1842–5.

Munakata, M. (1989), *Gijyutsu no Riron* (A Theory of Technology), Tokyo: Doubunkan. (in Japanese)

Murphy, G. P., R. P. Huben, J. M. Greco, M. Scott, J. L. Chin and H. A. deHaan (1987), 'Zoladex (ICI 118630): Clinical Trial of New Luteinizing Hormone-releasing Hormone Analog in Metastatic Prostatic Carcinoma', *Urology*, **29**, 185–90.

Nakagawa, K., N, Murakami, S. Yoshizaki, M. Tominaga, H. Mori, Y.

Yabuuchi and S. Shintani (1974), 'Derivatives of 3,4-Dihydrocarbostyril as β-Adrenergic Blocking Agents', *Journal of Medicinal Chemistry*, **17**, 529–33.

Nakajima, H., M. Hoshiyama, K. Yamashita and A. Kiyomoto (1975), 'Effect of Diltiazem on Electrical and Mechanical Activity of Isolated Cardiac Ventricular Muscle of Guinea Pig', *Japanese Journal of Pharmacology*, **25**, 383–92.

Nakaya, N., Y. Homma, H. Tamachi, H. Shigematsu, Y. Hata and Y. Goto (1987), 'The Effect of CS-514 on Serum Lipids and Apolipoproteins in Hypercholesterolemic Subjects', *JAMA*, **257**, 3088–93.

Namer, M., R. Metz, R. Tetelboum, R. Khater, L. Adenis, L. Mauriac, J. E. Couette and R. Bugat (1986), 'Clinical Results and Endocrinological Effects of Zoladex (ICI 118630), an LH-RH Analog, in the Treatment of Advanced Prostate Cancer: Results of a Multi-institution French Study', *European Journal of Cancer and Clinical Oncology*, **22**, 743.

Nelson, R. (1996), *The Source of Economic Growth*, Cambridge, MA: Harvard University Press.

Nelson, R. and S. Winter (1974), 'Neoclassical vs. Evolutionary Theories of Economic Growth: Critique and Prospectus', *Economic Journal*, **84**, 887–905.

Nelson, R. and S. Winter (1977), 'In Search of a Useful Theory of Innovation', *Research Policy*, **6**, 36–77.

Nelson, R. and S. Winter (1982), *An Evolutionary Theory of Economic Change*, Cambridge, MA: Harvard University Press.

Newall, C. E. (1985), 'Injectable Cephalosporin Antibiotics: Cephalothin to Ceftazidime', in S. M. Roberts and B. J. Price (eds), *Medicinal Chemistry: The Role of Organic Chemistry in Drug Research*, London: Academic Press, pp. 209–26.

Newton, G. G. F. and E. P. Abraham (1955), 'Cephalosporin C, a New Antibiotic Containing Sulphur and D-α-Aminoadipic Acid', *Nature*, **175**, 548–9.

Newton, G. G. F. and E. P. Abraham (1956), 'Isolation of Cephalosporin C, a Penicillin-like Antibiotic Containing D-α-Aminoadipic Acid', *Biochemical Journal*, **62**, 651–8.

Nicholson, R. I. and P. V. Maynard (1979), 'Anti-tumour Activity of ICI 118630, a New Potent Luteinizing Hormone-releasing Hormone Agonist', *British Journal of Cancer*, **39**, 268–73.

Nihon Sougou Kenkyusyo (1998), *Minkan Kigyou ni okeru Kenkyu Kaihatu Seikou Jirei ni Kansuru Cyousa* (Case Studies on Successful Research and Development in Japanese Private Companies), Tokyo: Nihon Sougou Kenkyusyo, pp. 274–5. (in Japanese)

Nihon Yakushi Gakkai (ed.) (1995), *Nihon Iyakuhin Sangyo-Shi* (A History of the Japanese Pharmaceutical Industry), Tokyo: Yakuji Nippou Sya. (in Japanese)

Niijima, T., Y. Aso and TAP-144-SR Study Group (1990), 'Clinical Phase I and Phase II Study on a Sustained Release Formulation of Leuprorelin Acetate (TAP-144-SR), an LH-RH Agonist, in Patients with Prostatic Carcinoma', *Hinyou Kiyou*, **36**, 1343–60. (in Japanese)

Noble, D. F. (1984), *Forces of Production: A Social History of Industrial Automation*, New York: Alfred A. Knopf.

Nonaka, I. and H. Takeuchi (1995), *The Knowledge-creating Company: How Japanese Companies Create the Dynamics of Innovation*, New York: Oxford University Press.

Numata, M. (1981), 'Sefemu-Kei Kousei-Zai no Doraggu Dezain ni Tuite' (On the Drug Design of Cephems Antibiotics), in-house documentation, Takeda Chemical Industries. (in Japanese)

Numata, M., M. Yamaoka, I. Minamida, M. Kuritani and Y. Imashiro (1978a), 'New Cephalosporins with 7-Acyl Groups Derived from β-Ketoacids. I: 7-(β-Ketoacylamino)Cephalosporins', *Journal of Antibiotics*, **31**, 1245–51.

Numata, M., I. Minamida, M. Yamaoka, M. Shiraishi and T. Miyawaki (1978b), 'New Cephalosporins with 7-Acyl Groups Derived from β-Ketoacids. II: Further Modifications of 7-(3-Oxobutyrylamino)-Cephalosporins', *Journal of Antibiotics*, **31**, 1252–61.

Numata, M., I. Minamida, M. Yamaoka, M. Shiraishi, T. Miyawaki, H. Akimoto, K. Naito and M. Kida (1978c), 'A New Cephalosporin. SCE-963: 7-[2-(2-Aminothiazol-4-Yl)-Acetamido]-3-[[[1-(2-Dimethylamino-ethyl)-1H-Tetrazol-5-Yl]-Thio]Methyl]Ceph-3-Em-4-Carboxylic Acid', *Journal of Antibiotics*, **31**, 1262–71.

O'Brien and M. Hibberd (1990), 'Clinical Efficacy and Safety of a New Leuprorelin Acetate Depot Formulation in Patients with Advanced Prostatic Cancer', *Journal of International Medical Research*, **18** (supplement 1), 57–68.

Odagiri, H. and A. Goto (1993), 'The Japanese System of Innovation: Past, Present, and Future', in R. R. Nelson (ed.), *National Innovation Systems: A Comparative Analysis*, New York: Oxford University Press, pp. 74–114.

Odagiri, H. and A. Goto (1996), *Technology and Industrial Development in Japan*, Oxford: Clarendon Press.

O'Donnell, T. V., H. H. Rea, P. E. Holst and M. R. Sears (1989), 'Fenoterol and Fatal Asthma', *Lancet*, **1**, 1070–1.

Ogawa, Y. (1999), 'R&D no Keii' (the Details of R&D), a document given by Dr Yasuaki Ogawa.

Ogawa, Y. and M. Fujino (1994), 'Zenritsusen Gan wo Naosu Kusuri –

Leuplin' (Leuplin, a Drug for the Treatment of Prostate Cancer), in H. Iwamura, S. Ogino, K. Matsumoto and Y. Yamada (eds), *Ima Wadai no Kusuri* (Drugs in the News), Tokyo: Gakkai Syuppan Center, pp. 173–90. (in Japanese)

Ogawa, Y. and H. Toguchi (1991), 'Sakusan Ryupurorerin Johousei Seizai no Sekkei Yowa' (Episodes in the Development of Leuprorelin Acetate Depot Formulation), *Human Science*, **2**, 20–3. (in Japanese)

Ogawa, Y., H. Okada, T. Heya and T. Shimamoto (1989), 'Controlled Release of LHRH Agonist, Leuprolide Acetate, from Microcapsules: Serum Drug Level Profiles and Pharmacological Effects in Animals', *Journal of Pharmacy and Pharmacology*, **41**, 439–44.

Oshima, H., H. R. Nankin, D.-F. Fan and P. Troen (1975), 'Delay in Sexual Maturation of Rats Caused by Synthetic LH-Releasing Hormone: Enhancement of Steroid Δ^4-5α-Hydrogenase in Testes', *Biology of Reproduction*, **12**, 491–7.

Otero, G. (1995), 'The Coming Revolution of Biotechnology: a Critique of Buttel', in M. Fransman, G. Junne and A. Roobeek (eds), *The Biotechnology Revolution?*, Oxford: Blackwell, pp. 46–61.

Otsuka Pharmaceutical Co. Ltd (1999), *Otsuka People Creating New Products for Better Health Worldwide.* (brochure), Tokyo: Otsuka Pharmaceutical Co. Ltd

Owen, G. (1999), *From Empire to Europe: The Decline and Revival of British Industry Since the Second World War*, London: HarperCollins.

Paget, G. E. (1963), 'Carcinogenic Action of Pronethalol', *British Medical Journal*, **2**, 1266–7.

Palmer, J. B. D. and M. M. Jenkins (1991), 'β_2-Agonists in Asthma', *Lancet*, **337**, 43.

Parker, K. L. and P. A. Lee (1989), 'Depot Leuprolide Acetate for Treatment of Precocious Puberty', *Journal of Clinical Endocrinology and Metabolism*, **69**, 689–91.

Patrick, G. L. (1995), *An Introduction to Medicinal Chemistry*, Oxford: Oxford University Press.

Pavitt, K. (1987), *On the Nature of Technology* (Inaugural Lecture given at the University of Sussex on 23 June 1987), Science Policy Research Unit, University of Sussex.

Pearce, N., J. Grainger, M. Atkinson, J. Crane, C. Burgess, C. Culling, H. Windom and R. Beasley (1990), 'Case-control Study of Prescribed Fenoterol and Death from Asthma in New Zealand, 1977–81', *Thorax*, **45**, 170–5.

Pearce, N., R. Beasley, J. Crane, C. Burgess and R. Jackson (1995), 'End of the New Zealand Asthma Mortality Epidemic', *Lancet*, **345**, 41–5.

Peel, E. T. and G. J. Gibson (1980), 'Effects of Long-term Inhaled Salbutamol Therapy on the Provocation of Asthma by Histamine', *American Review of Respiratory Disease*, **121**, 973–8.

Peeling, W. B. (1989), 'Phase III Studies to Compare Goserelin (Zoladex) with Orchiectomy and with Diethylstilbestrol in Treatment of Prostatic Carcinoma', *Urology*, **33** (Supplement), 45–52.

Phillipps, G. H. (1990), 'Structure–Activity Relationship of Topically Active Steroids: the Selection of Fluticasone Propionate', *Respiratory Medicine*, **84** (Supplement A), 19–23.

Pickering, A. (ed.) (1992), *Science as Practice and Culture*, Chicago: University of Chicago Press.

Pietro, D. A., S. Alexander, G. Mantell, J. E. Staggers and T. J. Cook (1989), 'Effects of Simvastatin in Hypercholesterolemia (Simvastatin Multicenter Study Group II)', *American Journal of Cardiology*, **63**, 682–6.

Pinch, T. (1996), 'The Social Construction of Technology: a Review', in E. Fox (ed.), *Technological Change*, Amsterdam: Harwood Academic Publishers, pp. 17–35.

Pinch, T. J. and W. E. Bijker (1987), 'The Social Construction of Facts and Artifacts: or, How Sociology of Science and the Sociology of Technology Might Benefit Each Other', in W. E. Bijker, T. P. Hughes and T. Pinch (eds), *The Social Construction of Technological Systems*, Cambridge, MA: MIT Press, pp. 17–50.

Pisano, G. P. (1997), *The Development Factory: Unlocking the Potential of Process Innovation*, Boston, MA: Harvard Business School Press.

Plummer, A. L. (1978), 'The Development of Drug Tolerance to Beta$_2$ Adrenergic Agents', *Chest*, **73** (Supplement), 949–57.

Poole, C., S. F. Lanes and A. M. Walker (1990), 'Fenoterol and Fatal Asthma', *Lancet*, **335**, 920–1.

Popielski, L. (1920), 'β-Imidazolyläthylamin und die Organextrakte. Erster Teil: β-Imidazolyläthylamin als mächtiger Erreger der Magendrüsen' (β-Imidazolylethylamine and the Organic Extracts. Part 1: β-Imidazolylethylamine as the Strong Stimulator of the Stomach Gland), *Pflügers Archiv für die gesamte Physiologie*, **178**, 214–36. (in German)

Porter, M. E., H. Takeuchi and M. Sakakibara (2000), *Can Japan Compete?*, Basingstoke: Macmillan.

Powell, C. E. and I. H. Slater (1958), 'Blocking of Inhibitory Adrenergic Receptors by a Dichloro Analog of Isoproterenol', *Journal of Pharmacology and Experimental Therapeutics*, **122**, 480–8.

Powell, W. W., K. W. Koput and L. Smith-Doerr (1996), 'Inter-Organizational Collaboration and the Locus of Innovation: Networks of Learning in Biotechnology', *Administrative Science Quarterly*, **41**, 116–45.

Powles, R., E. Shinebourne and J. Hamer (1969), 'Selective Cardiac Sympathetic Blockade as an Adjunct to Bronchodilator Therapy', *Thorax*, **24**, 616–18.

Prahalad, C. K. and G. Hamel (1990), 'The Core Competence of the Corporation', *Harvard Business Review*, May–June, 79–91.

Price, D. T., D. A. Schwinn, J. W. Lomasney, L. E. Allen, M. G. Caron and R. J. Lefkowitz (1993), 'Identification, Quantification, and Localization of mRNA for Three Distinct Alpha$_1$ Adrenergic Receptor Subtypes in Human Prostate', *Journal of Urology*, **150**, 546–51.

Prichard, B. N. C. (1964), 'Hypotensive Action of Pronethalol', *British Medical Journal*, **1**, 1227–8.

Prichard, B. N. C. and P. M. S. Gillam (1964), 'Use of Propranolol (Inderal) in Treatment of Hypertension', *British Medical Journal*, **2**, 725–7.

Prout, A. (1996), 'Actor-Network Theory, Technology and Medical Sociology: an Illustrative Analysis of the Metered Dose Inhaler', *Sociology of Health and Illness*, **18**, 198–219.

Rang, H. P., M. M. Dale and J. M. Ritter (1995), *Pharmacology*, 3rd edn, Edinburgh: Churchill Livingstone.

Raz, S. and M. Caine (1972), 'Adrenergic Receptors in the Female Canine Urethra', *Investigate Urology*, **9**, 319–23.

Redding, T. W. and A. V. Schally (1981), 'Inhibition of Prostate Tumor Growth in Two Rat Models by Chronic Administration of D-Trp^6 Analogue of Luteinizing Hormone-releasing Hormone', *Proceeding of the National Academy of Sciences USA*, **78**, 6509–12.

Redding, T. W. and A. V. Schally (1983), 'Inhibition of Mammary Tumor Growth in Rats and Mice by Administration of Agonistic and Antagonistic Analogs of Luteinizing Hormone-releasing Hormone', *Proceeding of the National Academy of Sciences USA*, **80**, 1459–62.

Redding, T. W., A.V. Schally, T. R. Tice and W. E. Meyers (1984), 'Long-acting Delivery Systems for Peptides: Inhibition of Rat Prostate Tumors by Controlled Release of [D-Trp6] Luteinizing Hormone-releasing Hormone from Injectable Microcapsules', *Proceeding of the National Academy of Sciences USA*, **81**, 5845–8.

Rees, J. (1991), 'β_2-Agonists and Asthma: Still the Mainstay of Symptomatic Treatment', *British Medical Journal*, **302**, 1166–7.

Reich, J. W. (1986), 'Drug Regulatory Affairs and Pharmaceutical Research and Development in Japan 1960–1985', *Drug Development and Industrial Pharmacy*, **12**, 1–51.

Reich, M. R. (1990), 'Why the Japanese Don't Export More Pharmaceuticals: Health Policy as Industrial Policy', *California Management Review*, **32**, 124–50.

Richards, E. (1988), 'The Politics of Therapeutic Evaluation: the Vitamin C and Cancer Controversy', *Social Studies of Science*, **18**, 653–701.

Rickwood, S. and A. Southworth (1995), *Human Hormones in Therapeutics*, London: FT Pharmaceuticals and Healthcare Publishing.

Rippel, R. H. and E. S. Johnson (1976), 'Inhibition of HCG-induced Ovarian and Uterine Weight Augmentation in the Immature Rat by Analogs of GnRH', *Proceedings of the Society for Experimental Biology and Medicine*, **152**, 432–6.

Rippel, R. H., E. S. Johnson, W. F. White, M. Fujino, I. Yamazaki and R. Nakayama (1973), 'Ovulation and LH-releasing Activity of a Highly Potent Analog of Synthetic Gonadotropin-releasing Hormone', *Endocrinology*, **93**, 1449–52.

Rippel, R. H., E. S. Johnson, W. F. White, M. Fujino, T. Fukuda and S. Kobayashi (1975), 'Ovulation and Gonadotropin-releasing Activity of a Highly Potent Analog of Synthetic Gonadotropin-releasing Hormone, [D-Leu^6, Des-Gly-NH$_2$^{10}, Pro-ethylamide^9]-GnRH', *Proceedings of the Society for Experimental Biology and Medicine*, **148**, 1193–7.

Rivier, C., J. Rivier and W. Vale (1978), 'Chronic Effects of [D-Trp^6-Pro^9-NEt] Luteinizing Hormone-releasing Factor on Reproductive Processes in the Female Rat', *Endocrinology*, **103**, 2299–2305.

Rizzo, M., T. Mazzei, E. Mini, R. Bartoletti and P. Periti (1990), 'Leuprorelin Acetate Depot in Advanced Prostatic Cancer: a Phase II Multicentre Trial', *Journal of International Medical Research*, **18** (supplement 1), 114–25.

Rosenberg, N. (1976), *Perspectives on Technology*, Cambridge: Cambridge University Press.

Rosenberg, N. (1982), *Inside the Black Box: Technology and Economics*, Cambridge: Cambridge University Press.

Rosenberg, N. (1994), *Exploring the Black Box*, Cambridge: Cambridge University Press.

Rothlin, E. and R. Gundlach (1921), 'Étude Expérimentale de l'Influence de l'Histamine sur la Sécrétion Gastrique' (an Experimental Study of the Influences of Histamine on the Gastric Secretion), *Archives Internationales de Physiologie*, **17**, 59–84. (in French)

Rothwell, R. (1994), 'Industrial Innovation: Success, Strategy, Trends', in M. Dodgson and R. Rothwell (eds), *The Handbook of Industrial Innovation*, Aldershot: Edward Elgar, pp. 33–53.

Rowlands, D. J., G. Howitt and P. Markman (1965), 'Propranolol (Inderal) in Disturbances of Cardiac Rhythm', *British Medical Journal*, **1**, 891–4.

Roy, P., L. Day and E. Sowton (1975), 'Effect of a New β-Adrenergic Blocking Agent, Atenolol (Tenormin), on Pain Frequency, Trinitrin Consumption, and Exercise Ability', *British Medical Journal*, **3**, 195–7.

Russell, S. and R. Williams (1988), 'Opening the Black Box and Closing It

Behind You: On Micro-sociology in the Social Analysis of Technology',
Edinburgh PICT Working Paper no. 3, Edinburgh: Research Centre for
Social Science, University of Edinburgh.

Ryman, K. S., S. H. Kubo, J. Lystash, G. Stone and R. J. Cody (1986),
'Effect of Nicardipine on Rest and Exercise Hemodynamics in Chronic
Congestive Heart Failure', *American Journal of Cardiology*, **58**, 583–8.

Saameli, K. (1967), 'Comparative Studies with β-Receptor Blocking Agents
and Quinidine', *Helvetica Physiologica Acta*, **25**, CR 432–3.

Sackett, D. L., H. S. Shannon and G. W. Brownman (1990), 'Fenoterol and
Fatal Asthma', *Lancet*, **335**, 45–6.

Sacks, J., A. C. Ivy, J. P. Burgess and J. E. Vandolah (1932), 'Histamine as
the Hormone for Gastric Secretion', *American Journal of Physiology*,
101, 331–8.

Sanders, L. M., J. S. Kent, G. I. McRae, B. H. Vickery, T. R. Tice and D. H.
Lewis (1984), 'Controlled Release of a Luteinizing Hormone-releasing
Hormone Analogue from Poly (*d,l*-lactide-co-glycolide) Microspheres',
Journal of Pharmaceutical Sciences, **73**, 1294–7.

Sandow, J. (1983), 'Clinical Applications of LHRH and Its Analogues',
Clinical Endocrinology, **18**, 571–92.

Sandow, J., W. von Rechenberg, G. Jerzabek and W. Stoll (1978), 'Pituitary
Gonadotropin Inhibition by a Highly Active Analog of Luteinizing
Hormone Releasing Hormone', *Fertility and Sterility*, **30**, 205–9.

Sankyo Co. Ltd (1996), *Mevalotin Story*, Tokyo. (in Japanese)

Santen, R. J., B. Warner, L. M. Demers, M. Dufau and J. A. Smith (1984a),
'Leuprolide Therapy for Prostatic Carcinoma', in B. H. Vickery, J. J.
Nestor and E. S. E. Hafez (eds), *LHRH and Its Analogs*, Lancaster: MTP
Press, pp. 351–64.

Santen, R. J., L. M. Demers, D. T. Max, J. Smith and L. M. Glode (1984b),
'Long Term Effects of Administration of a Gonadotropin-releasing
Hormone Superagonist Analog in Men with Prostatic Carcinoma',
Journal of Clinical Endocrinology and Metabolism, **58**, 397–400.

Sapienza, A. M. (1997), *Creating Technology Strategies: How to Build
Competitive Biomedical R&D*, New York: Wiley-Liss.

Sato, A., A. Ogiso, H. Noguchi, S. Mitsui, I. Kaneko and Y. Shimada
(1980), 'Mevalonolactone Derivatives as Inhibitors of 3-Hydroxy-3-
Methylglutaryl Coenzyme A Reductase', *Chemistry and Pharmacology
Bulletin*, **28**, 1509–25.

Schally, A. V. (1978), 'In the Pursuit of Hypothalamic Hormones', in J.
Meites, B. T. Donovan and S. M. McCann (eds), *Pioneers in Neuroendocrinology II*, New York: Plenum Press, pp. 347–66.

Schally, A. V., A. Arimura, C. Y. Bowers, A. J. Kastin, S. Sawano and T.

W. Redding (1968), 'Hypothalamic Neurohormones Regulating Anterior Pituitary Function', *Recent Progress in Hormone Research*, **24**, 497–580.

Schally, A. V., A. Arimura, Y. Baba, R. M. G. Nair, H. Matsuo, T. W. Redding, L. Debeljuk, and W. F. White (1971a), 'Isolation and Properties of the FSH and LH-releasing Hormone', *Biochemical and Biophysical Research Communication*, **43**, 393–9.

Schally, A. V., A. Arimura, A. J. Kastin, H. Matsuo, Y. Baba, T. W. Redding, R. M. G. Nair, L. Debeljuk and W. F. White (1971b), 'Gonadotropin-releasing Hormone: One Polypeptide Regulates Secretion of Luteinizing and Follicle-stimulating Hormones', *Science*, **173**, 1036–8.

Schally, A. V., A. Arimura, W. H. Carter, T. W. Redding, R. Geiger, W. König, H. Wissman, G. Jaeger, J. Sandow, N. Yanaihara, C. Yanaihara, T. Hashimoto and M. Sakagami (1972), 'Luteinizing Hormone-releasing Hormone (LH-RH) Activity of Some Synthetic Polypeptides. I: Fragments Shorter than Decapeptide', *Biochemical and Biophysical Research Communication*, **48**, 366–75.

Schally, A. V., A. Arimura and A. J. Kastin (1973), 'Hypothalamic Regulatory Hormones', *Science*, 179, 341–50.

Schmann, A. and H. Herxheimer (1971), 'The Bronchodilator Action of Salbutamol in Asthmatics', *Postgraduate Medical Journal*, **47** (Supplement), 92–9.

Schon, D. A. (1963), 'Champions for Radical New Inventions', *Harvard Business Review*, March–April, pp. 77–86.

Schuijt, C. and H. Staudinger (1995), 'End of New Zealand Asthma Epidemic', *Lancet*, **345**, 383–4.

Schwinn, D. A., J. W. Lomasney, W. Lorenz, P. J. Szklut, R. T. Fremeau, T. L. Yang-Feng, M. G. Caron, R. J. Lefkowitz and S. Cotecchia (1990), 'Molecular Cloning and Expression of the cDNA for a Novel α_1-Adrenergic Receptor Subtype', *Journal of Biological Chemistry*, **265**, 8183–9.

Scrip Yearbook (1991), Richmond, Surrey: PJB Publishing

Scrip Yearbook (1993), Richmond, Surrey: PJB Publishing

Sears, M. R. (1995), 'Is the Routine Use of Inhaled β-Adrenergic Agonists Appropriate in Asthma Treatment? No', *American Journal of Respiratory and Critical Care Medicine*, **151**, 600–1.

Sears, M. R. and D. R. Taylor (1992), 'Regular Beta-Agonist Therapy: the Quality of the Evidence', *European Respiratory Journal*, **5**, 896–7.

Sears, M. R. and D. R. Taylor (1993), 'Increase in Deaths during Salmeterol Treatment Unexplained', *British Medical Journal*, **306**, 1610–11.

Sears, M. R. and D. R. Taylor (1994), 'The β_2-Agonist Controversy: Observations, Explanations and Relationship to Asthma Epidemiology', *Drug Safety*, **11**, 259–83.

Sears, M. R., D. R. Taylor, C. G. Print, D. C. Lake, Q. Li, E. M. Flannery, D. M. Yates, M. K. Lucas and G. P. Herbison (1990), 'Regular Inhaled Beta-Agonist Treatment in Bronchial Asthma', *Lancet*, **336**, 1391–6.

Sears, M. R., D. R. Taylor, C. G. Print, D. C. Lake, G. P. Herbison and E. M. Flannery (1992), 'Increased Inhaled Bronchodilator vs Increased Inhaled Corticosteroid in the Control of Moderate Asthma', *Chest*, **102**, 1709–15.

Selwyn, S. (1980), *The Beta-lactam Antibiotics: Penicillins and Cephalosporins in Perspective*, London: Hodder and Stoughton.

Serizawa, N., K. Nakagawa, K. Hamano, Y. Tsujita, A. Terahara and H. Kuwano (1983a), 'Microbial Hydroxylation of ML-236B (Compactin) and Monacolin K (MB-530B)', *Journal of Antibiotics*, **36**, 604–7.

Serizawa, N., K. Nakagawa, Y. Tsujita, A. Terahara and H. Kuwano (1983b), '3α-Hydroxy-ML-236B (3α-Hydroxycompactin), Microbial Transformation Product of ML-236B (Compactin)', *Journal of Antibiotics*, **36**, 608–10.

Serizawa, N., S. Serizawa, K. Nakagawa, K. Furuya, T. Okazaki and A. Terahara (1983c), 'Microbial Hydroxylation of ML-236B (Compactin): Studies on Microorganisms Capable of 3β-Hydroxylation of ML-236B', *Journal of Antibiotics*, **36**, 887–91.

Serizawa, N., K. Nakagawa, Y. Tsujita, A. Terahara, H. Kuwano and M. Tanaka (1983d), '6α-Hydroxy-*Iso*-ML-236B (6α-Hydroxy-*Iso*-Compactin) and ML-236A, Microbial Transformation Products of ML-236B', *Journal of Antibiotics*, **36**, 918–20.

Shanks, R. G. (1976), 'The Properties of Beta-Adrenoceptor Antagonist', *Postgraduate Medical Journal*, **52** (Supplement 4), 14–20.

Shanks, R. G. (1984), 'The Discovery of Beta-Adrenoceptor Blocking Drugs', *Trends in Pharmacological Sciences*, **5**, 405–9.

Sharifi, R., M. Soloway and Leuprolide Study Group (1990), 'Clinical Study of Leuprolide Depot Formulation in the Treatment of Advanced Prostate Cancer', *Journal of Urology*, **143**, 68–71.

Sharp, M. (1991), 'Pharmaceuticals and Biotechnology: Perspectives for the European Industry', in C. Freeman, M. Sharp and W. Walker (eds), *Technology and the Future of Europe: Global Competition and the Environment in the 1990s*, London: Frances Pinter, pp. 213–30.

Sharp, M. (1995), 'Application of Biotechnology: an Overview', in M. Fransman, G. Junne and A. Roobeek (eds), *The Biotechnology Revolution?*, Oxford: Blackwell, pp. 163–73.

Shaw, R. W. and Zoladex Endometriosis Study Team (1992), 'An Open Randomized Comparative Study of the Effect of Goserelin Depot and Danazol in the Treatment of Endometriosis', *Fertility and Sterility*, **58**, 265–72.

Shepherd, G. L., M. R. Henzel and T. J. H. Clark (1981), 'Regular versus Symptomatic Aerosol Bronchodilator Treatment of Asthma', *British Journal of Disease of the Chest*, 75, 215–17.

Shepherd, G. L., W. J. Jenkins and J. Alexander (1991), 'Asthma Exacerbations in Patients Taking Regular Salmeterol, or Salbutamol for Symptoms', *Lancet*, 337, 1424.

Shida, T., K. Ito, T. Yagura, A. Hamada, Y. Yamamura *et al.* (1979), 'Shin β Jyuyoutai Shigekisei Kikanshi Kakucyouzai Procaterol no Kikanshi Zensoku ni Taisuru Yakkou Kentou, 2' (A Study on Efficacy of Procaterol, a New β-Receptor Stimulant Bronchodilator in Bronchial Asthma, 2), *Igaku no Ayumi*, 111, 544–58. (in Japanese)

Shimizu, K., T. Kumada and S. Okuzumi (1979), 'Cefotiam (SCE-963) ni Kansuru Kisoteki, Rinsyoteki Kenkyu' (a Basic and Clinical Study on Cefotiam (SCE-963)), *Chemotherapy*, 27 (Supplement 3), 255–61. (in Japanese)

Shiota, H., Y. Nakayama, S. Matsumoto, Y. Sakiyama, Y. Wagatsuma, K. Togashi, N. Nemoto, T. Yamaguchi, W. Yamada, M. Ayuse, K. Tateno, T. Akasaka, R. Tochigi, Y. Arai, N. Kobayashi, H. Hayakawa, K. Shiraki, F. Komota, C. Otaki, M. Baba, T. Mukoyama, Y. Tomita, H. Sugimoto, Y. Iikura, T. Nagakura, Y. Shirai, C. Naito, A. Nakajima, Y. Teramichi, T. Nemoto, T. Hirao, S. Torii, M. Yoshida, M. Ueda, H. Mikawa, K. Shinomiya, K. Seyama, S. Nishima and F. Nakajima (1981), 'Syouni Kikanshi Zensoku ni Taisuru Shin β$_2$ Jyuyoutai Shigekisei Kikanshi Kakucyouyaaku Procaterol no Yakkou Hyouka, 1' (A Study on Efficacy of Procaterol, a New β$_2$-Receptor Stimulant Bronchodilator in Children's Bronchial Asthma, 1), *Igaku no Ayumi*, 117, 1048–60. (in Japanese)

Siegel, S. C., R. M. Katz, G. S. Rachelefsky, M. L. Brandon and L. A. Borgen (1985), 'A Placebo-controlled Trial of Procaterol: a New Long-acting Oral Beta$_2$-Agonist in Bronchial Asthma', *Journal of Allergy and Clinical Immunology*, 75, 698–705.

Sievertsson, H., J. K. Chang, C. Bogentoft, B. L. Currie, K. Folkers and C. Y. Bowers (1971), 'Synthesis of the Luteinizing Releasing Hormone of the Hypothalamus and its Hormonal Activity', *Biochemical and Biophysical Research Communication*, 44, 1566–71.

Silver, L. L. and K. A. Bostian (1993), 'Discovery and Development of New Antibiotics: the Problem of Antibiotics Resistance', *Antimicrobial Agents and Chemotherapy*, 37, 377–83.

Silvis, S. E. (1985), 'Final Report on the United States Multicenter Trial Comparing Ranitidine to Cimetidine as Maintenance Therapy Following Healing of Duodenal Ulcer', *Journal of Clinical Gastroenterology*, 7, 482–7.

Simpson, F. O. (1974), 'β-Adrenergic Receptor Blocking Drugs in Hypertension', *Drugs*, **7**, 85–105.

Simpson, W. T. (1971), 'Initial Studies on the Human Pharmacology of Salbutamol', *Postgraduate Medical Journal*, **47** (Supplement), 35–8.

Singh, B. N., H. D. Nisbet, E. A. Harris and R. M. L. Whitlock (1975), 'A Comparison of the Actions of ICI 66082 and Propranolol on Cardiac and Peripheral β-Adrenoceptors', *European Journal of Pharmacology*, **34**, 75–86.

Siperstein, M. D. (1970), 'Regulation of Cholesterol Biosynthesis in Normal and Malignant Tissues,' in B. L. Horecker and E. R. Stadtman (eds), *Current Topics in Cellular Regulation*, vol. 2, New York: Academic Press, pp. 65–100.

Siperstein, M. D. and V. M. Fagan (1966), 'Feedback Control of Mevalonate Synthesis by Dietary Cholesterol', *Journal of Biological Chemistry*, **241**, 602–9.

Sloman, G., J. S. Robinson and K. McLean (1965), *British Medical Journal*, **1**, 895–6.

Smith, J. A., L. M. Glode, D. T. Max, J. N. Wettlaufer, D. Anbar, B. S. Stein, C. L. Jagst, A. G. Glass and G. P. Murphy (1985), 'Clinical Effects of Gonadotropin-releasing Hormone Analogue in Metastatic Carcinoma of Prostate', *Urology*, **25**, 106–14.

Smith, R. B. (1985), *The Development of a Medicine*, London: Macmillan.

Sneader, W. (1985), Drug Discovery: The Evolution of Modern Medicines, Chichester: John Wiley.

Sneddon, I. B. (1976), 'Clinical Use of Tropical Corticosteroids', *Drugs*, **11**, 193–9.

Soloway, M. S., J. A. Smith, G. Chodak, M. Scott, N. J. Vogelzang, G. Kennealey, N. L. Block, T. C. Gau, P. F. Schellhammer (1991), 'Zoladex versus Orchiectomy in Treatment of Advanced Prostate Cancer: a Randomized Trial', *Urology*, **37**, 46–51.

Speizer, F. E., R. Doll and P. Heaf (1968), 'Observations on Recent Increases in Mortality from Asthma', *British Medical Journal*, **1**, 335–9.

Spitzer, W. O. and A. S. Buist (1990), 'Case-control Study of Prescribed Fenoterol and Death from Asthma in New Zealand, 1977–81', *Thorax*, **45**, 645–8.

Spitzer, W. O., S. Sussa, P. Ernst, R. I. Horwitz, B. Habbick, D. Cockcroft, J. F. Boivin, M. McNutt, A. S. Buist and A. S. Rebuck (1992), 'The Use of β-Agonists and the Risk of Death and Near Death from Asthma', *New England Journal of Medicine*, **326**, 501–6.

Srivastava, S. C., H. A. Dewar and D. J. Newell (1964), 'Double-blind Trial of Propranolol (Inderal) in Angina of Effort', *British Medical Journal*, **2**, 724–5.

Staundinger, H. W. and J. F. Haas (1992a), 'Beta-Agonists: Friends or Foes?', *European Respiratory Journal*, **5**, 894–5.

Staundinger, H. W. and J. F. Haas (1992b), 'β-Agonists and Death from Asthma', *New England Journal of Medicine*, **327**: 354–5.

Steinmueller, W. E. (1994), 'Basic Research and Industrial Innovation,' in M. Dodgson and R. Rothwell (eds), *The Handbook of Industrial Innovation*, Aldershot: Edward Elgar, pp. 54–66.

Stephenson, R. P. (1956), 'A Modification of Receptor Theory', *British Journal of Pharmacology*, **11**, 379–93.

Stock, J. P. P. and N. Dale (1963), 'Beta-Adrenergic Receptor Blockade in Cardiac Arrhythmias', *British Medical Journal*, **2**, 1230–3.

Stone, T. and G. Darlington (2000), *Pills, Potions and Poisons: How Drugs Work*, Oxford: Oxford University Press.

Strange, P. G. and D. E. Koshland Jr (1976), 'Receptor Interactions in a Signalling System: Competition Between Ribose Receptor and Galactose Receptor in the Chemotaxis Response', *Proceedings of the National Academy of Sciences USA*, **73**, 762–6.

Strum, S. and B. Latour [1987] (1999), 'Redefining the Social Link: From Baboons to Humans', in D. MacKenzie and J. Wajcman (eds), *The Social Shaping of Technology*, 2nd edn, Buckingham: Open University Press, pp. 116–25.

Strum, W. B. (1983), 'Ranitidine', *Journal of the American Medical Association*, **250**, 1894–6.

Suissa, S., P. Ernst, J. F. Boivin, R. I. Horwitz, B. Habbick, D. Cockroft, L. Blais, M. McNutt, A. S. Buist and W. O. Spitzer (1994), 'A Cohort Analysis of Excess Mortality in Asthma and the Use of Inhaled β-Agonists', *American Journal of Respiratory and Critical Care Medicine*, **149**, 604–10.

Sweet, R. M. and L. F. Dahl (1970), 'Molecular Architecture of the Cephalosporins: Insights into Biological Activity Based on Structural Investigations', *Journal of the American Chemical Society*, **92**, 5489–5507.

Tait, J. and R. Williams (1999), *Policy Approaches to Research and Development: Foresight, Framework and Competitiveness*, Edinburgh: Scottish Universities Policy Research and Advice Network, Research Centre for Social Sciences, University of Edinburgh.

Takagi, T., M. Takeda and H. Maeno (1982), 'Effect of a New Potent H_2-Blocker, 3-[[[2-[(diaminomethylene)amino]-4-thiazolyl]methyl]-thio]-N^2-sulfamoylpropionamidine (YM-11170) on Gastric Secretion Induced by Histamine and Food in Conscious Dogs', *Archives internationales de pharmacodynamie et de thérapie*, **256**, 49–58.

Takayanagi, I., N. Kondo, H. Yamashita, T. Hongo and K. Takagi (1977),

'New Selective β_2-Adrenoceptor Stimulants 5-(1-Hydroxy-2-Isopropyl-Aminobutyl)- and 5-(1- Hydroxy-2-Ethylaminobutyl)-8-Hydroxycarbostyril Hydrochlorides (OPC-2009 and OPC-2030) and Cyclic AMP Concentration', *Journal of Pharmacy and Pharmacology*, **29**, 187–9.

Takeda Chemical Industries Ltd (1983), *Takeda Nihyaku Nen-Shi* (200 Years of Takeda), Osaka: Takeda Chemical Industries. (in Japanese)

Takenaka, T. (1974), '2, 6-Dimethyl-4-(3-nitrophenyl)-1, 4-dihydropyridine -3, 5-dicarboxylic acid 3-{2-(N-benzyl-N-methylamino)}-ethyl ester 5-methyl ester hydrochloride (YC-93) *no Noujyunkan ni taisuru Sayo*', *Kiso to Rinsyo* (Clinical Report), **8**, 51–64. (in Japanese)

Takenaka, T., S. Usuda, T. Nomura, H. Maeno and T. Sado (1976), 'Vasodilator Profile of a New 1, 4-Dihydropyridine Derivative, 2, 6-Dimethyl-4-(3-nitrophenyl)-1, 4-dihydropyridine-3, 5-dicarboxylic Acid 3-[2-(N-Benzyl-N-methylamino)]-ethyl Ester 5-Methyl Ester Hydrochloride (YC-93)', *Arzneimittel Forschung* (Drug Research), **26**, 2172–8.

Takenaka, T., K. Honda, T. Fujikura, K. Niigata, S. Tachikawa and N. Inukai (1984), 'New Sulfamoylphenethylamines, Potent α_1-adrenoceptor antagonists', *Journal of Pharmacy and Pharmacology*, **36**, 539–42.

Takenaka, T., T. Fujikura., K. Honda, M. Asano and K. Niigata (1995), 'Shinki α_1 Jyuyoutai Syadan-Yaku Ensan Tamsulosin no Kenkyu Kaihatu' ('Discovery and Development of Tamsulosin Hydrochloride, a New α_1 Adrenoceptor Antagonist'), *Yakugaku Zassi*, **115**, 773–89. (in Japanese)

Tanabe Co. Ltd (1994), 'Dokusouteki Sekaiteki na Iyakuhin - Herbesser' (Herbesser: an Original, International Drug), *Yakushigaku Zassi*, **29**, 275–6. (in Japanese)

Tara, E., L. Kellomaeki and A. Pylkaes (1971), 'Double-blind Comparison of Isoprenaline, Orciprenaline and Salbutamol Aerosols in Patients with Asthma', *Postgraduate Medical Journal*, **47** (Supplement), 61–3.

Taylor, D. R. and M. R. Sears (1994), 'Regular Beta-Adrenergic Agonists: Evidence, Not Reassurance, Is What Is Needed', *Chest*, **106**, 552–9.

Taylor, D. R. and C. S. Wong (1995), 'Asthma Morbidity and Mortality in New Zealand', *Thorax*, **50**, 1021.

Taylor, D. R., M. R. Sears, G. P. Herbison, E. M. Flannery, C. G. Print, D. C. Lake, D. M. Yates, M. K. Lucas and Q. Li (1993), 'Regular Inhaled β-Agonists in Asthma: Effects on Exacerbations and Lung Function', *Thorax*, **48**, 134–8.

Teece, D. J., G. Pisano and A. Shuen (1997), 'Dynamic Capabilities and Strategic Management', *Strategic Management Journal*, **18**, 509–33.

Temin, P. (1980), *Taking Your Medicine: Drug Regulation in the United States*, Cambridge, MA: Harvard University Press.

Thagard, P. (1999), *How Scientists Explain Disease*, Princeton, NJ:

Princeton University Press.

Thomas, L. G. (1990), 'Regulation and the Firm Size: FDA Impacts on Innovation', *RAND Journal of Economics*, **21**, 497–517.

Thomas, R. J. (1994), *What Machines Can't Do: Politics and Technology in the Industrial Enterprise*, Berkeley and Los Angeles, CA: University of California Press.

Thomke, S., E. von Hippel and R. Franke (1998), 'Modes of Experimentation: an Innovation Process – and Competitive – Variable', *Research Policy*, **27**, 315–32.

Thomson, A. P. D. and S. Zuckerman (1953), 'Functional Relations of the Adnenohypophysis and Hypothalamus', *Nature*, **171**, 970.

Timmermans, S. and V. Leiter (2000), 'The Redemption of Thalidomide: Standardizing the Risk of Birth Defects', *Social Studies of Science*, **30**, 41–71.

Todd, P. A. and K. L. Goa (1990), 'Simvastatin: a Review of its Pharmacological Properties and Therapeutic Potential in Hypercholesterolemia', *Drugs*, **40**, 583–607.

Toguchi, H., Y. Ogawa, H. Okada and M. Yamamoto (1991), 'Once-a-month Injectable Microcapsules of Leuprorelin Acetate', *Yakugaku Zassi*, **111**, 397–409. (in Japanese)

Tolis, G., D. Ackman, A. Stellos, A. Mehta, F. Labrie, A. T. A. Fazekas, A. M. Comaru-Schally, A. V. Schally (1982), 'Tumor Growth Inhibition in Patients with Prostatic Carcinoma Treated with Luteinizing Hormone-releasing Hormone Agonists', *Proceeding of the National Academy of Sciences USA*, **79**, 1658–62.

Tsuchiya, K., M. Kida, M. Kondo, H. Ono, M. Takeuchi and T. Nishi (1978), 'SCE-963, a New Broad-Spectrum Cephalosporin: *in Vitro* and *in Vivo* Antibacterial Activities', *Antimicrobial Agents and Chemotherapy*, **14**, 557–68.

Tsujita, Y. (1993), 'Development of HMG-CoA Reductase Inhibitors', *Chiryogaku*, **27**, 625–31. (in Japanese)

Tsujita, Y., M. Kuroda, K. Tanzawa, N. Kitano and A. Endo (1979), 'Hypolipidemic Effects in Dogs of ML-236B, a Competitive Inhibitor of 3-Hydroxy-3-Methylglutaryl Coenzyme A Reductase', *Atherosclerosis*, **32**, 307–13.

Tsujita, Y., M. Kuroda, Y. Shimada, K. Tanzawa, M. Arai, I. Kaneko, M. Tanaka, H. Masuda, C. Tarumi, Y. Watanabe and S. Fujii (1986), 'CS-514, a Competitive Inhibitor of 3-Hydroxy-3-Methylglutaryl Coenzyme A Reductase: Tissue-selective Inhibition of Sterol Synthesis and Hypolipidemic Effect on Various Animal Species', *Biochimica et Biophysica Acta*, **877**, 50–60.

Tsushima, S., M. Sendai, M. Shiraishi, M. Kato, N. Matsumoto, K. Naito and M. Numata (1979), 'A New Route to Semisynthetic Cephalosporins from Deacetylcephalosporin C. I: Synthesis of 3-Heterocyclicthiomethyl-cephalosporins', *Chemistry and Pharmacology Bulletin*, **27**, 696–702.

Tushman, M. L. and P. Anderson (1986), 'Technological Discontinuities and Organization Environments', *Administrative Science Quarterly*, **31**, 439–65.

Tushman, M. L. and L. Rosenkopf (1992), 'On the Organizational Determinants of Technological Change: Toward a Sociology of Technological Evolution', in B. Staw and L. Cummings (eds), *Research in Organizational Behavior*, vol. 14, Greenwich: JAI Press, pp. 311–47.

Twentyman, O. P., J .P. Finnerty, A. Harris, J. Palmer and S. T. Holgate (1990), 'Protection against Allergen-induced Asthma by Salmeterol', *Lancet*, **336**, 1338–42.

Utterback, J. M. (1994), *Mastering the Dynamics of Innovation*, Boston, MA: Harvard Business School Press.

Uvnäs, B. (1943), 'Some Chemical Properties of the Gastric Secretory Excitant from the Pyloric Mucosa', *Acta Physiologica Scandinavica*, **6**, 117–22.

Vale, W., G. Grant, J. Rivier, M. Monahan, M. Amoss, R. Blackwell, R. Burgus and R. Guillemin (1972), 'Synthetic Polypeptide Antagonists of the Hypothalamic Luteinizing Hormone Releasing Factor', *Science*, **176**, 933–4.

Van Cangh, P. J., R. J. Opsomer and F. X. Wese (1986), 'A Depot LH-RH Agonist (ICI 118630) as Primary Treatment of Advanced Carcinoma of Prostate', *European Journal of Cancer and Clinical Oncology*, **22**, 743.

van der Molen, T., D. S. Postma, M. O. Turner, B. Meyboom-de Jong, J. L. Malo, K. Chapman, R. Grossman, C. S. de Graaff, R. A. Riemersma and M. R. Sears (1996), 'Effects of the Long Acting β Agonist Formoterol on Asthma Control in Asthmatic Patients Using Inhaled Corticosteroids', *Thorax*, **52**, 535–9.

van Schayck, C. P. and C. L. A. van Herwaarden (1993), 'Do Bronchodilators Adversely Affect the Prognosis of Bronchia Hyperresponsiveness?', *Thorax*, **50**, 1021.

van Schayck, C. P., E. Dampeling, C. L. A. van Herwaarden, H. Folgering, A. L. M. Verbeek, H. J. M. van der Hoogen and C. van Weel (1991), 'Bronchodilator Treatment in Moderate Asthma or Chronic Bronchitis: Continuous or on Demand? A Randomised Controlled Study', *British Medical Journal*, **303**, 1426–31.

Vance, M. A. and J. A. Smith (1984), 'Endocrine and Clinical Effects of Leuprolide in Prostatic Cancer', *Clinical Pharmacology and Therapeutics*, **36**, 350–4.

Vaughan Williams, E. M. (1966), 'Mode of Action of Beta Receptor Antagonists on Cardiac Muscle', *American Journal of Cardiology*, **18**, 399–405.

Vilchez-Martinez, J. A., D. H. Coy, A. Arimura, E. J. Coy, Y. Hirotsu and A. V. Schally (1974), 'Synthesis and Biological Properties of [Leu-6]-LH-RH and [D-Leu-6, desGly-NH₂-10]-LH-RH Ethylamide', *Biochemical and Biophysical Research Communication*, **59**, 1226–32.

Vincenti, W. G. (1990), *What Engineers Know and How They Know It: Analytical Studies from Aeronautical History*, Baltimore, MD: Johns Hopkins University Press.

von Hippel, E. (1988), *The Sources of Innovation*, New York: Oxford University Press.

Wade, N. (1978), 'Rough Journey to a Nobel Prize'; 'Three-lap Race to Stockholm'; and 'A Race Spurred by Rivalry', *New Scientist*, **78**, 219–21, 301–3, 358–60.

Wade, N. (1981), *The Nobel Duel*, Garden City, NY: Anchor Press.

Wajcman, J. (1995), 'Feminist Theories of Technology', in S. Jasanoff, G. E. Markle, J. C. Petersen and T. J. Pinch (eds), *Handbook of Science and Technology Studies*, Thousand Oaks, CA: Sage, pp. 188–204.

Walker, K. J., R. I. Nicholson, A. O. Turkes, A. Turkes and K. Griffiths (1983), 'Therapeutic Potential of the LHRH Agonist, ICI 118630, in the Treatment of Advanced Prostatic Carcinoma', *Lancet*, **2**, 413–15.

Wanner, A. (1995), 'Is the Routine Use of Inhaled β-Adrenergic Agonists Appropriate in Asthma Treatment? Yes', *American Journal of Respiratory and Critical Care Medicine*, **151**, 597–9 and **152**, 823.

Warner, B. A., R. J. Santen, L. M. Demers and D. T. Max (1981), '[D-Leu⁶, Des-Gly-NH₂¹⁰, Pro-ethylamide⁹]-Gonadotropin-releasing Hormone (Leuprolide): a "Medical Castration" for the Treatment of Prostatic Carcinoma', *Clinical Research*, **29**, 666A.

Warner, B., R. J. Santen, D. Max and members of the Abott Study Group (1982), 'Successful "Medical Castration" with a Superagonist Analog of Gonadotropin Releasing Hormone (GnRH) in Treating Prostatic Carcinoma', *Clinical Research*, **30**, 493A.

Warner, B., T. J. Worgul, J. Drago, L. Demers, M. Dufau, D. Max, R. J. Santen, and members of the Abbott Study Group (1983), 'Effect of Very High Dose D-Leucine6-Gonadotropin Releasing Hormone Proethylamide on the Hypothalamic–Pituitary Testicular Axis in Patients with Prostatic Cancer', *Journal of Clinical Investigation*, **71**, 1842–53.

Waxman, J. (1984), 'Analogues of Gonadotrophin Releasing Hormone', *British Medical Journal*, **288**, 426–7.

Waxman, J. and A. Saini (1991), 'The Current Status of Scientific Research and Hormonal Treatment for Carcinoma of the Prostate', *British Journal of Cancer*, **64**, 419–21.

Waxman, J. H., J. A. H. Wass, W. F. Hendry, H. N. Whitfield, G. M. Besser, J. S. Malpas and R. T. D. Oliver (1983a), 'Treatment with Gonadotropin Releasing Hormone Analogue in Advanced Prostatic Cancer', *British Medical Journal*, **286**, 1309–12.

Waxman, J. H., J. A. H. Wass, W. F. Hendry, H. N. Whitfield, P. Bary, G. M. Besser, J. S. Malpas and R. T. D. Oliver (1983b), 'Treatment of Advanced Prostatic Cancer with Buserelin, an Analogue of Gonadotropin Releasing Hormone', *British Journal of Urology*, **55**, 737–42.

Waxman, J., A. Man, W. F. Hendry, H. N. Whitfield, G. M. Besser, R. C. Tiptaft, A. M. I. Paris and R. T. D. Oliver (1985), 'Importance of Early Tumour Exacerbation in Patients Treated with Long Acting Analogues of Gonadotrophin Releasing Hormone for Advanced Prostatic Cancer', *British Medical Journal*, **291**, 1387–8.

Webber, J. A. and W. J. Wheeler (1982), 'Antimicrobial and Pharmaco-kinetic Properties of Newer Penicillins and Cephalosporins', in R. B. Morin and M. Gorman (eds), *Chemistry and Biology of β-Lactam Antibiotics*, vol. 1, New York: Academic Press, pp. 371–436.

Webster, A. (1991), *Science, Technology and Society*, London: Macmillan.

Wein, A. J. (1990), 'Editorial Comments', *Journal of Urology*, **144**, 911–12.

Weisbach, J. A. and W. H. Moos (1995), 'Diagnosing the Decline of Major Pharmaceutical Research Laboratories: a Prescription for Drug Companies', *Drug Development Research*, **34**, 243–59.

Whelan, C. J. and M. Johnson (1992), 'Inhibition by Salmeterol of Increased Vascular Permeability and Granulocyte Accumulation in Guinea-pig Lung and Skin', *British Journal of Pharmacology*, **105**, 831–8.

Whipp, R. and P. Clark (1986), *Innovation and the Auto Industry: Product, Process and Work Organization*, London: Francis Pinter.

Whittaker, E. and D. J. Bower (1994), 'A Shift to External Alliances for Product Development in the Pharmaceutical Industry', *R&D Management*, **24**, 249–60.

Wick, W. E. (1967), 'Cephalexin, a New Orally Absorbed Cephalosporin Antibiotic', *Applied Microbiology*, **15**, 765–9.

Wiggins, S. N. (1981), 'Product Quality Regulation and New Drug Introductions: Some New Evidence from the 1970s', *Review of Economics and Statistics*, **63**, 615–19.

Wilcox, J. B. and G. S. Avery (1973), 'Beclomethasone Dipropionate Corticosteroid Inhaler: a Preliminary Report of its Pharmacological Properties and Therapeutic Efficacy in Asthma', *Drugs*, **6**, 84–93.

Wilding, P., M. Clark, J. T. Coon, S. Lewis, L. Rushton, J. Bennett, J.

Oborne, S. Cooper and A. E. Tattersfield (1997), 'Effect of Long Term Treatment with Salmeterol on Asthma Control: a Double Blind, Randomised Crossover Study', *British Medical Journal*, **314**, 1441–6.

Williams, D. I., D. S. Wilkinson, J. Overton, W. B. McKenna, J. A. Milne, A. Lyell and R. Church (1964), 'Betamethasone 17-Valerate: a New Topical Corticosteroid', *Lancet*, **1**, 1177–9.

Williams, M. R., K. J. Walker, A. Turkes, R. W. Blamey and R. I. Nicholson (1986), 'The Use of an LH-RH Agonist (ICI 118630, Zoladex) in Advanced Premenopausal Breast Cancer', *British Journal of Cancer*, **53**, 629–36.

Williams, R. and D. Edge (1996), 'The Social Shaping of Technology', *Research Policy*, **25**, 865–99.

Winfield, H. and J. Trachtenberg (1984), 'A Comparison of a Powerful Luteinizing Hormone Releasing Hormone Analogue Agonist and Estrogen in the Treatment of Advanced Prostatic Cancer', *Journal of Urology*, **131**, 1107–9.

Wiseman, R. A. (1971), 'Practolol: Accumulated Data on Unwanted Effects', *Postgraduate Medical Journal*, **47** (Supplement 2), 68-71.

Wolthers O. D. and S. Pedersen (1993), 'Short Term Growth during Treatment with Inhaled Fluticasone Propionate and Beclomethasone Dipropionate', *Archives of Diseases in Childhood*, **68**, 673–6.

Wong, C. S., I. D. Pavord, J. Williams, J. R. Britton and A. E. Tattersfield (1990), 'Bronchodilator, Cardiovascular and Hypokalaemic Effects of Fenoterol, Salbutamol, and Terbutaline in Asthma', *Lancet*, **336**, 1396–9.

Woolcock, A., B. Lundback, N. Ringdal and L. A. Jacques (1996), 'Comparison of Addition of Salmeterol to Inhaled Steroids with Doubling of the Dose of Inhaled Steroids', *American Journal of Respiratory and Critical Care Medicine*, **153**, 1481–8.

Yabuuchi, Y., S. Yamaashita and S.Tei (1977), 'Pharmacological Studies of OPC-2009, a Newly Synthesized Selective Beta Adrenoceptor Stimulant, in the Bronchomotor and Cardiovascular System of the Anesthetized Dog', *Journal of Pharmacology and Experimental Therapeutics*, **202**, 326–36.

Yagura, T., T. Shida, K. Ito, A. Hamada, Y. Yamamura *et al.* (1979), 'Shin β Jyuyoutai Shigekisei Kikanshi Kakucyouzai Procaterol no Kikanshi Zensoku ni Taisuru Yakkou Kentou, 1' (A Study on the Efficacy of Procaterol, a New β-Receptor Stimulant Bronchodilator in Bronchial Asthma, 1), *Igaku no Ayumi*, **111**, 196–215. (in Japanese)

Yakka Yakkou Hayamihyou (Tables of Drug Prices and Applications), 1994 edition, Tokyo: Sanraizu.

Yakuji Handobukku (Handbook of Pharmaceutical Affairs) (1997), Tokyo:

Yakugyo Jihou Sya. (in Japanese)

Yakuji Handobukku (Handbook of Pharmaceutical Affairs) (1999), Tokyo: Yakugyo Jihou Sya. (in Japanese)

Yamamoto, A. (2000), 'Lowering Cholesterol: 30 Years Experience in Clinical Lipidology', *Doumyaku Kouka*, **27**, 75–81. (in Japanese)

Yamamoto, A., H. Sudo and A. Endo (1980), 'Therapeutic Effects of ML-236B in Primary Hypercholesterolemia', *Atherosclerosis*, **35**, 259–66.

Yamanaka, H., T. Makino, F. Kumasaka and K. Shida (1984), 'Clinical Efficacy of (D-Leu^6)-Des Gly-NH$_2$^{10}-LH-RH Ethylamide Against Prostatic Cancer', *Hinyou Kiyou*, **30**, 545–60. (in Japanese)

Yamanouchi Co. Ltd (1994a), 'Harnal', *Yakushi-gaku Zassi*, **29**, 414–15. (in Japanese)

Yamanouchi Co. Ltd (1994b), 'Perdipine', *Yakushigaku Zassi*, **29**, 317–18. (in Japanese)

Yanagisawa, I. (1989), 'Hisutamin Jyuyoutai Kikkouzai no Kaihatsu' (The Development of Histamine Receptor Antagonists), in J. Kawada, H. Terada and T. Fujita (eds), *Souyaku no tame no Bunshi Sekkei* (Molecular Design for the Creation of New Drugs), *Kagaku Zoukan*, no. 116, Tokyo: Kagaku Doujin Sya, pp. 201–11. (in Japanese)

Yanagisawa, I. (1994), 'Syoukasei Kaiyou wo Naosu Kusuri – Famotidine' (A Drug for the Treatment of Peptic Ulcer: Famotidine), in H. Iwamura, S. Ogino, K. Matsumoto and Y. Yamada (eds), *Ima Wadai no Kusuri* (Drugs in the News), Tokyo: Gakkai Syuppan Centre, pp. 155–67. (in Japanese)

Yanagisawa, I., Y. Hirata and Y. Ishii (1984), 'Histamine H$_2$-Receptor Antagonists. 1: Synthesis of *N*-Cyano and *N*-Carbamoyl Amidine Derivatives and Their Biological Activities', *Journal of Medicinal Chemistry*, **27**, 849–57.

Yanagisawa, I., Y. Hirata and Y. Ishii (1987), 'Histamine H$_2$-Receptor Antagonists. 2: Synthesis and Pharmacological Activities of *N*-Sulfamoyl and *N*-Sulfonyl Amidine Derivatives', *Journal of Medicinal Chemistry*, **30**, 1787–93.

Yanaihara, N., C. Yanaihara, T. Hashimoto, Y. Kenmochi, T. Kaneko, H. Oka, S. Saito, A. V. Schally and A. Arimura (1972), 'Syntheses and LH- and FSH-RH Activities of LH-RH Analogs Substituted at Position 8', *Biochemical and Biophysical Research Communication*, **49**, 1280–91.

Yin, R. (1994), *Case Study Research: Design and Method*, 2nd edn, Thousand Oaks, CA: Sage.

Yoshizaki, S., K. Tanimura, S. Tamada, Y. Yabuuchi and K. Nakagawa (1976), 'Sympathomimetic Amines Having a Carbostyril Nucleus', *Journal of Medicinal Chemistry*, **19**, 1138–42.

Zeldis, J. B., L.S. Friedman and K. J. Isselbacher (1983), 'Ranitidine: a New

H_2-Receptor Antagonist', *New England Journal of Medicine*, **309**, 1368–73.

Zeneca (1999a), *Zoladex in Breast Cancer Monograph*, Macclesfield: Zeneca Pharmaceuticals.

Zeneca (1999b), *Zoladex in Gynaecological Disorders*, Macclesfield: Zeneca Pharmaceuticals.

Zenetti, C. L., H. H. Rotman and A. J. Dresner (1982), 'Efficacy and Duration of Action of Procaterol, a New Bronchodilator', *Journal of Clinical Pharmacology*, **22**, 250–3.

Zucker, L. G. and M. R. Darby (1997), 'Present at the Biotechnological Revolution: Transformation of Technological Identity for a Large Incumbent Pharmaceutical Firm', *Research Policy*, **26**, 429–46.

Index